Native Insurgencies and
the Genocidal Impulse
in the Americas

Nicholas A. Robins

Native Insurgencies and the Genocidal Impulse in the Americas

INDIANA UNIVERSITY PRESS

Bloomington and Indianapolis

This book is a publication of

Indiana University Press
601 North Morton Street
Bloomington, IN 47404-3797 USA

http://iupress.indiana.edu

Telephone orders	800-842-6796
Fax orders	812-855-7931
Orders by e-mail	iuporder@indiana.edu

The paper used in this publication meets the minimum
requirements of American National Standard for
Information Sciences—Permanence of Paper for Printed
Library Materials, ANSI Z39.48-1984.

Manufactured in the United States of America

Library of Congress Cataloging-in-Publication Data

Robins, Nicholas A., date
Native insurgencies and the genocidal impulse in the Americas / Nicholas A. Robins.
p. cm.
Includes bibliographical references and index.
ISBN 0-253-34616-9 (cloth : alk. paper)
1. Pueblo Revolt, 1680. 2. Yucatán (Mexico : State)—History—Caste War, 1847–1855. 3.
Peru—History—Insurrection of Tupac Amaru, 1780–1781. 4. La Paz (Bolivia)—History—Siege, 1781. 5.
Tupac-Amaru, José Gabriel, d. 1781. 6. Tupak Katari, 1750–1781. I. Title.
E99.P9R55 2005
303.6'4'0980903—dc22

2005001855

1 2 3 4 5 10 09 08 07 06 05

For Susan Halabi

Contents

Acknowledgments

During the years spent researching and writing this book, I have been very fortunate to have benefited from the support and kindness of many people. In Bolivia, I am especially indebted to Marcela Inch, director of the National Archive and Library of Bolivia, as well as her predecessors, Hugo Poppe Entrambasaguas, René Arze Aguirre, and the late Gunnar Mendoza. Researching there has always been a very pleasant and rewarding experience, in no small part due to the kindness, professionalism, and support of the staff there, especially, in my case, that of the assistant director, Joaquín Loayza Valdo, and Carminia Martínez, Judith Teran Ríos, Leonor Ferrufino, Candice León, Ana María Nava, Lidia Ortega, and María Renee Pareja Vilar.

My research at the Archdiocesan Archive-Library "Monseñor Taborga" has been greatly facilitated by its director, Guillermo Calvo Ayaviri, as well as his predecessor, Josep Barnadas. I would also like to thank Margoth Céspedes la Madrid for her patience and diligence. Their intimate knowledge of the collections, combined with their interest, support, and generosity, greatly facilitated the research of this work.

In Seville, I am indebted to the former director of the General Archive of the Indies, Pedro González García, as well as his staff, whose expertise and assistance were invaluable during my time spent researching there.

Earlier research for this work was also enabled by generous summer research grants from the Mellon Foundation and the Tinker Foundation. With the support of a Fulbright grant, I was able to complete much of the Bolivia-related research. During this time, I had the good fortune to have had the support of Don Terpstra, Peggy Bond, Cynthia Wolloch, Tamara Floyd, Carol Robles, Ralph Blessing, Cynthia Lloyd, and Carmen Pardo.

Many scholars have been most generous with their time and have offered comments and suggestions that have helped to form and refine my thoughts concerning ethnic conflict in Latin America. In this regard I would like to offer special thanks to Israel Charny, Roger Smith, Kurt Jonassohn, Adam Jones, Norman Cohn, and Peter du Preez. I have also benefited from the insights of Jan Szeminski, James Dunkerley, Xavier Albó, Terry Rugeley, Sinclair Thomson, Erick Langer, Fernando Cajías de la Vega, Sabine MacCormack, Claudio Andrade Padilla, Gertrude Yeager, Richard Greenleaf, and Roderic Camp.

I am immensely grateful to many people at Duke University who have enabled and supported my research there. I would like to offer my gratitude to John French, Natalie Hartman, Orin Starn, Deborah Jakubs, and Gil Merkx. I would also like to thank Rebecca Gomez and the staff of the Interlibrary Loan office at Perkins Library for their kind assistance.

I would also like to thank Bob Sloan, Jane Quinet, Marvin Keenan, and Elaine Durham Otto at Indiana University Press for their support during the publication of this work. It has been a pleasure to work with them.

I would also like to offer special thanks to my parents, Marjorie and Robert Robins, who have unwaveringly supported my research for many years. While many people have helped make this work possible, it simply never would have come into being without the enduring patience, immense support, and inspiring spirit of my wife, Susan Halabi. It is to her that this work is dedicated.

While I am deeply thankful to all who have helped make this book a reality, any omissions or errors in this work remain my responsibility.

Native Insurgencies and
the Genocidal Impulse
in the Americas

1   Introduction

In the predawn hours of August 10, 1680, the Pueblo Indians of present-day New Mexico rose up in a well-planned and highly coordinated effort to eliminate the Spanish presence in the Río Grande basin. Those Hispanics and their allies in the northern region who managed to flee the native fury and take refuge in Santa Fe would soon find themselves besieged in the main government building by an Indian force that vastly outnumbered them. Three days later, and increasingly weak from thirst, the Spaniards made a bold sally, killing many rebels and causing others to flee just as more insurgents were arriving to take their place. Recognizing that the tide of rebellion would soon surge again and overwhelm them, the Hispanics determined to make their way south. Shadowed and harassed by the Indians on their journey, they joined up with another band of refugees who had fled from the southern Río Abajo district. Together this group, numbering 1,946 people, was succored by a wagon train making its triennial journey north from Mexico City, and ultimately found sanctuary near El Paso. For the next twelve years the native peoples of the region north of the Río Grande would rule themselves, largely free of Spanish influence and intrusion.

One hundred years later, on August 6, 1780, Indians of the town of Macha, Upper Peru, now Bolivia, beheaded their curaca, or village chief, thereby igniting the Great Rebellion of Peru and Upper Peru. The insurgency would quickly spread and become the largest threat to Spanish rule in South or Central America prior to the Wars of Independence. Over the next sixteen months, bands of native insurgents would overrun many of the towns in the region, killing almost all non-Indians they encountered. Thousands of Spaniards, Creoles (those born in the New World of Spanish descent), and mestizos (those of mixed Spanish and Indian origin) and their allies were slaughtered in churches, homes, haciendas, or agricultural estates and on the roads as they sought refuge in larger towns. In Peru, having taken most of the rural towns, the Quechua leader Túpac Amaru led a brief and unsuccessful siege of Cuzco. In Upper Peru, after the death of the original leader, Tomás Catari, his cousins Dámaso and Nicolás Catari briefly besieged La Plata (present-day Sucre, Bolivia), having already dominated the surrounding area. La Paz, however, was to suffer a nine-month siege led by the mercurial Túpac Catari. More than 10,000 Hispanics and their allies died there, many of starvation when they had run out of dogs, cats, and leather to eat. Where native unity was not illusory, it was transitory, and Spanish offers of pardon only served to further divide them. This, as well as superior Spanish use of arms and native allies, enabled them to repress the uprising by January 1782. By then 100,000 people had lost their lives in this attempt to reestablish native rule in the Andes.[1]

Sixty-five years later in Yucatán, Mexico, on July 30, 1847, the Indian Cecilio Chi launched an attack on the town of Tepich, killing more than 100 Hispanics there in reprisal for an earlier Hispanic attack on the same town. In the Caste War of Yucatán that followed, Chi went on to attack settlements and haciendas in Yucatán in his relentless effort to eliminate those of Spanish descent and affinity from the region. The rebellion, in which Jacinto Pat and Bonifacio Novelo also figured as prominent leaders, devastated the peninsula and swelled Mérida and Campeche with thousands of panic-stricken refugees. Seeing little exit except the sea, and assisted by donations of money, arms, and munitions from abroad, the Creoles and their allies rallied in June 1848, their counterattack aided by the advent of the planting season, which depleted the rebel ranks. Now on the defensive and increasingly desperate due to mounting defeats, the rebels fled deep into the jungle and found inspiration in a putatively speaking cross that promised protection and salvation from their enemies. The town of Chan Santa Cruz sprang up around this oracle, inspiring widespread Indian devotion. Over time the focus of the rebels became less centered on the elimination of those of Spanish descent from the region and more on the defense of what became a de facto Indian state centered in what is now the Mexican state of Quintana Roo. Despite having their capital overrun several times by Creole forces, it was not until 1903 that the movement was definitively crushed under the Mexican general Ignacio Bravo.

Although spanning a continent and 223 years, these movements were of an archetypal nature: they were nativistic movements that were both millennial and exterminatory in their inspiration, means, and objectives. Benefiting from what they saw as divine assistance, the rebels sought to restore native rule and traditions to their societies and create an earthly paradise free from the depredations of the non-Indian. These were subaltern movements born of despair and oppression and sustained by the belief that they were forging a new world whose time had finally come. Indeed, in two cases, a new world came to be, for the Pueblo Indians did achieve independence for twelve years, and the natives of eastern Yucatán ran their own affairs for just over a half century.

These case studies examine the causes, course, nature, leadership, and goals of these movements, as well as their internal divisions. In so doing, this work identifies a genre of social uprising in Latin America, that of indigenous exterminatory millennialism, through examining the links that may sometimes be found, but are not inherent, between genocide, millennialism, and nativistic movements in this region in the colonial and early national periods. The fact that these movements sought to breathe new life into native culture by largely removing foreign influences put into motion a dynamic that resulted in killing based on race and ethnicity, ascribed or otherwise. They followed a brutal logic that was clearly and consistently demonstrated by rebel actions: the restoration of native rule and the primacy of native customs could only come about at the expense of the power, culture, and presence of their overlords; it was a zero sum game. In practice, by eliminating nonnatives and those who had sided with them, they were also eliminating the foreign influences that they embodied. This reflected the fact that genocide was a tool for the rebirth of native ways and rule, for the establishment of a native state, and for ensuring that the threat of alien domination would not return.

As with almost all messianic movements born of cultural conflict, some vestiges of the old society would remain.[2] That which survived generally would either contribute to the future survival or quality of life of the native society, such as the weapons, tactics, or foodstuff of their enemies, or underscore the dominance of the natives, such as keeping white women as slaves. In addition, some alien elements had already been assimilated into native culture to the point where they were no longer seen as intrinsically foreign. Most prominent in this regard is Catholicism. Although after the Pueblo Revolt Catholicism was rigidly suppressed by the victorious Indians, a century later the participants in the Great Rebellion had a much more syncretic approach emphasizing reformulation over outright rejection. By the 1850s, this orientation was even more pronounced, as we shall see with the cult of the speaking cross in the rebel state in Yucatán.

Amorphous Americas: Identity, Religion, and Upheaval

There are many ways to approach Indian rebellion in the Americas. All must, however, contend with ambiguities of identity, spiritual orientation, concepts of legitimacy, power relationships, and the varying motivations of rebels and loyalists alike. The range of these factors, the length of the colonial period, and the span of the continent further complicate the equation. Indians and other racial and ethnic groups were generally found among both insurgents and defenders of the Spanish crown, fighting both as conscripts and as volunteers. Such heterogeneity often reflected a degree of social, cultural, or ethnic paradox, and our ability to understand such movements is enhanced by the recognition of antinomy, or the idea that two things can be both in opposition and true. This stems from the fact that the colonial enterprise was laden with contradiction, whether cultural, religious, structural, or racial, all of which dialectically interacted to produce the synthesis that is Latin America. This mixing of cultures, religions, and races created inherent ambiguities that can be grasped even if they cannot be resolved. The result is that there are many truths which are not mutually exclusive and whose relevance and force varied by time, location, and strata.

One factor that complicates our understanding of native resistance is understanding who was actually rebelling. The degree of racial mixing and stratification in the Americas often defies efforts to categorize race, despite the Spaniards' persistent and complex efforts to do so. In this context, ethnic and cultural orientations played a vital role in determining individual self-identity. While many natives viewed themselves as members of an indigenous community with deep connections to the land and environment, many curacas and caciques, or leaders of Indian villages, were more absorbed into the orbit of the Hispanic world than that of those whom they commanded. Similarly, while some mestizos may have been oriented to the Hispanic world, others saw themselves essentially as natives. The slippery issue of ethnic identity is closely related to rearing and the degree of assimilation of Hispanic attributes by individuals, such as religion, language, occupation, place of residence, and dress.

Many scholars have explored the dynamic nature of native identity and the responses engendered by the forces to which it was subject. For example, Frances Levine, Carroll Riley, and John Kessell examine the efforts of the Pueblo Indians to defend their identity and traditions, while Daniel Reff traces the relations between conquest, disease, and cultural adaptation in colonial northern Mexico.[3] Similarly, Marcello Carmagnani focuses on southern Mexico in his examination of the efforts of natives in Oaxaca to defend their traditions and concept of self in the colonial context, while Norma Angélica Castillo Palma examines colonial ethnic relations in the region of Puebla, Mexico.[4] In the Andean context, Thomas Abercrombie and Brooke Larson also delve into the interplay between assimilation of Hispanic characteristics and changing indigenous identity over extensive time periods.[5] While Abercrombie traces the efforts of natives in the Lake Poopó region to preserve and perpetuate their traditions and culture in the face of Spanish efforts to eliminate them, Larson emphasizes not only the ambiguities of ethnicity but also the effect that integration into the colonial economy had in shaping intracommunity relations, class structure, and cultural expression. Such works illustrate how native peoples have endeavored to defend their identity and underscore the evolving nature of what they are defending. As we shall see in the case studies of this work, the Hispanic elements that were increasingly assimilated by the Indians were often, paradoxically, adopted for the purposes of their survival and autonomy as distinct peoples.

Native spirituality played an important role in expressing identity, although the degree to which such belief systems were fused with Christian beliefs is the subject of considerable debate. Studies of this nature include those of Lorenzo Huertas and Kenneth Mills, both of whom explore the enduring nature of

Andean belief systems and efforts to eradicate them.[6] While Huertas argues that native beliefs endured with minimal transformation in the colonial era, Mills pays greater attention to the ongoing interplay between indigenous religions and church policy that resulted in a distinctive form of Christian belief. Nicholas Griffiths examines not only the role of extirpation campaigns in the development of a syncretic Christianity in seventeenth- and eighteenth-century Peru but also how such campaigns could be used to political advantage by native leaders against their adversaries.[7]

In the Mexican context, Serge Gruzinski explores native religious expression and the differing popular and state responses to it, while William B. Taylor probes the relations between the clergy, civil officials, and native communities in the area of Mexico City and Guadalajara toward the end of the colonial period.[8] In the Yucatán region, Charlotte Zimmerman, Alfonso Villa Rojas, and Victoria Bricker trace and detail the interactions between Maya beliefs and Christianity.[9] While there were strong pressures to abandon traditional rites and to adopt Christianity throughout Latin America, it is important to recognize that many natives and Hispanics also viewed the Christian god as more powerful than those of the Indians. Not only did this help to explain the conquest, but in a traditionally polytheistic native context, to the extent that such powers could be co-opted by the Indians, they could be used to their own ends. Like an alloy of two metals, native beliefs and Catholicism could complement one another, adding to the Indians' supernatural arsenal.

Indian religions could also be imbued with utopian visions concerning the return of native rule to the region. In the context of the Pueblos, however, the syncretic influence was least influential among these case studies. Despite the repression of native rites by the colonizers, traditional Pueblo religion played a vital role in organizing, legitimating, and sustaining the uprising, issues which are detailed in the works of Andrew Knault, Carroll Riley, and Franklin Folsom.[10] The role of religion and millennialism in the Great Rebellion has received considerably more scholarly attention, however. Our understanding of the prophetic underpinnings of the movement has been greatly aided by the works of Marco Curatola, Alberto Flores Galindo, Manuel Burga, Rosalind Gow, and Mercedes López Baralt.[11] The millennial nature of the rebellion itself has been demonstrated through the works of Jan Szeminski, Steve Stern, Jorge Hidalgo Lehunde, Juan Ossio, and Nicholas Robins.[12] The broad messianic appeal of the Upper Peruvian leader Túpac Catari is also discussed in detail in the work of María Eugenia Valle del Siles.[13] Such millennial hopes found expression in public events in the Andes, a sphere studied by David Cahill and John Rowe.[14] Both demonstrate the vibrant nature of indigenous Andean identity in the seventeenth and eighteenth centuries, with Cahill positing that the colonial experience in Cuzco created a provincial, multiethnic identity based on shared experience. The scope of such an identity is questioned, however, by Ward Stavig, who highlights the differences and frictions among colonial actors in the Cuzco region prior to the Great Rebellion.[15] In the context of the Caste War of Yucatán, the role of the speaking cross in inspiring continued resistance by Indians is detailed in the works of Nelson Reed and Don Dumond.[16]

Indians contended with, and contested, their overlords not only through sustaining native culture, religious practices, and millennial hopes but also through consistent litigation against abuses by civil and religious authorities alike. Among the areas studied in this work, this was more prevalent in the Andes than among the Pueblo or Maya. Stavig has extensively studied litigation as resistance and the use of interethnic alliances to achieve shared objectives.[17] Both Túpac Amaru and Tomás Catari litigated extensively before raising the flag of rebellion, and their efforts are detailed in the works of Fisher, Válcarcel, Serulnikov, and Andrade.[18] The native was not a passive victim, as Indians and their communities engaged the colonial system through concerted and often furtive efforts to preserve their culture, religion, and folkways through the legal system, and through revolts and rebellions.

The accommodative relations between rulers and ruled which such efforts reveal came under increasing pressure especially in the mid- and late eighteenth century as the crown sought to make the colony more efficient and lucrative. Increases of both civil and ecclesiastical exactions, the expansion of the repartimiento de mercancías, or forced purchase of goods, as well as land encroachment, population pressures, and more rigorous collection of taxes all served to progressively undermine the increasingly tenuous dominance of the Hispanics throughout the region. Approaches emphasizing the role of economic forces have contributed much to our understanding of not only why rebellions happened but when they did. Scarlett O'Phelan Godoy and Sinclair Thomson stress the economic and political dislocations engendered by the Bourbon reforms in spawning the Great Rebellion, although Jürgen Golte takes a narrower approach focusing on the role of the repartimiento de mercancías, while Ward Stavig emphasizes the role of the mita, or system of forced labor, in the Cuzco region.[19] In Yucatán, much has been written concerning the expansion of sugar and henequen production and its role in spawning the Caste War there. Central in this regard is the work of Howard Cline, Nelson Reed, and Terry Rugeley.[20] Don Dumond, however, argues that both the role of race and the expanding economic frontier have received undue emphasis, and he highlights increasing peasant expectations dating from Mexican independence in the context of centuries of subjugation.[21]

Most uprisings in the Americas were neither millennial nor exterminatory, but rather localized responses to local grievances, and even when they became regional in scope, many rebels continued to be motivated by community issues such as exactions and abuses by officials. Studies that detail the role of such local issues include those of William Taylor, Eric Van Young, and Kevin Gosner.[22] It was in rebellions, however, that repressed Indian desires and their own definitions of ethnicity and what it meant to be Indian came to the fore. Charles Walker describes how in the late colonial and early national periods, nativist influences shaped Indian concepts of protonationalism in the region of Cuzco, juxtaposing it with the more conservative objectives of the Creoles.[23] In Mexico, Eric Van Young also stresses the gaps between the independence objectives of Mexican Creoles and the more localistic orientations of the rural peasantry in the Mexican war for independence.[24] He stresses the native desire to defend their culture and communities, and the religious inspiration of many rebels, over class-based explanations. Gosner, however, uses the concept of moral economy and the increase of civil and religious exactions to help explain the rise of the millennial Tzetzal revolt in Chiapas in 1712.[25] Similarly, Paul Vanderwood examines the economic and religious bases of the anti-Porfiran rebellion of Tomochic, Chihuahua, at the close of the nineteenth century.[26]

Despite their varying orientations, foci, and emphases, the study of Indian identity and rebellion is, ironically, united by two conflicting forces: the defense of native tradition and the concomitant assimilation of Hispanic culture. Whether through litigation, concealing their limited resources, or rebellion, the native sought to defend that which served as the basis of their identity, whether it was community traditions, language, religion, or land and other resources. This was a dynamic, assimilative process, however, in which the identity that they were defending was itself evolving as a result of generations of colonialism. Part of the defense of this evolving identity was the affirmation of its indigenous roots through rites, processions, ceremonies, and also rebellion. Indeed, native uprisings threw into high relief their sources of discord, their sense of legitimacy, their desires, and their own perceptions of who was and was not an Indian.

This work does not suggest that every Indian rebellion in the Americas was a nativistic movement, nor was every nativistic movement millennial or exterminatory. In addition, this study recognizes that the Indians were victims of genocide as well as ethnocide (or the effort to eliminate a culture but not its people) committed by the Hispanics.[27] In many revolts there were specific grievances, such as against a particularly exploitative corregidor (district governor) or village priest. Some uprisings, however, had aims that went much farther and incorporated millennial and genocidal goals which sought the maximal affirmation of native identity through the elimination of those deemed to be non-Indians. These were not smooth processes but, rather, ones laden with discord, division, and competing objectives on both sides. Nevertheless, an exterminatory response should not be surprising, given the internal dynamics of such movements and the generations of exploitation, abuse, and humiliation suffered at the hands of their oppressors. There was, in the eyes of many rebels, an inherent incompatibility between the return to native rule and the continued presence of most non-Indian people and ways in the region. Leaders such as Túpac Amaru in Peru and Jacinto Pat in Yucatán, who favored multiethnic coexistence, found themselves at odds with their followers who were generally much more radical in terms of the exterminatory nature of their objectives. Leaders such as Popé in New Mexico, Túpac Catari in Upper Peru, and Cecilio Chi in Yucatán were much more aligned with the aspirations of their followers and had little interest in controlling their excesses and genocidal impulses.

While this work focuses on the exterminatory dimension of three rebellions, it also recognizes that, as with identity and religion, these insurrections were by nature heterodox in terms of their origins and objectives. The exterminatory strand was one among many, and the use of ethnicity to determine who lived and who died reveals what it meant to be an "Indian" in different places and time. In the end, our understanding of native resistance movements in Latin America will be enhanced by exploring and, where relevant, recognizing the degree to which genocide was part of the ideology or practice of other such movements. In the case studies examined here, the exterminatory impulse was a significant tendency of the insurgencies, although to differing degrees at differing times among different people.

Within this context, the use of the term *caste war* requires examination. The term is something of a misnomer, as *casta* referred to one of mixed descent, such as mestizos, mulattos, or individuals of mixed white and African ancestry, and numerous other mixed race groups. A caste war in this sense would refer to a war among people of mixed ancestry or between one or many castes and some other nonmiscegenated group. Ethnicity was an expression of one's identity, and it involved attribution, or the imputation of characteristics, by others. Skin color aside, one's occupation, social status, place of residence, primary language, and style of dress all were criteria that determined whether one would be considered "Indian" or Hispanic by insurgents in these conflicts. In this context, ethnicity helped to clarify the ambiguity of miscegenation, and one's ethnic orientation was often more important than mixed parentage. Although Cecilio Chi was an Indian, Túpac Amaru was a mestizo, and Túpac Catari was said to be light-skinned for an Indian, ethnically they were all Indians and they fought and died for the rebirth of native ways. In cases of mixed ancestry, ethnic identity clearly superseded genotypes, and these wars were fought to reestablish the political, economic, social, and cultural dominance of one ethnic group and the physical and cultural elimination of another. Thus, a caste war is the violent effort of one racial or ethnic group, self-identified or otherwise, to eliminate another. It is, simply put, an exterminatory conflict.

Documentary Discord

This research is based largely on primary sources. Some may argue that many contemporaries sought to stress the racial element of these conflicts in order to promote unity among not just Spaniards and Creoles but also mestizos, a large "swing vote" whose loyalties could have an important impact on the outcome of a conflict. But it is also possible that these contemporaries were simply reporting what they saw and had no need to exaggerate. Indian actions spoke for themselves, and writers of the time often understated, not exaggerated, "unspeakable deeds that cause horror even in the imagination," "outrages that the pen is horrified to repeat," and "shocking desecrations and insolences that [are] . . . indecent to mention."[28] The fact that an atrocity which "horrifies the tongue" or "scandalizes the ears" is often only alluded to suggests that things were in fact much worse than reported, not less so.[29]

The critical use of primary sources can identify and compensate for their biases. For example, in *Guerra de castas de Yucatán: su origen, sus consecuencias y su estado actual, 1866,* the anonymous chronicler of the Caste War, believed to be General Severo de Castillo, had a difficult time concealing his disdain for his enemies. He viewed them simply as barbarians who needed to be exterminated. Given his hostility, his positive comments concerning his adversaries, such as their bravery, tenacity, and organization, have special import.

While Spaniards and Creoles mediated native expression in the documents through the questions they asked as well as through translators and scribes, Indians did speak through them, most notably through confessions and through demands communicated in negotiations. Most importantly, they spoke through their actions, which are also recorded. Although confessions were usually extracted through force or the threat of it, they clearly had value for the interrogators and still do for historians who explore them critically. While some prisoners may have told their captors what they believed the Spanish expected to be told, others felt that they had nothing to lose by telling the truth.[30] As Alonso Guigui, the Indian governor of Jemez in New Mexico, asserted his innocence concerning the 1696 rebellion, in answer to a question he said that "he would say so if he knew, since he knew he was going to die, and he denied everything he was asked."[31] Other prisoners offered information that underscored the millennial inspiration and genocidal goals either of themselves or their compatriots. If the Spanish and Creole interrogators did not feel that interrogations and confessions were of value in terms of gathering and corroborating information concerning uprisings, they would have been less inclined to take the time and effort to extract them. The value of interrogation was shown in 1680 in New Mexico when Governor Otermín first learned from one prisoner that not all of the Hispanics in the region had been killed and, later, another revealed where other refugees had gathered.[32]

Peace negotiations also pose their own special problems. Often the insurgents engaged in them in order to buy time, for example, to finish a harvest, gather reinforcements, or amass weapons. Even if conducted in good faith, they often give more insight into the objectives of the leadership than into those of the insurgents as a whole. Many leaders, such as Túpac Amaru and Jacinto Pat, were much more conservative than those whom they led. They had a hard time controlling the actions of those who acted in their name, especially as distances increased. As a result, their leadership was in many ways titular, and their statements, in peace negotiations or otherwise, cannot be assumed to reflect those of most insurgents.

While rebel statements do offer insights into their objectives, rebel actions in the field offer additional material through which to examine their hopes and aspirations and, in the case studies which follow, the exterminatory impulse that characterized these movements. Actions were in many ways the words of the rebel masses, for most of them left no written record. Actions were also occasionally chosen and calculated and laden with a strong symbolic content. For example, during the Great Rebellion in the area of La Paz, the rebel Andrés Túpac Amaru commanded that whenever rebels found medals emblazoned with the bust of Carlos III on them, the medals were to be hung from a gallows.[33] First, this action is calculated: it takes time to do this, and it is not arbitrary. Second, it is imbued with symbolism, communicating both that Spanish rule had been executed and that the same fate would await those loyalist curacas to whom the medals had been granted. Other actions were not symbolic, yet they articulated rebel goals clearly. Killing every non-Indian man, woman, and child, in village after village, says a lot about rebel objectives.

There is, in the end, only a limited amount of source material, copious though it may be. Other studies of these rebellions draw from it and form the basis for our understanding of these movements. To impugn the conclusions drawn critically from these documents is to impugn the conclusions of many studies on these rebellions. If such sources are not valid for one, they are not valid for another. Furthermore, the sources often corroborate each other, especially concerning the specific course of events, even when written from different, and mutually hostile, perspectives. Finally, the statements of contemporaries on both sides of each conflict are further corroborated by the symbolic expression of insurgents through which they cogently expressed their intent and articulated their goals. Such symbolic expression is explored in detail in chapter 7. The events of these rebellions and the symbolic language they reveal tell a tale of native peoples who did not want reforms to an oppressive system, but rather wanted its elimination and the elimination of those who operated and benefited from it. Genocide was not only consistent with rebel actions, it was among their objectives.

2   Millennialism, Nativism, and Genocide

The concept of millennialism derives from the reference in the book of Revelation (20:4–6) to the promised 1,000-year reign of peace prior to the Judgment Day following the Second Coming of Christ. Millennial movements, however, are not limited to those of Christian orientation and are archetypal expressions of hope, usually born of desperation. While focusing on millennialism in Western Europe between the eleventh and sixteenth centuries, Norman Cohn characterizes them as movements that offer salvation to the faithful as a whole through the divinely assisted establishment of an earthly utopia. The birth of this promised land is "imminent, in the sense that it is to come both soon and suddenly; [and] total, in the sense that it is to utterly transform life on earth, so that the new dispensation will be no mere improvement on the present but perfection itself."[1] Such movements are often organized along clan lines, promise the birth of a "simultaneously sacred and profane paradise," and are frequently found in "societies [that] . . . do not . . . sharply demarcate the secular and religious realms."[2] The new order is often heralded by disasters such as military conflicts, pestilence, crop failures, and social decay, which both presage the new order and prepare people to accept it.[3] Millennial movements can assume different forms, such as those of "national liberation," which are the focus of this study, as well as a more peaceful variant that seeks reform or the defense of traditional cultural values. In addition, there are also class-based, as opposed to clan-based, millennial movements, such as communism.[4]

Many social movements may have millennial qualities, including those referred to as being "nativistic" in nature. Ralph Linton coined this term, defining it as a "conscious, organized attempt on the part of a society's members to revive or perpetuate selected aspects of its culture."[5] Linton, however, emphasizes the role of cultural conflict, and thus cultural interaction, in spawning such movements, and he notes that usually they will incorporate elements of the alien culture in their vision of the future. While not inherently millennial, they often develop such characteristics. There are subgroups of nativistic movements that reflect the degree of cultural stress a society is subject to and the tactics of its leader. Revivalistic nativism seeks to breathe new life into a culture or aspects of it that are in decline, while perpetuative nativism seeks to strengthen a culture that is not already in decline. These movements may be of a magical or rational nature. Magical nativism is characterized by a belief in and reliance upon divine or supernatural assistance and often has millennial qualities. Such movements generally are led either by one who claims to be the messiah or by a prophet who announces the arrival of the savior. In contrast, rational nativistic movements rely much less on divine assistance while seeking the revival or perpetuation of cultural practices and symbols.[6] Critics have suggested that these divisions are cumbersome and instead propose that they be divided into three forms: dynamic movements, which would subsume revivalist movements; passive movements, which are nonviolent; and reformative nativistic movements, which have a culturally syncretic approach.[7] In addition, Lanternari argues that Linton fails to recognize the degree to which such movements are opposed to "Western culture" and, it should be added, Western people.[8]

Nativistic efforts are, paradoxically, movements of adaptation. On the one hand, they reject almost all aspects of alien rule or influence, and the movement is in that sense a rejection of adaptation to such forces. On the other hand, the stresses to which the native society is subjected usually not only are unique but threaten the very survival of the people and their culture.[9] Adapt they must, or face the extinction of ways of life that they have known for centuries or millennia, or of life itself. In an anticolonial context, such movements

> all involve a belief in society's return to its source, usually expressed in terms of the expectation of the millennium and the cataclysms . . . that are to precede it, and also embody a belief in the rising of the dead, in the reversal of the existing social order, in the ejection of the white man, in the end of the world, and in its regeneration in an age of abundance and happiness.[10]

In areas such as Latin America, the propagation of Christian belief can generate or reinforce preexisting millennial beliefs through its emphasis on persecution, individual sacrifice, resurrection, collective salvation, and an afterlife.[11] This reflects the fact that both Christianity and anticolonial millennial movements have "all . . . arisen equally from crisis and dilemmas, and they all convey a message of salvation and hope. . . . The messianic message of old appears now in a new garb."[12]

Such movements, however, are rarely successful, and they are likely to have twin and contradictory results. One is extensive repression of the subject group, although this is often done in the context of the introduction of more moderate or ameliorative policies regarding extraction or the allocation of resources.[13] Nevertheless, memories of the movement may live on and inspire future uprisings. For example, in 1779 Túpac Amaru took his name from his ancestor, who was killed at Spanish hands in 1572, and in the late twentieth century guerrilla groups in Peru and Bolivia took their names, respectively, from Túpac Amaru and Túpac Catari.[14] In the end, "[h]istory obeys its own law, which is that the road to the future upon which it travels cannot be short-cut by any outside force striving to lead it back onto the road of the past."[15]

Leadership

The combination of severe social, economic, spiritual, or cultural decay or even collapse, in conjunction with the emergence of a charismatic leader, can precipitate social violence. Indeed, leadership is essential for the development of millennial movements.[16] Out of the rubble of tradition, such a leader both explains the reasons for its collapse and offers a way which he or she promises will inexorably lead to an invulnerable utopian society.[17] In the colonial context, this often involves a return to old ways and the limited absorption of certain elements of the alien society.[18] The descriptive and prescriptive nature of the leader's appeal underscores its ideological nature.[19]

The perceived wisdom of the leader is not ascribed to chance; rather, it is seen as the product of divine inspiration. Charismatic leaders often claim the ability to communicate with deities and to control the elements. During the siege of La Paz, Túpac Catari was eager to draw his saber and do battle with the "dust devils" that develop frequently on the altiplano. Their transitory nature helped to define him as one who had power over nature. Many leaders also claim to embody "sleeping emperors," or revered figures who, though dead, are expected to return to lead the faithful in the creation of the new order.[20] In Peru, Túpac Amaru was perceived by many Indians as Inkarrí, the long-awaited savior who would restore native rule to the land.[21] Often it is the suggestibility resulting from the upheaval caused by such events as droughts, famines, plagues, and military defeat that predisposes people to listen to and heed the message of the leader, facilitating his or her rise.[22] Like the movements he or she often leads, the charismatic leader responds to the need to combat these threats, calling for and making a break with established norms and institutions.

The charismatic leader has a synergistic relationship with followers, both promoting and accepting the qualities ascribed to him or her. According to Max Weber, the adepts follow a charismatic leader out of a genuine devotion flowing from a faith in supernatural powers, not as a result of coercion.[23] While this may initially be the case, we shall see in the case studies which follow that as the conflict intensifies and the pressures on the group increase, so do the recourse and reliance on coercion to maintain unity. Furthermore, in traditional societies, shamans tend to be "feared rather than loved."[24] Often in mass movements, not just those of a millennial or nativistic nature, people are drawn to join them out of a sense of social and individual alienation, or the erosion or elimination of previously held principles or expectations, and they willingly forsake "autonomy, responsibility, and decision making to their group and leaders."[25] Part of the appeal of joining is that membership in the movement offers a sense of community and a new identity as well as the opportunity to change the larger society.[26] "Conversion rituals" often mark the entrance of people into millennial movements and involve antinomian actions violating previously existing social norms and morals while demonstrating their commitment to and acceptance by the new movement.[27] In addition to underscoring their acceptance into the movements, such initiation rites are the point of no return, serving to symbolically purge members of their old beliefs while uniting them through shared experience and the creation of "collective guilt" among them.[28]

In order to maintain credibility, charismatic leaders must make good on at least some of their promises or otherwise demonstrate their special powers.[29] It is the role of the leader that determines whether a movement is messianic or prophetic. While the messianic leader claims to be the savior, prophetic leaders announce the coming of the redeemer.[30] In most cases, the leaders draw from the well of traditional beliefs, hopes, and expectations to galvanize and mobilize followers. As such, they personify, reflect, and reinforce the aspirations of their followers. According to Vittorio Lanternari, the leader is "the point at which the past and the future converge. He gives creative impulse to a prospective 'moment' of history, and into him, in turn, flows the tradition that is history's moment of retrospection."[31]

It is interesting to note that often the leaders of movements seeking the end of alien influences and people in a region are those who apparently have assimilated many of these same influences. Not only have they often been among a displaced native elite who have attended colonial educational institutions, but they often have had roles as "cultural brokers," such as interpreters or intermediaries between colonial authorities and subjects. They know the system, they are both its subject and enforcer, and rebellion can reflect their hope of social and personal redemption and advancement. Many are also comparatively well traveled, having journeyed beyond their hometowns as healers, traders, or advocates for their people. Furthermore, although they often have encountered significant personal obstacles or challenges in their lives, optimism tends to characterize their outlook.[32] Some rely almost exclusively on supernatural assistance or the spontaneous actions of their followers. Such "pure" millennial leaders in essence "expect [the revolution] to make itself, by divine revelation . . . by a miracle" with a minimum of strategic or tactical planning. It may be that such leaders are more prevalent in areas where there is a rich eschatological heritage and numerous prophesies concerning the inexorable victory of rebel forces.[33]

Leaders give voice to the aspirations of their people as well as their frustrations.[34] More important, they "divinate" the actions of the insurgents. Rebelling and killing become actions that have not only divine approbation but protection. As a result, like lightning joining heaven and earth, the millennial rebel becomes, in their eyes, an agent or channel for a higher power. The utopia is within grasp, born of a divine cataclysm enacted through the hand of the insurgent.[35] Only rarely, however, are such movements successful, and this study will examine two that were. Nevertheless, sooner or later, the better technology of their enemies, combined with their ability to exploit native divisions and often intermarriage between alien and native, takes its toll and leads either to the defeat of the insurgents or the metamorphosis of the movement into one of a more passive and nonviolent nature.[36]

Nativistic Millennialism and the Exterminatory Impulse

Anticolonial millennial movements may develop a genocidal element, something that is frequently overlooked in the literature. Clearly, "mass movements can rise and spread without belief in a God, but never without belief in a devil."[37] In the context of ethnic conflict, very often that "devil" is either an alien or otherwise ethnically distinct.[38] Such exterminatory impulses are not, however, confined to the colonial environment and can be found where one ethnically distinctive group controls another. In the Caste War of Yucatán, the region had secured independence from Spain, and in fact at the outbreak of the uprising Yucatán had seceded from Mexico. From the Indian perspective, however, little had changed materially; a small white elite still controlled almost all aspects of society and ruthlessly exploited them. When the ethnic element is injected into revitalization and millennial movements, as is likely in a colonial or quasi-colonial context, the risk of the movement assuming an exterminatory dimension increases. The oppressors are not just the enemies of the rebels; they are mortal enemies in a zero sum game. They believe that they must kill their enemies, or their tattered world will end, and along with it, sooner or later, themselves. The result is genocidal millennialism, where a salvationist movement "boils over" and develops an exterminatory dimension. The "ejection of the white man" in a violent movement often involves killing based on racial criteria.[39] Those who are "ejected" are the lucky ones; the others are killed.

Exactly what constitutes genocide is the subject of considerable debate. Chalk and Jonassohn observe the lack of a "generally accepted definition [of genocide] . . . in the literature."[40] Given the increased attention paid to genocide in recent years, and efforts to hold perpetrators accountable in international legal tribunals, it is not surprising that a considerable amount of what is written on the topic focuses on the contentious issue of definitions.[41] The term *genocide* was originally developed by the Polish jurist Rafael Lemkin, in his study of Nazi jurisprudence in conquered areas, *Axis Rule in Occupied Europe*. Building on the Greek word for race, *genos*, Lemkin defined genocide as "the destruction of a nation or an ethnic group" that is "effected through a synchronized attack on different aspects of life of the captive people." The objective of this is the eradication of the "essential foundations of the life of national groups, with the aim of annihilating the groups themselves. The objectives of such a plan are the disintegration of the political and social institutions, of culture, language, national feelings, religion and the economic existence of national groups, and the destruction of the personal security, liberty, health, dignity and even the lives of the individuals belonging to such groups."[42]

Lemkin influenced what in 1948 would become, and remains, the United Nations' definition of genocide. Under international law, genocide is held to be

> acts committed with intent to destroy, in whole or in part, a national, ethnical, racial or religious group, as such:
> (a) Killing members of the group;
> (b) Causing serious bodily or mental harm to members of the group;
> (c) Deliberately inflicting on the group conditions of life calculated to bring about its physical destruction in whole or in part;
> (d) Imposing measures intended to prevent births within the group;
> (e) Forcibly transferring children of the group to another group.[43]

This is a broad definition, indeed, and its scope, as well as its omission of mass killing based on political orientation, generated considerable criticism. Excluding political killings from the definition reflected the influence and interests of the Soviet Union in not having its actions against political opponents fall under this rubric.[44]

Harff and Gurr fault the UN definition for failing to recognize mass murder based on political affinities as a form of genocide, but also find the reference in section (b) to acts "causing serious bodily or mental harm to members of the group" too wide-ranging. Many scholars argue that only states are capable of committing genocide. For example Harff and Gurr assert that it is an "accepted principle" that genocide is "an act of the state," and they thereby limit their definition of genocide to "the promotion and execution of policies of a state or their agents which result in the deaths of a substantial portion of a group."[45] In a similar vein, Irving Louis Horowitz defines genocide as the "structural and systematic destruction of innocent people by a state bureaucratic apparatus."[46] Dadrian recognizes, but does not explicitly limit his definition to, the frequent role of the state in genocide, defining it as "the successful attempt by a dominant group, vested with formal authority and/or with preponderant access to the overall resources of power, to reduce by coercion or lethal violence the number of a minority group whose ultimate extermination is held desirable and useful and whose respective vulnerability is a major factor contributing to the decision for genocide."[47] As we shall see in the case studies that follow, while the state is often the perpetrator of exterminatory policies, this is not a prerequisite. Furthermore, the contemporary rise of decentralized conflicts and the proliferation of weapons of mass destruction and independently financed terrorist organizations highlight the fact that while the state may conduct or facilitate genocides, state involvement is not a precondition for their possible occurrence.

Other scholars, such as Yehuda Bauer, do not stress the paramount role of the state in their definitions, but limit them on the basis of time period. Bauer characterizes genocide as

> the planned destruction, since the mid-eighteenth century, of a racial, national or ethnic group by the following means: (a) selective mass murder of elites or part of the population; (b) elimination of national (racial, ethnic) culture and religious life with the intent of "denationalization"; (c) enslavement, with the same intent; (d) destruction of national (racial, ethnic) economic life, with the same intent; (e) biological decimation through the kidnapping of children, or the prevention of normal family life, with the same intent.[48]

The definition is a sound one, if one omits its temporal restrictions. To do otherwise is to ignore scores of genocides that occurred before 1750, especially given that, as Dadrian points out,

> [I]n Biblical times . . . it was more or less in the spirit of the times (Old Testament) to resort to devastation and destruction as a matter of course in warfare . . . [which] rendered particular types of genocide common behavior which was mostly taken for granted by both perpetrators and victims.[49]

Chalk and Jonassohn offer a more nuanced definition of genocide as "a form of one-sided mass killing in which a state or other authority intends to destroy a group, as that group and membership in it are defined by the perpetrator."[50] They note that only rarely do perpetrators of genocide actually succeed in eliminating whole populations, and for that reason they use the term *mass killing*. By characterizing such killings as "one-sided," they seek to exclude victims of conventional combat. They also observe that the victims of genocide usually have "no organized military machinery that might be opposed to that of the perpetrator."[51] The case studies that follow call into question these latter assertions. In all cases the rebels were engaged in "two-sided" combat, and fighting an organized, if poorly disciplined, military.

Other scholars have avoided the limitations noted above and offered definitions that recognize the various forms that genocides can assume. Pieter Drost offers a concise definition of genocide as "the deliberate destruction of physical life of individual human beings by reason of their membership in any human collectivity as such."[52] Peter du Preez largely follows this model, characterizing genocide as "the deliberate killing of people primarily because they are categorized as being of a certain kind, with certain attributes."[53] Helen Fein elaborates upon this idea, asserting that genocide involves "the calculated murder of a segment or all of a group defined outside of the universe of obligation of the perpetrator by a government, elite, staff or crowd [where the universe of obligation is] the range of people to whom the common conscience extends: the people toward whom rules and obligations are binding."[54]

The case studies in this work illustrate that a state is clearly not the only entity capable of committing genocide. In all cases the rebels did establish some form of rule in the areas under their control. In Peru and Upper Peru this was brief and subject to the fluidity of ongoing combat, but in New Mexico Indian self-rule continued for twelve years, and in Yucatán it endured for just over fifty. But genocide was the means to create this rule, and in all cases native rule was highly fragmented and often decentralized. In none of these cases during the course of the insurrection did the rebels have a "preponderant access to power," and the genocides were committed in anything but a "bureaucratic" manner.[55] Furthermore, these case studies demonstrate that the victim group can become the victor and that perpetrators are not always better armed.

In addition to the definitions of genocide above, there are other specific forms which scholars have developed. These include "linguicide," or the destruction of a language, as a form of ethnocide, or the destruction of a people's culture but not their lives.[56] Dadrian refers to cultural extermination as "cultural genocide," which has as its objective the elimination of the victim group's culture and many of its members, and the limited inclusion of survivors into the victor culture.[57] Reflecting the occurrence of killing based on political affinities, "politicide" refers to the extermination of political opponents or a political class.[58] Finally, "ecocide" refers to mass killings caused by environmental destruction.[59] Ecocide and linguicide pose special problems that highlight the role of intent in the perpetration of genocide. Linguicide, ecocide, and even genocide may occur, although intent is lacking. Generally, however, intent is seen as a necessary condition for the perpetration of genocide. Although not always easy to demonstrate, Chalk and Jonassohn assert that intent "may be imputed by analyzing the inherent logic of the situation and the processes occurring in the environment."[60] The "logic of the situation" found in many movements against alien domination leads them to be prone to developing genocidal qualities.

A unified approach would reflect the common denominator of these definitions, extermination, and would consider as exterminatory movements such undertakings which had or have as their object, or result in, the total or practical elimination of a people, ethnically or racially defined, class, group, culture, belief system, or language. The approaches and emphases above are largely consistent with this, and such an approach recognizes that genocide deals with the elimination of human beings based on certain characteristics. It also recognizes that while cultural elimination, or ethnocide, can involve genocide, this is not a necessary condition. Finally, it recognizes that the state is not the only entity capable of such policies, that genocides are not bound by any time period, and that genocide can be perpetrated by subaltern and resistance movements.

There is more agreement on classifications of genocide, which tend to be built around motive and are not always mutually exclusive, than there is on exactly what is being classified. "Latent genocide" is genocide without intent and may also be referred to as "negligent genocide." In contrast, "retributive genocide" utilizes genocide as a means of punishing a victim group for perceived wrongs, while "utilitarian genocide" has economic advancement as its motive. Finally, "optimal genocide" is "indiscriminate . . . sustained [and] aims at [the] total obliteration" of the victim group.[61] Roger Smith notes that retributive genocide can be institutionally integrated in military organizations and can as a result become common in warfare. He also notes that genocides can reflect diverse motives; for example, retributive genocide may also serve such "utilitarian" ends as capturing resources or power. "Monopolistic" goals of political domination also are found among the causes of genocide, which Harff and Gurr refer to as "hegemonial" genocide, an example of which are the Chinese policies in Tibet in 1959.[62]

Chalk and Jonassohn summarize the tendencies of genocides to seek "to eliminate a real or perceived threat . . . to spread terror among real or potential enemies . . . to acquire economic wealth . . . [and] to implement a belief, a theory, or an ideology."[63] Such "ideological" genocides, which seek social salvation through the elimination of target groups, were a hallmark of the twentieth century. They are usually oriented toward a domestic group and include those of Turkey in 1915, Ukraine in 1931–32, Nazi Germany in 1940–45, Indonesia in 1965, Burundi in 1972–73, and Cambodia in 1975–78.[64] Overlapping with ideological genocide is "xenophobic" genocide conducted "in the service of doctrines of national protection or social purification which define the victims as alien and threatening."[65] Du Preez notes that the colonization and decolonization processes often are associated with genocide. Apart from the conquest of Latin America, such "genocides of colonization" would include that of the Herero between 1904 and 1911 in present-day Namibia, and those of "decolonization" would include that of the Ibo in Nigeria in 1966–67. There are also "developmental" genocides, which have as their goal the elimination of a people who are held to be "less advanced."[66] Kuper further divides genocides on the basis of whether they are oriented domestically or internationally.[67]

For chiliasts, genocide may be used as a weapon in the creation of the promised land. Utopian visions will often include a world largely free of the enemy, while those who survive are subordinated in roles that the oppressed know only too well. To pave the way for the genocide, leaders, chiliastic or otherwise, seek to denigrate or dehumanize their adversaries, while amplifying the perceived threat that they pose to the point where they are seen as mortal enemies. Projection also may play an important role, if the victim group "has been seized on as the object of projections of what people fear and dislike in themselves."[68] The blaming of problems on the victim group facilitates this process, as can the habituation to murder.[69] Other risk factors for genocide include a conspiratorial orientation among the perpetrators and political polarization. In addition, forces that promote social violence may lead to genocide, such as a long history of animosity between perpetrator and victim groups, natural or demographic disasters for which the victim group may be blamed either directly or indirectly, and economic hardship.[70]

Whatever the type of genocide, one reason why some observers emphasize the role of a bureaucratic apparatus in its execution is that it usually requires some degree of coercion and obedience to implement.[71] What may be surprising is that "normal" people can become agents in the commission of genocide. Israel Charny notes that "genociders are not generally distinguishable as 'sicker' than most people," and individuals will often do things in a group that they would not otherwise do alone.[72] The potential to commit genocide is, in his view, inherent to the human condition, and as a result genocides are "runaway, pathological, cancerous exaggerations of an originally normal process."[73] Swept up in the tide of events, responding to a "historic moment of opportunity," and forced to conform, individuals can also claim that they were simply defending themselves or responding to a higher authority, whether it be a leader, institution, or ideology.[74] In addition, group activity makes individual responsibility hazier.[75] Other factors that induce people to become perpetrators include opportunities for material advancement, a sense of obligation to exact revenge for past abuses, a clear distinction between the victim and perpetrator groups, the belief that they are creating a better world, and the desire to demonstrate membership and shared identity in the perpetrator group.[76]

There appears to be a tendency to avoid recognizing genocides. Chalk and Jonassohn assert that "until very recently scholars have participated in a process of pervasive and self-imposed denial" that involves "the ignoring of these events in historical reporting, or their glossing over by the use of vague or ambiguous terminology," such as "razing" a city or referring to the "Final Solution."[77] In the context of Latin America, the euphemistic approach prevails. Referring to the genocide by the Pueblo Indians, one author notes that they had the goal of "eliminating the Spanish presence in New Mexico."[78] What is left unstated is that extermination was the means to achieve this. This "collective denial" can lead to individuals, institutions, and nations standing by and doing little or nothing to prevent genocides, as was seen in Burundi in 1972–73 and Rwanda in 1994, where the international community did little to prevent or stop them.[79] Other examples of de facto neutrality include the genocides of Cambodia in 1975–78 and East Timor in 1975–76.[80] Charny argues that denial offers people a means of "blunting [the] pain" of a problem that they feel incapable of solving.[81]

This "collective denial" is also found in the Americas, where the Indian is with few exceptions seen as a victim of genocide and not a perpetrator. There is no question that the Spanish colonial enterprise resulted in the genocide of millions of native people, and a concerted policy of ethnocide sought the cultural extermination of those who survived. Genocide may have predated the Spanish, however. Referring to the mass killings of the Anasazi in southwest Colorado and northern New Mexico and the Iroquois attack against the Huron Indians in 1649, Chalk and Jonassohn observe that "this seriously raise[s] the probability that the Indians of the Americas knew genocide before the coming of the Europeans."[82] Whether or not they did, Indian-led millennial, nativistic exterminatory movements have punctuated the history of the region.

3 Creation through Extermination

Native Efforts to Eliminate the Hispanic Presence in the Americas

The Pueblo Revolt: The Colonial Bargain in New Mexico

The Pueblo Revolt of 1680 was the culmination of decades of endemic resistance by the Pueblo Indians to Spanish rule. Numerous conspiracies had been uncovered and broken up by the Spaniards over the years, and had it not been for the extraordinary organization and coordination of the rebels, the rebellion of 1680 would have met a similar end. By then, however, the natives had learned from their mistakes, but not in the way the Spaniards had hoped. The Pueblo Indians had not only plenty of time to learn, their first contacts with the Spanish dating back to 1538, but also plenty of reason. Since the arrival of the colonizers, Pueblo populations had consistently and precipitously declined as the military-backed missionary frontier expanded northward, and those who survived recurring epidemics brought by the Hispanics were subject to economic, religious, and physical oppression.[1]

Despite the eventual presence of Franciscans in almost all of the pueblos, the small number of friars and their persistent tendency not to master the native languages helped to minimize their impact on native ways.[2] Nevertheless, they fervently and consistently sought the extermination of traditional native beliefs and religious practices. Indian unwillingness to accept the way of the friars was paralleled by an unwillingness by many Hispanics to acquiesce to the Franciscans' efforts to dominate both religious and civil affairs. The lack of extractable natural resources in the region, and competition over Indian labor, only exacerbated endemic civil-religious discord.[3] Civil authorities could influence mission life through laws concerning native labor, tribute levels, and their decisive influence on local pueblo government.[4] Nevertheless, the friar, perhaps with a few Hispanic soldiers, was often the only Spaniard living in a pueblo, and this presence enabled the clergy to monopolize the best lands in the area for cultivation and grazing.[5]

The economic power of the friars was enhanced by considerable political power, much of it mediated through the office of the custodian, established in New Mexico in 1616. The custodian, who served a three-year term, functioned as a prelate, as there was no bishop assigned to New Mexico. In 1625, the appointment of Friar Alonso de Benavides as commissary, or agent, of the Holy Office of the Inquisition in New Mexico, and the announcement there of the same in January 1626, further consolidated the power of the clergy. It was strengthened again in 1633 by the establishment in the region of the Santa Cruzada, which investigated improper sales of indulgences. While the authority of the Holy Office was limited to the Hispanics, it was not uncommon for the custodian to serve as the commissary of the Inquisition at the same time. Further adding to the power of the clergy was the fact that they were relatively free of internal divisions. All were Franciscans, and as a result there were no other orders or secular clergy with which to compete.[6]

In this context, not only were the Indians forced to convert to Catholicism and attend catechism and mass, but they were also required to support all of the religious and temporal needs of the resident priests. This included building a church and living quarters, farming mission lands, raising livestock, cutting firewood, and serving as cooks, personal servants, carriers, bell ringers, and even concubines.[7] It was not unusual for scores of natives to be employed in such occupations, and because such service exempted them from tribute, it also reduced the availability of labor to, and the income of, local crown authorities and other settlers.[8] Within the pueblo, those most affected by Hispanic and Catholic intrusion were the Indian medicine men, whose status and the religious traditions they embodied were under constant attack by the friars.[9] In 1661, the custodian led a crackdown on native rituals, and in the ensuing sweep, over 1,600 masks and other associated religious and ceremonial items were destroyed.[10] While underscoring the enduring nature of native rites, such efforts also caused considerable unrest. As one contemporary noted in 1680, the "Indians wished to rebel because they resented it greatly that the religious and the Spaniards should deprive them of their idols, their dances, and their superstitions."[11]

In addition to the friars, the Indians had to contend with the Spanish encomenderos, a small but highly exploitative group that received crown grants of Indian labor.[12] Generally in this region in the 1630s the encomenderos received a blanket, six palms square, valued at six reales, and one fanega of corn, valued at four reales, usually collected, respectively, in May and October. Sometimes a finished animal hide would substitute for one of the other products, and many encomenderos would make more frequent and additional demands upon the Indians, especially for foodstuffs such as corn.[13] Further burdening the Indians was the repartimiento, a system of forced labor for the settlers.[14]

The arrival of the Hispanics also severely complicated the relations between the Pueblo Indians and the nomadic Athapaskan plains Indians, which included numerous Apache and Navajo bands. Relations with the nomadic tribes had long been characterized by a tenuous ambivalence between persistent conflict and occasional trade conducted under the auspices of a temporary truce. As early as 1600, the rapid acquisition of horses by the Apaches and Navajos accentuated their advantage against their sedentary brethren, for now they could attack more rapidly, carry away more, and withdraw to more distant parts. In addition, as they learned of Spanish agricultural tools, products, and livestock, their appetite for these goods increased. With the pueblos having less to trade due to the surpluses extracted by the Hispanics, the Apaches and Navajos were more inclined to steal what was not traded. An Apache or Navajo attack on a pueblo may mean desolation to the town and its inhabitants, but it also offered an opportunity to the local Hispanic settlers to lead punitive slaving expeditions, furthering a cycle of violence in which the Pueblos were the vortex.[15]

Worse than the new demands of their overlords and the depredations of the Indians to the north, the pueblo population was riddled with disease. This process began as early as the 1530s as Cabeza de Vaca and his companions journeyed through the region, and it would only get worse. While in 1539 there were between 110 and 150 pueblos, by 1581 disease had played a significant role in reducing this number to about 60. In 1638 the population was estimated to be 40,000, a number that would plummet to 16,000 in 1678. Excluding the Hopi, by 1706 the total population had fallen to 6,440.[16] While much of the population decline can be attributed to the ravages of smallpox, repeated droughts and ensuing famines exacerbated the situation. One of the worst famines was that of 1666–69, and hundreds if not thousands of natives died, while many of the Spanish, Creole, and mestizo settlers were reduced to eating roasted or boiled leather.[17] Their weakened state also made the Hispanics less able to defend the Pueblo Indians from Apache attacks, which increased markedly after 1671 with the advent of another regional famine.[18]

Seeing their authority increasingly challenged through such raids, as well as through the continuing practice of native rituals, the Hispanics reinvigorated their efforts to "stamp out every vestige of native rites," especially under the administration of Governor Juan Francisco Treviño (1675–77).[19] In 1675, charging that several medicine men had cast a spell on Friar Andrés Durán in San Ildefonso, as well as others in Taos, Acoma, Zuni, and elsewhere, Treviño arrested forty-seven curanderos, or medicine men, from throughout the region. All were flogged, and four were sentenced to hang. In the end, only three suffered this fate, the fourth escaping the noose through suicide.[20] The others, sentenced to be sold into slavery for a period of ten years, were released at the aggressive insistence of a delegation of seventy Christian Indians who threatened to attack the Hispanics or flee the region if the captive curanderos were not released.[21]

Rather than crushing their will, the oppression and demographic decline suffered by the Indians inspired numerous revolts before 1680. Some rebellions had been local affairs, such as an uprising in Jemez in 1623, the killing in February 1632 of the Friars Arvide and Letrado at the hands of the Zuni Indians, and the 1633 poisoning death of Friar Porras by the Moqui Indians.[22] In 1639 the Indians of Taos had also revolted, killing Friar Pedro de Miranda and two Spaniards. The natives of Picurís also plotted to kill their friar, who, tipped off, fled before the plot could be realized.[23] In 1644 and again in 1654, the Spaniards uncovered new conspiracies among the Jemez.[24] In 1650, the Spaniards unraveled an intrigue involving both Tewas and Apaches to kill the friars and Hispanics of the region. Nine of the ringleaders were hanged, and the others involved were sold into a ten-year term of slavery.[25]

During the administration of Governor Hernando de Ugarte y la Concha (1653–56), the Indian medicine men were perhaps the most active in fomenting rebellion, and many were hanged for it.[26] According to one Indian, Pedro Naranjo, the Spanish-speaking rebel from San Felipe, rebellions in the 1650s were planned "by advice of the Indian wizards; [and] . . . while in some pueblos their messages were received, at others they did not agree to it."[27] After Governor Ugarte uncovered one of these conspiracies, he hanged "seven or eight [Indians and] the restlessness ceased."[28] At least for a while, although soon after emissaries of rebellion from Taos were dispatched to surrounding towns, carrying "two deerskins with some drawings thereon depicting conspiracies according to their method, summoning the people to a new revolt."[29] As before, the Indians were divided in their opinions. In Moqui the leaders "refused to admit them, and thereupon the covenant they were entering upon ceased for the time being, but always retaining in their hearts the desire to carry the same into execution."[30]

That desire again found expression in the mid-1660s, under the administration of Governor Villanueva (1665–68). Esteban Clemente, the Indian governor of Las Salinas, spoke six Indian languages and was popular not only among the Indians in many villages but also among the Hispanics. Clemente lived in the pueblo of Abó and operated a mule train and trading enterprise with the Apaches. He was hanged after it was discovered that "the whole kingdom secretly obeyed" him and supported his plot to "destroy the whole body of Christians . . . sparing not a single friar or Spaniard." His plan was simple and would become a formula for many future uprisings: the Indians would give chase to the horses, leaving the Hispanics on foot and much easier prey. The plot especially surprised the colonial authorities, as Clemente had been prosperous and well regarded by them.[31] Although these conspiracies and rebellions were uncovered or suppressed, they repeatedly demonstrated to the Indians the need for secretive planning, precise coordination, and broad support from the native leadership. These lessons would be skillfully applied in 1680.

The Pueblo Uprising of 1680

Among the forty-seven medicine men arrested in Governor Treviño's roundup in 1675 was one by the name of Popé, which translates from Tewa as "ripe squash," so named because he was said to be born at the time of harvest.[32] His lack of assimilation into the Hispanic culture is suggested by the fact that he apparently had no Christian name. He had been planning a regional rebellion since at least 1674 and perhaps as early as 1668.[33] Popé remains an enigma, and his origins and even his race are not known with certainty. Some have suggested that he was in fact a mulatto named Diego de Santiago, who had come from New Spain as a servant or slave in the 1630s. Subsequently, he had married an Indian and lived in Taos. Others argue that his real name was Domingo Naranjo.[34] Irrespective of his origins, by the time he had been apprehended under orders of Governor Treviño, he knew what to expect; it was the third time he had been arrested for sorcery, and he would be fortunate to get away with a flogging. In addition, his brother had been sold into slavery.[35] Although he was released with the others at the insistence of the Indian delegation previously described, his hatred for the Hispanics had only increased. Even after gaining his liberty, he continued to be harassed by the governor's secretary of government and war, Francisco Xavier, who was widely hated by the Indians. As a result, Popé fled from his home in San Juan and took up residence among the Tiwa in Taos, long a hotbed of resentment and resistance to the Hispanics.[36]

There he continued to craft his rebellion, spending considerable time in the Taos kiva, or subterranean ceremonial center. Perhaps under the influence of peyote, he was said to communicate with three deities in the form of Indians: Caudi, Tilini, and Theume.[37] What is perplexing is that these three deities are drawn from Nahua mythology, not that of the Pueblos, suggesting that he had southern origins.[38] Our understanding of this report is further complicated by the degree of mediation of these descriptions. It was reported by many Hispanic and Indian contemporaries that the three deities with whom he communicated would spew fire from their bodies and that Popé was black and had large yellow eyes. While it is possible that Popé was of African descent, these images also reflect the manner in which the devil was depicted in this period and may very well be Hispanic distortions of the events.[39] Furthermore, missionaries and others often viewed native unrest as machinations of Satan.[40]

In any case, Popé inspired his followers, partially through hope and partially through fear.[41] He promised that the Indians would again rule themselves and that "the God of the Spaniards was worth nothing and theirs was very strong, the Spaniards' God being rotten wood."[42] No wonder the Spaniards viewed him as the devil incarnate.[43] Popé's plan called for the rebels to "put an end to as many [Hispanics] as possible, sparing neither men, women, children, nor missionaries," and was crafted with the expectation that the Manso Indians to the south would finish off any who might escape.[44] Fearful that this plot would be uncovered as had so many in the past, Popé even ordered the murder of his brother-in-law, Nicolás Bua, the pro-Spanish governor of San Juan, who had learned about the conspiracy.[45] Popé carefully wove a web of support for his plot, sending runners to convince other leaders that rebellion was not only possible but necessary. The messengers would carry a knotted rope of maguey fiber, with the number of knots corresponding both to the number of days before the uprising and the number of villages that remained to visit. Under the threat of death, village leaders would untie one knot to express their support for the plan, when it would be passed on to the next village. Smoke signals further confirmed their commitment to the conspiracy.[46]

Among those who became involved in the plot were several who would assume leadership roles in it, such as Antonio Malacate of the Keres, El Jaca of Taos, and Luis Tupatú from Picurís, who later would rule much of the region. In addition to other leaders of Pecos, Jemez, and San Lorenzo, Popé garnered considerable support from mixed-race people who lived among the Indians. Among these were the Coyotes, or individuals of Indian and mestizo descent, Francisco "El Ollita" and Nicolás Jonva of San Ildefonso, Alonso Catiti from Santo Domingo, and the mulatto Domingo Naranjo from the pueblo of Santa Clara. Although support and participation would be widespread, the Tanos and Keres leaders were reported to have been reluctant to join, even though their people were supportive of the uprising. All of the conspirators were male, and left out of the conspiracy were the Piro villages whose inhabitants were believed by the plotters to be sympathetic to Spanish interests.[47]

Popé's timing was as good as his planning. Given the repeated difficulties the Indians had encountered in their tenacious efforts to shake off the Spanish yoke, and the fact that the conspiracy of 1680 was also uncovered prior to its outbreak, things went surprisingly smoothly for the rebels. As originally planned, the uprising was to occur simultaneously in all of the pueblos that supported it on August 12, 1680. The idea was to have it erupt before the wagon train from Mexico City arrived, which would bring food and munitions to the Hispanics, as well as the escort that had been sent south to meet it near the Río Grande.[48]

As a result of the hesitation of some Indian leaders to join the conspiracy, word of it leaked out to Spanish authorities. On August 9, 1680, the Indian governors of San Cristóbal, San Marcos, and La Ciénega notified Governor Antonio Otermín that they had captured two Tewa couriers from Tesuque, named Catua and Omtua, who were attempting to garner support among the Tano for the uprising. Otermín learned from them and in subsequent reports that the messengers were telling the leaders in the towns they visited that "all of them in general should rebel, and that any pueblo that would not agree to it they would destroy, killing all the people." He also learned of the rebels' "desire to kill the ecclesiastical ministers and all the Spaniards, women and children, destroying the whole population of the kingdom."[49]

Although Otermín knew there was a conspiracy, he did not know the date for which it was set. This was because once the Indian messengers realized that the leaders of San Cristóbal, San Marcos, La Ciénega, and Pecos opposed the revolt, they misled them by telling them that it was planned for August 13, not the original date of August 12. Realizing the danger and quick to respond, Otermín immediately alerted all of the alcaldes mayores, or district officials, to the plot and ordered the Hispanics south of San Felipe, in the Río Abajo region, to make a stand in La Isleta and those in the northern jurisdictions to do the same in either Santa Cruz de la Cañada, Taos, or Santa Fe. Many either did not receive this warning or failed to heed it, "as is apparent from the ease with which [the rebels] captured and killed people."[50]

Learning that the plan had been discovered, and knowing that the Spanish reaction would be swift and severe, Popé advanced the date for the rebellion, ordering that it begin immediately, the night of August 9–10. That night and early morning the Indians of Taos, Pecurís, San Ildefonso, Santa Clara, San Juan, Tesuque, Pojoaque, and Nambé attacked the missions and ranches in their respective regions in a well-coordinated offensive. In Picurís the rebels were led by Luís Tupatú, while those of Taos were led by El Jaca.[51] Although Tupatú's followers killed one Hispanic along with his mulata slave and her son, things were much worse in Taos. There the rebels killed Friars Francisco de Mora and Matías Rendón, who had fled from Picurís, as well as Friar Antonio de Pro, and the alcalde mayor with about fourteen troops "along with all the families of the inhabitants of that valley, all of whom were together in the convent."[52] In the Taos Valley alone sixty-eight of the seventy Hispanic settlers were killed. There as elsewhere, the rebels also set fire to the churches and looted and destroyed Hispanic properties. The two Hispanics who survived the slaughter in Taos, Sebastián de Herrera and Fernando de Chávez, quickly made their way southward. A week later, having seen the ruins of La Cañada, they would reach the outskirts of Santa Fe, and seeing it under siege, continued their journey, eventually making it past Isleta where they ultimately found succor when they joined up with the lieutenant general of Río Abajo, Alonso García.[53] In Galisteo, the rebels had killed Friar Domingo de Bera, Joseph Nieto, Juan de Leiva, Nicolás de Leiva, and four Hispanic women, as well as "all their daughters and families," among others. In addition, they captured four Hispanic women, who were later killed in retribution after heavy Tano losses during the siege of Santa Fe.[54]

Throughout August 10, many of the remaining towns rose up, including Santo Domingo, Jemez, and San Lorenzo. Also on August 10, Governor Otermín learned of the rebellion to the north in Picurís, the killing of two Spaniards in Santa Clara, and the looting of the surrounding ranches. As these and other reports came in, the governor sent Maestre de Campo (Field Marshall) Francisco Gómez and a detachment of soldiers to reconnoiter the region. Upon their return two days later, they brought confirmation that many Hispanics had sought refuge in La Cañada and that Friar Tomás de Torres had been killed in Nambé, as well as his brother Sebastián, his wife, and their child, in addition to several others there. In Pojoaque, they found numerous Hispanics dead, including Doña Petronila de Salas with her ten children. In all of the towns they visited, the convents and haciendas had been burned and the horses and livestock taken.[55]

Realizing that the rebels would soon advance on the Spanish capital and that the only hope of those in the rural areas lay in Santa Fe, Otermín ordered that the Hispanics gathered in both La Cañada and Los Cerillos come immediately to Santa Fe, where he gathered the residents in the casas reales, or governor's compound, to prepare to fight. He ordered the digging of trenches, and moved many sacred articles from the church there for safekeeping. Animals were also brought inside for the Hispanics to better endure a siege, and two cannons were placed near the main doors, aimed at the corners of the plaza where it was anticipated the Indians would attack. As these preparations were being made, the refugees from Los Cerillos arrived in Santa Fe on August 12, while those from La Cañada would arrive the following day.[56]

Also on August 13, Otermín sent the first of three notes to Lieutenant General Alonso García in Río Abajo, ordering that he send troops to assist in the defense of Santa Fe.[57] None of these messages would arrive, however, as one courier was killed by the Indians, and the other two could not advance past Santo Domingo.[58] Their journey there was full of foreboding, for on the road they encountered the bodies of six Hispanics, and upon their arrival in Santo Domingo they found the bodies of three friars, the alcalde mayor Andrés de Peralta, and all of the guards there.[59] Also on August 13, Otermín had sent two trusted Indians to the Tanos and Keres areas to bring letters to the alcaldes mayores there and to report on Indian movements. The next morning they returned, confirming his concerns of an imminent Indian attack, by reporting that there were about 500 Indians from Pecos, San Cristóbal, San Lázaro, San Marcos, Galisteo, and La Ciénega gathered in a field just outside of town. Other rebels were stationed across the river from Santa Fe, and all were "armed and giving war whoops."[60] According to Gómez, they intended to "attack it and destroy the governor and all the Spaniards, so that the whole kingdom might be theirs. . . . They were saying that now God and Santa María were dead . . . and that their own God whom they obeyed had never died."[61]

The Indians gathered there were awaiting more support from those of Taos, Picurís, and other pueblos, in addition to Apaches with whom they had formed an alliance.[62] The governor learned that one of the rebel leaders was an Indian named Juan from Santa Fe whom he knew and had earlier entrusted to carry a note to Galisteo. On August 15, Otermín offered Juan safe conduct to negotiate, and in the ensuing conversation, the governor learned that the rebels were carrying two banners, one of which was white and the other red. Juan told the governor that he must choose between them, and to choose the white one indicated that he and the Hispanics agreed to abandon the region, whereas choosing the red one indicated that they would fight. The emissary also demanded the release of all non-Hispanics under the governor's control, which included Juan's wife and child. Seeking a third way, Otermín offered to pardon the rebels of their crimes if they would return to their homes and swear obedience to crown and cross. Rejecting this, the emissary returned to the rebels where "his people received him with peals of bells and trumpets, giving loud shouts in sign of war."[63]

During these discussions, Indians led by Luís Tupatú had begun looting the Analco neighborhood and hermitage very near Santa Fe, and subsequently they began to move on the capital. Seeking to stop their advance, the governor dispatched about 100 soldiers to do battle, which included both Hispanics and some loyal "servants of the citizens."[64] The confrontation lasted most of the day and at one point required Otermín to lead a relief force to succor his men.[65] Although many Indians were killed, several Hispanics were injured, as many of the rebels were "on horseback, armed with arquebuses, lances, swords, and shields, which they had accumulated in the despoiling of the people whom they had killed."[66] Just as the Hispanics were getting the upper hand and many of the rebels were taking flight, insurgent reinforcements arrived from Taos, Tesuque, and Picurís. They quickly dominated a height that allowed them to shoot into the courtyard of the casas reales where the Spanish and their allies had gathered.[67]

The next morning, August 16, the Indians descended upon the town, and Otermín led a sally to engage them. Soon the rebels withdrew to their more advantageous position above, and apart from some minor skirmishes to prevent some buildings from being burned, a standoff ensued as the rebels waited for still more reinforcements. By the next day, having been joined by natives from Taos, Pecurís, Jemez, and elsewhere, the rebel ranks had swelled to about 2,500. Emboldened by their numbers, they again advanced into the center of town, entrenching themselves in strong positions and diverting the water supply that ran in front of the casas reales, an action which would make the situation of the Hispanics progressively desperate in the days ahead.[68] From their new positions, they began to loot and burn numerous buildings, and they attempted to set fire to the doors of a tower that was part of the casas reales. Governor Otermín led several fruitless efforts to restore the defenders' access to water, although he was successful in preventing the rebels from setting fire to the casas reales. Also on August 17, as the insurgents increased the pressure, they almost succeeded in capturing the cannons that the defenders had placed at the doors of the governor's house. They promised the Hispanics that soon Apaches would join them in the siege, and they "began a chant of victory, and raised war-whoops, burning all the houses of the villa . . . [such that at night the] whole villa was a torch and everywhere were war chants and shouts."[69]

Inside the casas reales were about 1,000 men, women, and children, in addition to a large number of horses, cattle, and goats, many of which began to die of thirst. Of the people inside, only about 100 were capable of fighting, and they were "surrounded by . . . a wailing of women and children, with confusion everywhere."[70] It was by now apparent that reinforcements from Río Abajo were not going to arrive, and the increasing boldness of the rebels and their own lack of water had made their situation desperate in the extreme. In a junta de guerra, or war council, on August 19 they decided to fight their way out and head south. On the next morning, after mass and confession, Otermín led his forces against the rebels, charging the house of Maestre de Campo Francisco Xavier, which had become an insurgent headquarters. The governor's move surprised the Indians with its boldness, and while they resisted the first charge, after repeated assaults the rebels there and elsewhere in the town began to retreat. The royalists then redirected their energies to burning the houses where other Indians had barricaded themselves, and although some did surrender, others died fighting.[71]

Five Hispanics perished in this encounter, and others were wounded, including the governor, who had received two arrow wounds to the face and a gunshot wound to the chest.[72] Despite their losses, they had killed over 300 rebels and captured, interrogated, and subsequently executed 47. The governor was "a little relieved by this miraculous event" of their victory.[73] Knowing that it would only be a brief time before the rebels regrouped and were joined by the Apaches, he decided to make as orderly a retreat as possible toward Isleta.[74] After sating their thirst, the "routed, robbed, and starving" refugees began their march south on August 21, taking with them over 400 head of livestock. By August 23 they had reached San Marcos, and following the course of the Río Grande, arrived in Isleta on August 27.[75]

During their exodus the refugees were shadowed by groups of rebels who kept an eye on their movements from heights along the way and planned two ambushes which the Hispanics foiled.[76] In Santa Fe, Otermín had learned from interrogating a captured rebel that Lieutenant General García and others in Río Abajo had gathered in Isleta, and now he learned from another captive that many of the Hispanic residents of Sandía, Jemez, Zía, and Isleta had now fled south, some to El Paso and others as far as El Parral. Enraged that García had not organized a force to rescue him in Santa Fe, he dispatched Friar Francisco Farfan and an escort to capture and bring him to Otermín.[77]

Overall, those in Río Abajo, which had the largest number of Hispanic settlers, fared much better than those to the north. As a result of the initial warning they received from Otermín, many there managed to escape the Indian wrath by taking flight to Isleta, the only Tiwa pueblo that remained loyal.[78] The Indians of Puaray, Sandía, and Alameda, however, joined their brethren in the rebellion on August 10, looting and killing those who had not fled, and bringing the booty to Sandía, which served as the rebel base in Río Abajo. Lieutenant General García made a foray into Zía, Santa Ana, and Sandía, where he managed to rescue some Hispanic women and children and bring them to Isleta, where they joined the band of about 1,500 refugees "on foot, without clothing or shoes." In all, about 120 Hispanics were killed in the Río Abajo region.[79]

The loyalty of the Indians in Isleta was tenuous at best, and they showed increasing signs of hostility, perhaps out of fear of Indian reprisals for not joining the insurrection, or out of support for the rebellion, or both. With only 120 men who could fight, few supplies, and even less ammunition, García decided to march his band south in the hope of encountering the northbound wagon train under Friar Ayeta.[80] Several days into the march, on August 20 at El Alto, García encountered Sebastián de Herrera and Fernando de Chávez, the two Hispanics who had escaped the massacre in Taos, seen the fighting in Santa Fe from a distance, and finally found some succor. They also provided the first information that anyone in the Río Arriba region to the north had survived the rebellion. On August 24, after being shadowed by Apaches, García's band of refugees finally arrived in Socorro, having been joined on the way by many Piro Indians who had not been invited to join the uprising.[81]

Fearing attack by the Socorro Indians, García again decided to continue southward, reaching Fray Cristóbal, about 180 miles north of El Paso, on September 4. There, Friar Farfan brought more news of the survival of those in the north and a letter ordering him to present himself to Otermín.[82] Two days later Otermín and García met up in El Alamillo, and subsequent to the inquiry that immediately followed, García was found innocent due to the general belief that all of the Hispanics in the northern region had been killed. In addition, he had sent three messages to Otermín, none of which reached him.[83] By September 13, both groups of refugees were united at Fray Cristóbal, and together they made their way to La Salineta, twelve miles north of El Paso, where by

September 29 they had all arrived. Although there had been two missions and a few Hispanic settlers in this area, the arrival of the refugees here and their subsequent relocation just to the south would mark the beginning of the development of El Paso as a large-scale settlement.[84]

On September 29, Otermín ordered a muster of the survivors at La Salineta. Of the 1,946 people who were counted over the next several days, there were only 155 men who could bear arms. In addition to 954 Hispanic women and children, there were 837 natives. Five hundred of these were Indian servants, and the remainder were Piro Indians from Senecú, Socorro, Alamillo, and Sevilleta who, fearing reprisals from the rebels for their partiality to the Hispanics, fled with them.[85] Of the 155 men who could bear arms, only 36 had guns, the "remainder being totally disabled, naked, afoot, unarmed."[86] Up to 1,000 people had already violated Otermín's orders and had fled farther south to the province of Nueva Vizcaya.[87] The refugees lacked provisions, were still vulnerable to Indian attack, had "lean and disabled" horses, and were facing the onset of winter.[88]

According to Otermín's calculations, in addition to 19 Franciscan friars and two lay brothers, 380 Hispanics had been killed in the rebellion in the entire region, including 285 women and children. Thirty-four towns had been razed, in addition to numerous haciendas and ranches.[89] Among the rebels, thorough organization and effective communication allowed them to survive the discovery of the plot, and with the flight of the Hispanics, the "Pueblos . . . had accomplished what no other Amerindian society had achieved on such a scale before them, and what none would achieve after, a complete setback of European expansion in the New World."[90] They then began what would be twelve years of independent rule, a period which will be examined later in this work. Despite the hopes of many Indians, it would turn out to be a time of great hardship during which they continued to be subject to Apache and Yuta attacks, arbitrary authority, periodic Hispanic incursions, drought, famine, and internecine division.

From Hispanic Retreat to Reconquest

After arriving near the Río Grande and being succored by the wagon train, groups of Hispanics continued to flee farther south, preferring the risk of execution by the crown for violating orders to stay in the region over the risk of being killed by the Indians. Those survivors who remained depended on supplies from the outside and lived in three settlements of "huts . . . of sticks and branches," each about six miles apart, with Otermín living in San Lorenzo and friars administering those of San Pedro de Alcantará and Santísimo Sacramentado.[91] Having escaped the rebels to the north, the Hispanics were in no rush to attempt a reconquest. Such was their reluctance that when in November 1680 the order came from the viceroy to retake the region, Otermín essentially had to force-march the able-bodied men from the settlement before even holding a muster. From November 1680 to early February 1681, they ventured north, parleying with some rebels who feigned an interest in peace and plotted to kill them, finding many destroyed villages, and ultimately returning to the refugee settlement with nothing to show for their efforts.[92]

While the Hispanic settlement would stabilize and a presidio, or garrisoned fort, would be constructed in the following years, it would not be until after the arrival of Diego de Vargas Zapata Lujan Ponce de Leon as governor ten years later that the Hispanics would effectively reinsert themselves in the Pueblo region. The relative success of Vargas's two expeditions into the area, in 1692 and 1693, owed more to his reliance on political skill, the creation of godparental linkages with the Indians, and symbolic submission than on force of arms.[93] In the first "reconquest," he secured declarations of loyalty from twenty-three pueblos, rescued seventy-four prisoners, and baptized 2,214 people, all, as he proudly stated, without using "an ounce of powder or unsheathing a sword, and without it costing the royal treasury a single maravedi."[94] Encouraged by the apparent success of this entrada, on October 13, 1693, Governor Vargas led a group of seventy families, totaling more than 800 people, in an ultimately successful effort to resettle Santa Fe.[95] Despite the apparently promising nature of his earlier entradas, Vargas would spend much of the coming years in a constant effort to suppress Indian conspiracies.[96]

By 1695 it was clear that there was a plot of regional scope, and friars consistently reported that "a rebellion and general uprising of the Indians of this kingdom is certain," especially as the Indians knew that the Hispanics "lack provisions, many weapons, and military supplies."[97] By March 1696, the Indians had shown increasing disrespect for the friars, and in anticipation of war, many had begun to relocate to the mesas for better protection from eventual retaliation.[98] For their part, the priests of many pueblos left their missions to seek security in Santa Cruz, Bernalillo, and Santa Fe.[99] Portending the future, and noting that often plots were to be carried out on a full moon, Friar Miguel Trizio wrote that there will be "many more full moons, and we do not know which one will become waning for us and the crescent for them."[100]

On June 4, 1696, the pueblos did rise again, led by the Tiwas of Taos and Picurís, the Tewas of San Ildefonso and Nambé, the Tanos of Jemez and San Cristóbal, and the Keres of Santo Domingo and Cochiti, killing five priests and twenty-one Hispanics.[101] Most of the Indians of Santa Ana, San Felipe, Zía, Pecos, and Tesuque, however, remained loyal to the Hispanics and assisted in suppressing the revolt.[102] As before, after the rebellion was suppressed the insurgents fled to the mesas or other defensive locations or to live among the

Apaches.[103] Apart from the human toll, the rebellion exacerbated the effects of a drought and famine, and as a result many Hispanics were facing starvation and eating dogs and "roasted cowhides," which were "scarce."[104]

In the years after the Spaniards had reasserted their authority, they moderated their religious and exploitative zeal to some extent, having gone from "self-assured intolerance to despairing accommodation." Time brought more tolerance, and by 1776 Friar Atanasio Domínguez viewed native religious ceremonies as "not essentially wicked," and called the kivas "council rooms." The encomienda system, whereby conquistadors or colonists were granted native labor in exchange for formally Christianizing their charges, was also ended and godparental relations between Hispanics and Indians increased. The native population continued to decline, however, to the point where in the 1750s there were more Hispanics than Indians in the region.[105] Despite all of their efforts and transitory success, the Indians were unsuccessful in permanently eliminating the Hispanic presence from their lands.

The 1780–82 Great Rebellion of Peru and Upper Peru: The Late Colonial Context and the Decline of Accommodative Relations

One hundred years after the Pueblo Revolt, the Spanish colonial system was well-entrenched throughout Latin America. Political monism, expressed through a centralized, authoritarian, bureaucratic, patrimonialist, Thomistic state, was melded with economic monism based on mercantilist theory and state-mandated monopolies. Although the encomienda had been phased out, the natives remained subject to forced labor, forced purchases, and increasing civil and ecclesiastical exactions.

In Peru and Upper Peru, the mita system was generally oriented to silver and mercury extraction, the latter of which was used in the amalgamation process. The mita was an adaptation of an Incaic labor conscription system of the same name, and under the Spanish one-seventh of the recorded male population between 18 and 50 in twenty-nine designated provinces was liable for one year of forced labor. As a result, in theory, an Indian would only serve as a mitayo, or mita laborer, once every six years. In practice, however, they often had to serve every two or three years because labor obligations were assessed at the community level, and the infrequent nature of census taking did not take into account the demographic decline in that area during much of the sixteenth and seventeenth centuries. Not all labor was done through mitayos, however, and much economic activity also included wage laborers, slaves, and yanaconas, or hacienda-bound Indians. Given that many of the haciendas and obrajes, or textile-making centers, in the region were tied to, and dependent on, the demands of the mining industry, there was considerable competition for Indian labor in the generation prior to the Great Rebellion.[106]

In addition to the mita, one of the forms of exploitation most despised by the Indians was the repartimiento de mercancías, under which originario men, or those who lived in their original hometowns, between 18 and 50 were forced to purchase goods at highly inflated prices. Some of these goods came from Europe, while others were produced locally, and they often included items of little or no use to the Indians such as razors for shaving and blue hair powder. Generally they were distributed by the corregidor, or district governor akin to the alcalde mayor in New Mexico, or his agents, who received them on consignment. The reparto, as it was also known, had been utilized since the late seventeenth century. When it was legalized in 1751 as part of the Bourbon reforms, it expanded considerably in scope and scale. It was forced upon many Indians who were technically exempt from it. This exacerbated the coercive nature of Hispanic-Indian relations and saddled the Indians with yet more debt. By artificially expanding the internal economy, it also led to an increase in demand for Indian labor, most notably in obrajes, or textile centers, and haciendas, or agricultural estates, both of which after 1720 were no longer allocated mita laborers. Such was the resentment engendered as a result of this system that rebellions in the region were most prevalent following the legalization of the reparto and in areas that utilized extensive Indian labor in obrajes.[107]

Although the corregidor was among the most vigorous exploiters of the Indians, other royal officials, such as scribes and tax collectors, acted similarly.[108] Priests also played a critical role in the exploitation of the Indians. As in New Mexico, they were often the only nonnative resident in a village, and as a result they had considerable power and autonomy. They also received significant income from their parishes, which like the corregimientos, or civil districts, were evaluated on the basis of their revenue potential. For the clergy, much of this came in the form of diezmos, or tithes, primicías, or first fruits, and various fees for baptism, marriage, burial, and other services such as those related to the festival held in honor of a village's patron saint. Although these fees were fixed in 1754, clergy routinely charged more.[109] The natives were also made to supply the priest with food, firewood, and household services, and concubinage with village girls was commonplace.[110] Not surprisingly, the stream of complaints against the reparto, corregidors, scribes, and tax collectors was paralleled by one against village priests.[111] The Spanish judge Benito Mata Linares summed it up well when he characterized the cofradías, or religious brotherhoods, as "a pretext covered with the veil of religion to suck from the Indian what he has," and noted that "the corregidor [can begin] the destruction of the Indians, but the priest annihilates them."[112]

The curaca was the intermediary between the Hispanic and Indian worlds, and while some tried to defend those under their charge from the depredations of Hispanic authorities, others embraced their position as a road to riches.[113] Both the corregidor and priest depended upon the curaca to organize the mita and collect tribute, dues, debts, and other payments and services, and the curaca, in turn, often worked through the jilaqatas, or originario-elected councils, of the villages under their jurisdiction.[114] One reason why curacas increasingly favored the exploitation, as opposed to the defense, of their subjects was that by the 1770s the position was increasingly filled by mestizos on an indefinite "interim" term, appointed by the corregidor. Previously, it had been a hereditary position where the individual had an organic connection to the communities under their jurisdiction.[115]

The Great Rebellion

The Great Rebellion of 1780–82, which engulfed much of Peru and Upper Peru, sought the elimination not only of Spanish rule but of Hispanics and much of their culture as well. It was a highly confederated rebellion, and as a result was quite heterodox. Leadership was critical, but even more critical was what was often imputed to it and the response such beliefs elicited among the masses. Generally its objectives became more radical over time, on the battlefield, and as the original leaders were captured and executed.

The increasing tendency to impose pliable "interim" curacas on local Indian communities resulted in increased levels of exploitation and engendered resentment among community members and those hereditary curacas who were displaced. Among those was Tomás Catari, an Aymara-speaking Indian from the town of Macha, in Chayanta Province in Upper Peru. What Catari lacked in formal education (he was illiterate and did not speak Spanish) he more than compensated for in his unrelenting determination to assume his hereditary position as leader of his community and to improve the abysmal conditions of his people.[116] Between 1778 and 1780 he would journey repeatedly to Potosí and La Plata, and even to Buenos Aires, where he met with the viceroy, in a tenacious effort to eliminate abuses in tribute collection and have himself confirmed as curaca of Macha. The royal officials he met on these trips were sympathetic, but offered little of substance, and upon his return to Macha he was flogged and repeatedly imprisoned by the corregidor of Macha, Joaquin Alós.[117] By February 17, 1779, after twice escaping from jail with the aid of his supporters, he returned to Macha, abandoned the legalist approach, and decided to take things into his own hands. He claimed that he had been confirmed as curaca and that he had royal support to reduce tribute levels by about one-third, which was the amount corrupt officials were shorting the treasury. News of these actions spread quickly and landed Catari in jail again, ultimately in La Plata, from June 10 until August 29, 1780.[118]

Seeking his release, Catari's supporters in Macha refused to pay tribute and captured the "interim" curaca of Macha, Blas Bernal, hoping to exchange him for Catari. Corregidor Alós could not or would not free Catari, and as a result Bernal was executed on August 6, 1780. The Great Rebellion had begun and would only intensify in the coming months.[119] Seeking a more valuable hostage, on August 26, the rebels captured Corregidor Alós in the village of Pocoata.[120] The Indians gave the authorities four days to confirm Tomás Catari as curaca of Macha, and release him to serve as such, in exchange for Alós's life. The risky move paid off, and on August 30, 1780, Catari arrived in Macha to an exuberant welcome, accompanied by his parish priest, Gregorio Josef de Merlos. Alós was released, and he journeyed to La Plata.[121]

Buoyed by their success, word spread among the Indians in Chayanta, Paria, and Yamparáez provinces that Catari, putatively acting under orders from Carlos III, not only had reduced tribute levels but had also announced the end of the reparto, the mita, civil taxes, and religious dues.[122] By September, Indian rebel groups were operating throughout this region, looting haciendas and "killing the Spaniards, mestizos, and the very Indians" who did not support the rebels.[123] Curacas were an early target of the rebels, and everyone in Chayanta province was a mestizo, except in the villages of Moscari, Sacaca, and Acacio. Some managed to flee, although many curacas were captured and killed, putatively under the orders of Tomás Catari.[124]

The Great Rebellion in the Region of Cuzco, Peru

As the rebels in Upper Peru sought out and killed curacas, and increasingly Hispanics, rebellion was also about to engulf much of Peru to the north and west. Although the Great Rebellion erupted in Upper Peru, it is often referred to as the Túpac Amaru Rebellion, after its most prominent leader, José Gabriel Condorcanqui y Thupa Amaro, who was born in 1742 in Tinta province. Although his leadership became increasingly nominal as one ventured beyond the Cuzco region, he nevertheless played a vital role in mobilizing both Quechua- and Aymara-speaking insurgents throughout the region and provided them with a figure upon which to project their own aspirations. Despite the role he would play in an Indian insurgency, and underscoring the role of ethnic identity in the conflict, it is notable that Túpac Amaru was a mestizo, not an Indian. On his mother's side, he descended from Felipe Túpac Amaru, the last Inca ruler whose execution in Cuzco in 1572 symbolized the final consolidation of the Spanish conquest of the region.[125]

Like all curacas, Túpac Amaru was subject to the unremitting demands of the local corregidor, in his case Antonio de Arriaga. Unlike many, however, in 1777 he went to Lima on behalf of the natives in his district and several others, and litigated for relief from the abuses of the reparto and limitations on the mita.[126] He would return home to Tungasuca a year later with nothing to show for it, except his strengthened resolve. The inability to secure legal redress, as well as his exposure to Enlightenment ideas in Lima, apparently led him to rebel. Upon his return he began to weave a web of conspiracy with the aid of his muleteer network, and as preparations progressed he began to stall on collecting reparto debts and tribute payments, to the increasing vexation of Corregidor Arriaga.[127] After being threatened with death by Arriaga, and perhaps concerned that his plot would be discovered as a result of the unrelated eruption over two months earlier of the rebellion led by Tomás Catari, Túpac Amaru decided it was time to act.[128]

On November 4, 1780, when Arriaga was returning from Yanacoa to nearby Tungasuca, Túpac Amaru and a group of adherents seized the corregidor and forced him to write a series of letters to Hispanics and curacas, telling them to come to Tungasuca. As a result, over 200 would arrive in Tungasuca over the following days. On November 10, Túpac Amaru gathered and surrounded them with about 4,000 Indians "all with slings in hand," and in a well-choreographed ceremony in which he too claimed to be acting under Spanish royal orders, he had Arriaga's slave, Antonio Oblitas, execute the corregidor.[129]

Túpac Amaru lost no time in seizing Arriaga's property and distributing it among his followers, nor in taking the weapons there and marching on the province of Quispicanchis. On the way hundreds of Indians joined the insurgency, looting Hispanic houses, stores, haciendas, and obrajes. Túpac Amaru had tapped into the centuries of hatred and resentment harbored by the Indians, and its measure was the blood that flowed. In short order, the provinces of Quispicanchis, Tinta, Cotabambas, Calca, and Chumbivilcas came under rebel domination as Túpac Amaru decreed the abolition of the reparto, the mita, numerous taxes, and the position of corregidor. Enticed by the opportunity for vengeance and booty, the ranks of the rebels continued to grow, leaving in their wake death, desolation, and embers.[130]

Just over a week after Corregidor Arriaga's death, on November 18, 1780, in the town of Sangarará the rebels confronted over 1,300 Hispanic and Indian loyalist troops dispatched from Cuzco.[131] Surprising them, Túpac Amaru ordered an attack, and in the ensuing slaughter all 578 Hispanics died, the church was destroyed, and the rebels availed themselves of weapons and loot.[132] Apart from a boost in morale and materiel, the rebel victory at Sangarará had several effects. Not only did it demonstrate that the Inca was unable to maintain effective control over his followers, but the massacre, and accompanying reports of cannibalism, shocked the Hispanic community in Cuzco and elsewhere, dried up any Creole support that may have been forthcoming, and led to the excommunication of Túpac Amaru and all those who supported him.[133]

Progressively recognizing the inviability of the multiethnic approach, native symbols increasingly dominated the movement. Túpac Amaru unveiled a rebel flag and commissioned a portrait of himself and his wife, Micaela Bastidas, an important rebel leader herself, as Inca king and queen. He also began to sign documents as Inca king and united and spoke to his troops at huacas, the shrines of minor Andean deities. The indigenous motif, long important in rallying forces for the rebellion, now came to dominate almost exclusively.[134]

After Sangarará, he led his followers back toward Tungasuca, killing Hispanics and their supporters, looting, and adding to his forces along the way. By early December he had conquered the provinces of Azángaro and Carabaya while consolidating his control over those of Tinta, Quispicanchis, and Calca. By mid-December he was in his hometown, making weapons and other preparations to seize the prize of Cuzco, while the Hispanics there prepared its defenses and fretfully awaited reinforcements from Lima.[135] Soon the Hispanic and native worlds would again collide in the ancient Inca capital. Túpac Amaru marched for Cuzco on December 19, adding to his troops as he made his way through the towns of Quiquijana, Paylla, Urcos, Andaquilas, and Oropesa. Arriving on the outskirts of Cuzco on December 28 with approximately 40,000 followers, he set up camp at nearby Picchu. While directing the siege against the city, he also consolidated his grip on the surrounding area, gaining more adherents in the process, and continued to issue calls to more distant provinces to join the uprising.[136]

Less than a week after Túpac Amaru arrived at the outskirts of Cuzco, on January 1, 1781, the first group of soldiers from Lima arrived. Although consisting of only 200 troops, they brought 400 guns, 500 swords, 12,000 bullets, a professional military commander in the person of Colonel Gabriel de Aviles, and a big boost in morale. While Hispanics commanded the defense of the city, most of the 12,000 people actually defending it were Indians. Having reinforced the defenses, Colonel Aviles decided to test the mettle of the rebels, engaging in two inconclusive skirmishes on January 3 and 6. Having probed and tested their adversaries, the Hispanics led a much larger force against the insurgents on January 8, undeterred by poor weather and reinforced by the arrival of 8,000 mostly Indian loyalist troops from Guancaro. Although there was initially no clear victor in this engagement either, the next morning the fog lifted from the battlefield and rebel positions to reveal that the insurgents had withdrawn.[137]

While Túpac Amaru had been conducting what amounted to a tepid siege of Cuzco, his cousin, Diego Túpac Amaru, had dominated the provinces of Calca, Paucartambo, and Urubamba at the head of about 6,000 rebels. His advance was stopped, however, with successive defeats at Huaran, Yucay, and Pau-cartambo. Defeated but not captured, Diego Túpac Amaru made his way back to Tungasuca where he rejoined Túpac Amaru on January 18. Regrouping from their respective setbacks, they prepared themselves and their troops for the impending counteroffensive as troops under General del Valle made their way toward the rebel's lair.[138]

Regional Radicalization

Although Cuzco was free from the threat of imminent Indian domination, the rebellion raged in the surrounding region. As with Túpac Amaru in Peru, in Upper Peru Tomás Catari had unleashed forces which he had a hard time controlling. As his adherents embellished his orders and increasingly ravaged the countryside, Catari continued to proclaim his "blind obedience" to Carlos III. In a letter to the king, he sought pardon for those who had rebelled, and promised that he and his supporters would continue to pay tribute and taxes and serve the mita.[139] His appeal is significant as it not only underscores that Catari was in essence a reformist but also shows that he was well aware that while he claimed to act with the king's blessing, he knew he did not.

Tomás Catari's time was running out, however. Soon after the royalists had broken the siege of Cuzco, Tomás Catari was captured, and on January 8, during the march to La Plata, his supporters tried to free him by staging an ambush at Chataquila about ten miles from the city. Vastly outnumbered, and refusing to surrender, the leader of the escort, Juan Antonio Acuña, had Catari and his scribe Isidro Serrano shot on the spot before they themselves fell victim to the rebels.[140] Given his previous escapes and his messianic appeal, it is not surprising that there were many rumors that Catari had yet again dodged his demise. His cousin Dámaso went to Quilaquila, where Catari and Serrano had been interred, "with the object of verifying [that] the death of his relative was true, as there were rumors running among the Indians that he had resuscitated."[141]

The Amaristas in Peru continued to suffer setbacks of their own. By April 4, Túpac Amaru and the troops immediately under his command were surrounded between Tinta and Sangarará. Hunted and running out of supplies, the rebel forces planned a counterattack in Langui. Claiming to be going to gather more reinforcements, a rebel colonel, Ventura Landaeta, instead joined up with another rebel, the captain Francisco Cruz, organized a small force, and captured the Inca, much of his family, and thirty-two of his captains. After being handed over to General del Valle, the prisoners arrived in irons in Cuzco on April 14, 1781, and were executed on May 18, 1781.[142]

The decentralized nature of the rebellion in both Peru and Upper Peru, and the commitment of those who led and participated in it, meant that the capture and death of Tomás Catari and Túpac Amaru did not stop the rebellion. Instead, it entered a more radical phase. In the region between Cuzco and Puno, Diego Cristóbal Túpac Amaru assumed leadership of the insurgency and increasingly targeted Creoles and their interests, in addition to Spaniards. The fall of Puno on May 7, 1781, and the subsequent capture of Caravaya on May 26, underscored the fact that the rebellion was far from over.[143]

Diego Cristóbal Túpac Amaru was not the only one of the original Amaristas operating in Upper Peru. His 19-year-old nephew, Andrés Mendagure Túpac Amaru, was leading 11,000 rebels from Omasuyo, Larecaja, and Sicasica provinces in the siege and subsequent capture of Sorata.[144] Between March and July 1781, they laid siege to Sorata, while its inhabitants held out in the hope of succor, eating horses, dogs, and cats as the months wore on and the food ran out. By late July, however, Andrés Mendagure had his troops dam up the water coming from the Cerro de Tipoani, constructed canals toward the city, and unleashed a violent surge of water that flooded the adobe town. After five days, the walls of many buildings and defensive trenches began to collapse or wash away.[145]

With the city weakened and now fatally exposed, the rebels assaulted it at around 6:00 A.M. on August 5, "not sparing women or children . . . in the streets or houses." Most of the residents, however, had sought refuge in the church, and when the rebels stormed it, they took the men one by one out to their deaths, "leaving the streets filled with horror and bodies." The women were stripped, and their lives were spared by Andrés Túpac Amaru, who stipulated that henceforth they must "chew coca [and] dress in cotton [and] walk without shoes."[146]

To the south, on January 15, 1781, the corregidor of Paria province, Manuel de Bodega, was in the village of Challapata making a second attempt to collect tribute, backed up by seventy-eight armed men. His previous efforts had been unsuccessful as the Indians there, following both their desires and orders imputed to Tomás Catari and Túpac Amaru, had refused to pay their hated overlord.[147] Not only did they again refuse to pay, but they attacked the royalists, threatened to burn the church, and in the end captured Bodega and had his slave execute him at the rollo, or stone column, that symbolized Spanish authority.[148] Hispanics, curacas, and their supporters continued to be a focus of rebel wrath throughout the region during this time. Ten days later, on January 26, the corregidor of Carangas, Mateo Ibañez Arco, was killed in Corque, also while trying to collect tribute.[149]

The radicalization of the rebellion in Upper Peru is similar to the trajectory in the Cuzco–Lake Titicaca region, where the extended family of Túpac Amaru rose to fill his place and presided over an increasingly extremist movement. In Upper Peru, the cousins of Tomás Catari, Dámaso and Nicolás, took his place and led an effort to "finish off with all those who were not Indians and with those who opposed" them.[150] Indeed, February and March were months of horror for the Hispanics of Upper Peru and unprecedented hope for the natives. While the rebels initially generally targeted curacas and mestizos, they now increasingly began to kill Hispanics and their sympathizers, such as happened on February 2 when rebels overran the town of Carangas.[151]

Just as Cuzco was the prize sought by the Amaristas in Peru, La Plata, as a pre-Hispanic Indian town and seat of colonial authority, was coveted by the followers of the Cataris. In the second week of February, rebels led by Sancho Acho began to mass on the town, while its military commander, Ignacio Flores, redoubled its defenses.[152] On their way to implement the siege of the city, on February 12, Dámaso Catari and Ramón Paca invaded the village of Yura and killed the local curaca, although they allowed the priest and two of his assistants to flee after they were made to strip.[153] Likewise, the many statues in the church were stripped of their clothes. Paca executed a similar attack in nearby Anansayas, leading the invasion during mass, killing the curaca and his children, and allowing the priest and his assistants to escape after threatening to kill the cleric and attacking him "on the very altar with threats, shouting and shots from the slings, [with the Indians] ripping off the sacred vestments until [he was] naked in the sacristy."[154]

By the next day Dámaso Catari had arrived outside of La Plata, and he took command of the 4,000 rebels who had gathered there. Playing native horns, they shouted and expressed their plan to raze the city and kill all non-Indians except for the priests. After a skirmish on February 17, Flores led the loyalist forces to La Punilla on February 20, successfully breaking the siege but failing to capture any of the rebel leaders.[155] The loyalist momentum continued to grow, spurred on by subsequent rebel defeats, bounties on rebel leaders, and offers of pardon. The Indians of Pocoata, who always had reservations about the rebellion, as well as some Indians from Macha captured the leaders in the following month and handed them over to royal authorities. Dámaso was hanged on April 27, and Nicolás on May 7, in the main plaza of La Plata.[156] The capture and execution of the Cataris may have revealed rebel divisions and dampened the insurgency's momentum, but it failed to stop it. Much of this resilience is because the rebellion, in both Peru and Upper Peru, was highly decentralized and in effect a loose regional confederation of local level uprisings.[157]

Despite the fact that Hispanics were increasingly the target of rebel attacks in the region, the Creoles of the mining town of Oruro sought an alliance with them to expel the Spaniards. Chafing from economic decline and outraged over his ouster from political office, the wealthy miner Creole Jacinto Rodríguez organized Indians, Creoles, and mestizos to kill the fifty Spanish residents of the town on February 10, 1781, just days before the siege of La Plata began. At around noon on February 11, after most of the Spaniards had been killed, large groups of Indians who had previously been invited by the Creoles to join the rebellion began to arrive in Oruro. The increasing numbers of Indians so alarmed the Creoles that they dispatched twenty-five messengers to intercept other groups of Indians on their way and dissuade them from entering the town.[158]

Although initially the relations among Creoles, mestizos, and Indians were positive, things quickly began to deteriorate. By dusk of February 11 there were over 4,000 intoxicated natives in the town looting houses and dancing "over [the Spanish corpses] with happiness and [abusing] them again with rocks, knives, and garrotes."[159] All this was happening as more Indians from the region continued to arrive, their numbers growing in the coming days to 9,000, and then 15,000, in a town of sixteen square blocks. Things quickly escaped the control of the Creoles as the Indians ignored pleas from clerics and began to storm and desecrate churches and convents as they searched for and killed any Spaniards they could find.[160]

The Creole-Indian alliance was breaking apart quickly as the radical aims of the Indian rebels increasingly came to the fore, and they soon began to focus their hostility on the Creoles.[161] Not only did the rebels target Creole property for looting, but they demanded under penalty of death that they give up their weapons and that all of the residents of Oruro wear only indigenous clothes, chew coca, and address people in the traditional native manner.[162] As still more Indians arrived under Juan Rodriguez, Jacinto's brother, the rebels demanded that they be given the lands not only of the dead Spaniards but also of the Creoles and clerics. As with the other demands, these were quickly acceded to.[163] The Indian insistence for land is indicative of the widespread hope among the rebels that the death of their Hispanic overlords would, among other things, result in the regaining of their lands. José Gabriel Túpac Amaru, Andrés Túpac Amaru, and Simón Castillo, among others, all promised land for their adherents.[164]

It was clear to the Creoles, however, that their concessions were not dampening the ever-growing hostility of the Indians. With the support of an Indian ally, curaca Lope Chungara of Challapata, they captured and killed those who had been looting Creole property. Seeing the resolve of the Creoles, the Indians slowly began to depart the town. It was a rancorous departure, however, and some Indians promised that they would be back and "drink chicha in the skull" of Jacinto Rodríguez.[165] By February 16, a week after the Creoles had begun the insurrection, Oruro was finally back in their hands. The dead included twenty-seven Spaniards, thirteen Negro slaves, one Creole, and one Frenchman. Slaves were victimized because they were seen as loyal to the Europeans and in some cases also because they were not Indians. In addition, nineteen Indian rebels had died, for the most part at each other's hands.[166]

Smarting from their eviction from Oruro, and outraged that curaca Chungara had backed the Creoles, the Indians of Paria killed and replaced him with Santos Mamani, a former alcalde of Challapata. In the coming weeks, Mamani would besiege and repeatedly attack Oruro, presiding over an alliance that fractured more each time they were defeated by the Creoles.[167] Despite their setbacks, so confident were some rebels of victory, not only in Oruro but in the region, that they claimed that "the ruin of Oruro would serve as lunch, for dinner they would do the same with Potosí, for a snack, Chuquisaca, and [they] would finish off dining with Cochabamba."[168] Their appetite would not be sated, however, and on April 7, 1,000 royalist troops under Commandant José Ayarza arrived from Cochabamba, broke the siege, and entered a quiet, desolate Oruro.[169] Ayarza did not arrest the Rodríguez brothers, who now began to assist the royalists, and Jacinto wrote a letter to Viceroy Juan José Vertíz in which he sought to exculpate himself.[170] Around May 24, as the royalist troops continued to reestablish their dominance in the region, the Indians of Challapata and Poopó sought pardon and turned in Santos Mamani to Jacinto Rodríguez.[171] For his part, Rodríguez would be arrested in January 1784. He died the next year in jail while awaiting trial with numerous other Creoles in Buenos Aires.[172]

In the province and area of Cochabamba during February and March 1781, rebellion also raged as the insurgents attacked Tinquipaya, Colcha, Tacopaya, and Quirquiavi.[173] As in Oruro and elsewhere, the corpses were left unburied, the villages were looted, and those few taken prisoner were forced to serve the Indians and wear native clothes.[174] The day after the Colcha massacre, on February 22, other insurgents attacked the village of Palca in Misque province. After gaining entry into the church, they executed over 400 Hispanic men, women, and children, leaving "some on top of the others, and even on the altars [and] many in a shameless position." The village priest, Gabriel Josef Arnao, would later be found in his "sacred vestments stained with his own blood [and his body] ripped apart."[175] In the neighboring villages of Calliri, Machaca, and "others of less security," similar events played out and there was "no shortage of bloodshed."[176]

One of the worst attacks in this region came on February 25, in the town of Tapacari, about twenty-five miles from Cochabamba. The rebel Tomás Flores and about 2,000 Indians from Paria, Corque, and the vicinity of Tapacari gathered around the town on February 21, 1781, looting surrounding haciendas and killing curacas and Hispanics. As mass was being held, the insurgents stormed the town, killing those they found outside of the church. They then assaulted the church and began to slaughter people in the "altars, choir, and tower" until "not a man was left."[177] One did escape, however, to report that "the blood ran like streams from those who were beheaded there," while Indian men and women danced over and flogged the naked corpses, threw babies from the church tower, and reportedly drank the blood of their enemies.[178] After the carnage, the rebels took all of the religious statues and objects to the plaza and made a pyre of them.[179] Three days after the killings in Tapacari, on February 28, Indian rebels led by Marcos Churata simultaneously attacked the village of Tarata and the surrounding haciendas, killing all the Hispanics they encountered.[180]

The rebellion reached quite far south in Upper Peru, encompassing the provinces of Chichas, Lipes, and Porco, although it was not on the scale of that to the north.[181] In Chocaya, the Creole lawyer Lorenzo Antesana had a plan similar to his brethren in Oruro. He had sent purported edicts of Túpac Amaru as far south as Atacama, in present-day Chile, fomenting rebellion. However, when the rebels invaded Chocaya on March 6, 1781, despite already being in Indian dress, he was put to death before he could even get a putative rebel edict sparing Creoles out of his pocket.[182] The largest town in the southern region to fall, however, was Tupiza, in the province of Chichas. In a scene also reminiscent of Oruro, the rebellion there was led on March 7, 1781, by the mestizo militia sergeant Luís Laso de la Vega, who organized a mob to kill the few Spaniards in the town.[183] Hedging his bets, Laso de la Vega sent a letter to royal authorities in Santiago de Cotagaita saying that the corregidor had died in a riot and pleading for help to avoid an imminent Indian massacre. Simultaneously, he proclaimed himself governor and captain general of the province in the name of Túpac Amaru, sending decrees to neighboring towns calling for support and ordering death to those who opposed the uprising.[184]

While it took somewhat longer to suppress the rebellion to the north, the royalists rapidly reasserted their command in this area. Much of this was due to the fact that a royalist column under José de Reseguín was heading north, ultimately to break the siege of La Paz. Tipped off by refugees fleeing the area, on March 17, at around 4:00 A.M., he stealthily surrounded the town, led a group of soldiers up the main street, and arrested a surprised Laso de la Vega, who had answered his door half-naked. By afternoon, Reseguín had rounded up 160 prisoners, 23 of whom would shortly be hanged, with more to follow in the coming week.[185]

Farther to the north, in Chayanta province, while the insurgents enforced their siege of Oruro in March 1781, the rebel Simón Castillo began final preparations to attack the small town of San Pedro de Buenavista. Castillo had raided haciendas in the region and occupied the town twice before, in October and December 1780, looting, searching for curacas and mestizos, and presenting an order said to have been written by Túpac Amaru abolishing all religious fees.[186] This was, however, only the prelude. In early March 1781, over 2,000 Indians from the vicinity of San Pedro, Moscari, Cana, Pocoata, and Macha began a siege of the town, cutting off communication, food, and water supplies. Although this was orchestrated by Castillo from a hacienda about twelve miles away, it was led by the rebel curaca Pasqual Tola, Santos Yujra, Bernabe Cuchillo, and Sebastían Puntado. Castillo not only promised his followers that Túpac Amaru would arrive in May "without fail" but ordered the rebels to "kill from the priest down" through the mestizos.[187] On March 5, the Indians entered the town, and despite fear, fatigue, thirst, and a seemingly endless hail of rocks, the Hispanics, gathered yet again in the village church and adjoining cemetery, fired upon and held off the rebels.

The standoff lasted until March 9, 1781, the same day that Santos Mamani led his first attack on Oruro, when the rebels, concerned about a reported advance of loyalist troops from Cochabamba, decided to mount an all-out attack. Initially, the besieged seemed to have some success in repelling the assault, but the tide quickly turned to the insurgents' favor with the arrival of about 2,000 Indians from Moscari, gathered by Castillo and led by Marcos Colque. A new rain of stones descended upon the church, shattering the roof and silencing the weapons of those inside. As the Indians broke away the church door, Father Ysidro Herrera begged for mercy for those inside. The rebels told him it was futile, that they planned to kill everyone. Losing all hope, the priest opened the church doors and the Hispanics "hand[ed] themselves over to the arms of death."[188]

Father Herrera was the first to leave, holding the sacrament. He was greeted by shouts of "Kill, kill the priest," beaten to death, and then beheaded.[189] Almost every person inside the church, who in all numbered about 500, including four other priests as well as several infants, was then killed, although the rebels did spare some Hispanic women to serve as slaves. Inside the church, they left "not [an] . . . altarpiece standing," and they stripped religious images before destroying them.[190] The scene of carnage and destruction was, for the rebels, one worthy of celebration, and Castillo arrived the following day to join in the festivities. For the next few days, the rebels celebrated in the town and church, "with flutes and drums [and] dancing" while "mimicking the sacred ceremonies," drinking chicha from silver chalices before casting them aside.[191]

Ten days after the San Pedro massacre, on March 19, 1781, just as the siege of Sorata was gearing up in Peru, the rebel Tomás Callisaya entered the village of Tiquina on the shore of Lake Titicaca. He called for the death of all Hispanics, including priests, corregidors and other crown officials, curacas, and all of their families. Seeking the immediate end of both Hispanics and their culture, he further commanded the Indians not to attend any Catholic services or to eat bread or drink water from fountains.[192] Callisaya had tapped a wellspring of Indian support, and as Indians flocked to his side, the Hispanics fled to the church. His prey corralled, he told the Hispanics that they were going to die, and he would burn the church if they did not surrender.

As in San Pedro de Buenavista, the Hispanics soon lost hope and came out, each carrying a crucifix or other religious object, and "we had hardly walked to the gallows . . . when the Spanish men were carried off by the Indian men, and the Spanish women were carried off by the Indian women . . . forming in that theater a funeral lake of blood . . . of one hundred souls . . . of both sexes, children . . . Indians . . . collectors [and] dependents of the corregidor."[193] The massacre at Tiquina was typical, and similar events were repeated in Chucuito, Juli, and Copacabana as well as many other villages in the region.[194]

Not far from Tiquina, in La Paz the rebels had begun a siege beginning on March 14, 1781. It was led by the Indian Túpac Catari, who was born around 1750 as Julián Apasa in the village of Ayoayo, in Sicasica province. Of very modest origins, it appears that he was orphaned as a child and raised by the village sacristan. Despite the religious context of his upbringing, like Tomás Catari in Chayanta, he never learned to read or to speak Spanish, and instead spoke only Aymara.[195] His background is hazy, although he did intercept a letter from Túpac Amaru to Tomás Catari. Subsequently, he adopted the nom de guerre of Túpac Catari in an effort to draw adherents from both rebel leaders. After the deaths of these leaders, he claimed at times to be their reincarnation.[196]

In January and February 1781, he was active in Sicasica and Pacajes provinces, where his genocidal radicalism attracted many supporters. By March he led them to start the siege of La Paz, and at his height he commanded about 40,000 followers principally from the provinces surrounding Lake Titicaca and La Paz, in addition to others who had participated in uprisings in the provinces of Paucarcolla, Cochabamba, Chayanta, Oruro, Paria, Carangas, Pacajes, and Porco. They enforced the first siege until June 30, 1781, when loyalists under Commandant Ignacio Flores managed to lift it.[197] During this time, the commitment by the rebels to their cause impressed the commander of the forces defending the city, Sebastián de Segurola, who noted that the insurgents fought with "a spirit . . . so horrible that . . . it can serve as an example as the most valiant nation."[198]

But it was not combat that killed most people in La Paz. In excess of 10,000 people, or about one-third of the population, would perish, mostly from starvation, before the city was firmly back in Spanish control. The effects of combat and hunger were so extreme that "there was not one" who was not injured or affected, and the residents were compelled to eat "not only the horses, mules, and donkeys but also (after having run out of dogs and cats) leather and trunks served as the best subsistence."[199] One priest who survived alluded to cannibalism among the besieged, offering that some had eaten "meat, perhaps or perhaps not of people, of which there is no shortage of people who assure me of this."[200] While Flores managed to lift the siege and bring provisions into the devastated city, he was soon beset by numerous desertions as his unruly troops chafed under attempts to discipline them. Having at least offered succor to the city, and seeing his forces rapidly dwindling, he retreated to Oruro in late July. The rebels monitored their movements, and by August 5 they had again placed the city under siege and resumed hostilities, now in the company of rebels led by Andrés Túpac Amaru, fresh from his victory in Sorata.[201]

While Catari officially proclaimed his allegiance to Andrés Túpac Amaru, the two forces not only kept separate camps but suffered such severe frictions that Catari expressed his intent to expel the Amaristas and Quechua speakers from the region upon his victory.[202] In mid-September, Diego Túpac Amaru had Andrés come to Azángaro to assist him there, and dispatched another cousin of the Inca, Miguel Bastidas Túpac Amaru, to El Alto in his stead. Finally, on October 17, 1781, forces led by Josef Reseguín managed to definitively break the siege. The Aymara rebel was betrayed and captured after a feast early the following month. Like Túpac Amaru, he was sentenced to be ripped apart by four horses, which was carried out on November 13.[203]

Just as leadership was critical for the outbreak of the insurgency, so was its widespread elimination or co-optation vital for its suppression. The capture and death of Túpac Amaru and Tomás Catari, and then Dámaso and Nicolás Catari, Santos Mamani and Simón Castillo, and numerous other rebel leaders, were the result of their betrayal by their erstwhile followers who sought to take advantage of the amnesty.[204] Many curacas, and the communities they led, remained loyal to the Spanish and were given both symbolic and material rewards for their fealty.[205] By January 1782, only isolated resistance remained, and most of the rebels who had not been captured or killed signed the Peace of Sicuani.[206] Approximately 100,000 people, or 8 percent of the population, perished in the insurgency, and approximately 40,000 of them were Hispanics.[207]

To the extent that the colonial experience had been initiated by genocide against the Indians and further advanced through ethnocide, the latter trait returned to the fore with a vengeance. There was soon a concerted effort under way by the Spanish authorities to eliminate indigenous customs and identity. The position of curaca was formally abolished, and Indian communities came under even closer supervision by Hispanics. Symbolic expressions of native heritage were likewise banned, such as Incaic paintings, royal garb, flags, literature, and drama concerning the pre-Hispanic past. Underscoring the depth to which the Spanish sought the elimination of indigenous culture was the redoubling of earlier efforts to eliminate native languages, which began in 1774, with the prohibition of the use of Quechua.[208]

In an effort to mitigate any resistance such measures might incite, the crown sought to address some of the major causes of the rebellion. Viceroy Jáuregui reduced mita demands, and his successor, Viceroy de Croix, abolished the legal reparto and introduced the intendant system in place of that of the corregidores in 1784. Later, in 1787, an audiencia, or district court with executive powers, was established in Cuzco. While the Spanish recognized three of the causes of the rebellion in these acts—the mita, reparto, and ineffective legal redress— the effects of the edicts were minimal. Indians continued to be exploited by their local overlords, and subintendants continued in the same tradition of the corregidors who preceded them. Túpac Amaru had succeeded in officially eliminating the reparto and securing the establishment of an audiencia in Cuzco, but the "success" was not only Pyrrhic but also hollow and did not in any substantive way improve the conditions of the natives.[209]

The Caste War of Yucatán: The Dialectics of Independence and Economic Development

Like the Pueblo Revolt of New Mexico, the 1848–1901 Caste War of Yucatán was successful in reclaiming for indigenous peoples the independence that had been lost through Spanish conquest. Unlike in New Mexico, however, the Indians maintained their independence for just over a half-century, controlling roughly the area of the present-day Mexican state of Quintana Roo. It was, according to Reed, "the most successful revolt by native people in the new world."[210] Given the length and changing nature of the conflict, this section does not offer a detailed military history. Rather, it focuses on the pivotal events that underscore its different phases.[211]

The roots of the Caste War stretch back through the colonial experience, although events in the early national period set it in motion. In 1821 independence from Spain brought both challenges and opportunities to all residents of the peninsula. The closure of the market in Spain and Cuba, which remained under Spanish control, for rice, cotton, cattle, and logwood products exported from Yucatán, and the temporary end of Indian tribute initially reduced tax revenues and economic productivity.[212] This downturn, however, was short-lived, and, aided by the introduction of tax incentives in 1823, Yucatán experienced a growth of sugar cultivation that responded to international demand and the decline of imports from Cuba.

Shortly afterwards, the cultivation of henequen for twine also expanded significantly, and like sugar, it was largely cultivated for export. By 1846, only thirteen years after the establishment of the first henequen plantation, the crop had become the second-most valuable export, and the sector employed the greatest number of people in Yucatán. Sugar remained the largest crop in terms of value until it was eclipsed by henequen in 1870.[213] The export-oriented growth of henequen and sugar brought tens of thousands of settlers to frontier towns, eroded the traditional paternalistic and internally oriented nature of the hacienda, encroached on native lands, and led to increasing contacts between Hispanics and the Huits, Maya who had long been isolated from external forces.[214]

While in New Mexico it was the expansion of the missionary frontier, and its attendant settlement and exploitation patterns, that paved the way for conflict, in Yucatán it was the expansion of the economic frontier that had the same effect. As a result, the expansion of the sugar frontier, which was central to the economic program of the liberal ruling elite, would also contribute to their downfall.[215]

Independence also brought severe dislocations to the Church as a result of the forced sale of Church lands and, beginning in 1843, the abolition of tithes and many obventions, or religious exactions.[216] Nevertheless, the civil taxes and the fagina, or levy of forced labor of four to six days per year, continued, the latter now used to build roads to open and link the frontier to the larger cities.[217] Although formally freed from tithes and obventions, the Indians saw dramatic increases in baptism, marriage, and other fees, continuing taxes for catechism and church maintenance, as well as increasing Church encroachment on Indian lands.[218] As in Peru and Upper Peru in the 1770s, these efforts by the Church to make up lost revenue, as well as the widespread promiscuity of priests and their frequent absence from their parishes, served to alienate the Indians from the Church.[219] The native elite was also negatively affected by the anticlerical reforms of the era, as native leaders and those who worked for the Church had been exempt from many ecclesiastical and civil taxes. Less revenue for the Church in the form of obventions meant less revenue for Indian headmen from commissions and also less social distinction between those formerly exempt and those who had not been.[220]

On both a regional and national level, the primary political fault line was between liberalism, which favored a more decentralized, federalist, and secular approach to nation-building, and conservatism, which supported a strong central government and was more respectful of the traditional prerogatives of the Church. By 1835, the wily Mexican leader Santa Anna, who had come to power as a liberal, had abandoned these views in favor of conservatism. Reflecting the conservative, and his own, preference for centralized power, he appointed state governors as he endeavored to consolidate his authority. The apprehensions of liberals in Yucatán, many of whom were sugar producers, concerning tax increases decreed in Mexico City were realized when Santa Anna increased export duties and taxes on intrastate commerce and tobacco, largely to fund the war with the United States over Texas. The greatest irritant to Yucatecos, however, was the sending of their men to fight in Texas. Fearing such a fate, in May 1839 Santiago Imán, a merchant and captain in the Yucatecan militia in Tizimin, revolted with the support of army deserters, some citizens of Tizimin, and blacks from the San Fernando ranch. After successive defeats, and recognizing the urgent need for more widespread support, Imán appealed to the Indians for support. To arouse their sympathies, he promised a permanent end to obventions and, implicitly or explicitly, lands for his supporters and a reduction of civil taxes. This had the effect he sought, and as native support for his rebellion quickly grew, his fortunes changed, and with their help he soon took Chemax and Valladolid. He then established a provisional government, reinstated the liberal 1825 constitution, and replaced the obvention with a religious tax of 12 reales per year applied to male Indians between the ages of 14 and 60. Reflecting the support for liberalism in the region, on February 18, 1840, Mérida proclaimed independence from Mexico, pending the restoration of federalism in the republic.[221]

According to one contemporary, with the mobilization of the natives and the fall of Valladolid to Imán's forces, the Indians "for the first time . . . measured their power and their force with that of the whites," and by enlisting Indian support the "Yucatecans, in a moment of delirium, took from his nest the serpent that in a short time would devour them."[222] Now independent, Santiago Méndez assumed the governorship of Yucatán, and Miguel Barbachano became vice governor. Despite the liberal nature of the 1841 constitution that was subsequently promulgated, in frontier zones it was not political principles but the expansion of sugar and henequen which shaped Hispanic-Indian relations.[223]

The price of Yucatán's independence was steep, as the Mexican authorities closed their ports to Yucatecan products, and in 1843 Santa Anna moved to force the reintegration of the peninsula into Mexico. Again, the Indians were called to arms, this time by Barbachano, who had replaced Méndez as governor and, who like Imán before him, promised land and an end to civil taxes for those natives who joined. Again defeated by Yucatecan forces, the central government negotiated and, in December 1843, agreed to recognize Yucatán's autonomy, exempt the Yucatecans from military service in Texas, and reopen ports and markets to Yucatecan products. The Hispanics had obtained what they wanted, but the Indians were still waiting to be rewarded for their loyalty. Just as Imán and Barbachano did not keep their promises, neither did Santa Anna, who soon reneged on the agreement. As a result, in December 1845 Yucatán again declared its sovereignty.[224]

As American forces invaded Mexico the following year, Barbachano agreed to reintegrate Yucatán into Mexico to help repel the U.S. invasion, after Santa Anna had reinstated the liberal 1824 constitution and agreed to honor the 1843 agreement of reunion. This, however, enraged the leaders of Campeche, and in November 1846, Domingo Barret, a supporter of Méndez, or Mendecista, led a revolt against Barbachano to maintain their independence from Mexico.[225]

Antonio Trujeque, the Mendecista political boss of Peto, raised a largely Indian army of 3,000 in Tihosuco and led them to Valladolid on January 15, 1847. After the garrison of 300 men under Lieutenant Colonel Claudio Venegas refused to surrender, Trujeque led the assault.

Soon the Indian troops could not be controlled by their Hispanic organizers. Among those leading the Indians were Cecilio Chi and Bonifacio Novelo, two men who would figure prominently in the Caste War. This second assault on Valladolid turned into a rampage and was marked by widespread looting, rapes, and reports of cannibalism. The Indians killed "without respecting sex nor age," destroying "what they could not rob." Victims "were paraded in triumph through the streets, and when the executioners were done insulting them," many were tossed into bonfires lit with furniture and official documents.[226] The savageness of the attack stunned the Hispanics and emboldened the Indians and their native leaders. Amid fears of "a general uprising of the indigenous race against that of the white," Barbachano surrendered power to Domingo Barret on January 22, 1847, and soon departed to Havana. By July, Barret had resigned in favor of his ally Santiago Méndez, who, instead of rewarding the Indians for their support, disillusioned them by restoring obventions.[227]

In July 1847, already heightened fears of a race war were again fanned when Manuel Antonio Ay, the Indian batab, or chief, of Chichimila, who had also been involved in the most recent carnage in Valladolid, was arrested for conspiring to organize an Indian uprising. During the trial that followed, the breadth of the plot, involving Cecilio Chi, based in Ichmul, Jacinto Pat, the wealthy federalist batab of Tihosuco, and Bonifacio Novelo, a rural merchant based in Valladolid, came to light.[228] Ay was soon found guilty of plotting rebellion and executed in Valladolid on July 26, 1847. To Chi, Pat, and Novelo, it became clear that, unlike Hispanic rebels who were usually exiled, Indian insurgents would not be so lucky.[229]

The Caste War of Yucatán

Meanwhile, on July 28, Antonio Trujeque marched to Tepich in an effort to capture Chi. Although they did not find him, the troops beat several Indians, looted, and raped at least one young girl there. Unknowingly, in so doing Trujeque and his troops had lit the spark that would ignite the Caste War.[230] On July 30, Chi led a retaliatory attack on Tepich, killing between twenty-five and thirty Hispanic families who had neglected to follow Trujeque's counsel to increase the town's defenses.[231] The Caste War had begun. Troops were again sent to Tepich where, among other actions, they locked many Indian women, children, and elders in houses and burned them alive.[232] The Indian response was not long in coming, and within days they attacked the town of Ekpedz and the surrounding area, killing the Hispanics they encountered, seizing weapons, and looting and burning houses before retreating to Chunbob.[233]

Fearful of the spread of rebellion, in Mérida and Campeche the Hispanics rapidly and unsuccessfully tried to patch up their differences while preparing their defenses. Between December 1847 and January 1848, Governor Méndez decreed martial law, prohibited the sale of gunpowder and lead, ordered the seizure of all Indian arms other than machetes, and offered pardon to those rebels who surrendered immediately.[234] Accompanying this was what amounted to a witch hunt against Indians, especially batabs who were suspected of supporting the rebellion. Many were executed, such as those of Chicxulub, Motul, Yaxkukul, Concal, Uman, and Acanceh, while over 108 others were sent to prisons in Campeche or Veracruz. Speaking of the actions of the Hispanic authorities, Baqueiro notes that "innumerable innocents [were made] victims of [Hispanic] delirium."[235]

Despite the increasing repression, the war intensified throughout August and only worsened in September as a result of the withdrawal of troops from frontier towns to augment the factions in the continuing conflict between Mérida and Campeche.[236] This would become a pattern in the years ahead, and the rebels lost no time in filling the vacuum. Rebels invaded Tixcacalcupul, killing the local priest and "almost all" of the whites there, including many women and children.[237] Soon afterward, Tinum, Sabán, Chikinoonot, and Sacalaca fell and were put to the torch, and while many of the Hispanics were able to flee in advance of the rebel offensive, many others were captured and killed.[238] After razing the hamlets and haciendas around Tihosuco, the rebels attacked and laid siege to the town on November 8, 1847. Vastly outnumbered, the garrison and residents fought their way out to Peto two days later, handing the rebels an easy victory. It was the rebels' first conquest of a large town, and apart from a boost to morale, it yielded guns, ammunition, livestock, alcohol, and up to 16,000 pesos.

By late November, such was the rebel advance that they controlled the entire area between Peto and Valladolid.[239] Generally, they preferred to raze a town instead of trying to hold it, while the Hispanics sought to retake and reoccupy what had been lost. Tihosuco was not destroyed when it fell to the insurgents, however, as it was Jacinto Pat's hometown.[240] The rebels soon advanced on the town of Ichmul, attacking it unsuccessfully on December 5. Having purchased more munitions in British Honduras, they again besieged it on December 19. On Christmas Eve, the surviving Hispanics fought their way out of town, joining Colonel Eulogio Rosado and his 2,500 troops in Peto. The rebels celebrated their victory in Ichmul on Christmas Day by looting and burning the town.[241] Indians under Jacinto Pat now set their sights on Peto, where the ferocity of Indian combat continued to consume Hispanic morale. Having lost over half of his troops through desertion, Colonel Rosado decided it was time to retreat and regroup. On February 6, 1848, he abandoned Peto, leading a ragged, panic-stricken column of 2,000 people to Tekax.[242]

As the rebels under Pat were preparing to attack Ichmul in early December

1847, rebels under Cecilio Chi had launched an offensive in the area of Valladolid, with the town as the ultimate objective. With the capture of Popolá, the last road out of Valladolid and which led to Izamal fell under Indian control. Not only did this isolate the larger towns, but the booty gained in the process provided goods such as silver, cotton, and honey, which they took south to British Honduras to trade for weapons and ammunition. Having dominated the area, they attacked Valladolid unsuccessfully on December 4, 1847.[243] Repulsing the assault did not break the siege, however, which continued through February as the will of the defenders progressively eroded. On the night of March 18, the Hispanics made the decision to abandon the town the next day.[244]

Despite the plans and orders to ensure an orderly exit, it quickly turned into a free-for-all. The rebels swept into the vacuum of the retreating Hispanics, killing all those they could. As Ancona notes, "Soldiers, women and children fell bathed in their blood, and the screams, the moans, and curses which escaped the lips of the victims were mixed with the cries of victory" of the Indians.[245] As the band of 10,000 refugees and over 100 carriages lumbered over the next three days on their thirty-mile journey to Espita, the Indians kept up the pressure and the soldiers deserted in droves, leaving the defenseless to the Indian will. Those who survived eventually made it to the haven of Mérida, via Espita and Temax.[246] In the coming months, Tizimin, Río Lagartos, Espita, Dzilam, Dzidzantún, Yaxcabá, Tunkás, Pixoy, Tinún, Dzitás, Mani, Sotuta, and Sitilpech would also fall to the insurgents.[247]

As the tide of war swept ever closer to Mérida and negotiations with the Indians yielded nothing, Méndez stepped down as governor, ceding the post to his rival Miguel Barbachano, who, it was believed, had more influence among the rebels.[248] Barbachano, as governor, now sought a permanent peace treaty with Pat, the rebel leader most willing to negotiate. In April they agreed not only to an end of the head tax and reduced fees for religious services but also that the debts of hacienda laborers would be forgiven, Indians could use state lands, the weapons seized from the Indians would be returned, and there would be no taxes on alcohol production. To guarantee that the treaty would be honored, and with Barbachano's blessing, Pat also insisted that Barbachano would be governor of Yucatán for life and that Pat would likewise be governor for life of the Indians of the region.[249] To symbolize the treaty, Barbachano sent Pat a staff and a white sash of office, upon which was emblazoned in gold letters "Gran Cacique de Yucatán." The reach of Pat's political ambition had exceeded his grasp, and other rebel leaders were outraged. Cecilio Chi, with the support of the rebel leaders Florentino Chan and Venancio Pec, wasted no time in sending his lieutenant, Raimundo Chi, at the head of 1,500 troops to Pat in Tzucacab. Before all of the "Gran Cacique's" troops, Chi seized and tore up the treaty, took the staff and sash of office, and burned them all.[250]

To underscore that there would be no peace, Cecilio Chi prosecuted the war with a vengeance, concentrating his forces outside of Izamal, while also laying siege to Sitilpech, five miles east. The loss of at least 350 men from Izamal in an effort to aid Sitilpech, the most in a single battle, broke the will of the Hispanics there. After a week of siege, the Hispanics decided to abandon Izamal on May 28, 1848. As in Valladolid, Ichmul, Peto, and elsewhere, as the 1,000 soldiers made their exit, the Indians entered the town, killing all they could, looting and burning what stood. The irony was that they abandoned the town the night before the Indians planned to lift the siege. Bacalar, to the south on the Río Hondo, had also fallen to rebels led by Venancio Pec, Juan Pablo Cocom, and Teodoro Villanueva the same day. Only two days earlier, Colonel Cetina had abandoned Ticul in the face of a determined siege by rebels under Pat, who was seeking to regain his legitimacy as a leader after being tainted by the peace treaty.[251]

By the end of May 1848, the rebels had taken 250 towns and villages and were masters of over 80 percent of Yucatán, and more than ever, Mérida and Campeche were "colonies in a foreign country," tenuously connected by one road. The rebels were advancing and soon were within three miles of Campeche and eighteen miles of Mérida.[252] Mérida was bursting at the seams with refugees, and those who could not find accommodations as guests in homes lived in churches, government buildings, plazas, and the streets. The population of Mérida was now double what it was in peacetime and held 100,000 of the 140,000 whites and mestizos in the peninsula.[253] Things were not much better in Campeche, where, according to Baqueiro, the number of refugees was "a sure thermometer of what has happening" and the town was "filled with people of different classes and conditions, of strange dress, and also different manners."[254] Certainly the "thermometer" had risen in that area in April after 3,000 rebels led by José María Barrera had conquered the Chenes area, situated in and to the south of the Puuc mountain range, swelling their ranks with yet more recruits and Campeche with yet more refugees.[255]

The Hispanic Counteroffensive

By May 1848, the planting season was approaching, and this would be a major factor in turning the tide of the conflict. The Indians had to plant to survive, and increasing numbers slipped away to return to their milpas, or cornfields. In addition, the extremity of the plight of the Hispanics was becoming known outside of the region. In Veracruz, New Orleans, and Havana, groups sympathetic to the Hispanics organized relief efforts, gathering and sending food, money, and weapons. The silver and jewels of the church in Yucatán were seized by the Hispanic authorities and sold in Cuba, the proceeds used to buy more weapons. Fortunately for the Hispanics, the western Maya had not risen to the extent of their brethren in the east. As Dumond notes, "Successful recruitment stopped as the rebel advance stalled . . . the rebels had reached the heartland of the original Spanish colony, the region longest under close Spanish domination, the area of the heaviest fully settled population, and also—as it turned out—home to the campesinos most loyal to the status quo." Although Mérida and Campeche were clearly under serious threat, it was not, according to Rugeley, a "Maya near-miss" as the rebels were overextended, encountered less support in this region, and increasingly faded back to their cornfields.[256]

In the summer and early fall of 1848, the Hispanic counteroffensive got under way and soon bore fruit, as Tunkás, Maní, Sotuta, Cenotillo, Hocabá, Pustunich, Oxkutzcab, Teabo, and Tabi, or what remained of them, came back under their control.[257] In the region around Campeche, where the rebel Juan de Dios May was active, the Hispanics retook Xtocbiakal and Sahcabá, where May was killed, as well as Hecelchakán and Bolonchénticul.[258] By early fall, about the only settlement the insurgents still controlled was Bacalar, which had become a vital rebel entrepôt for the supply of munitions from British Honduras.[259] Coinciding with the counteroffensive was Yucatán's reintegration into the Mexican union in August 1848. With it came a promise of 14,000 pesos a month for support of the war effort, in addition to an immediate payment of 150,000 pesos and 2,000 rifles.[260]

The increase of money, munitions, and even American mercenaries greatly improved Hispanic morale, as did a continuing string of victories. In December 1848, they retook Peto, Dzonotchel, Ichmul, Tihosuco, and Valladolid, while January 1849 yielded Cuncumul, Ebtun, Dzitnup, Temoson, Tizimin, Espita, Sabán, and Tinum.[261] The Hispanics also now better understood Indian tactics and the value of flanking patrols to defeat them, and in March 1849 they began to sell rebel captives as slaves in Cuba. Despite the rapid and dramatic pace of their counterattack, and the fact that many rebels took advantage of an amnesty, it led not to outright victory but to a stalemate. Fifteen thousand troops spread out in garrisons along the frontier were under nearly constant attack or siege, especially in the area between Sabán and Tizimin.[262] The Hispanic offensive was also not without its setbacks. Between December 1848 and January 1849, the insurgents seized Kancabdzonot, Santa María, Yaxuná, Calchén, Tabí, Tahchibichén, and Tixcacaltuyú.[263]

Also helping the Hispanics was the fact that the rebel war machine had slowed, as so much had been looted and destroyed over the last year that there was less booty to seize. Less loot meant less ability to buy weapons, shot, and powder in British Honduras. It did not, however, mean that the rebels fought with less determination.[264] Seeking to strangle the rebel supply lines, on April

20, 1849, Governor Barbachano dispatched Colonel Cetina with 800 men from Sisal to retake Bacalar. By early May he and his forces had wrestled it from forces under José María Tzuc, Isaac Pat, and Cosme Damían Pech.[265] For the rebels, the loss of Bacalar and increased Hispanic patrols on the Río Hondo made getting munitions more difficult, but not impossible, as they made better use of other trails and created new supply lines originating in Ascención Bay.[266] The isolation of Bacalar, other troop demands, and continuing civil discord in Yucatán meant that for the next eight years, despite occasional relief forces, the Bacalar garrison would basically be ignored until the Indians retook it in February 1858.[267] By late summer 1849 such was the progress of the Hispanics that Izamal, Peto, Sitilpech, Sacalaca, Ticul, Tunkás, and Tekax were again under their control.[268] Many of these towns, however, such as Tihosuco, Sabán, and Bacalar, were subject to months of rebel sieges.[269]

The Hispanic counteroffensive that began in the early summer of 1848 shifted the entire balance of the war. The rebels were now often literally on the run, and a great number were starving. Apparently in December 1848, though no later than September 1849, they had also lost their most radical leader, Cecilio Chi, who had been killed by his mestizo secretary, Atanacio Flores, who had been having an affair with Chi's wife.[270] Jacinto Pat's spirit was largely broken by the loss of his son, Marcelo, who was killed in the battle for Oxkutzcab.[271] His title of Gran Cacique de Yucatán stripped, his son dead, two of his daughters in Hispanic hands, and the tide of battle against him, he increasingly found solace in alcohol.[272] In September 1849, Pat's willingness to negotiate, as well as his efforts to generate money to buy weapons by taxing his subjects, led to his assassination by forces loyal to Florentino Chan and Venancio Pec at Holchén, about fifteen miles from Bacalar.[273] While José María Barrera led the troops in the south that had previously recognized Pat, the movement was considerably more fragmented than it had been before the deaths of Chi and Pat.[274]

As the dry season, from September to April, arrived in 1849–50, the Hispanics sought to unleash a new offensive to finish off their enemies under General Manuel Micheltorena, who replaced General López de Llergo as commander of the Hispanic troops. In their push southward, the Hispanics advanced through Iturbide, Becanchen, Kampocolche, and all the way to the rebel supply point of Cruz Chen on Ascención Bay, which had helped to compensate for the loss of Bacalar.[275] Despite the string of Hispanic victories, "neither the frightful misery in which . . . [the rebels] lived in the wilderness, nor the constant defeats that they were suffering, nor the tenacious persecution in all places by the Yucatecan troops, were capable of making them submit."[276] They fought on, "in the middle of their disasters, their families prisoners, deprived of their wives and sons, their fields ruined, their houses burned, ceaselessly pursued, and almost always defeated."[277] Though on the defensive, the insurgents kept up the pressure on the Hispanics, and in November 1850 alone they attacked Tekax, Xil, Bolenchenticul, and Hopolchen.[278]

The Speaking Cross

The rebels, increasingly plagued by starvation, had lost almost all that they once had conquered, as well as many of their original leaders. They needed something not only to reunite them but to inspire them against the odds. The rebel leader José María Barrera knew this as well as anyone and perhaps reflected upon it as he fled south from Hispanic forces in Kampocolche. Legend has it that at one of the small springs that dot the Yucatán, at a place that would come to be called Chan Santa Cruz, or Little Holy Cross, he encountered a small cross carved in a mahogany tree. Perhaps it was created by a Huit, or by Barrera himself; we may never know.[279]

In any case, Barrera erected another cross nearby, and with the assistance of Manuel Nahuat, gifted in the art of ventriloquism, he convinced the Indians that it spoke the word of God. Its words were a salve to the spirits of the rebels, and while it commanded them to launch an attack on Kampocolche, it also promised that the rebels would not be harmed by the bullets of the Hispanics. "A delirious fanaticism sprang from the hearts" of the rebels, who now became known as the Cruzob, or followers of the cross, and they attacked the town at 3:00 A.M. on January 4, 1851, "with a valor which in much time they had not shown."[280] Despite their failure to take the town and the loss of 108 Indian lives in the effort, the cross retained its appeal, and increasing numbers of rebels flocked to hear its putative revelations. Some rebels had been captured in Kampocolche, and as a result Colonel Novelo learned of the cross and its promises. On March 23, he led the first of what would be many attacks on the new rebel base of Chan Santa Cruz, killing Nahuat and bringing the cross, along with other captives, to Kampocolche.[281]

Barrera had seen the effect of the speaking cross during its brief tenure, and he wasted no time in creating another. Since Nahaut was dead, he had Juan de la Cruz Puc of Nabalam serve as scribe for the cross, interpreting and recording its putative will. As expressed through Puc, the cross was irate over the recent setbacks and said it would not speak again but would transmit its wishes through Puc. It called for a vengeful attack on Yalcoba, which lay eighty miles to the north, in an effort to liberate the original cross, which they mistakenly believed had been taken there. Again, the rebels were assured of divine protection with the promise that three supernatural beings would assist them and ensure victory.[282] There is some confusion over exactly how many crosses there were, though it appears that there were three which emerged after the capture of the original one erected by Barrera.[283] While the speaking cross clearly had a vital role in uniting a desperate and almost vanquished group, the rebel leaders also saw that it had value "to avoid responsibility for unpopular or risky decisions."[284]

While the written word of the cross elicited respect, it did not rival the veneration aroused by a speaking cross. Barrera saw this and, seeking to enhance the appeal of the cult, constructed a church in Chan Santa Cruz. In it was an inner sanctum, called La Gloria, where the three crosses were kept on the altar. Behind it was dug a cavity, into which a person could fit, along with a cask which, when spoken through, gave the voice a mysterious, echoing, ethereal quality. The fact that almost no one was allowed in La Gloria, and that the church was under constant guard, further imbued the cult with a mystique.[285] While it did not give the Indians what they most needed, food to relieve their famine, it did offer something almost as important, hope, as well as a literal rallying point. Natives were attracted to it from as far north as Valladolid and from the region of Bacalar in the south.

Not all those in the south, however, were interested in the promises of the cross or, for that matter, wanted to continue fighting. In Chichenha, during August 1851, the rebel Angelino Itza was negotiating a peace with the Mexican authorities through the good offices of the mayor of Peten, Modesto Méndez. Barrera attended these negotiations, which in essence proposed to grant autonomy to Chichenha in exchange for the recognition of the authority of Mexico. While Itza and his followers accepted the terms and became known as the Pacíficos del Sur, or Peaceful Ones of the South, Barrera headed home to Chan Santa Cruz. To underscore his opposition to such negotiation, he returned a month later, razed Chichenha, and took Itza and his lieutenants as prisoners back to Chan Santa Cruz.[286]

Meanwhile, despite his policy of unremitting attacks on the rebels, General Micheltorena was unable to defeat them. In September 1850, he resigned as a result of the government's refusal to provide the financial support he believed was necessary to win the war. In his stead came General Rómulo Díaz de la Vega at the head of fresh troops, arriving in Mérida in late March 1851. As the rainy season tapered off, Vega began his offensive, arriving in Chan Santa Cruz on February 24. What he found was astonishing. The little settlement had grown into a town with a church, barracks, and leaders' residences, all built around a plaza in the Spanish fashion. He also found many Indians dead from starvation, and with Indian prisoners watching, he cut down the mahogany tree upon which was carved the "mother of crosses."[287] From there he marched on to Bacalar, where 621 troops had died since May 1849.[288] Despite his efforts, he failed to deal the rebels a decisive blow, and in fact his foray led to Indian attacks on Tekax and the settlements of Chunhuas and Nohbec as a result of soldiers being shifted from garrisons there to join his march. In mid-June 1852, his forces returned to Chan Santa Cruz, where they killed Venancio Pec and Juan Bautista Yam, in addition to rescuing numerous prisoners and capturing rebel weapons.[289]

Stalemate and an Indian State

It is hard to say when the Caste War actually ended. Rather than an end point, it is more appropriate to compare it to an illness, the worst of which is past but chronic symptoms remain. That is where Yucatán was in mid-1852. Not only had Mérida and Campeche avoided desolation, but Mérida was on the rebound. Most of the other major towns had been reoccupied by the Hispanics, defensive lines were maintained, many Indians had been forcibly resettled into towns under Hispanic control, and henequen production rebounded. For their part, the rebels battled repeated Hispanic offensives, as well as hunger and internal divisions.[290]

Despite being on the defensive, even in their stronghold of Chan Santa Cruz, the Cruzob—also now referred to as the indios bravos, or warlike ones, by Mexican authorities—were 35,000–40,000 strong, far from giving up, and quick to exploit weaknesses in Hispanic defenses, especially when troops were drawn from them to suppress the ongoing intra-Hispanic discord in the region.[291] In August 1853, during the Molas-Cepeda Revolt, a liberal uprising directed against Santa Anna and his governor, General Díaz de la Vega, the Cruzob attacked and razed Tacdzibichén, Uaymax, Sacalaca, Sabán, Dzonotchel, Chikindzonot, Ichmul, Tihosuco, Tixcacaltuyú, Santa María, and Yaxcaba.[292]

In the years to come, the Hispanics would attack Chan Santa Cruz numerous times while otherwise seeking to destroy rebel harvests in Cruzob territory, while the rebels kept the pressure on towns such as Tihosuco and Peto.[293] The year of 1855 saw numerous Indian attacks, such as those on Pachmul, Yaxcupil, Xpichil, Xbubucax, San Pedro, San Pablo, and Polunquil, the taking of considerable loot and numerous prisoners back to Chan Santa Cruz, and the death of more than 1,000 Hispanics in various engagements. Although both sides of the conflict could inflict substantial damage upon the other, neither could obtain a decisive advantage and the war remained stalemated. The rebels, though not free of their enemies, had indeed achieved autonomy.[294]

In addition to the military and religious aspects of running what amounted to their own country, there were commercial considerations. All were interrelated, as the sale of logging rights to enterprises in British Honduras, loot, and the breeding of draft animals and livestock were the oxygen that kept their military machine and independence alive. While Cruzob groups would often go to Bacalar and Ascención Bay to trade with people from British Honduras, other traders from British Honduras would make the journey to Chan Santa Cruz, selling not only powder and ammunition but also salt and manufactured goods from the south.[295] By the mid-1850s the Cruzob were better off than ever before. In 1856 they had a good harvest, which had been allowed to ripen due to a reduction in Hispanic incursions. They also had plenty of weapons and were eager to use them.[296] In April 1856, the rebels attacked Yaxcabá, Tibolon, Tiholop, Kaua, and Kancabdzonot, killing scores of people and, as usual, looting and burning what they could.[297] In 1857 the rebels also attacked Ekpedz, Chikindzonot, and Tekax.[298]

The raid on Tekax occurred during a new round of conflict between Mérida and Campeche. The spies of the Cruzob had learned of the discord, and the Tatich, or spiritual and overall leader of the Cruzob, ostensibly following the will of the speaking cross, sent 2,000 fighters under Crescencio Poot, the General of the Plaza, the Cruzob military leader, to Tekax. Into the town of 5,000 they marched on September 14, 1857, in uniform, in formation, and with some light-skinned men dressed as officers, all proclaiming for Campeche.[299] Those who thought the invading troops were Campechanos "soon come out of their sad hallucination to be sacrificed."[300] Poot turned his people loose on the town, and over 1,100 Hispanics were killed over the next few hours as the rebels entered houses, stores, and government buildings, killing almost everyone they could, including many women who were raped before being shot or hacked to death. By dawn, "all of the streets of the city were found colored with blood." Poot packed up the loot and much alcohol and left town, ultimately selling and trading much of it for powder with traders from British Honduras.[301]

Emboldened, and still chafing from the loss of Bacalar and the resulting pressure on their supply routes, the Cruzob sought to recapture the outpost on the Río Hondo. On February 21, 1858, soldiers under Venancio Puc assaulted the town and fort, surprising and quickly defeating its garrison of 300 soldiers. Over 250 defenders were killed in the storming of the town, and although some of the defenders managed to cross the Río Hondo and find sanctuary in British Honduras, most surrendered, believing that they would be allowed to abandon the town after giving up their arms, as had happened when the town fell to the rebels in 1848. Instead, many, including women, were immediately killed, while most others were executed in the days ahead.[302]

The continuing turmoil of Yucatecan politics in 1857 and 1858 had forestalled organizing reprisals for the loss of Tekax and Bacalar. In twenty-six months, Yucatán had six governors. It was a period, according to one contemporary, in which "governors rose and fell with the rapidity of buckets in a well."[303] Such was the distraction of the Mexican authorities that the rebels had been "burning and robbing with the greatest tranquility" the towns they assaulted.[304] By January 1860, however, the Hispanics had sufficiently organized their affairs to launch another attack on Chan Santa Cruz. On January 12, 1860, forces under Colonel Acereto arrived there with 2,850 soldiers, the largest group ever sent. As usual, the Cruzob abandoned their capital instead of defending it, and it took Poot about a week to gather his forces, including those from the regions of Bacalar and Peto. Perhaps because he had a strong force, or perhaps because they were very well armed, Poot did not engage in the usual siege but rather attacked and shattered the Hispanic troops, who, in the face of unrelenting assaults and continuing defeats, were clamoring to retreat. Fearing not only the Cruzob but also the rising internal dissension, Colonel Acereto ordered a retreat. In all, over 1,500 of the invaders would die, and the Cruzob had turned adversity into strength by capturing all of the enemy artillery, 2,500 rifles, 300 pack animals, and even the military band. No further efforts would be made to attack Chan Santa Cruz for some time.[305]

Still quite strong, in 1861, the Cruzob attacked several frontier towns, such as Ekpedz, where sixty Indians kidnapped the entire population, Sacalaca, which they razed while exterminating the retreating garrison, and Dzonotchel. In September 1861, in Tunkás, Poot repeated the tactic that had worked so well in Tekax, marching his people into town "perfectly uniformed like the Yucatecan[s] . . . marching with the regularity of well-ordered troops."[306] The first group was led by Claudio Novelo, a son of Bonifacio Novelo, who greeted and "was calling by their names the well known residents of the town."[307] Following close behind were more troops under Lorenzo Briceño and Crescencio Poot. Once the 300 Cruzob had entered the town, they gathered up the residents and mockingly forced them to shout their support for an uprising in Campeche, while the other rebels looted almost 50,000 pesos in silver and goods and burned the town. Only two people were killed during this assault. The rebels took the remaining Hispanic population of about 500 captive.[308] A few months later, the towns of Dzitás and Pisté suffered the same fate, the thirty inhabitants who were caught joining those already in the Cruzob capital.[309] The border between the Maya and Hispanic worlds was now very well defined, as the towns of Ekpedz, Sacalaca, Sabán, and Ichmul were all forsaken by the Hispanics to the jungle. Soldiers were the only residents of Tihosuco and Tixcacalcupul, while the few residents in Tekax, Peto, and Yaxcaba lived in constant fear of the Cruzob. Having faced annihilation in 1850, the Cruzob had carved a kingdom, repulsed all forays into their territory, vanquished Hispanic and even Indian enemies, and between 1858 and 1861 captured or killed in excess of 4,000 people.[310]

The appearance of the supreme power of the speaking cross masked, but did not prevent, numerous internal divisions among the Cruzob leadership. Several generals were critical of the cult of the speaking cross, perhaps because it limited their own power or forced them to undertake military actions that they did not support. On December 23, 1863, Venancio Puc was deposed and subsequently beheaded in a coup d'état, led by the mestizo general Dionisio Zapata Santos. The main issue was peace, and Zapata favored a negotiated settlement with the Mexicans. This was still a heretical idea to most of the Cruzob, and as the Mexican authorities sent a peace commission to British Honduras in the hope of negotiating with him, Zapata was killed in another coup. This one brought one of the few remaining original leaders, Bonifacio Novelo, to power as Tatich, replacing Augustín Barrera. Crescencio Poot replaced Leandro Santos as General of the Plaza, a post he would hold until 1885, and Bernabé Cen also ascended to the ruling inner circle.[311] By 1867, Novelo informed the visiting British arms merchant John Carmichael that while the cross still commanded respect, it no longer spoke.[312]

Around 1870, Bonifacio Novelo died, apparently of natural causes. Juan de la Cruz, who had served as secretary of the cross, rose to the position of Tatich, and in the early 1880s Crescencio Poot became General of the Plaza. Poot knew as well as anyone the dangers of favoring any accommodation with the Hispanics, though this did not stop him from entering into a peace treaty with Mexico, which he signed in Belize City in January 1884. Like the treaties with the Pacíficos, it codified the status quo, allowing Poot to continue as ruler, prohibiting any authorities to be imposed on the Cruzob without their permission, and providing for bilateral extradition of criminals. The price, as in the past, was recognizing the formal authority of Mexico. This appeared to work, but there was considerable resentment of it among other Cruzob leaders.

In August 1885, the opposition became manifest, and Aniceto Dzul led a coup in which Poot was killed. Dzul subsequently relocated his base of operations twelve miles south of Chan Santa Cruz. It is interesting to note that Juan de la Cruz remained as Tatich, in Chan Santa Cruz. He may have supported Dzul, or the internecine conflict may have been a strictly military matter.[313] It did, however, demonstrate the fragmentation in the region and the increase of the power of the generals over religious leaders. Shadowing this was the continuing decline in the Cruzob population. Whereas in the 1860s they numbered about 40,000, by 1890 the population was approximately a quarter of that. Dzul saw this decline during his rule, which ended when he died naturally in the late 1880s or early 1890s. He was succeeded by his trusted second in command, Román Pec, who in February 1886 had kept the pressure on the Hispanics by leading attacks in the region of Valladolid.[314]

As the Cruzob splintered from within, they were also increasingly negatively affected by changing geopolitical pressures. With the rise of British investment in Mexico, especially under Porfirio Diaz, the British government increasingly favored removing irritants to relations. The border between Mexico and British Honduras was one of them, and the continued sales of munitions by people in British Honduras to the Cruzob was another. Despite fears of Cruzob attacks as they improved their relations with Mexico City, the British negotiated and in July 1893 signed the Spencer-Mariscal treaty in which Mexico recognized British Honduras as British territory and clearly established the border between the two.[315]

Things were changing, and there was little Pec could do about it. Between the signing of the treaty in 1893 and its final ratification in Mexico in 1895, trade continued between British Honduras and the Cruzob, though on an increasingly modest scale. Pec tried to hold things together, executing his lieutenant, Crescencio Puc, and others who he believed favored peace. Isolated, Pec was killed in yet another coup, this one led by Felipe Yama, who now became General of the Plaza. Although the end was still to come, the fact that the beginning of the end had arrived was symbolized when, in January 1898, the armed barge Chetumal anchored in Mexican waters not far from Bacalar and closed the primary Cruzob trade route.[316]

Pressures had also been quietly building in the north. Henequen production had exploded in the northwest, responding to increasing demand not only for rope for ships but, beginning in 1880, for twine to be used for bundling wheat harvested in the United States by the McCormick reaper. Whereas in 1875 the henequen harvest was 6 million kilos, by 1885 this had climbed to 43 million, and by 1900 it had reached 81 million. The peninsula was further integrated by the expansion of rail and telegraph lines to Motul, Peto, Tekax, Tecoh, and Ticul.[317] In 1898 the Mexican government pushed their own frontier eastward, repopulating Ichmul, Sacalaca, and Tihosuco with military garrisons that would serve as a line of bases for the final subjugation of the Cruzob. The native kingdom was also pressured from the north, as La Compañía Agrícola and La Compañía Colonizadora obtained natural resource concessions on the north coast. The former had access to salt deposits, while both cultivated sugar, bananas, cocoa, and cotton in addition to extracting chicle, the base of chewing gum.[318] The isolation from which the Cruzob had benefited for so long was fast eroding.

In October 1899, 70-year-old General Ignacio Bravo arrived in Progreso to lead the final suppression of the Cruzob. In 1900 the Indians had come under the spiritual leadership of a new Tatich, Pedro Pascual Barrera, grandson of José María Barrera, the cult's originator.[319] By September 1900, Peto and Mérida had finally been linked by rail, and work continued to push it south, through Cruzob territory, to Ascención Bay. Progress cutting through the jungle was slow, only about one-third of a mile per day, and done under very heavy guard with repeating rifles and cannon, both of which the Cruzob had a hard time resisting. An epidemic of measles also took its toll, as did the flight of many Cruzob to British Honduras, and by February 1901, the Cruzob population in Yucatán was only around 800.

The end was clearly at hand, and Bacalar fell to the Mexicans on March 21,

1901, and on March 23, the battered Cruzob fought their last engagement, fifteen miles from Chan Santa Cruz, which General Bravo entered and found abandoned on May 4 or 5.[320] Symbolizing the end of the Cruzob was the renaming of Chan Santa Cruz to Santa Cruz de Bravo, after its conqueror, and in November 1902, the state of Quintana Roo was established, encompassing most of what had been the Indian state. Later Santa Cruz de Bravo would be renamed Felipe Carillo Puerto, and today it is the capital of Quintana Roo.[321] Indian independence, long riddled by internal factionalism, had come to its end, and the former Cruzob were now subject to the Mexican state.

4 Nativism, Caste Wars, and the Exterminatory Impulse

The three insurgencies that are the focus of this work were each a "conscious, organized attempt on the part of a society's members to revive or perpetuate selected aspects of its culture."[1] Each responded to a complex of "stresses" within their society and culture that either threatened their cultural or physical survival, such as in the case of the Pueblo Revolt, or were exacerbations of ongoing processes that had resulted in differing degrees of cultural decimation, such as in the case of the Great Rebellion and the Caste War of Yucatán.[2]

In all cases, this nativism was a response to ethnocide, or the effort to eliminate a culture but not a people, by the Hispanic colonizers or their descendants. Ethnocide is commonly viewed as a form of genocide, although in theory it is possible to conduct ethnocide without mass killings.[3] The point here is to recognize that ethnocide was inherent to the colonial experience in Latin America and continued to shape Hispanic-Indian relations in the postcolonial period as well.

In Latin America generally, and New Mexico specifically, the conquest resulted in genocide, with millions dying in its wake. While pre-Hispanic population figures are difficult to determine with precision, in some places this demographic implosion resulted in the deaths of up to 95 percent of the population. Here again a definitional issue arises, as the Spaniards generally sought to dominate and exploit, not exterminate, the native groups. The desire to dominate was often superseded, however, by genocidal objectives in cases where native groups refused to submit to Spanish rule. Furthermore, from the cultural perspective, the Spanish clearly had ethnocidal objectives, and in this sense they were exterminatory. In terms of the cost of human life, however, it appears that most natives died from diseases introduced by the Spanish to which they had no immunity, and others died from overwork and suicide. Nevertheless, as David Stannard writes, "deaths from disease *may* have exceeded those deriving from any other single cause but . . . [they] were in fact caused by intertwined and interacting *combinations* of lethal agents, combinations that took different forms in different locales."[4] Although the Spanish need for Indian labor attenuated the intent of genocide, certainly there was genocide, and the 1680 rebellion in New Mexico occurred in this context. There, population levels had fallen from about 130,000 in 1581 to about 60,000 in 1600. By 1638 the pueblo population was approximately 40,000, a number that would continue to fall to approximately 15,000 in 1678 and 7,000 by the early 1700s.[5]

One example of the link between Hispanic domination, native rebellion, and genocide was underscored during the 1681 entrada to New Mexico, when Juan Domínguez de Mendoza threatened the people of Alameda. There he told an elderly woman that unless the people of the pueblo showed fealty to the Hispanics, "not one stone will remain upon another in their pueblo, nor will any of them be left."[6] In the cases of the Great Rebellion and the Caste War of Yucatán, however, the effects of the genocide of the Spanish conquest had long passed. Nevertheless, as in New Mexico, native peoples in these areas were engaged in a struggle for physical and cultural survival and affirmation. In all cases, within this preexisting context of Hispanic-led genocide and ethnocide, the insurgents led millennially inspired nativistic movements in which the practical if not total extermination of Hispanics was both a means and an end.

The Past as Future: Nativism in New Mexico

The Pueblo Revolt was the most successful of a series of often wide-ranging conspiracies to eliminate the Hispanic presence in the Pueblo region.[7] Even after the 1680 revolt, many Indian groups continued to seek the extermination of Hispanics. Between 1680 and 1684 there were at least five conspiracies in the El Paso region with these aims, mostly led by Manso, Jano, Suma, Jocome, and Chinara Indians, often with support from the pueblos in the north.[8] Unlike almost all native uprisings in the Americas, the success of the Pueblo Revolt and the ensuing period of self-rule offers considerable detail concerning its nativistic quality.

After the Hispanics had been killed or expelled, Popé moved quickly to consolidate his authority and to systematically eradicate all nonnative influences in the region. Wearing Indian regalia and a bull's horn on his forehead, he began by visiting all of the towns that participated in the revolt, often in the company of Luís Tupatu of Pecurís, El Jaca of Taos, Alonso Catiti of Santo Domingo, and "a large retinue of people."[9] He commanded all Indians who had been baptized to bathe and scrub themselves, symbolically purifying themselves of the taint of baptismal waters. In addition, as many Indians had been forced by the friars into marriages, he told them that they were now free to leave their spouses and marry whomever they chose.[10] Popé prohibited the utterance of the names Jesus and María, along with the entire Spanish language, and specifically ordered the natives to abandon their Christian names. He further banned Catholicism and all things associated with it, and commanded people "to immediately break up and burn the images of the Holy Christ and of the Virgin Mary, and those of the other saints, crosses and all other things touching Christianity, and to burn the temples, [and] break the bells."[11]

Popé also ordered that "in no manner should they ever pronounce the name of God, the Blessed Sacrament, the Blessed Virgin, or the Saints, imposing great punishment, particularly that of the lash, should they do so."[12] Flogging was only one punishment, and those who had not supported the rebellion or who refused to comply were killed or enslaved.[13] Few rebels needed the lash to apostatize them, and the rebel disdain for Catholicism was evident during the siege of Santa Fe. As they burned the houses and church of the town, the Hispanics heard "the ridicule which the . . . Indian rebels made of the sacred things, intoning the alabado and the other prayers of the church with jeers."[14] In Jemez, when Lieutenant General Alonso García and his group fled south, he noted that "as we left the pueblo, the Indians mockingly rang the bells and scoffed at us."[15]

The elimination of Catholicism and Hispanic culture cleared the way for the resurgence of native religion and ritual and the social and political structure associated with it. Religion is the nexus where a group's concepts of origin, identity, social organization, customs, and relation to the cosmos interact, and the unbridled Hispanic assault on native religions following the conquest had struck at the heart of native identity. Simmons notes that in New Mexico the Hispanics "through interference with native ritual had upset the delicate balance between man and the forces of nature, thereby precipitating cosmic disaster."[16] Scholes also observes that in "the Pueblo system religion, village government and social institutions were so closely interrelated that it was impossible to abolish any part without destroying the whole."[17]

Seeking to reverse this "cosmic disaster," Popé "immediately upon the departure of the Spaniards . . . ordered their estufas constructed, these being the houses where they practice idolatry, and throughout the entire kingdom the Cachina was danced."[18] Native rites were now practiced openly, and the Indians "built their temples on the four sides and in the center of the plaza with small enclosures of piled rocks, where they offered up flour, plumes and seeds of the maguey, corn and tobacco . . . giving the children to understand that henceforth they should all do likewise."[19] Often these were "enclosed very carefully" to prevent their being trampled by animals.[20] By making offerings at these sites, the Indians believed that they "would have anything that they wished."[21]

Although the instruments of Catholic worship were systematically destroyed and many churches were burned, churches continued to be used by the Indians, though not in the manner originally intended. For example, in Sandía, much of the mission had been destroyed except for the "guard room . . . with the two cells that follow it. . . . in the third cell there is hanging from the whole circumference of the walls, arranged very carefully, . . . a large number of masks," which the Indians had "left with particular care for their dances."[22] In addition, "in the circumference of the cloister, the private oratory, and the refectory they attempted to make their dwellings, and in the principal cell of the three that I have mentioned, they have set up a forge with very good bellows and with a ploughshare as an anvil."[23] In Santo Domingo much of the mission had been "destroyed" in the rebellion, although some of it had "been rebuilt for a fortress and living quarters."[24] Even during the uprising in 1696, church buildings continued to serve a function for the Indians. In San Cristóbal the church was employed as "a smithy and stable, and it also serves as a place for them to gather and talk."[25] In Taos the church had also been converted to a stable and a forge, and in Picurís there were "diabolical figures," probably kachina dancers, painted on the walls.[26]

Such was Popé's zeal to extirpate Hispanic influences among the masses that he prohibited the cultivation of any crops that had been introduced by the Spaniards.[27] As a result, watermelons, cabbage, cucumbers, turnips, garlic, radishes, onion, wheat, peas, grapes, and peppers were banned, along with peach, plum, apricot, cherry, apple, and citrus trees. The only crops permitted were squash, beans, and corn. Likewise, pigs, cattle, cats, chickens, and sheep were to be killed, although horses had proved so valuable for transport and warfare that they were assimilated.[28] Despite the threat of severe punishment or even death, many people continued to cultivate crops introduced by the Spaniards. According to one contemporary, "They had obeyed in everything except with regards to the seeds."[29] Given the continuing famine, this may have been looked upon with a blind eye by the Indian leaders. Even ten years later, when Governor Vargas entered Cochiti on September 11, 1692, he saw fields of corn, melons, and squash.[30]

In 1681, despite famine, disease, and inter- and intratribal frictions, the general perception of the Hispanics after Otermín's entrada was that the Indians preferred the vagaries and hardships of independence to life under the Hispanics and that they were "very well content with the life they are living."[31] An elderly Indian told the Spanish that he believed "the life the [Indians] . . . led was better than among the Spaniards."[32]

The road to the nativistic, millennial utopia of the Pueblo Indians was that of genocide. Indeed, the utopia that they envisioned could only be forged through the elimination of the Hispanic population. Indian rule and Hispanic presence were in the eyes of the rebels clearly antithetical, and as such, genocide was inherent to the objectives of the rebellion. In San Diego de Jemez, an Indian messenger from Tesuque arrived on the night of August 10, 1680, calling upon the residents to "kill the Spaniards and friars who are here," and assuring them that "none of the Spaniards will remain alive" there or anywhere else in the region.[33] Just days before the revolt, the loyalist Pecos chief Juan Ye tipped off the Hispanics that there was a conspiracy afoot to "kill all the Spaniards and religious."[34]

Two loyal messengers sent by Governor Otermín to reconnoiter the Tano and Keres region immediately before the rebellion came running back the day the siege of Santa Fe began, reporting that Indians from Pecos, San Cristóbal, San Lorenzo, San Marcos, Galisteo, and La Cienega were "on the way to attack it and destroy the governor and all the Spaniards" and that they planned to "sack the said villa all together and kill within it the señor governor and captain-general, the religious, and all the citizens."[35] During the interrogations of prisoners just before the Hispanics abandoned Santa Fe, many asserted that Popé had ordered that they kill "the priests and the Spaniards, so that only the women and children would be left. They said that all the remaining men must be killed, even to the male child at the breast, as they have done in other parts where they have been."[36] In 1681, a Tanos Indian informed the Hispanics that Popé had "given them to understand that the father of all the Indians, their great captain, who had been such since the world had been inundated, had ordered the said Popé to tell all the pueblos to rebel and to swear that they would do so; that no religious or no Spanish person must remain."[37] The cabildo, or city council, of Santa Fe also noted "that many times . . . the revolting Indians . . . declared that not one [Hispanic] in the entire kingdom should escape with his life."[38]

The rebel Pedro Naranjo reported that Alonso Catiti had ordered him and the people of San Felipe "to assemble in order to go to the Villa to kill the governor and all who were with him."[39] Another Indian reported that the residents of San Felipe had gone to Santo Domingo "to kill the friars, the alcalde mayor, and the other persons who were there."[40] An elderly Indian, Pedro Gamboa, told his Spanish interrogators that he "has heard . . . that the Indians do not want religious or Spaniards" and during the attack on Santa Fe they sought to "destroy the governor . . . and all the people who were with him."[41] Another deponent, the Tiwa Jerónimo, likewise told his Hispanic captors that Popé had ordered the Indians to kill all priests and Spaniards.[42]

A Tewa Indian servant to the Hispanics named Antonio, who had been with them in the casas reales during the siege of Santa Fe, managed to escape before being recaptured by the Hispanics. Asked why he fled, he said it was "because he thought that the Spaniards would all be killed," given that the insurgents had insisted "the Spaniards must perish."[43] He further informed them that the rebels were planning an ambush "at the junction of the hills and the Río del Norte near the house of Cristóbal Anaya, and [would] there attack the Spaniards when they attempted to cross over, and annihilate them."[44] At this point of their journey southward with Governor Otermín, another captured Indian told the Hispanics that Indians from Tesuque had told those in San Cristóbal that the "Indians want to kill the Custodian, the Fathers and the Spaniards, and have said that whoever kills a Spaniard shall have an Indian woman as wife, and whoever kills four shall have as many wives, and those killing ten or more shall have as many wives. They have said that they will kill all the servants of the Spaniards and those who talk Castilian, and have ordered everyone to burn their rosaries."[45]

In Jemez, a rebel messenger urged the inhabitants to kill any Hispanics they encountered, assuring them that of those who had already fled south "not one of them will escape." In his journey southward, Lieutenant General García passed through Santa Ana, which was populated by women who informed him that the men "had left to kill the Spaniards."[46] According to Hackett, a year later, in 1681, when the Hispanics had resettled in the region of El Paso, the Pueblo Indians "were continually deliberating plans for the total extermination of the Spaniards."[47]

When Vargas returned to Santa Fe in September 1692, the Indians from Galisteo who occupied the town told him that "they were ready to fight for five days, [and that] they had to kill us all, we must not flee as we had the first time, and they had to take everybody's life."[48] As his reconquest continued in 1693, the Indians at Ciéneguilla promised Vargas that they "would fight . . . until they left us all dead, once and for all."[49] When Vargas finally retook Santa Fe in December 1693, it was only after the Indians there expressed their will to "fight until all of the Spaniards die" and promised that "not one will escape us. The friars will for a short time be our servants, we will make them carry firewood and bring it from the woods, and after they have served us we will kill all of them just like when we threw out the Spaniards the other time" in 1680.[50] The besieged Indians also promised "that they were going to kill them and make slaves of their women and children."[51] Such goals persisted, and in 1694 an Indian woman named Lucía testified that the natives were plotting to feign a peace and then kill Vargas and the religious who accompanied him.[52]

In the lead-up to the uprising in 1696, Friar Francisco de Vargas reported that "the missionaries are afraid" because the Indians are plotting to "take the lives of both the religious and the Spaniards . . . seeing that they lack provisions, many weapons, and military supplies."[53] As fears of a March 1696 uprising increased, the priest José Diaz was told by a loyalist Tano that "at the next full moon they planned to kill the Spaniards."[54] In Cochiti in April, an Indian woman told Friar Alfonso Jiménez de Cisneros:

"Take notice, Spaniards, the Indian has not said once that there will be a revolt and that they plan to kill all of the Spaniards. Do not tire, because what the Indian says once, he always carries out, so do not trust them; when the least you expect it they will strike you over the head." These are the exact words said by the Indian woman.[55]

One conspirator who was caught in 1696, Diego Umviro of Pecos, expressed his desire to kill the intruders "because the Spaniards were of a different blood."[56] The Indian Francisco Témprano of Tajique confessed that the inhabitants of San Cristóbal had asserted that "the day had come when the fathers and Spaniards had to die" and that they should be ready to "kill all the religious and whichever Spaniards might be in those pueblos at that time."[57] Another prisoner, an Indian from Keres who defiantly refused to give his name, stated that the Tanos were urging Indians to rebel as "the Spaniards had to die now."[58] Also in 1696, in San Juan de los Caballeros, the rebel Juan Griego told the residents and the Tewa governor there, Miguel Saxete, that "everyone in all the pueblos was going to rise up that night and kill all the religious and Spaniards, and they had to do the same thing."[59] Such statements concerning the genocidal intent of the uprising were not bluff or bluster on the Indians' part, but ultimately were expressed through concerted action as the events of the 1680 and 1696 rebellions demonstrate.

Prophecy, Nativism, and the Great Rebellion

As with the Pueblo Revolt, the Great Rebellion of Peru and Upper Peru was a millennially inspired attempt to reinstitute Indian rule, society, and customs, and the exterminatory impulse was a key component of these objectives. Although it is important to recognize that the rebellion was quite heterodox and, as in the other rebellions, not every Indian supported the extermination of the Hispanics or the elimination of their culture, great numbers did. Evaluated in terms of the consistent actions of combatants, genocide was an important and defining element of the uprising.

Although the conquest ended the Inca Empire, it did not end the strong, indigenous oral history tradition in the region or hopes for the reestablishment of Indian rule, and from this emerged numerous prophesies promising its restoration. The fact that the natives, both Quechua and Aymara speakers, had a cyclical concept of time not only helped to explain why the conquest had occurred, as part of the periodic destruction and rebirth of their world, but also assured them that eventually the cycle would run its course and native rule would be restored. Most important to the Indians in this regard was the prophesy of Inkarrí, a divine Andean hero-savior who would defeat the intruders and implement a utopian era of indigenous rule in the region. As with the conquest, this shift, which was nothing less than a changing of time cycles, would be announced by a pachacuti, or cataclysmic destruction of the established order. By the 1750s, the belief in the Inkarrí legend was widespread among Indians throughout Peru and Upper Peru.[60]

Reinforcing this prophesy of a "sleeping emperor" who would return to redeem the native race was the belief among many Indians that Túpac Amaru I, the last Inca leader and executed in 1572, was slowly regenerating underground and would one day return to redeem his people. In this legend, Túpac Amaru I was occasionally confused with the Inca Atahualpa, who was killed by the Spanish during the conquest. Túpac Amaru and Túpac Catari both used such popular beliefs to foment their charismatic image.[61] Christian influences also contributed to the prophetic environment. Chief among these were prophesies attributed to Saint Francis Solano (1549–1610) and Saint Rose of Lima (1586–1617) that foretold the destruction of Lima and the death of its Hispanic citizens by a tidal wave which would not harm the Indian quarters. The destruction wrought by this catastrophe would give rise first to harbingers of the new order such as famine, illness, and turmoil, and then ultimately a native Catholic rule.[62]

Many contemporaries of the rebellion recognized the role of prophesy and popular historical memory in sparking and sustaining it. In Oruro, one Hispanic asserted that the natives adhered to their prophesies just as the Jews awaited "the coming of the Messiah." He also noted that with the eruption of the rebellion, for the Indians, the "day they were waiting for had arrived," and the "Sun . . . had come out for them."[63] The Franciscan friar Josef Antonio Cervantes, who was held captive by insurgents from Poopó, Paria, Sorasora, and Challapata under Santos Mamani from January to April 1781, not only noted the imminence with which Túpac Amaru's arrival in the area was expected but also was asked by Mamani if he "did not know that the time had arrived in which the Indians would be alleviated and the Spaniards and Creoles would be annihilated."[64] The statement that the "time had arrived" suggests a prophetic element concerning the elimination of the Hispanics in the region, while his asking the friar if he "did not know" about it suggests that it was a belief widely held among the insurgents.

Another captive, this one held by Túpac Amaru, reported that the Inca had promised his followers that "there had come the time of Sta. Rosa's prophecy when the kingdom would return to the hand of its previous possessors."[65] A captive of Túpac Catari during the siege of La Paz, the priest Matías de la Borda, reported that Túpac Catari had one of his scribes write that "it was already time that they fulfill the prophesies . . . which he also explained to the Indians in their language so that they would not dismay in the business of winning the city."[66] Borda also overheard Catari tell his followers that "the time had been completed to fulfill the prophecy that the kingdom would return to be theirs" and added that the Indians operated "exactly under the hope which was suggested to them by those leaders."[67] In one letter, Túpac Catari asserted that "everything will return to its owner, as have predicted first Santa Teresa to San Ignacio de Loyola [that] what belonged to the Inca King would be returned to him."[68] This statement appears to refer, erroneously, to the prophesy of Saint Rose of Lima.

One contemporary believed that the native "memory of their previous kings" was among the causes of the insurgency.[69] Likewise, in Paria and the surrounding region, Commandant Ignacio Flores, who led much of the royalist offensive in Upper Peru, observed that the natives had an enduring "devotion to their Incas."[70] In 1782, the Council of the Indies also recognized that the Indians had striven "to conserve the memory of their ancient Pagan Kings." In addition, they were cognizant of the utopian nature of Garcilaso de la Vegaìs's *Royal Commentaries of the Incas,* noting that "the Indians have learned many harmful things" from it and ordered that all copies of it "be gathered up . . . even if [it requires] purchasing the issues through third persons [in] secret." It appears that this was one among numerous such works as the same edict directed that "similar documents" also be removed from the public.[71]

Such prophesies of divine assistance in the creation of a utopian Indian society formed part of the millennial milieu from which the exterminatory tendency of the insurgency developed. As with the Pueblo Revolt and the Caste War of Yucatán, inherent to the reestablishment of Indian rule and the supremacy of their culture was the elimination of all but a few Hispanics, their allies, and their culture. It was in this process that millennialism "boiled over" into genocide, and it underscores the "total" difference between the old colonial society and the new native millennial society.[72] In all of the rebellions, to be Hispanic meant support for, participation in, or adherence to the Spanish system of domination and their culture. A mestizo, or even an Indian, could be considered a "spiritual Spaniard" in rebel eyes if they dressed in the Hispanic fashion. Likewise, occupations had an ethnic component, with the ranks of mine owners and hacendados usually filled with Spaniards, Creoles, and occasionally mestizo or Indian curacas.[73] While Hispanic society was very attentive to status differences, the rebels saw Spaniards and Creoles simply as "Spaniards," and race and ethnicity were the easiest ways to determine who was a member of the exploiting elite. Race-based killing increasingly put the masses at odds with more conservative leaders such as Túpac Amaru and Tomás Catari, and underscores that these two leaders had little control over those who acted in their name in what was a highly confederated and decentralized rebellion.[74]

The rebels were seeking to totally transform their world, but they believed that the birth of the new society was imminent. In fact, the rebellion itself was the pachacuti, and in addition to prophesies concerning divine assistance and the inevitability of the new order, many rebels believed that leaders such as Túpac Amaru, Tomás Catari, and Túpac Catari had divine protection. This will be explored further in the section below concerning leadership. Many rebels also believed that they would be resurrected if they died during the rebellion. This promise of enjoying an earthly utopia, as opposed to some other form of afterlife, also reflects the millennial nature of the rebellion.[75] In witnessing the execution of a group of rebels in Cochabamba province in 1781, one contemporary wrote that the condemned arrived at the gallows "with the same presence of spirit that [they bring] to one of their feasts." Another witness added that "if in other circumstances it was a sad spectacle to see such a rigorous execution, here it was reduced to fun and pastime." He noted that "there were those who at the foot of the gallows were eating. . . . This was the effect of the persuasion which the rebel Tupa Amaro gave them that they would always resuscitate."[76] Campbell asserts that Túpac Amaru promised that he would resurrect those of his followers who died three days after he was crowned Inca king in Cuzco, although Szeminski asserts that the Inca promised that the dead would resurrect five days after his coronation.[77]

As in the other rebellions under study here, the almost total elimination of Hispanics was inherent to the creation of this new order. When the rebellion exploded in Chayanta and the surrounding region in August 1780, much of the rebel wrath was initially directed at the curacas, who were in this region with few exceptions mestizos. Most had been chosen by the corregidor due to their willingness to serve Hispanic interests and had no organic connection to the communities over which they held sway. They had also progressively alienated their charges due to their unrelenting exploitation that had been given even more impetus by the expansion of the reparto in the years preceding the rebellion.[78] The degree to which mestizos were victims of rebel wrath appears to be dependent upon their degree of assimilation into Hispanic society and their involvement in the colonial system of exploitation. Many mestizos were among the rebels, and prominent in this regard were Túpac Amaru and also Luís Laso de la Vega in Tupiza. When Nicolás Catari led the assault on Aullagas, he had many mestizos in his ranks, and the mestizos in Oruro switched their allegiance from the Creoles to the Indians as the rebellion there radicalized.[79] It is important to recognize that not all mestizo—or, for that matter, Indian—participation in the rebellion was voluntary, as conscription was widespread, and many probably joined out of fear of being considered "Hispanic." In addition, in some cases those classified as "mestizos" were so only in the legal sense, because that racial category was exempt from tribute and the mita, and many Indians understandably sought to have themselves so categorized.[80]

While mestizos were an early target of the rebels in Upper Peru in August and September 1780, by October the focus of aggression had notably broadened in many cases to include Spaniards, Creoles, and those of light skin color. One contemporary observed that soon after Tomás Catari had been freed and named curaca of Macha in late August 1780, those who acted in his name started to kill the Spaniards and mestizos.[81] Likewise, a royal official believed that Túpac Amaru had ordered the rebels to kill "as many Spaniards and mestizos as they could get their hands on."[82] In September and October 1780, when rebels led by Simón Castillo occupied San Pedro de Buenavista, they insisted that the priest there surrender not only the curacas but also all of the mestizos. Later they would kill almost all of the Hispanics there.[83] In October 1780, Manuel de Bodega, the corregidor of Paria who would die in the rebellion two months later, wrote that the rebels were killing "any Spaniard and cholo that they find in the towns . . . so that there will be no person to subject them."[84] In Tola-pampa, in Porco province, an edict reputedly from Nicolás Catari circulated that commanded the rebels to "kill all the corregidors, priests, miners, Span-iards, and mestizos." Some rebels reported that after the death of Tomás Catari, Dámaso and Nicolás directed the Indians to "finish off with all those who were not Indians and with those who opposed" them.[85]

Some victims were literally dressed to be killed, as in many cases people who wore Hispanic clothing were killed on that basis. This tendency, and the effort to avert its consequences, was very clear in Oruro, as the Hispanics began to dress in the Indian fashion and chew coca. Similarly, in Chocaya, Arque, Colcha, and Sacaca, the rebels banned the use of Hispanic clothing and forced all sur-vivors to dress in the native manner.[86] In the town of Sicasica the Indians were killing "those of their nation who used shirts and were not immediately mov-ing to their dress."[87] Likewise, Túpac Catari in La Paz and Tomás Callisaya in Tiquina ordered the death of anyone who ate bread or drank water from foun-tains, as well as those who did not speak Aymara or dress in the native fashion.[88]

In Oruro, after the natives had overrun the town, their wrath was increas-ingly directed against Hispanics generally, as opposed to only Spaniards. The rebel order that no Creoles be allowed to carry firearms or be among their ranks, as well as attacks on Creole people and interests, underscores the shift, which may also have encouraged many mestizos to side with the Indians.[89] A similar situation prevailed in Arque, where a Creole wrote Jacinto Rodríguez asking if "it was true that he had given orders that the Indians kill all whites without distinction" between Creoles and Spaniards.[90] The shift was complete by the time the Indians lay siege to Oruro and indicated their intent to kill all Hispanics there, including women, the young, and priests.[91] Throughout the region engulfed by the rebellion, threats such as these were translated into action as thousands of Hispanics died in towns such as Sorata, Juli, Tiquina, Colcha, Palca, San Pedro de Buenavista, Carangas, Ayopaia, Arque, Tarata, Tapacari, and Tupiza.[92]

Often in cases of genocide, perpetrators and victims will give differing views as to the objectives of a movement. In Peru and Upper Peru, however, both groups explicitly recognized the exterminatory nature of the rebellion. In Upper Peru, one royal official erroneously believed that Túpac Amaru had commanded that all Hispanics die and that his followers supported his desire for the "extermination" of non-Indians.[93] The cabildo of Cochabamba expressed their belief that the rebels desired that "there not remain in this vast kingdom any other kind of people than that of their own caste."[94] One observer asserted that "they killed with more cruelty all those that had white faces," and in Chayanta a Hispanic believed that the Indians sought to kill "as many Spaniards as they could find."[95] In Chocaya, Florentín Alfaro saved his life by fleeing in the belief that the rebels were trying to "finish off all of the Spaniards and mestizos."[96]

The thinking of Sebastián de Segurola, who led the defense of La Paz during its siege, changed with time. As the rebellion flared, he reflected that Túpac Catari sought "not just to kill the corregidors and Europeans, as I thought at the beginning, but rather all those who were not legitimately Indians."[97] The priest Matías de la Borda, who had considerable opportunity to observe the rebels in El Alto as he was held prisoner by Túpac Catari, wrote that the Aymara rebel wanted the "total extermination of the Spanish people, both patrician and European, and of the[ir] life, customs and Religion."[98] The priest Josef de Uriate, a prisoner of the rebels around Sicasica, noted that the insurgents planned to "pass under the knife the Spaniards and mestizos without sparing the priests, women nor children, and [to] extinguish the cattle and seeds of Spain." In addition, they had even issued their own coins in order "not to see the royal face."[99]

Indian confessions and statements indicate that such assertions were not simply Hispanic exaggerations to promote unity but rather descriptions of events. When he led the siege of La Paz, Túpac Catari demanded that the Hispanics destroy their defenses and surrender "all of the corregidors . . . Europeans . . . priests and their assistants, the royal officials, the customs tax collectors, hacendados and firearms."[100] In one communication he ordered "that all the Creoles die," and indicated that he planned to "finish off everyone with the objective that there will not be mestizos."[101] His sister, the rebel Gregoria Apasa, stated plainly that the rebels sought "to take the lives of the whites whenever they had the opportunity."[102] The rebel Augustina Zerna, who was the consort of Andrés Túpac Amaru when he participated in the siege of La Paz, said that the rebels wanted to "finish with all the Spaniards or white faces."[103] The insurgent Josefa Anaya confessed that the rebels sought to "kill the corregidores, the Europeans and bad Creoles, although in reality they always killed everyone they found."[104] Diego Quispe corroborates this with his statement that the rebels wanted to "kill absolutely all the whites without distinction" between Spaniard and Creole.[105] Still in the region of La Paz, the rebel Diego Estaca confessed that "the principal objective of the uprising was to get rid of all of the white people," and in Tiquina, Tomás Callisaya ordered in Túpac Catari's name "that all corregidores, their ministers, caciques, collectors, and other dependents be passed by the knife, as well as all the chapetones, Creoles, women and children, without exception of sex or age, and all persons who are or look Spanish, or at the least are dressed in the imitation of such Spanish."[106] Like Túpac Catari, he also commanded the Indians to "totally separate themselves from all of the customs of the Spanish."[107] Many rebels who participated in the siege of La Paz had journeyed there from the southern provinces, and as a result events there reflect the objectives of Indians from diverse areas.[108]

One rebel who was involved in the massacre in San Pedro de Buenavista acknowledged that he was motivated by "the express desire of taking the lives of the Spaniards," and another in Cochabamba confessed that the rebels in the region wanted to kill "white people" and take their property.[109] In the village of Carasi, the mestizo rebel Andrés Gonzales confessed that he wanted to kill all of the Hispanics "from the priest on."[110] In Poroma, the rebel Sebastían Morochi stated in his confession that the rebels sought to kill "everyone [there] including the priest," and the rebel Sencio Chamsi also confessed that the insurgents planned to "destroy" all of the Hispanics there.[111] In Tapacari, the insurgents wanted to kill not only the curaca but also his relatives "up to the fifth generation."[112] In the region of Sillota and Oruro, other rebels, such as Diego Calsina, Juan Solis, Cruz Tomás, and Manuel Mamani, also confessed to wanting to kill all Hispanics.[113] Also in Sillota, the insurgent Casimiro Ramos confessed that the rebels there wanted to "exterminate" the Hispanics in the town, and the rebel Eusebio Padilla acknowledged that he sought to kill "Spaniards, mestizos, blacks and all except the tributary Indians" there.[114] Similarly, the rebel Ascensio Taquichiro confessed that in Challacollo he sought to "burn the town and kill the inhabitants without leaving one alive who was not an Indian."[115] While these confessions were in all likelihood extracted by force or threat of it, they are also consistent with events on the battlefield and, as we shall see in chapter 7, further corroborated by rebel symbolic actions.

The rebel treatment of priests and Catholicism generally offers further insights as to the nativistic goals of the insurgents. At the outbreak of the insurgency, between August 1780 and January 1781, the rebels generally honored the tradition of church sanctuary and often abided by the pleas of clerics to avoid escalating violence. In Pocoata, following the capture of Corregidor Alós, the rebels did not assault the church and kill those inside, and instead heeded the plaintive calls of the priests to permit the soldiers inside to withdraw from the town after they had given up their clothes, weapons, and property.[116] Even in San Pedro de Buenavista, which the Indians occupied three times between September and December 1780, the village priest managed to resist Indian demands that he hand over the curacas who had sought refuge in the church there.[117] Father Merlos, with Tomás Catari in Macha, was successful in persuading the rebels to spare the lives of several captive curacas who had been brought there for judgment.[118] Clergy were not always successful in this regard in the early months of the rebellion, however, and in Macha the curaca Pasqual Chura was forcibly taken by the rebels from the church and killed, and the curaca Florencio Lupa was taken from Merlos's custody and executed.[119]

With the death of Tomás Catari on January 8, 1781, the insurgency in Upper Peru took a decidedly radical turn. Sometimes priests were still able to prevent the storming of churches and to spare those inside, for example, in Ocuri and Pintatora.[120] Such restraint was increasingly the exception to the rule, however, as the slaughter of people in churches became the norm. In January in Challapata, the rebels rejected the cleric's plea for mercy for Corregidor Bodega and killed him after he exited the temple holding a monstrance and desperately clutching the priest.[121] Soon nothing Catholic was sacred, and not only were people systematically killed in churches, but liturgical artifacts were also deliberately destroyed, as in the massacres of San Pedro de Buenavista, Oruro, Tapacari, Yura, Colcha, Palca, Tarata, and many other villages.[122] This declining respect for the servants, symbols, and sanctuary of Catholicism suggests a spreading belief that the pachacuti was indeed under way, the power of native deities was on the rise, and the power of the Catholic god was on the wane.[123]

Consistent with this tendency was the increasing focus of rebel wrath on clerics. Initially, they were subject to threats of violence, such as in January and February 1781 in Macha when Dámaso Catari attributed at least some of the blame for Tomás's death to Father Merlos and ordered him to leave town or be killed. As Merlos and his party made their way to La Plata, they were stoned by the rebels.[124] In Yura, on February 12, 1781, Dámaso Catari and Ramón Paca allowed the priest to flee only after he had been made to strip. The same thing happened subsequently in Anasayas.[125] At almost the same time, the rebels killed a priest in Poopó, Victór García, who boldly ignored a local rebel prohibition on holding mass. In Oruro, at least one priest was killed by the rebels, many were struck by stones as they appealed for calm, and others were reported killed "in the surrounding area."[126] In Colcha, three priests were killed by the insurgents, along with others in Palca and Tapacari, while sacristans and lieutenant priests were murdered in Tinquipaya, Tacopaya, and Quinquinavi.[127] In San Pedro de Buenavista and neighboring Aymaia, six priests were killed as the rebel forbearance of the previous months vanished.[128] To the north, in Tiquina, Tomás Callisaya commanded that the Indians "pass under the knife the priests . . . and ordered [that] they do not hear masses, confess or adore the sacrament."[129] In Songo, outside of La Paz, the priest Félix Gisbert met this death at rebel hands, as did the cleric Sebastián Limanchi in Guaqui and the priest of Juli, José Arrescurrenaga, near Acora.[130]

The pachacuti was in some ways a self-fulfilling prophecy, since by creating the upheaval of the rebellion, the insurgents were also creating the pachacuti, which then became evident in the carnage of the rebellion. The killing of priests also followed a similar logic, for by killing them the rebels were demonstrating the rising power of native gods. To them, it was clear that the Catholic god, who still had some power, could no longer protect his ministers. It may be that not only did many Indians increasingly believe that the Catholic god had lost his power relative to the native deities, but that it was the Hispanics who were the sinners, not the Indians.[131] As the perceived power of the Catholic god waned, so did respect for Catholicism generally. As one priest noted in Oruro, they "worked all . . . afternoon with exhortations, tears, [and] beseachment . . . without the least fruit" to end the violence.[132] Not even parading the statue of the Christ of Burgos calmed the mob, and one rebel is recorded as saying that it was "nothing more than a piece of wood."[133] After the rebels assaulted the San Augustín convent there, they cast the statues of the saints to the ground and lit local cigars from the candles in the church.[134] As Santos Mamani led the siege of the town, one rebel referred to the Virgin as a "witch" and other rebels stated that they planned to "cut off the head of the image of Our Lady of Rosario" once they had overrun the town.[135]

When the surge of rebellion reached Palca, in Cochabamba province, one rebel held the host as he ran down the street, shouting that it was nothing more than bread that anyone could make with flour.[136] The rebels also filled the monstrance there with coca leaves, thereby "conscripting" it into the service of worship of native gods.[137] Other rebels in Poopó, Colcha, and Arque refused to permit or attend mass or to confess, while rebels in Tatasi only allowed the priest there to flee if he promised to leave the parish permanently.[138] Priestly persuasion, Catholic rites, and church sanctuary were not the only casualties. So were ecclesiastical wealth and revenue. In Oruro, the rebels demanded church lands and the abolition of diezmos and primicías. Some rebels still had some respect for, or fear of, the Catholic god. In Oruro, perhaps hedging their bets, when Father Menéndez absolved the Indians after distributing silver outside of town, many of the rebels kneeled.[139]

There are other indications that many rebels held the belief that the pachacuti of revolution was aided by and reflected the resurgent dominance of indigenous deities, and that they had a role to play in breaking the spiritual power of Catholicism. The treatment of Catholic symbols, especially those with limited utility outside of the church, is one such indicator. In San Pedro de Buenavista, while the rebels took the silver and jewels from the church, they denuded the statues of Mary and Jesus and then broke them and the monstrance into pieces.[140] Similarly, in Condocondo the insurgents destroyed a monstrance through stoning, and after the slaughter in Tapacari, the rebels carried the religious statues to the plaza and burned them.[141]

To the north in Puno, in December 1780, numerous rebels who had been fatally wounded in battle refused to have the last rites or to "take between their lips the sweet name of God."[142] Likewise, in La Paz, one observer wrote, "There is no Indian who is not a rebel, all willingly die . . . without remembering God. . . . On the 26th of October they beheaded 12 rebels and none of these could we get to say Jesus, and the same has happened with another 600 who have been executed in both sieges."[143] As Szeminski suggests, this may reflect a rebel belief that Túpac Amaru had promised resurrection to rebels only if they did not mention Jesus when they died.[144] Although Túpac Amaru was strongly influenced by Catholicism, his more nativist followers may have imputed such an order to him. The rebels did not necessarily believe that the Christian god was entirely powerless. Rather, they believed that he had been cast into the underworld and thus weakened, and to call for his assistance would mean that an individual would join him there and not share in the earthly utopia that they believed would follow the pachacuti.[145]

Centuries of abuse by clerics had created a wellspring of resentment among many Indians. Of the rebels who slaughtered people in San Pedro de Buenavista, many asserted that one of the reasons they hated priests was because of the financial and other demands they so frequently made on the Indians. In October 1780, Simón Castillo showed a purported edict of Túpac Amaru which ended all ecclesiastical dues, although in fact the Inca wanted to continue many such taxes in a more modest way.[146] When the cleric Dionicio Córtes was killed in Aymaia, one rebel exclaimed, "Priest! Thief! It is because of you that we are naked."[147] In Tapacari, before the rebellion, the Indian residents sought to mitigate the demands placed upon them by their resident priest by sending a delegation to Cochabamba to seek a reduction of their religious financial burdens.[148]

The enduring nature of native religion was not lost on Hispanics who lived through the rebellion. The royal official Benito Mata Linares asserted that the "Indian is as lacking of the true religion [today] as in the beginning of the conquest . . . he has only changed names, but it is idolatry."[149] Referring to the region of Chayanta, another Hispanic wrote that the "Indians prefer their hidden ceremonies" to those of Catholicism, as they "firmly believe [in their] superstitions [where] every squeak and animal movement has mystery and significance."[150]

In the creation of the new native utopia, ensuring that the Hispanic order would never return was just as important as destroying it and preventing the resurrection of their enemies. In order to achieve this latter aim, Túpac Amaru had prohibited the burial of Corregidor Arriaga for four days, and many rebels followed the example, which also was a means of showing their support for the Inca. The beheading of enemies was also a traditional means of preventing their resurrection.[151] All of these events and tendencies underscore the scope, depth, and permanence of the ethnic, social, political, and religious transformation envisioned by the rebels.

Genocide and the Nativist Domain in Yucatán

Like the Pueblo Revolt, the Caste War of Yucatán was also a successful exterminatory nativistic movement.[152] Unlike the Pueblo Revolt, however, the Maya rebels had assimilated much more of Hispanic culture by 1848 than the Pueblos had in 1680. Unlike most millennially inspired nativistic movements, and as in New Mexico, we are able to examine the traits of the new society that they created.

Although the cult of the speaking cross was born of despair, the town that grew around the place of its origin became a symbol not only of Indian strength but also of independence. Chan Santa Cruz grew rapidly and copied the Hispanic tradition of a church and arcaded official buildings facing a plaza. By 1866, its population was 4,000–5,000, and that of their domain was 15,000–20,000.[153] While the architecture reflected Hispanic influences and even included windows and doors brought up from Bacalar, the social structure was the inversion of that under the Hispanics, with the Indians as the ruling class.[154] Over the years, thousands of non-Indians were brought there as prisoner-slaves. In 1859 alone there were 500 prisoners captured, although 200 would be killed soon afterward. Many Hispanic men worked as the Indians had in Hispanic society, as field laborers with little or no hope of a better life. Others who had other skills of value to Cruzob society were somewhat better off, serving as scribes, masons, or instructors of military arts. In 1860, the Cruzob captured the entire military band from Colonel Acereto's retreating forces, and it performed for the Cruzob and taught them to play various instruments. It is important to note that Hispanics were not the only slaves among the Cruzob. Other Indians were captured from rival groups, such as the Pacíficos of Chichenha, as well as about 100 Chinese contract laborers who had fled British Honduras in 1866 due to their dissatisfaction with working conditions there.[155] White women were often held as concubines by the rebels, especially by the leaders. Interestingly, all children born of prisoners were free.[156]

The Indian society outwardly appeared to have strong Hispanic influences. Certainly, the layout and architecture of Chan Santa Cruz were heavily influenced by the Hispanic heritage, the cult of the speaking cross had Christian influences, and the military ranks largely followed those of their enemies. In almost all other aspects, however, it was the native influence that dominated. The syncretic cult of the cross, according to Charlotte Zimmerman, was in essence "a pre-Christian religious outpouring which is related to Christianity only by this absorption of forms."[157]

In 1888, the British explorer William Miller marched from Bacalar to Chan Santa Cruz, noting, "The Santa Cruz Indians have a very bad name and there are a good many murders recorded against them, which cause people to be very careful about going into their country."[158] Passing through Bacalar, which was surrounded by a stone wall and ran "along the lagoon for about two English miles, and is about one mile broad," he noted numerous mounds of bones in various parts of the church. Overall the town was being retaken by the jungle, and the sixty-man Indian garrison, which rotated every two months, rejected living in the crumbling stone houses, opting instead to reside in huts they had constructed.[159]

The road north to Chan Santa Cruz was rocky, about eight feet wide, and, in the Hispanic tradition, marked every three miles by a cross. With his Cruzob escort, Miller passed through various villages on the way to the Indian capital, each of which

> has its church, and it is the custom to lodge in them when traveling. They are merely leaf roofs with walls of stick carried only half-way up to the roof. At one end a table is placed for an altar, on which are twelve or fifteen crosses. . . . they have no priests but remember a few prayers taught them by the Spaniards, and these they sometimes chant before their altars.[160]

In San Pedro, twelve miles from Chan, he met the native leader Aniceto Zul. Zul had lost sight in one eye and, believing a man and woman had cast a hex on him, had had them executed the day before Miller's arrival. To any question Miller asked, Zul would reply, "Why do you wish to know?"[161] Zul ruled from San Pedro, and Miller noted that "the last chief of the Santa Cruz Indians was killed, together with about twenty other chiefs, by . . . Don Anis, about four years ago, and the said Don Anis now reigns in his stead and will continue to do so until some other chief contrives to get a party sufficiently strong to kill him in his turn."[162]

Upon entering Chan Santa Cruz, he found it "very similar to Bacalar, and . . . occupied by a garrison of about 150 men, but nobody lives there permanently. The chiefs meet there for consultation and for settling the affairs of the nation. They are armed with Enfield rifles and machetes."[163] The Cruzob were dressed

> in cotton trousers and shirt and straw hat, sandals on the feet, and when on duty as soldiers they have two leather straps, one over each shoulder

and crossing the breast. One strap supports the machete and the other the cartridge-box. These straps are held in to the waist by a belt passing outside them [and] . . . give them quite a correct military appearance. The trousers are made very wide in the legs, and when traveling they are rolled up high on the thigh, and when off duty they frequently leave off the shirt and then appear only to have on a waist-cloth.[164]

Twenty-one years previously, John Carmichael had offered a description of a more populated but otherwise similar Chan Santa Cruz. He noted that in "the neighborhood of the plaza, the buildings are all stone, many of them with pretensions to architecture. The style is that usually adopted in Mexico, viz., flat roofs with arched piazzas in front. The windows are faced with iron bars, and the doors are loop-holed for musketry. . . . Facing the temple stands the palace of the Patrón, which is a magnificent building built of stone, with arched piazzas in front and at the back, and occupies an entire side of the plaza. The remaining two sides are occupied by the barracks, the prison and the council house. In the center of the plaza on a rock stands a sapodilla tree, under which their prisoners are executed, being cut to pieces by machetes or cutlasses." The residences just outside of Chan were "made of . . . poles with thatched roofs and are at a little distance from the road, surrounded with orange and fruit trees, while the lot is always enclosed by a stone wall."[165]

The Pacífico communities to the south and west contained many former Cruzob, and according to one explorer, Carl Berendt, who visited them in the late 1860s, they were "quiet settlers, laborious and orderly, submitting to their self-elected local authorities, honest in their dealings, rigorous [with] criminals among them, and by far the best class of people in" either Peten or British Honduras.[166] Like the Cruzob, the Pacíficos traded extensively with British Honduras for manufactured goods, exporting oxen, cattle and their products, horses, moccasins for loggers, as well as palm leaves and some coffee.[167] The settlement of Ixkanha was organized militarily in a similar manner as Chan Santa Cruz, although this was of a more defensive nature, and they did not have a speaking cross. Commercially, it was oriented toward Campeche. By 1904 they had suffered an epidemic of smallpox, and their population had declined to about 8,000.[168]

Over time the other Pacífico communities declined as well. The bamboo wall around Icaiche offered only limited defense, and in 1892 smallpox and whooping cough cut the population there in half. By 1904 they numbered only about 500 as a result of declines from "war, rum and pestilence." By this time many of those who survived were involved in the harvesting of chicle.[169] Although noting the Indian taste for alcohol and the more bellicose demeanor of the Cruzob, in 1902 the explorer Karl Sapper wrote:

As to the character of the independent Mayas, I can make an almost wholly favorable report from my own experience. . . . I was particularly impressed by the reliableness of these Maya, by the punctuality with which they fulfilled a promise once given, and by the fidelity which they showed to me on my journey. . . . Everywhere, even in the most isolated hut, we found hospitable entertainment . . . [and they were] very quick to appreciate a harmless jest. It is often said of the Mayas that they are honest in important matters, but that they readily steal trifles; I have never had the least thing stolen from me during my travels in Maya territory.[170]

By the 1930s, Icaiche had been abandoned.[171]

Many observers had noted the valor and stoicism of the Cruzob. As early as 1813, the priest José Bartolomé del Granado Baeza noted that "for more than 45 years I have attended them during their final illnesses, and very rarely have I seen tears shed over the death of parents, children, spouses or relatives. Much more commonly I have seen them with their eyes dry and serene in all circumstances."[172] Baqueiro sums it up well, noting that "the Indians are accustomed to die with an inexplicable stoicism, with an imperturbability almost unknown among other races . . . they would come serenely out of their prisons, arrive at the gallows, rise its stairs with a firm step, take the noose and perfectly place it around their neck, and then they would wait with the same serenity . . . to be strangled. They would not beg nor cry before their executioners; on the contrary, if they saw a family member present, they would take their leave from them and give them the last hug with valor."[173] Another contemporary characterized the Indians as "austere by nature . . . reserved . . . valiant and tenacious. . . . They are fatalistic and await death with a stoic indifference."[174]

To some extent this reflects that to "the native people the supernatural world is very real and very close. Gods, spirits, and crosses are present whenever the native moves, and permeate almost all his thinking." The figure of the cross had over the centuries gained a position of special reverence, and "the symbol of the cross is so deeply ingrained on the mind of the native that he sees crosses everywhere he looks: in the intersections of the beams and poles which form the framework of his house, . . . in the meeting of two paths, . . . in the natural formation of stones and trees."[175] Less visible, but also important, are pre-Hispanic indigenous spirits "who are felt to be present in the very bush and villages . . . [and] help the native most directly in his daily struggle for existence."[176] The Catholic and indigenous deities have differing qualities and abilities, and are not seen as inherently contradictory. While H-men, or medicine men, direct relations with native gods, the maestro cantor usually serves as the intermediary with the Catholic deity.[177]

As in all of the rebellions studied here, the genocidal tendency was quite pronounced during the Caste War of Yucatán, and although the Hispanics were referred to as whites, as elsewhere ethnicity was intimately linked with racial orientation, language, clothing, and occupation. At the beginning of the national period over half of the rural Hispanics were part Indian. Dumond argues that "anyone who spoke Maya and could pass as a campesino," or peasant, was seen as an Indian by the rebels.[178] The insurgents, however, also killed Indians who, due to their support of the Hispanics, were considered "spiritual Spaniards" and were often relatively well-off compared with the mass of rebels. In the late August 1847, during the attack on Acambalam, the rebels killed the Indian foreman and his family. Likewise, in January 1848, the rebels killed the cacique of Popolá, who had supported the Hispanics.[179]

Rebel leaders sought to unite the genocidal objectives of the rebellion with divine mandate and protection. In a letter written in 1847 or early 1848, Bonifacio Novelo noted that "this is not an uprising that we are making, but rather an order from Jesus Christ that we are obeying, so that we can have liberty here in Yucatán."[180] In 1850, representing the speaking cross, Juan de la Cruz wrote to his followers that "the moment has arrived of a general uprising of the indigenes against the whites," and promised that "although you may hear the boom of the shotgun of the enemy above your heads, nothing will happen to anyone" in the coming offensive "against the whites." He assured them that the cross will be "with you at all hours, I go ahead of you, protecting you from the enemies so that nothing happens to you." He added, "My father has already told me . . . that the enemies will never win and only the crosses will win."[181] He went on to reiterate that "the hour for Yucatán to rise up against the whites once and for all has arrived."[182] As late as 1887 a sermon of the cross promised the faithful that "my lord has already told me, children, that the enemy will never win, that only the crosses will win, for this reason my beloved men I will not abandon you to the enemy." The omnipresence of the cross and its commitment to the faithful were reinforced when de la Cruz wrote, "I am walking at all hours, my throat and my whole stomach are dry with unquenchable thirst, which I have from walking in Yucatán to defend you."[183] In 1888, a message from Juan de la Cruz, still acting as the intermediary for the cross, stated that "there will not be peace neither for the foreigners nor for the Christians [Indians], then, it is desperately necessary to throw them [the whites] out once and for all from the land . . . so that there can be happiness among all the beings of the land forever."[184] Overall, the speaking cross united "the contents of the pre-Hispanic Maya cross: the tree . . . of life and water, bridge between heaven and earth, refuge of men after death."[185]

While the sermons of the cross inspired the rebels, the belief in divine assistance and the inevitability of Indian victory was reinforced by the Mayas' cyclical view of time in which "the events in one cycle would be repeated in all successive cycles as they had been repeating since time immemorial."[186] The rebels may also have been inspired to varying degrees by the Chilam Balam of Maní, a sacred Maya text, in which the "king of the Itza would return one day and drive the foreigners into the sea."[187] According to Bartolomé and Barabas, however, it is the Chilam Balam of Chumayel that is the basis of the "prophetic, millenarianist and messianic ideology" of the Caste War and it, too, is based on a cyclical concept of time. Central to this is, much like the Andean pachacuti, "the destruction of the world and the disappearance of the foreigners," which will lead to a new time cycle of Indian self-rule. All of this would follow a "cataclysm, product of the presence of the Anti-Christ (the God of the Whites), [that] will be preceded by the arrival of a Savior, who would come to impose justice on earth. This savior will be the true Jesus Christ, who would come down from the forest of the Maya to guide the great battle against the usurpers. Afterwards the land will be reborn, the dead will arise, and violence will not reign but rather the will of God." Bartolomé and Barabas argue that such prophesies were known throughout the colonial era and inspired the 1761 revolt of Jacinto Canek. Whether or not they did, in a letter sent by Manuel Antonio Ay, he also signed it in Canek's name, thereby creating a prophetic link between the native and Hispanic religions when he wrote that "the whites think these things have ended, but they will never be finished. This it says in the book of Chilam Balam, and thus has said Jesus Christ."[188]

As in the other cases, the clearest indication of the exterminatory aims of the rebels was expressed in their actions and sometimes in their words. Civilians and those identified as Hispanics were clearly rebel targets. In January 1847, when the Indians nominally led by Antonio Trujeque stormed Valladolid, some shouted, "Kill those who have shirts!"[189] Six months later, an Indian spy for the Hispanics reported that the natives gathering at Jacinto Pat's hacienda at Culumpich were organizing "a great conspiracy against the white race."[190] At the outbreak of the rebellion, on July 30, 1847, the rebels screamed, "Perish the Whites!" as they attacked Tepich.[191] During this time they were also "announcing their war of extermination."[192] Indian prisoners from the siege of Peto in January 1848 acknowledged "the existence of a conspiracy" to exterminate the Hispanics.[193] In town after town, such as Kancaboonot, Santa María, Valladolid, Sitilpech, and others, the rebels killed people on the basis of race or perceived racial affinity.[194] Typical was the attack in April 1848 of Maní, where the rebels killed "more than two hundred people in their houses, in the streets, and in the very temple" and left "the bodies in pieces."[195]

During Father Antonio Sierra's captivity among the rebels in May 1848, the rebel Francisco Puc recognized, but tried to distance himself from, the genocidal nature of the rebellion, telling the priest that "it pains me much to spill the blood of the whites," and he promised to try to kill Bonifacio Novelo to open the way for peace.[196] Later, in 1857, although the manner in which the rebels under Crescencio Poot invaded Tekax by posing as supporters of a pro-Campeche rebellion was somewhat unusual, its outcome was typical because the rebels systematically killed people "of all ages, sexes and conditions."[197]

The exterminatory nature of the uprising was certainly clear to its contemporaries. It was more description than hyperbole when, in August 1847, Governor Barret stated that the Indians had given "the cry of death against the whites" and were killing "unarmed men and innocent children of the white race."[198] Despite his own desire to exterminate the rebels, General Severo del Castillo noted that after the Indians under Santiago Imán attacked Valladolid, "for the first time they satisfied their implacable hate of the white race, there awakened in their heart . . . the desire for vengeance, the desire for extermination, and that of their independence."[199] He further noted that the plot hatched by Ay, Chi, and Pat sought to "behead all of the whites of the peninsula."[200] Baqueiro notes that in early 1848 the rebels had a "pernicious plan of extermination of the white race" and refers to the conflict as the "war against the whites."[201]

In February 1848, Felipe Rosado must have been having second thoughts about the wisdom of having withdrawn to his ranch in Sucsucil when, reversing his earlier view that the uprising was an expression of Hispanic political factionalism, he noted simply that the Indians "want to finish off the white race."[202] At around the same time in Tekax, José Domingo Sosa, in a letter to Santiago Méndez, wrote that many whites had believed, as had Felipe Rosado, that the Indians were supporting Barbachano. Guided by that belief, many there had sought to join the rebels and instead were killed by them as Chi "wants nothing to do with the whites."[203] Also in February 1848, as fears of an Indian attack grew in Bacalar, the Hispanic commandant of the garrison there requested that the superintendent of British Honduras allow Hispanic refugees to settle in Punta Consejo because of the rebels who were "devastating entire towns, and killing all classes but their own . . . with a view to the extermination of the whites in order that they [the Indians] may remain alone in the country."[204] In June 1848, the Hispanic military leader Manuel Puerto noted that the Indians have "given the cry of desolation and general extermination to those who are not of their same race. They judge that with the towns converted to ashes . . . there will not exist a single white person, as unfortunately they have achieved in most of the State, [and as a result] they will be owners of the land."[205]

The governor of Jamaica, referring to complaints of Governor Barbachano about the flow of munitions to the rebels from British Honduras, referred to the Indian "war against the white population of that province."[206] Later, again noting the racial nature of the conflict, he referred to it as a "War of Colours."[207] Despite the generally positive relations the British maintained with the Cruzob, in 1868 the officials in Belize City nevertheless "view[ed] with concern their constant success in the war of extermination against all Mexican factions. . . . They are laying waste the whole country. They aim at extinguishing the European Race and re-establishing Indian Dominion."[208]

Later historians have also recognized the genocidal nature of the rebellion. Ancona asserts that the goal of the Indian rebels was to "exterminate the other races that inhabited the peninsula" and that they often specifically targeted women and children.[209] As fears spread in Mérida of a planned uprising on August 15, 1847, there was widespread concern that the Indians led by Chi would then "finish off all of those people who did not belong to their race."[210] In the 1860s, Carl Berendt referred to it as a "war of races" in which the Indians "are by no means hostile to the white man in general; their hatred is directed against the Mexican and Spaniard only."[211] Villa Rojas observes that the goal of the Caste War of Yucatán was "to rid the peninsula of the Whites" and that this policy "was, without regard to age or sex, translated into . . . relentless action."[212] Similarly, Howard Cline described the Caste War as "a war of attempted extermination of non-native populations."[213]

As with many genocidal movements, some among the race marked for extermination were spared. Most of these had skills from which the rebels could benefit, such as in the operation of weapons or as scribes, stone workers, field hands, and musicians.[214] For example, Sergeant José María Echeverría, who was a prisoner of the Cruzob in Chan Santa Cruz from 1853 to 1856, was spared because he knew how to read and write.[215] Sometimes children were spared, and when the rebels took Bacalar in February 1858, the six children who were spared could read and write.[216] Even the most radical of rebel leaders, Cecilio Chi, had a mestizo secretary, who would later be his assassin.[217]

Although the tendency was for the rebels to kill all Hispanics when the rebellion began, as Chan Santa Cruz became more established there was a shift, though far from uniform, toward enslaving noncombatants rather than killing them. This began as early as March 1853, when the Cruzob took many prisoners from Tixcacaltuyu, and it was more pronounced by September 1861 with the kidnapping and enslavement of the Hispanic population of Tunkás and much of that of the surrounding area.[218] A few months later the same happened on a smaller scale in Dzitás and Pisté when the residents of these villages were also brought to Chan Santa Cruz to serve as slaves.[219] This may have reflected the desire of the Cruzob for labor and increased agricultural productivity, as well as their desire to invert previous social and power relationships. As with the Pueblo Revolt, it appears that paternity was important in establishing ethnic status. A child of a Cruzob father and Hispanic mother was considered Cruzob, something not unusual in a population that was already highly miscegenated. As a result, in addition to reversing the previous order, the sparing of white women and their use as concubines by the rebels led to an increased Cruzob population.[220]

The Hispanic forces seeking to crush the Yucatecan insurgency were themselves determined to "exterminate the Santa Cruz Indians."[221] Baqueiro notes that in late 1848, "the Yucatecans for their part exclaimed 'War of Extermination'."[222] In a proclamation seeking to encourage peace negotiations in February 1848, Barbachano blustered that while he was willing to address rebel demands, the Hispanic forces had "sufficient power . . . to exterminate [the rebels] in one strike."[223] In September 1848, according to Baqueiro, Colonel Eulogio Rosado had orders to "attain the complete extermination of the rebels."[224] In early December 1848, when the Hispanics retook Tixméhuac, they bayoneted many Indians, and "a great part of these victims were women and innocent children."[225] In September 1849, defending the sale of Maya as slaves to Cuba, the government of Yucatán recognized the racial nature of the rebellion and argued that "while the population of the rebellious Indians is not diminished by a third or a fourth part, at least, there will be neither peace nor quiet, nor security for the whites."[226] As Melchor Campos notes, many conservatives in Yucatán, such as General Severo del Castillo, sought "the extermination or forced expulsion" of the rebels.[227]

Even a Hispanic military commander recognized that "barbaric and cruel actions were as common among the whites as the Indians, such that both bands burned towns occupied by the enemy, laid waste to the countryside, and worked on attaining the great plan of extermination and destruction conceived and put in full execution by the Indians."[228] He also referred to the war as a "double war of extermination."[229] Rape of Indian women by Hispanic men was also an instrument of war against the natives, although Baqueiro preferred to "keep silent on this," as "the language denies us its rich words, if we were to propose to explain in detail what . . . we have gathered of the tradition of this."[230] Prisoners were treated similarly by both sides in the conflict: those who could not make a march were executed, and those who survived were generally enslaved.[231] But while the Indians had no real need for the Hispanics, the Hispanics needed Indian labor. Justo Sierra O'Reilly, in an article in the periodical *El Fénix* in December 1850, plainly stated that "we have the sad understanding that without [Indians] we can do nothing in agricultural life, nor could the richness of the country ever develop."[232] While the rebels initially sought the extermination, and later the enslavement, of the Hispanics generally, the Hispanics were more focused on ethnocide and politicide, that form of genocide which focuses on the extermination of opposition groups.[233]

Conclusion

While not every nativistic movement is millennial or even violent, the Pueblo Revolt, the Great Rebellion, and the Caste War of Yucatán were millennially inspired. Out of this desire to create an Indian-ruled society, free from the burdens, abuses, and presence of the Hispanics, evolved the genocidal element of these rebellions. All of these conflicts were exterminatory, on both sides, in the sense that they had as their object the total or practical elimination of a people, class, group, culture, belief system, or language. In the case of the Indians, self-identified or otherwise, this was directed against those they identified as Hispanics and their sympathizers, along with most of their culture, language, and belief system. Due to their dependence on Indian labor, the exterminatory aims of the Hispanics were focused on the leading rebels, as opposed to all Indians, as well as their culture, belief system, and (in the case of Peru and Upper Peru) their language. The repeated use of amnesties by Hispanic officials in all of these rebellions highlights the targeted nature of their exterminatory aims.

These uprisings were also genocidal in terms of the definitions advanced by Lemkin, the United Nations, Fein, and Drost. In coining the word *genocide,* Lemkin defined it as "the destruction of a nation or an ethnic group" that is "effected through a synchronized attack on different aspects of life of the captive people" which has the "aim of annihilating the groups themselves."[234] Likewise, it is consistent with the definition of the United Nations, broad and controversial though it is, which defines genocide as

> acts committed with intent to destroy, in whole or in part, a national, ethnical, racial or religious group, as such:
> (a) Killing members of the group;
> (b) Causing serious bodily or mental harm to members of the group;
> (c) Deliberately inflicting on the group conditions of life calculated to bring about its physical destruction in whole or in part;
> (d) Imposing measures intended to prevent births within the group;
> (e) Forcibly transferring children of the group to another group.[235]

The events in these studies also conform to Helen Fein's definition of genocide as involving "the calculated murder of a segment or all of a group defined outside of the universe of obligation of the perpetrator by a government, elite, staff or crowd [where the universe of obligation is] the range of people to whom the common conscience extends: the people toward whom rules and obligations are binding."[236]

They also are consistent with the definition offered by Pieter Drost and Peter du Preez, respectively, that genocide is "the deliberate destruction of physical life of individual human beings by reason of their membership of any human collectivity as such" and the "deliberate killing of people primarily because they are categorized as being of a certain kind, with certain attributes."[237] These rebellions are also consistent with the definition of Bauer if we omit its temporal restrictions, who defines genocide as

> the planned destruction . . . of a racial, national or ethnic group by the following means: (a) selective mass murder of elites or part of the population; (b) elimination of national (racial, ethnic) culture and religious life with the intent of "denationalization"; (c) enslavement, with the same intent; (d) destruction of national (racial, ethnic) economic life, with the same intent; (e) biological decimation through the kidnapping of children, or the prevention of normal family life, with the same intent.[238]

It is also largely consistent with Chalk and Jonassohn's definition of genocide as "a form of one-sided mass killing in which a state or other authority intends to destroy a group, as that group and membership in it are defined by the perpetrator," and who usually have "no organized military machinery that might be opposed to that of the perpetrator."[239] The events in this study do, however, indicate that genocides can occur in two-sided, as opposed to "one-sided," conflicts, and in all cases studied here the victim groups as a whole did have the ability, and made the effort, to defend themselves.

The events of this study also urge a refining of the definition advanced by Dadrian, who argues that genocide is characterized by

> the successful attempt by a dominant group, vested with formal authority and/or with preponderant access to the overall resources of power, to reduce by coercion or lethal violence the number of a minority group whose ultimate extermination is held desirable and useful and whose respective vulnerability is a major factor contributing to the decision for genocide.[240]

The rebels in all of these case studies did not hold formal authority at the outbreak of the insurgencies, nor did they have a "preponderant access to the overall resources of power."[241] They did, however, seek the elimination of a minority group whom they perceived as vulnerable. While both Indian and Hispanic actions in these conflicts were on the whole genocidal on the basis of these definitions, the primary distinction was in the scope of action. While Hispanic actions were informed by their recognition that they depended on Indian labor for their survival, the native rebels sought a much more thoroughgoing extermination due to their history of relations with the Hispanics, the zero sum game nature of the situation, and their view, with the partial exception of the Cruzob, that independence and Hispanic presence were irreconcilable.

These events also urge a reevaluation of the state-centered arguments of Harff and Gurr and Horowitz which, respectively, posit that genocide involves "the promotion and execution of policies of a state or their agents which result in the deaths of a substantial portion of a group" and the "structural and systematic destruction of innocent people by a state bureaucratic apparatus."[242]

While all of these rebellions did result in the creation of insurgent authority in the areas under their control, however briefly as in the case of the Great Rebellion, genocide was not only an expression of this authority but also the means through which it was created.

Finally, from the typological aspect, these genocides had multiple and overlapping characteristics. They were retributive and focused on decolonization, seeking vengeance for decades and centuries of ruthless exploitation and loss of independence. Retribution could also involve the sparing and enslavement of Hispanics, the vestiges of the old order underscoring the fundamental difference of the new. Overall, however, the taking of prisoners was the exception. Most Hispanics in these conflicts were simply killed. In their effort to rid their respective regions of Hispanics and much of their culture, they were also xenophobic. Related to this were the monopolistic tendencies seeking Indian control of economic resources, political power, and social status.[243] The fact that in these rebellions not every Hispanic was killed, nor every vestige of their culture extirpated, does not mitigate their exterminatory nature. Very rarely do genocides succeed in the total elimination of a targeted group, and effort and intent are almost as important as outcome.[244] In addition, the imperatives of survival and the ability to resist in the future, combined with limited assimilation resulting from alien domination, help to explain why these and other nativistic movements, genocidal or otherwise, retain certain elements of the alien group.[245]

5   Rebellion and Relative Deprivation

Millennial movements in traditional societies are reactionary, seeking to re-create a legendary golden age often through cultural, and occasionally genetic, purification. On the other hand, they are fundamentally revolutionary in that their ideological agenda can usually only be implemented through the removal of a certain strata of society.[1] They are also revolutionary in the true sense of the word, for they often seek a recurrence of a time past, however idealized. Two elements run through revitalization, nativistic, and millennial movements: their emergence in a context of stress, broadly defined, and their leadership by charismatic individuals who explain why things have gone the way they have and who can lead the way out. If all is well, and there is no general perception of a crisis, radical prescriptions for the future tend to fall on deaf ears.

The stress that does cause people to view the world in a new way comes in many forms and is central not only to the rise of millennialism but to the rise of social violence generally. Both can erupt as a result of intense and socially widespread frustrations in a context where people feel they lack the means to achieve their aspirations. Relative deprivation theory offers a valuable tool for understanding the outbreak of social violence.[2] Relative deprivation is a gauge of social discontent that refers to the gap between one's expectations, or those "events, objects, and conditions" that one believes he or she should be able to have or experience, and one's ability to attain them. Means are critical here. It is not the difference between what people have and what they want but between what they have and what they reasonably believe they can achieve. Relative deprivation is thus predicated on both individual perceptions and what are culturally specific and socially accepted definitions of "reasonable." Furthermore, it requires some benchmark, or norm, upon which to measure variation. There are three basic types of values, both tangible and intangible, around which people's aspirations develop: those of welfare, power, and an "interpersonal" nature.[3] Welfare values concern standard-of-living issues, physical health, and mental development, whereas power values concern issues of individual or group autonomy, control by others, and political participation. Finally, interpersonal values concern one's position and participation in a community and relations with others.[4]

Several factors determine the likelihood of social unrest. These include the degree to which the gap between expectations and abilities is felt in a society, in terms of numbers of people and the strength of the perception, the rapidity with which the gap develops, and the degree of the perception that relationships are based on a zero sum game. As all of these factors increase, so does the risk of social violence.[5] Other facilitating factors include the degree to which socialization practices promote the perception that violence is a legitimate currency for the expression of frustration, the leadership promoting or discouraging it, and the legitimacy, vitality, and coercive resources of a regime.[6] The amount of violence that these forces produce will depend on the available avenues of political articulation, the cohesion of the regime's coercive resources, the degree of organization, discipline, and unity among the opposition, and the intelligence-gathering abilities of each side.[7]

One form of relative deprivation often associated with nativistic millennialism is decremental deprivation, which reflects the gap between relatively stable expectation patterns and a relatively sudden and dramatic drop in the ability to meet them. Abilities drop while expectations remain the same.[8] Displaced native elites, suddenly relegated to minor if any roles in a colonial arrangement, experience decremental deprivation. This is often the harbinger of more to come, as the extractive nature of the relationship between colonial rulers and their subjects creates significant economic hardships for the masses, who often had only modest surpluses to begin with. When ethnic differences are superimposed on exploitative relationships, the risk of an uprising assuming an exterminatory dimension increases. Other sources of stress causing decremental deprivation include policies concerning agricultural production, labor, religion, tribute, and taxation.[9]

Related to decremental deprivation is the concept of "moral economy," which examines the perceived legitimacy of accommodative relationships between rulers and ruled.[10] While resentment of colonialism may be constant, unrest is not. However, when the "colonial bargain" is changed, for example, when taxes are increased or new ones imposed, the decremental deprivation that such policies spur can have the effect of undermining this accommodative relationship.[11] Overall, "[e]conomic deterioration by slow degrees can become accepted by its victims as part of the normal situation. What infuriates peasants . . . is a new and sudden imposition or demand that strikes many people at once and is a break with accepted rules and customs."[12] Such actions reflect the inherent frictions of unequal relationships and may also be indicative of declining vitality and legitimacy of the regime. Devitalization may result from less frequent contact between dominant and subject groups, internal divisions, and a decline of leadership or administrative abilities within the dominant group. Accommodative relations can also be undermined through resource depletion, increasing repression of native religions, and the increased power of subject groups, whether internally or externally generated.[13] Generally, the undermining of accommodative relationships through stress is a marker on the road to social violence.

Also relevant here is prospect theory, an approach to the study of decision making which posits that individuals are willing to take greater risks to avoid losses than they are willing to take to make corresponding gains. Like relative deprivation, it requires a reference point from which to measure change. It also posits that people will persist in losing ventures, or continue "throwing good money after bad," in a tenacious effort to regain a previous reference point.[14] In addition, prospect theory predicts that people will adjust, or establish new reference points, more readily as a result of gains than they will as a result of losses. Applied to social violence, it suggests that people are more prone to violence to defend against or recoup losses than they are to make similar gains.

Disasters, and even the decay of tradition, are a source of decremental deprivation. The feelings of helplessness and hopelessness that they engender provide the basis of the appeal of the leader who can fill this vacuum not just with renewed hope but with the promise of imminent perfection. Increased suggestibility is often a result of a disaster, or "a severe, relatively sudden, and frequently unexpected disruption of normal structural arrangements within a social system."[15] Such traumatic events make those who experience them submissive and more open to new ways of viewing the world, while at the same time undermining traditional authority patterns. To spawn a millennial movement, irrespective as to whether it is revitalistic or nativistic, a disaster must be profound in its scope and affect whatever people regard as personally vital. Of course, not every disaster spawns a millennial movement; it "is a necessary rather than a sufficient condition." Disasters that have limited impact, or whose effects can be rapidly mitigated, tend not to result in millennialism. This helps to explain why urban areas are less prone to millennialism, as authorities can respond more rapidly and in a more concerted manner to disasters in these areas. Furthermore, urban areas tend to be heterogeneous and people there are not as bound to the natural world as in the countryside. In contrast, rural areas are often more homogeneous and vulnerable to economic and environmental shocks that facilitate the outbreak of such movements, and their isolation assists in their consolidation before they come in conflict with opposing forces.[16]

Michael Barkun argues that disasters of such long duration that they establish new norms, and disasters among people with cyclical, nonteleological views of time, are not millenigenic. Among the former, Barkun argues that over time, the effects of a disaster are accepted by people, and that eventually the postdisaster situation becomes a new reference point, the new norm. He asserts, "One cannot really regard constant deprivation either as a form of relative deprivation or as disaster . . . for it is neither sudden nor unanticipated, but simply 'there.' "[17] As we shall see in the cases of the Great Rebellion in Peru and Upper Peru and the Caste War in Yucatán, this is not always the case, and preconquest reference points can be enduring.[18] Native peoples were reminded every day of the effects that the conquest had on them. While the initial disaster itself may have passed, its effects continued. It still retained a relative quality, as legends and oral histories perpetuated often idealized memories of how things once were. Combined with this, the incessant and pervasive reminders of colonial or alien elite rule, coupled with a lack of means for, and hope of, self-improvement, serve to make the disaster an ongoing one. In addition, prophesies may reflect a cyclical view of time, in which the world is on occasion destroyed and re-created by higher powers. This not only helps them to comprehend the initial disaster of conquest but also helps them to endure it by serving as a light at the end of the tunnel. Indeed, a cyclical concept of time, prophesies of a better world, and the perception that life under alien rule is an ongoing disaster are vital materials for the charismatic leader who can seize upon them to place himself or herself at the intersection of the perceived grandeur of the past, the misery of the present, and hopes of a divinely ordained and perfect future.

While decremental deprivation may be closely associated with nativistic millennialism, this is not the only cause. As Leon Trotsky noted, "The mere existence of privations is not enough to cause an insurrection; if it were, the masses would always be in revolt."[19] Social unrest and revolution may also come about in a context of prosperity, where economic growth or other improvements create expectations for continued growth. Alexis de Tocqueville concurred: "It is not always in going from bad to worse that one falls into revolution. It happens most often that a people, which had supported the most crushing laws . . . rejects them violently when their burden is lightened."[20] In conditions of progressive deprivation, these rising expectations, based on the new norm of growth, are shattered when suddenly the growth or improvements decline.[21] Related to progressive deprivation is accelerated deprivation, where both expectations and abilities are increasing, although expectations increasingly outstrip abilities. As the discrepancy between them continues to increase, so do the possibilities of social violence.[22]

Another form of relative deprivation is aspirational deprivation. Here people's expectations increase while their abilities remain the same. This often occurs in a context of intercultural contact, and communications technology such as the transistor radio, satellite television, and the Internet contribute to the development of new desires. A population long shut off from the world is exposed to new influences that prompt an increase in their expectations, although their abilities remain unchanged. This can happen suddenly and through the introduction of new ideas and belief systems, as opposed to material goods. In such cases, "conversion" takes place, with the "abandonment of . . . the preexisting norms and beliefs that establish existing expectation levels . . . and their re-placement by new beliefs that justify increased or different expectations."[23] Disasters can also spur conversion through demonstrating the inefficacy of pre-vious belief systems. In addition, relative deprivation can occur in a context of "value disequilibrium," where people seek harmony between various values. For example, a person of high social rank may also seek to have a correspond-ing level of material wealth.[24]

We should also note that social violence can result from the gap created by increasing expectations and the decline of previously stable abilities, a form of relative deprivation that could be termed "divergent deprivation." This differs from progressive and accelerated deprivation in that both of these forms are based on increasing, not previously stable, abilities. Divergent deprivation can occur on two levels and, due to the intensity of the gap and the rapidity with which it is created, may create an especially volatile situation. On one level, divergent deprivation can occur within one value context, such as welfare val-ues. The decline of previously stable abilities concerning a standard of living in a context of increasing expectations in this regard would create divergent deprivation. Similarly, different values can be experiencing differing forms of relative deprivation, both within and between sectors of the population. This, too, can produce divergent deprivation within a population segment. In a co-lonial context, for example, decremental deprivation may result from new ex-tractive demands and native elite displacement, and aspirational deprivation may emerge following exposure to the goods introduced by, and lifestyle of, colonizers. In this situation, expectations may increase while abilities decline, especially among those who have greater interactions with the alien elites. This is similar in some respects to conversion, but plays out over a longer time frame.[25] Despite the differing forms of relative deprivation, decremental, progressive, and divergent deprivation appear to be most likely to spur social unrest in less developed areas.[26] Prospect theory helps us understand this, as people are will-ing to take inordinate risks to retain or regain what they have or had.[27]

Demography, Depletion, and Decremental Deprivation among the Pueblos

In the Pueblo region, the stresses created by colonialism and cultural conflict precipitated decremental deprivation, or a declining ability to satisfy stable, precolonial expectations.[28] The scope of this was expansive, as all of the pueblos under Spanish dominion were subject to the same forces, which be-came more severe after the establishment of Santa Fe in 1610. Perhaps most important was the intensity of these forces in the context of the demographic collapse of the native population. By 1680 the 16,000 Pueblo Indians were "facing extinction"; their population had fallen by up to 80 percent since preconquest times.[29] It is important to recognize that not only did disease, famine, and social decay under Spanish rule combine to weaken the natives, but these forces were mutually reinforcing, progressively undermined accommodative relationships in a zero sum game situation. Those natives who did not die were ruthlessly exploited by Hispanic missionaries, authorities, and settlers, attacked by Apaches, and were witnesses to the continual erosion of native ways. In this context, the rebellion is also consistent with the idea that people will take inordinate risks to avert losses, as prospect theory holds.[30]

Since the conquest, all social groups had seen historically stable welfare values collapse, as surpluses consistently eroded, labor demands increased, and the population continued to plummet.[31] The introduction of horses exacerbated the problem, as the Pueblo were less able to resist more frequent incursions by Apache and other nomadic bands of Indians, who often attacked in retaliation for slaving expeditions of the Hispanics and now could attack faster, carry more booty, and flee faster and farther than before.[32] The Hispanic presence also led to decremental deprivation in terms of Indian labor and surplus. Whereas previously surplus could be used for sustenance in times of drought or for trade, it had become a zero sum game situation as it was appropriated by the encomenderos, friars, and others whom the Indians viewed as illegitimate usurpers. Likewise, native labor was increasingly dedicated to satisfying the demands of the Hispanics and not for personal or community benefit. As one rebel put it, the natives had rebelled "because of the hardships suffered at the hands of the Spaniards and Religious; because they were not allowed to till their lands or do anything for their own benefit."[33] Another rebel, Pedro García, reported that the Indians rebelled because "they were tired of the work they had to do for the Spaniards and the religious because they did not allow them to plant or do other things for their own needs."[34]

Within this context of demographic and natural disasters, severe decremental deprivation, and an environment where violence was seen as a legitimate currency of expression, the Indian village caciques were hard hit in terms of the decline of power and, to a lesser degree, interpersonal values. Although their authority was circumscribed by the official recognition of Indian governors who served as the link between the pueblos and the Hispanic officials, they retained considerable status in their communities. Nevertheless, time had shown that they were powerless to reverse the decline of their societies, a factor in the continuing erosion of their status. Those most affected in terms of interpersonal and power values, or their autonomy, social status, and relationships with others, however, were those medicine men such as Popé who led the rites and rituals and served as the link with the native spiritual world. Despite occasional periods of increased tolerance of native rites by civil authorities, the medicine men were not only forced to practice surreptitiously but generally persecuted by Hispanic religious and civil authorities alike. Their decline was emblematic of the decline of native religion generally and with it the social fabric and traditions upon which it rested and was reinforced.[35] This appears to have been brought to a head with Governor Treviño's roundup of the medicine men, including the future rebel leader Popé, in 1675 and the ensuing abuses by Governor Otermín's secretary of war, Francisco Xavier, as he and other officials "molested and burned" many kivas.[36]

It appears that this concerted assault caused the medicine men to fear for the continued existence of their own lives, as well as their religion and society. This, however, occurred, in a context where there had been periods of liberalization, such as those under Governors Eulate (1618–25) and López de Mendizabal (1659–61). As a result, while the secular trend was one of decremental deprivation, the periodic rising of hopes through liberalization only accentuated the frustration when the screw again tightened. A captive, the elderly Pedro Gamboa, stated that the natives had rebelled "because the Spaniards had punished their medicine men and idolaters, [and] the Teguas, Taos, Picuries and the Pecos Xemes tribes had formed a conspiracy to kill the Spaniards and Religious." He added that

> the Indians did not want any Spaniards or Religious in their country [and that] . . . a strong sentiment had existed among the Indians since this Kingdom was discovered against the Spaniards and Religious, because they had been deprived of their idols and witchcraft, which had been handed down to them from generation to generation.[37]

He further asserted that he had "heard this resentment spoken of since he was of an age to understand."[38] One thing that worked to the Indians' advantage was the obvious and continuing severe frictions among the Hispanics themselves. Their devitalization and internal division, both before the rebellion and after the Hispanic reconquest, as well as the relatively small numbers of Hispanics in the region, translated into some hope and strength for the pueblos. While the 1675 roundup of the medicine men undermined the accommodative relationship with the Hispanics and led them and many in their communities to fear for the continued existence of their lives, rituals, and society, which in their view depended upon such worship and ceremonies, the successful Indian demands for the release of the captive curanderos also demonstrated that they did have some ability to influence events.[39] In sum, while the Pueblo Indians generally suffered from decremental deprivation, and all experienced a decline of welfare values, among medicine men and caciques this was compounded by the decline of power and interpersonal values. These forces, combined with native planning and opportunity, formed the basis of the Pueblo Revolt.

Economic Pressures, Expectations, and the Great Rebellion

In Peru and Upper Peru, the series of revenue-enhancing and administrative measures commonly referred to as the Bourbon reforms set in motion a dynamic that would precipitate the Great Rebellion. These changes had been gradually implemented over about a generation, including the legalization of the repartimiento de mercancías, the introduction of taxes on Indian staples, and more aggressive revenue collection, among other administrative and military measures. The 1770s, however, saw a marked increase in their intensity, the expansion of the internal economy, increased demand for Indian labor, greater divisions among the ruling elite, and the decline of Lima as a commercial center with the establishment of the Viceroyalty of La Plata in Buenos Aires in 1776.[40]

Throughout the period of their implementation, within the Indian population there were differential effects. Among the native elite, many were involved in muleteering and other forms of commerce and, in the area of welfare values, were especially subject to progressive deprivation, or the partial reversal of socioeconomic betterment in a context of increasing expectations engendered by the previous improvement.[41] The "renaissance" of native culture and increasing expressions and appreciation of Incaic heritage is also indicative of a trend and desire for greater cultural affirmation and autonomy on the part of the Indians, especially those of the elite.[42] While such expressions increased aspirations, especially in a prophetic environment predicting the inevitable return of native rule, they also underscored the fact that they were a subject race. Overall, we find a form of divergent deprivation at work that was formed by aspirational deprivation with increased interpersonal value aspirations in a context of stable abilities paired with progressive deprivation in terms of welfare values as a result of the increases in the alcabala, or sales tax, and other exactions and more vigorous efforts to collect them. We should also note that for those of the hereditary curaca class, replaced by "interim" curacas, power value decremental deprivation was especially severe.

When organizing and propagating the rebellion, however, Indian leaders recognized that the mita and reparto were much more deeply rooted grievances among the mass of Indians.[43] Upon this bedrock of resentment, the Bourbon reforms heightened the sense of a zero sum game between Indians and Hispanics and led to welfare value–based progressive deprivation. Increased taxation, often on items formerly exempt; increased demand for labor and services by corregidor, curaca, and priest alike; and increased encroachment on native lands all affected native welfare values as they reversed the advances previously under way against the backdrop of increasing expectation. While the new exactions affected different sectors of the population in different ways and created divisions among the ruling elite, taken as a whole the reforms engendered significant and very widespread resentment, something recognized by both rebels and loyalists as an important cause of the rebellion.[44] When mixed with a lack of effective avenues of redress and a vibrant, cataclysmic, prophetic tradition and a charismatic leader, the frustrations caused by these new exactions were a recipe for rebellion.

Despite the gulf between them, Creoles and Indians did share an increasing frustration with the colonial system, although for different reasons. A firmer and more intrusive royal authority, increasing and efficiently collected taxes, and mounting competition for native labor and surplus not only assaulted Creole welfare values but also increased Creole frustration with the broader social and political prerogatives held by peninsulares, or those from Spain.[45] This frustration was heightened as a result of the increasing spread of enlightenment ideas, most notably those emphasizing individual liberty.[46] The clandestine importation and printing of books espousing such ideas grew, as did the frustration of royal authorities in their efforts to intercept them. In 1754, the priest Pedro Logu lamented the fact that the "introduction of prohibited books . . . is so free that the diligence practiced here [by] the Santo Tribunal" was ineffective in controlling them.[47] While limited in their diffusion, some of the Indian elite were also exposed to enlightenment ideas, including Túpac Amaru, who spent a year in Lima in 1777 litigating to reduce demands on his people and defending his lineage. It was during that time, according to his wife, Micaela Bastidas, that he "opened his eyes."[48]

It was not just the spread of enlightenment ideas and heightened frustration with new royal demands that aroused Creole desires for change, but also the realization of these ideas through the United States war for independence. This simultaneously reaffirmed the value of such concepts, while delegitimizing Spanish rule, and spurred power- and interpersonal value–based aspirational deprivation.[49] To the extent that these forces interacted, they promoted "conversion," or "the abandonment of some or all of the norms and beliefs that establish existing expectation levels . . . and their replacement by new beliefs that justify increased or different expectations."[50] Again, we find divergent deprivation in force, formed by a combination of power and interpersonal value aspirational deprivation matched with welfare value–based decremental deprivation produced by the Bourbon reforms.[51]

The threat of war with Britain led many Creoles to perceive Spain as vulnerable. It also led to the expansion of militias, which subsequently fostered a nascent nationalism among Creoles.[52] That such forces were at play is evidenced by numerous Creole-led rebellions before the Great Rebellion, such as those in La Paz between 1776 and 1780, in Arequipa in January 1780, in Cuzco and Cochabamba in April 1780, and in Chuquisaca in March 1780.[53] Lewin sums it up well when he observes that "we can say that there existed, at the time, two American revolutionary movements: one Creole and another indigenous."[54] These two strands only rarely intersected, and when they did, such as in Oruro in February 1781, or in Túpac Amaru's promises to protect the wealth of Creoles who joined him, it quickly became apparent that their goals and interests inherently conflicted. The Creoles wanted an elitist political revolution, while the Indians sought a political, social, economic, and cultural transformation.

Dashed Hopes, Liberal Policies, and the Economic Frontier in Yucatán

In the Caste War of Yucatán, the expansion of the economic frontier and especially of sugar, policies reducing the power of the Church, and the involvement of natives in Hispanic political conflicts had far-reaching effects. Among the native elite, such policies helped to spawn divergent deprivation, or the decline of previously stable welfare and interpersonal value abilities in the context of increasing power value aspirations. Welfare values were affected as a result of declining commissions from collecting increasingly unstable religious taxes, while their interpersonal values reflected the parallel decline in their status, as there was increasingly less to distinguish them from the mass of Indians.[55] Rugeley notes that the "importance of the batabs' crumbling status cannot be overestimated" in tracing the origins of the conflict, adding that "the gradual expansion of non-Maya elites in rural areas tended to crowd the batab out of available opportunities and qualify the prestige he had once enjoyed."[56] At the same time, however, their involvement in Hispanic conflicts, such as the war of independence, Imán's 1839 revolt, Barbachano's call in 1843 for their support in resisting the reincorporation of Yucatán into Mexico, and their involvement in the 1847 Mérida-Campeche conflict, created new welfare and power value aspirations while legitimating violence as a political currency. Their involvement in these conflicts produced conversion and the establishment of a new reference point based on their demonstrated power while also stimulating a desire to exercise it more fully.[57] Inverting the social order was no longer a dream but rather an imminent possibility. As a result, while power value aspirations had consistently increased, welfare and interpersonal values had declined.

Likewise, the Indians whom the elite led also suffered from divergent deprivation, though in a more pronounced form. Having not only been involved, but having been decisive, in the numerous conflicts cited above, they too realized the power of the machete and how, once raised, it could make the Hispanics cower in fear. With power and interpersonal value aspirations on the rise, they too saw the reversal of the social order, or the elimination of the Hispanics, as a realistic possibility. While both of these power and interpersonal values reflected increasing aspirations, the majority of Indians saw their material standing coming under increasing pressure, as the economic frontier expanded and churches progressively encroached on community lands and raised fees for services such as baptism and marriage. The increase of such extractive demands was widely felt, and served to further delegitimate Hispanic authority. While taxes, church dues, forced labor, and land pressures all contributed to the outbreak of the insurgency, taxes and church dues were the central issues for many rebels.[58]

The effect of these forces was also exacerbated as these increases were implemented in a context where the natives had repeatedly been led to believe that obventions and many civil taxes would be eliminated and that they would be given land. This began in 1813–14 when obventions and the fagina were briefly abolished, their restoration dashing the "millenarian expectation" that it had engendered.[59] In 1839, Imán promised, and largely failed to deliver, an end to obventions, a reduction of civil taxes, and land for those who supported him. Again, in 1843, Governor Barbachano promised, and failed to deliver, the abolition of obventions and tithes in his efforts to enlist Indian support against Santa Anna's forces.[60] Indian involvement in these conflicts also led many to believe that violence was the only effective means of political articulation. While the 1841 constitution provided the vote for the Indians, in the end the document was little more than an expression of ideals as opposed to a viable mechanism for nation building.[61] These events not only created frustration, and welfare value aspirational deprivation, but had a heightened effect due to the fact that there were repeated cycles of such disappointment.[62]

The Huit population, which had for the most part remained outside of the Hispanic world and were prominent in the rebellion, were increasingly and reluctantly brought into the Hispanic world and economy as a result of the expansion of the sugar frontier.[63] With it came decremental deprivation because it became increasingly difficult to fulfill long-standing expectations as public lands and water rights, upon which they had long depended for sustenance, were increasingly sold to Hispanics. As a result, most Huits were left with few alternatives except working on a hacienda, fleeing deeper into the forest, or fighting to reverse the situation.[64] As Reed notes, "What was dangerous was not long oppression, but sudden acculturation, the forced march from one world to another."[65] Overall, after so many broken promises and dashed hopes, it was apparent to many Indians that Hispanic words could not be trusted, violence worked, and that they were in a zero sum game situation. Their hand was further strengthened by the continuing divisions and discord among the Hispanics.[66]

In all of these uprisings, relative deprivation was central to their outbreak and often affected different social sectors in different ways. Whereas in the Pueblo Revolt, decremental deprivation in all value areas played an especially important role, in the Andean and Yucatecan examples, divergent deprivation helped spawn the rebellions. In the context of prophecies concerning the return of native rule in Peru and Upper Peru, among the Indian elite divergent deprivation was caused by a mix of unsated power and interpersonal value aspirations and decremental deprivation in terms of welfare values. Among the mass of Indians, decremental deprivation had even greater force as a result of the erosion of welfare values through new and better-collected exactions and increased demand for their labor. In Yucatán, the welfare and interpersonal values of the Indian elite declined in a context of increasing power value aspirations. Divergent deprivation also had an impact on Indians, who like the batabs experienced welfare value decremental deprivation and power value aspirational deprivation.

6   Leadership and Division

Despite the differences in time and place, these rebellions were all led by charismatic individuals who promised divine protection for their salvationist endeavor. These leaders not only helped to imbue the movements with millennial qualities but also, with varying degrees of success, offered a degree of cohesion that mitigated the divisive nature of the forces that they led, nominally or otherwise. For their part, the Hispanics were plagued by internal divisions, yet were adept at exploiting those of the natives to their own benefit and, ultimately, victory.

In New Mexico, although a healer, Popé was unlike many charismatic leaders, as he had not been assimilated into the alien culture.[1] He cultivated the belief that he communicated with Indian deities, received guidance from them, and that he and the rebels benefited from divine intervention in the establishment and sustenance of the new order. Leadership played a critical role both in organizing the insurgency and in subsequent efforts to consolidate native authority. Popé not only cultivated the belief that he had divine powers but linked them to the origin of his people and their rebirth under his rule. He claimed that he received his instructions

> from the ca[u]di and the other two who emitted fire from their extremities at the said estufa of Taos, and that thereby they remained as of old, the same as when they came out of the laguna de Cópala; that that was the best mode of living and the one they desired, because the God of the Spaniards was worthless and theirs was very powerful, and that of the Spaniard was nothing but rotten pieces of wood, and this was heeded and obeyed by all, save some, who, moved by Christian zeal, repudiated it. And these were immediately put to death by order of the said Popé.[2]

Popé had also "given them to understand that the father of all the Indians, their great captain, who had been such since the world had been inundated, had ordered the said Popé to tell all the pueblos to rebel and to swear that they would do so . . . and that after this they would live as in ancient times."[3]

The divine assistance promised by Popé was not only to ensure the success of the rebellion itself but would lead to an earthly utopia. He promised his followers that after the rebellion they would be "regaled like the religious and Spaniards, and would gather a great many provisions and everything they needed."[4] In addition, the rebel Pedro Naranjo noted the widespread belief that by living under the laws of their ancients they would raise a great quantity of corn and beans, large bolls of cotton, pumpkins and watermelons of a great size and musk melons, and that their houses would be filled, and they would have good health and plenty of rest; and . . . the people . . . [would be] overjoyed, living in pleasure.[5]

Another Indian, a Tiwa named Jerónimo, said that Popé promised "large crops of grain, maize with large and thick ears, many bundles of cotton, many calabashes and watermelons, and everything else in proportion."[6] Another native reported that Popé promised that if people followed his commands, "they would thereby be assured of harvesting much maize, cotton, and an abundance of all crops, and better ones than ever, and that they would live in great ease."[7] It is interesting that it was imputed to, or expressed by, Popé that the future would include an abundance of melons and grain, which had been introduced by the Spaniards.

This perfect world was also to benefit from divine protection from further Hispanic intrusion, as the spirits "of the estufa of Taos had given them to understand that as soon as the Spaniards moved upon this kingdom they would warn them of it, so they could assemble and prevent their getting any of them."[8] Hubert Bancroft also notes that Popé claimed "supernatural powers" and that the Castillos "were not to be feared, for he had built walls up to the skies to keep them away."[9]

Popé's minimal integration into colonial society also differentiated him from many other Native American leaders. Kessell notes, "The native leader who had risen highest in the Spaniards' eyes, who had learned most about the dominant culture and its flaws, and who seemingly had profited to the greatest extent from the colonial system, often sought to overthrow it."[10] In 1680, Fray Antonio de la Sierra noted that "the Indians who have done the greatest harm are those who have been most favored by the religious and who are the most intelligent."[11] The Indian named Juan who presented Governor Otermín with the options of choosing the red or white banners had earlier been sent by him as a messenger, and the governor lamented the fact that this Indian, "who spoke our language, was so intelligent, and had lived all his life in the villa among the Spaniards, where I had placed so much confidence in him . . . was now coming as a leader of the Indian rebels."[12] While the origins of Popé are ambiguous, many other leaders of the rebellion were of mixed origin.[13] Alonso Catiti and Francisco "El Ollita" were both Coyotes, or of Indian and mestizo parentage, while the rebel Antonio Bolsas was described as "very ladino," or Hispanicized.[14] In 1694, one of the Indians who opposed Vargas's reconquest of Jemez was "a ladino Indian named Diego."[15] This diversity underscores the fact that ethnicity was as important as race in the rebellion, and while some rebels may have had some Spanish blood, ethnically they were Indians.

Having expelled the Hispanics and dominated the region, Popé soon began to repeat many of the practices of those whom he abhorred. In his visits to the pueblos with other rebel leaders, he insisted that people kneel in his presence and that he be received with the same pomp and formality as the Spanish governor, with the addition that he would bless his subjects by casting corn flour on them.[16] Not only did he demand tribute of cotton and other goods from all of the towns under his dominion, but he moved into the former Spanish governor's residence in Santa Fe and took to riding in the governor's carriage there. On at least one occasion, in Santa Ana, Popé hosted a banquet with "the foods that the religious and governors used to use, and a large table, after the style of the Spanish," during which he played the role of the Spanish governor, and Alonso Catiti played that of the custodian, offering praise and toasts to one another with silver chalices.[17]

This spectacle highlights that just as many Indians continued to cultivate crops introduced by the Spanish, the leaders often continued to use these and other Spanish imports. After the rebellion, the rebel chiefs were quick to appropriate and distribute the livestock of the Hispanics and missions among themselves.[18] Popé and the other rebel leaders often kept chalices and other religious artifacts for their own use.[19] In Santo Domingo, during his entrada in December 1681 with Governor Otermín, Juan Domínguez de Mendoza found much Spanish property and that "most of the things that had been in the church and the offices of the convent" had been taken and kept in the house of the rebel leader Alonso Catiti and his immediate neighbor, Diego el Zapatero. In Alameda he also found some religious articles in homes, while in Puaray he "found many valuable things that they had stolen from the Spaniards, in two houses in particular," which included a silver lamp and a "Turkish" carpet. In houses in San Felipe, he found a censer and broken crosses alongside ceremonial masks.[20] Such assimilation is not unusual among nativistic or anticolonial millennial movements. Generally it appears that whatever is assimilated either favors the defense, survival, and reproduction of the nativists or underscores their new dominance over their erstwhile rulers.[21]

After less than a year and a half, by November 1681 Popé had alienated so many people over "the amount [which] in his frequent visits he made them contribute" that he was ousted by Luís Tupatu of Picurís. One Indian named Juan, who in 1681 asserted that he was over 100 years old and "that he remembers distinctly, as if it were yesterday, when the Spaniards entered this kingdom, and that when he was baptized he was able to stand on his own feet," stated that as a result of the drought and famine many Indians were unhappy, as "everyone is perishing." Popé might have been able to continue in power had he delivered on some of his promises concerning the blissful nature of life after the rebellion. The mutually reinforcing effects of a continuing drought, famine, disease, and raids from the Apache and Yuta Indians also contributed to his downfall. Overall, these forces would continue to bedevil Tupatu, and the unity that enabled the rebellion disintegrated. The fact that the natives of the region had never been subject to a centralized rule before the Spanish arrived acted as a catalyst for the reemergence of their autonomy.[22]

Although Popé would again rule in 1688, he died soon afterward, and Tupatu reemerged as the dominant figure. Of the most prominent rebel leaders, he was one of the few remaining, for Alonso Catiti had died before 1688. The circumstances were unclear, for it was said that upon entering a kiva, "he burst suddenly, coming out in everyone's view, all of his intestines."[23] By the time Vargas arrived in 1692, dissent among the pueblos was such that Tupatu was more interested in punishing his native adversaries than in repelling the Hispanics, and he quickly entered into an alliance with them. He may also have retained some Spanish characteristics, or appeared to do so for effect: when he met Vargas, in addition to his mother-of-pearl crown, shotgun, and powder horn, he was "dressed in the Spanish style."[24]

Polarization among the Pueblos

If the lifting of Hispanic oppression and the promise of a nativist utopia were not enough inducement to join the Pueblo Revolt, rebel leaders readily fell back on coercion. This to some degree masked and mitigated divisions between those of different generations, between Indian military leaders and medicine men, and traditional rivalries between pueblos, all of which were exacerbated by famine and attacks by nomadic Indians. When the rebellion was being organized, it was opposed by the Tanos leaders, although the Indians subject to them supported it. Also opposing the rebellion were the Pecos Indians and the leaders of San Cristóbal, San Marcos, and La Cienega. The latter two and the Tanos chiefs were among those who alerted Governor Otermín to the plot.[25] In organizing the rebellion, Popé reportedly promised that "the pueblo that failed to obey would be laid waste."[26] Others who were unsupportive were killed. In San Felipe, as the rebellion erupted, a group of rebels asked the Indian Bartolomé Naranjo, "'Have you the courage to help the Indians and take part with them in killing the friars and Spaniards?' And he refused to accede to it . . . and having left him for a while they then secured him and in a perfidious and treacherous manner clubbed and killed him."[27]

Another native noted in 1681 that "all of [the Indians] did not voluntarily revolt," and many joined the uprising "on account of the fear" they had of Popé, who "communicates with the devil, and on that account they were afraid of him."[28] Popé also used such fear to his advantage after the rebellion, when

> in order to terrorize the people into obedience . . . an order came from the three demons, spoken of by the said Popé, to the effect that anyone who still carried in his heart the priests, governors and Spaniards, would show it in the dirt of his face and clothes worn by him, and that such should be punished; and that if they observed the commands of the aforesaid four nothing would be lacking to them.[29]

As we have previously seen, in the midst of an ongoing famine, there were also divisions over the orders concerning the cultivation of crops introduced by the Hispanics and the tribute demands of Popé.[30]

Inter- and intratribal conflicts were a continual affliction of the independent pueblos. The Jemez, Taos, Picurís, and Tewas were especially subject to Yuta raids, whereas Apaches caused devastation in Alameda, Puaray, Sandía, San Felipe, and Santo Domingo. As a result, many communities abandoned their towns in search of food or greater security.[31] The forces of famine and external attack also stimulated the resurgence of the autonomous tendencies in Pueblo society. Under Popé, the Keres, Taos, and Pecos had conflicts with the Tewas and Tanos, who were led by Luis Tupatu. When Tupatu was ousted in 1688 and Popé returned to power with support of Tewa pueblos, he was not recognized by the inhabitants of Jemez, Taos, Pecos, Cochiti, Santa Ana, Zía, San Felipe, or Santo Domingo. When Tupatu met and sided with Vargas in 1692, part of his goal was to punish the Pecos, Keres, Jemez, and Tanos Indians who had failed to recognize him. In addition, as disintegration supplanted confederation, the Tiwas and Piros were repeatedly attacked by the Tewas, Keres, and Jemez Indians because the Tiwas and Piros were seen as sympathetic to the Hispanics.[32]

By late 1681, Tanos, Tewas, Keres, and Jemez Indians were planning an attack on Isleta for December 12, for which they "were in arms to come and kill the people" there and seize their corn.[33] The rebel Pedro Naranjo had been dispatched to Isleta as part of this plan. Although he was captured by the Spaniards before he could implement it, he had been instructed to tell the people of Isleta to send their youths to Taos to collect cattle, which would be given to them to assuage their hunger. While they were there, the rebels would attack Isleta and "kill all the old men who remained and capture the women and children in order to give them to the Apaches in recompense for their people whom the Spaniards had killed in the wars, so that they might make friends with them." Those who had been sent to Taos were likewise to be killed, all as punishment for those of Isleta, as they had not participated in the rebellion.[34]

Concerning the Indians' response to the Hispanics' return to the region during Otermín's entrada of 1681, one Indian acknowledged that although "it is true that there were different opinions among them," he believed that most would resist the Hispanic reentry into the region. The mass of Indians "stood in great fear" of their leaders, and in 1681 the younger warriors were especially opposed to any accommodation with the Hispanics. How to respond to the Hispanic incursions was not the only source of discord, as "every time that the Apache enemy came they blamed the leaders of the revolt, saying [that after the uprising] they had lived in continual restlessness.[35] Dissension is also suggested when, as Mendoza and his group struck out from the main body of troops during the 1681 entrada, he learned that the Indians of Alameda, Puaray, and Sandía had gone to the mountains outside of Sandía, and many of those from Alameda were "weeping loudly" as they left, fearful both of Spanish reprisals and of living in a winter wilderness.[36] In 1689 an Indian reported to the Hispanics that the inhabitants of Acoma had taken refuge in the mountains due to numerous conflicts with those of neighboring Laguna.[37]

Vargas skillfully used Indian divisions to his advantage in his reconquest of the region. Schisms in native society were nothing new and were noted by Coronado as early as 1540. Kessell asserts that "whether this intramural dissension resulted from competing generational, occupational, or social factions, it evidently was endemic."[38] It does appear that in the reconquest, while native military leaders may have supported the Hispanics as a means to dominate their enemies, the pueblo religious leaders resisted such changes, as there was no way they could come out ahead through an alliance with the interlopers. Among those who sided with the Hispanics in 1692 were the former rebels Bartolomé de Ojeda, Luís Tupatu, and Cristóbal Yope of San Lorenzo.[39]

As Vargas passed near Santo Domingo in September 1692, his band captured an Indian from San Felipe who told them that the Tewas and Tanos were "making war against them [and that they] celebrated the coming of the Spaniards and would help them go and kill Tewas." Generational gaps were also evident in late September 1692, when Vargas approached Pecos. There an Indian woman captive told him that the younger Indians "wanted neither to go see [Vargas] nor allow the older people of the pueblo" to do so, although many of the elders wanted to negotiate. Another Indian told Vargas that the pueblo was so divided over how to deal with the Hispanics that the young were about to kill the old of the community. The residents of Taos had alienated many through their rule, and such were the divisions that in early October 1692 Vargas wrote that the "Tewa, Tano and Picurís . . . have asked me to destroy these rebels [of Taos] once and for all and burn their pueblo."[40]

In December 1693, as Vargas camped in the cold outside of Santa Fe, the Indians from Galisteo who occupied the town were divided over whether they should cede the town to the Hispanics or "fight until all of the Spaniards are dead." On New Year's Eve in 1693, the erstwhile rebel from Zía, Bartolomé de Ojeda, informed Vargas that Antonio Malacate and other Jemez Indians were trying to enlist the support of the Keres and Navajos to attack the Hispanics, but Zía, Santa Ana, and San Felipe were opposed to the plan and as a result were under attack by them. In January 1694, many of the Indians from San Ildefonso, Puguaque, Cuyamunque, Jacona, Tesuque, San Cristóbal, San Lorenzo, and Santa Clara who had retreated to the Mesilla de San Ildefonso in anticipation of a Hispanic attack wanted to return to take advantage of Vargas's pardon, as a result of "what they were suffering and what they could expect of a crude and drawn out war." Their captains, however, "fearing what they deserved . . . threatened them through all means."[41]

Among the Pecos, in a planned rebellion of August 1695, only "half" of them supported it, and their leaders would be executed the following year.[42] Four years later, however, resentments and divisions continued there.[43] In San Cristóbal in 1696, some of the inhabitants opposed the rebellion, but "the leaders of this treachery silenced them and chided them."[44] In the same year in Nambé, the cacique executed one Indian "because he was a friend of the Spaniards, knew how to speak Castilian, and reported what they were dealing with in their conversations and meetings."[45] In Tesuque in 1696, the inhabitants were ready to join the rebels in Chimayo, but after the cacique Domingo "became angry with them, they calmed down, became silent, and agreed to die at the Spaniards' side."[46] For his part, Domingo was targeted for death by the Indians of Santa Clara and San Ildefonso because he was pro-Spanish.[47] In July and August 1696, Vargas learned that the Tewas, Picurís, Taos, and Tanos Indians did not want to participate in the rebellion which, like that of 1680, was being organized on a regional level.[48] Also like the 1680 rebellion, the organization of that of 1696 relied to some degree on coercion. In August 1696, a captured Tewa, Miguel Saxete, reported that the rebel Juan Griego had insisted on the night of the rebellion that "everyone in all the pueblos was going to rise up that night and kill all the religious and Spaniards, and they had to do the same thing."[49] Overall, Juan Griego was "greatly feared and obeyed" by "all the Tewas from San Juan pueblo."[50]

A Tenuous Coalition: The Hispanics in New Mexico

Although long-standing and bitter civil-religious divisions were somewhat muted in the aftermath of the rebellion, overall the Hispanics continued to be riddled by factionalism. Before the uprising, it was not an easy task to maintain a stable Hispanic population in New Mexico. Such was the discontent in the colony in 1680 that some families had wanted to leave for the past three years, and five months previous to the revolt, forty families had planned to move away, but the governor had "managed to quiet them." He did so by "persuasion and prudent measures, without being able to resort to the force of the law even to punish the gravest crimes, for all were relatives and he had no paid men whom he could use."[51] While fear of the rebels united the Hispanics, it also caused many to flee. Making his way north from Mexico City, as Father Ayeta approached the Río Grande in his effort to aid the refugees, six of his wagoneers fled because they had "little liking to go to war." Meanwhile, as the Hispanics made their way south, Governor Otermín found that "the people . . . coming with him [were] reluctant to stop, and consequently he has much more fear and misgiving about controlling the division that is going ahead and is in Fray Cristóbal."[52] Indeed, up to around 1,000 people crossed the Río Grande and kept on going, preferring the risk of punishment to the risk of staying in the region.[53]

Once in the El Paso area, during a junta de guerra on April 5, 1681, although a few Hispanics suggested resettling in Isleta or undertaking an entrada, most agreed that they should get provisions from Nueva Vizcaya and await orders from the viceroy or king before reentering the region.[54] Even getting provisions from Casas Grandes was difficult "because of the little or no assistance given on the part of the" refugees. Of the ten men ordered to accompany Pedro de Leiva on his journey there, only one did; he then abandoned Leiva in Casas Grandes and returned to El Paso.[55] Gambling by the refugees also was a source of discord, and in October 1681, the governor complained that many "with . . . great audacity and shamelessness have gambled with the horses and other things that they have," and ordered that no one "dare to gamble with any of the arms, horses, or clothing" and that all winnings be returned to their original owners.[56]

When an entrada north was finally ordered in September 1681, Otermín had great difficulty organizing a muster as "up to the present the inhabitants and natives of this kingdom who . . . have been ordered to come have not done so."[57] Most of those present claimed that they were too old or ill to participate.[58] On September 9, when Otermín read the order to undertake the entrada, Fray Francisco de Ayeta noted that no one was eager to go and that "even before Otermín finished reading the dispatch . . . there were not lacking those who began to raise difficulties and obstacles. . . . He became cognizant of the fact that all the most courageous and fervent promises and desires to return to the conquest exhibited in La Salineta . . . had changed to cold indifference." He further noted that "there were not lacking teachers who inculcated dismay in the place of encouragement" in a "camp . . . composed of people of whom the number of disgruntled ones exceeded the number who were content."[59]

The wealth of some of the refugees was also a source of friction. Of those who escaped from the Río Abajo region with Lieutenant General Alonso García, many had managed to get out with their property "without showing their faces to the enemy or discharging a harquebus."[60] Many of these same people also received support from the crown as refugees. Maestre de campo Francisco Gómez noted that "those who have distinguished themselves most with their complaints and clamor to receive the best cattle and be given maize first . . . they themselves have enough to support others from their own property . . . [and are] the families of the said Thóme Domínguez and don Pedro de Chávez. . . . They carry off more than their numbers entitle them to, taking it from the poor." Gómez added that "Francisco Domínguez left with a flock of 400 or more sheep, which he was taking to El Parral to sell, and on the road the . . . father fray Francisco de Ayeta bought them" and brought them back to the refugee colony."[61]

Governor Otermín also noted that the same families who were comparatively well-off were reluctant to join the entrada. While most were refusing to present themselves "on pretext of being ill," "others have said that they are extremely poor and destitute, they being the ones who have property and a comfortable living, and all alike are aiming not to leave their comforts and interests, thus impeding the royal service with their bad example and teaching, they being persons of popularity and influence."[62]

When, in early November, he finally held muster, he did so three days' march from El Paso. He had not done it before as "up to the present time not only the citizens who left the said provinces [of New Mexico] in former times, but many of those who came out with them, have remained absent, with the exception of some six persons . . . [and] it is true that the forces which I have at present are not adequate" for a reconquest. This was because he had "many undisciplined soldiers, boys without experience, due to the absence of the soldiers who have not desired to appear and of others who have stayed away maliciously."[63] He had earlier said that "in order to keep all of them in this plaza de armas and its environs . . . I have overlooked many things with reference to the aforesaid persons." Despite being ready to begin the entrada, Otermín decided to briefly delay it "in order to avert a disturbance—they being men who have a following of sons, sons-in-law, and relatives—that this be suspended and that they be heard, I acting with all possible deliberation and tolerance."[64]

Indiscipline and division characterized the entrada once it was finally under way. In December 1681, as they approached Isleta, Otermín ordered that looters would be executed and that any property of the Hispanics they recovered should be brought to him. Subsequently, those under Domínguez's command ignored the order with "audacious impudence and effrontery," and overall it was "an offense so general that at present there is no remedy for it."[65] In addition, Otermín was "displeased," to say the least, by Domínguez's diplomatic way of dealing with the Indians. Instead, he wanted to pursue a much more punitive approach, but, as Father Ayeta noted, when he presented this to the other soldiers he "found some of them so rebellious and others so inclined to object that he believes it impossible." Following the entrada, in March 1682, several Hispanics defied Otermín's prohibition on leaving the refugee colony, and journeyed to Mexico City to lodge complaints against him.[66] Overall, when also considered against the backdrop of the long-standing schisms among the Hispanics, these divisions were illustrative of the "epidemic of hatred in these parts against any person who governs and commands."[67]

The Methods of Pueblo Warfare

The rebels of New Mexico earned the grudging respect of at least some of their adversaries. Just after the rebellion, the cabildo of Santa Fe wrote that "many of them are intelligent, are skillful on horseback, and able to manage firearms as well as any Spaniard; and they have a knowledge of all the territory of the kingdom."[68] Indeed, despite their abhorrence of the Hispanics and most of their culture, the rebels showed no reluctance in using Hispanic weapons, body armor, and horses to gain the upper hand in the rebellion. They knew from experience how effective horses were in giving one's force an advantage, and many of their plots had an almost formulaic quality that involved capturing or giving chase to the horses to make the Hispanics more vulnerable to attack.[69] Much of their success had to do with the meticulous planning that went into the rebellion and, to a lesser degree, their use of psychological warfare to demoralize the Hispanics and to encourage cohesion among the Indians.

As the rebel siege of Santa Fe began, Otermín was initially under the impression, as a result of what Indians had told him from the battle lines, that all of the Hispanics in the region, including Río Abajo, had been killed in the uprising.[70] This tactic was also employed against Sergeant Major Sebastian de Herrera as he led an expedition to the north. When the Indian governor of Taos came to try to kill him, Herrera was told, "Now we have killed the governor and Xavier [Otermín's secretary of war], and all the rest; now there are no more Spaniards, and we shall kill you."[71] In the south, the rebels played the same trick, spreading rumors that reached Lieutenant General Alonso García that all of the Hispanics in Río Arriba had been killed. As the group he led departed from Zía, they believed that the governor and capitan general were dead.[72]

In Santa Fe, as Otermín interrogated the forty-seven captives he took just before abandoning the capital, he learned that not only were some Apache groups allied with the rebels but that those in Río Abajo had in fact not been killed but had taken refuge in Isleta.[73] As they made their way south, Otermín learned from another Indian captured on the way that García's group had left Isleta and were continuing their march south.[74]

False information was also used to inspire other natives to rebel. In Jemez, around noon on August 10, 1680, an Indian arrived "highly elated and saying, 'Now we have killed the Spanish governor and a great many other Spaniards, and all of them are already destroyed, even to the friars, children and women. We have killed them all from Los Taos to the pueblo of Santo Domingo; and there lacks [only] Río Abajo where the enemies of the Spaniards are now attacking. Not one will be left alive . . . therefore take up arms and kill these Spaniards and friars who are here.' And this, in fact, the said Jemez Indians did." They then attacked the soldiers and priests there, pursuing them for six miles before they linked up with García.[75] García later remarked that the rebels there had promised that "not one of them will escape" from Jemez.[76]

In addition to using disinformation to demoralize the Hispanics and to inspire ambivalent Indians to rebel, the rebels used it in an effort to maintain cohesion after expelling the Hispanics. During Otermín's entrada of 1681, Luís Granillo reported to Otermín that the Tanos had gone to Galisteo and told the inhabitants there that the Hispanics were coming to kill them all.[77] In November 1692, as Vargas approached Acoma, the inhabitants were reluctant to negotiate because the Navajos, Apaches, and Mansos had led them to believe that the Hispanics would slaughter them after a feigned pardon. The Indians of San Bernardo de Aguatuvi had been told the same thing by the Apaches.[78] Even Hispanic allies contributed to the rumor mill. In the 1692 entrada, an interpreter, Pedro de Tapia, told the Tewas and Tanos that Vargas was going to have all of the rebel leaders "beheaded" after they finished rebuilding the missions. In December 1696, a Piro Indian in Cochiti told the governor of Tesuque that Vargas "was to go with all the Spaniards to Pecos and the rest of the pueblos in the kingdom and kill all the men, leaving only the boys. This was why the Spaniards had come. The Piros and Tiwas were in El Paso to help the Spaniards carry this out." After the 1696 rebellion, an Indian prisoner, Juan Domingo from Cuyamungue, said he had participated because he and others in his town had heard from Tewa and Tano Indians that "the Spaniards were about to slit everybody's throat and take away their women and children."[79]

Leadership, Discord, and the Andean Insurgency

The numerous prophecies concerning the return of native rule to Peru and Upper Peru both reflected and promoted the eschatological hopes of the Indians while facilitating their perception of prominent rebel leaders as protected and aided by divine powers. As channels of divine will, such leaders were the fulcrum upon which the pachacuti would occur, initiating a new time cycle of harmony and native rule.[80] Túpac Amaru not only derived legitimacy from his Incaic lineage but also claimed to benefit from "God's grace." In Quechua, the word *Amaru*, and in Aymara, the word *Catari*, both mean "serpent." This has symbolic meaning, for the Incas often associated heroes with serpents. In Túpac Amaru's case, these characteristics reinforced the idea that the legend that Túpac Amaru I would return as Inkarrí was finally being realized.[81] Szeminski asserts that Túpac Amaru was viewed as indomitable by the Indians, and due to his Incaic origins he possessed a "divine character as the son of the sun [yet also] acquired a new trait, he was the one who would return order to the world" as Inkarrí. The fact that many viewed him as a demigod is suggested by the fact that many of his followers kneeled when in his presence.[82]

The leadership of Túpac Amaru and Túpac Catari had elements of what Eric Hobsbawm refers to as a "pure" millennial leader, who believes that the revolution will "make itself" as a result of divine intervention or the unprompted action of participants. During the short and lackluster siege of Cuzco, the Inca rebel appears to have placed little emphasis on strategic or tactical planning. He was scolded by his wife and fellow rebel leader, Micaela Bastidas, for not moving more aggressively against the city, especially given that he had 40,000 troops and it was immensely more advantageous to attack before the arrival of the reinforcements that they knew were coming from Lima. Leon Campbell also describes Túpac Amaru as a "pure" leader, asserting that he "believed that he 'owned' the Cuzco provinces and expected them to fall naturally under his sway . . . [and he wanted] to be welcomed there as a Liberator rather than a military conqueror."[83]

Despite their many differences in origins and objectives, Túpac Catari acted in a similar manner, and like the Inca rebel Tomás Catari, all had traveled extensively in their respective regions and extensively utilized kin in organizing and prosecuting the rebellion.[84] Although Túpac Catari had a comparable number of rebels as Túpac Amaru under his command for close to six months, he never ordered a direct and decisive assault on the city; instead, the conflict was characterized by large-scale skirmishes.[85] As a result of many defections of Indians from the city, he was aware of the starvation and weakness of the population there, which in the end led to the death of about 10,000 people, or a third of its population.[86] As a result, he appears to have believed, with somewhat more reason than Túpac Amaru, that it would fall on its own due to the protracted nature of the siege. "Pure" millennial leadership is also found in Juan Santos Atahualpa, who led a resistance movement against Spanish rule between 1742 and 1761. He shied away from direct attacks on centers of Hispanic population, believing that the masses would rise up spontaneously and, with divine assistance, would end Spanish rule in the region.[87] It is possible that the strong eschatological beliefs in the Andean region led leaders to rely more on supernatural assistance than on military planning.

Tomás Catari also demonstrated charismatic leadership, and popular beliefs of his invincibility may have emerged from, and been reinforced by, his re-peated escapes from captivity.[88] In addition, like Túpac Amaru, his peaceful efforts to obtain redress through the colonial legal system may have led many to esteem him as a champion of his people.[89] When he was finally appointed by Spanish officials as curaca, he was received in Macha as a "messiah," and the natives addressed him "sometimes [as] your highness and others [as] your ex-cellency."[90] One contemporary who saw him during this time in Macha said that the natives "look upon him with distinction."[91] The rebel Nicolás Catari, in his confession, recognized that the Indians "venerated [Tomás Catari] as a superior, but he would not admit those respects."[92] Distance may have led to exaggeration, as a recruiter/conscripter for Tomás, named Tomás Coca, was said to have "publicly" claimed that the messiah of Macha would "sit on a seat with a red cape calling himself king."[93]

Royal officials also asserted that Tomás Catari had proclaimed himself king "and other divine names" and that the rebels saw him as "the oracle to whom [they] consult their doubts and questions" while looking upon "him as the Re-deemer of his people."[94] We may never know if Catari actually called himself king or claimed divine protection, but it is clear that his supporters viewed him in a like manner. His cousin Dámaso Catari may also have seen himself as hav-ing the support of the heavens, as when in his showdown with Joaquín Alós on August 26, 1780, he reputedly defied the corregidor to "Kill me now so that I may go to the Sun and give my orders."[95] Simón Castillo appears to have had charismatic qualities. One contemporary observed that "the Indians venerate him [and] there is nothing that he says which is not the Gospel," while another asserted that he assured his adepts that he would "remedy everything and put it in order as absolute master of these places."[96] Similarly, in Lipes and Chichas provinces, the followers of Pedro de la Cruz Condori had "so much veneration for him that they kneel and prostrate themselves on the ground when they see him."[97]

Many rebels believed their leaders to be immortal, and such conviction helped to mitigate the effect that a leader's death had on his followers' morale. When, after Tomás Catari's death, Corregidor Bodega went to Challapata to collect tribute, he noted that many natives there refused to believe that Catari had in fact perished. Dámaso even went to Quilaquila to see whether or not he had been resurrected, as many believed.[98] Visitador General José Antonio de Areche recognized that many natives "believed the rebel [Túpac Amaru] to be immortal" and that among the reasons he was beheaded was to disabuse witnesses and others of such hopes.[99] As we have seen above, many rebels be-lieved that they would benefit from resurrection in the event they died in the rebellion.[100]

Of all the leaders in the Great Rebellion, it was Túpac Amaru who most instilled a sense of imminence in the creation of the new order. Many rebels in Oruro, Cochabamba, and other regions believed "as articles of faith" that he had conquered Lima.[101] Other insurgents were of the opinion that he had already been crowned in Cuzco, although many rebels thought he was making a triumphant journey south from La Paz to ensure a rebel victory in the region of Upper Peru.[102] Even as early as January 15, 1781, the rebels of Challapata planned to deliver the head of Corregidor Bodega "to their Inca King who they know has already entered La Paz."[103] Bernardo Franco, a Creole who was held as a prisoner and scribe of the rebels in Chayanta, stated that the insurgents were anticipating that their "King Don Josef Gabriel Tupacamaru Ynga" would arrive in the area shortly.[104] In Chocaya, the rebels thought that Túpac Amaru was "about to enter" the village.[105]

In February 1781, as the Creoles desperately sought to get the Indians to leave Oruro, they met some success after they told the rebels that Túpac Amaru had been crowned king, was on his way from La Paz, and would arrive in the Oruro region in eight days.[106] Numerous rebels not only had portraits of the Inca but also then left hoping to meet him on his supposed journey southward.[107] The sense of the imminent creation of a new society was brought to new heights when the Creole rebel Jacinto Rodríguez told the rebels that Potosí, La Plata, and La Paz had already fallen to the rebels.[108] The sense of imminence not only served as an inspiration for insurgents but also caused some to join the rebellion. The rebel Pedro Choque stated in his confession that he became a rebel "because they were expecting the curaca Túpac Amaro whom they had as their king," and the Indian Ventura Pinto asserted that he had joined the rebellion because he understood that Carlos III had died and that the Inca was now king.[109]

When Oruro was under siege, rebels there as well as in the vicinity of Colcha and San Pedro de Buenavista stated that they had joined the insurgency because they believed that Túpac Amaru had "expressly commanded them to do so," and that after their expected victory they planned to kill all of the inhabitants and send their heads to the Inca, "whom [they] were expecting [and] had as their king."[110] The rebels in Tupiza also wanted to send the head of Corregidor Francisco García de Prado to Túpac Amaru.[111] Dámaso Catari confessed that although he did not know the whereabouts of Túpac Amaru, he understood that the Inca was on his way to Oruro with 8,000 Creoles and 6,000 Indians.[112] It is interesting that he understood the Inca's forces to be predominantly Creole. For his part, Nicolás Catari stated that the Inca was "very far advanced in his conquests and was making haste toward Oruro."[113] Such was the Inca's popularity in Upper Peru that one contemporary wrote that if "Túpac Amaro flees from Cuzco . . . he could in our viceroyalty accomplish . . . what he appears not to have accomplished in that of Lima."[114] Some rebels sought to honor Túpac Amaru and the Cataris of Chayanta, and add to their popular appeal, by adopting their names. In Ubina, Chocaya, Portugalete, Santa Catalina, and Tatasi, three rebel brothers operating there called themselves Túpac Amaru and Dámaso and Nicolás Catari, and José Reseguín at first believed that the two putative Cataris were the half-brothers from Chayanta.[115]

Despite, or perhaps because of, Túpac Amaru's appeal in the region, there was friction between the Amaristas and Túpac Cataristas during the siege of La Paz. Túpac Catari said that he planned to kill Andrés Túpac Amaru and eliminate Quechua influences in the region upon the anticipated victory of his forces.[116] Although there may have been some resentment of pre-Hispanic Inca domination in Upper Peru, this does not seem to have been a factor among the rank and file of rebels in Upper Peru. Instead, Quechua- and Aymara-speaking Indians were united by the shared goal of eliminating Hispanic rule, blood, and influences in the region, and also perhaps by the fusing by many Indians of the ideas of "Indian" and "Inca" beginning in the 1650s.[117]

The most mercurial of the major rebel leaders, Túpac Catari, was also one of the most charismatic. He sought to hold a monopoly on divine power, whether it was through controlling a weakened Christian god, through relations with native deities, or through controlling the elements. The idea that the Catholic god was weakened, but still had some power, partially helps to explain the ambivalent attitude that Túpac Catari had concerning Christianity. No doubt this attitude was also shaped to some degree by his upbringing by the sacristan of Ayoayo and his exposure there to Catholic rites. The Aymara rebel held priests captive in order to hold mass daily, and many of his adepts believed that he had a halo around his head when he first called upon the natives to rebel. By having priests as his captive servants he also held captive the power that remained of the Catholic god. He was willing to demonstrate his power over them, and by extension their god, as shown by his ordering the execution of a priest when he repudiated Catari's order to absolve him after confession.[118]

In his camp in El Alto, Catari had a primitive chapel furnished with looted religious objects and an organ. During mass, however, he ordered his followers not to remove their hats as well as "orders equally scandalous." Mass was also a vehicle for Catari to demonstrate his own putatively divine powers. During the ceremony he was known to look into a mirror for divine guidance while making expressions that "appeared laughable." On other occasions, he would hold to his ear or look into a silver box which he always had with him, as he asserted that "God himself spoke into his ear," and as a result of the revelations that he received he "was not capable of error in the prosecution of the war." He also derived divine guidance from the Virgin Mary. One contemporary, Esteban Losa, observed that when Catari entered churches, "he was regularly received with great pomp under a canopy [and he] persuaded his followers that an Image of Our Lady spoke . . . [and] whose consultation resulted in the death or pardon of prisoners." Reflecting his stature and power, after services a trumpet would sound and the congregation would kneel and kiss his hand.[119]

At times Catari was blunt in his claims of divine protection, once stating that he was "sent by God and no one has the power to do anything" against him, and insisting that "everything I say is the word of the Holy Spirit."[120] He also claimed, "I already have the favor of God" and "God will help us."[121] He further asserted that "it is from above that we must finish all, it is the will of God in all and for all, because as they say the bad fruit one must cut from the roots and that way we will finish all."[122] In addition to his assertion of protection by the Christian god, he also claimed that he exercised control over natural events. As Esteban Losa noted, "To prove it he would take out his saber and attack the whirlwinds which regularly form in the Puna, and would make the Indians see that he made them go away with ease stabbing them without being hurt."[123] This action may also have had symbolic significance, as many Indians viewed the dust devils as a link with the underworld from which the whites were said to have come, and thus by destroying it Catari also impeded the Christian god from assisting the Hispanics.[124]

Catari sought to maintain a monopoly on his reputed powers over nature. He learned that in Sicasica province an Indian by the name of Guarachi had claimed that he had the power to make the "sun come down in the sky" and had commanded that the Aymara leader come to meet him. Catari appeared to obey the order, although he arrived with a retinue of bodyguards. When he and his escort met Guarachi, who "shouted like a child" and exercised his putative powers from behind a drape, they quickly shot and stabbed him to death.[125] In addition to claiming to control the elements and have the support of the Catholic god, Catari claimed to be in contact with and assisted by native ancestors. Losa wrote that he "would go to the ancient sepulchers of the Pagans, whose ruins exist in all of Peru, and in a loud voice say, 'It is now time for you to come back to the world and help me.'"[126]

Catari's followers apparently believed that he did indeed possess divine powers, protection, and guidance. Sebastián de Segurola observed that "the Indians have a blind and loyal obedience" to him, while Losa said that he had "a particular ability to subjugate his followers."[127] The captive cleric Matías de la Borda also noted how Catari's adepts "practiced blindly his orders . . . and attended to him as if he was in fact a God."[128] Father Borda also wrote that "his commissioners exceeded in fulfilling his orders."[129] This underscores the point that while Túpac Catari's radicalism more closely reflected the popular Indian will than did Tomás Catari or Túpac Amaru, even he was sometimes more conservative than his supporters. Rebel treatment of ecclesiastics is one example of this. Although generally Catari utilized clerics as his religious servants, other rebels in the area were more inclined to kill them. For example, the clerics Félix Gisbert in Songo, Matías de Aresenaga in Chucuito, and Sebastián Limanchi in Guaqui were all killed by the insurgents, and when the cleric Juan de la Buena Muerte went beyond the frontlines, he was caught by the rebels and "killed on the spot."[130] On April 12, 1781, the captive Franciscan Antonio Barriga was also killed by Catari's supporters, without the leader's approbation, because they believed that Barriga had cast a curse on them during a mass, subsequent to which they were defeated in a battle.[131] While they believed the Catholic god was weakened, they also believed that he still could muster some power.

Divided We Fall: Rebel Divisions during the Great Rebellion

One striking fact of the rebellion was the degree of internal divisions within each of the opposing forces. This highlights the role of antinomy, or an apparent contradiction of equally valid principles or conclusions, in the rebellion, which was in the end a highly fragmented and heterodox enterprise. Clearly, great numbers of rebels sought the realization of their eschatological dreams in the rebellion. Many natives, however, were reluctant rebels or lackluster loyalists, as widespread conscription on both sides of the conflict imbued it with an element of a native civil war.

Like the Pueblo Indians, the rebels found that disinformation could be used to their advantage. One effective method to build the rebel ranks was to present the rebellion to Indians as an act of loyalism through asserting that the Indians were simply implementing the orders of Carlos III concerning ridding the region of abusive officials and priests. After his return from Buenos Aires, Tomás Catari utilized such an approach when he claimed that a royal decree had confirmed him as curaca of Macha and ordered a reduction of tribute. Many Indians held the view that Catari had in fact gone to Spain and met with the king, although it is not clear if Catari himself actually made such claims.[132] Again, such inferences by large groups of Indians and their subsequent effect are more important than whether or not Catari made such statements. In addition, rebels in the region of Chayanta often took such claims one step further by asserting that not only had Catari journeyed to Spain but that he had persuaded Carlos III to authorize him to abolish the repartos and mita and to name curacas of his choosing. In such a view, those who resisted such demands were considered "rebels" and executed.[133] One thing, however, is clear: Tomás knew that he had not gone to Spain, nor had he met with Carlos III. This is evident from a letter he wrote to the king in November 1780, in which he asked for pardon for himself and the rebels, begged for an end to the hated reparto, and insisted that the members of the La Plata audiencia and "other Spaniard and mestizo" governors were the real traitors to the crown.[134] Dámaso Catari, in his confession, also acknowledged that he was aware no royal order had been issued concerning tribute reduction.[135]

The effort to mask rebellion as loyalism is found in Peru as well, where Túpac Amaru initially asserted that his actions were the implementation of royal orders. Andrés and Diego Túpac Amaru also made claims, to Indians as well as to royal officials, that they had been ordered by Carlos III to end the mita, reparto, and numerous taxes and to kill corregidors and Spaniards. At the outset of the rebellion, Túpac Amaru and Andrés Túpac Amaru also would issue edicts in the name of the Spanish king.[136] In the region of La Paz, Túpac Catari asserted that he had received the putative royal order abolishing all repartos and taxes that he said had been granted to Tomás Catari.[137] Cloaking rebellion as loyalism suggested that many individuals would join the insurrection only if they felt that doing so was an act of loyalty. For those uninspired to join either voluntarily or through feint, the rebel leadership was quick to resort to conscription.

In Chayanta, Tomás Coca, a recruiter for Tomás Catari, extensively utilized forced induction to enlist those who could fight but had not volunteered to do so.[138] In the vicinity of Pintatora and Ocuri, the rebel recruiter Cárlos Pacaja confessed that he had used the threat of death to recruit over 1,000 natives to fight under Nicolás Catari.[139] Both Dámaso Catari and his supporter Antonio Cruz conscripted Indians and mestizos to assist in the siege of La Plata.[140] In Colcha, adherents of Tomás Catari threatened to kill and burn the homes of all who did not join them. It was not an idle threat, as one Hispanic contemporary there wrote that the rebels were "killing and sacking the . . . Indians who did not join them."[141]

In the vicinity of Yura, Potolo, Moromoro, Macha, and elsewhere in Upper Peru, natives who refused to participate in the rebellion were killed by the rebels.[142] In his conscription efforts in Yura, the rebel Ramón Paca relied on a purported edict from Túpac Amaru which demanded that "those that don't rebel . . . be finished off," and in Tomabe, Dámaso Catari demanded that all those able to fight come to Macha or be killed.[143] Similarly, Simón Castillo ordered the execution of anyone in San Pedro de Buenavista who did not join the rebellion, and in Chocaya, the rebel Pedro de la Cruz Condori threatened that Indians who did not join him "would experience rigorous punishment."[144] He also claimed to be the "true ambassador of his Majesty" Túpac Amaru, and promised that anyone who failed to recognize him as such would suffer the "corresponding penalty."[145] Also in Chocaya, the insurgent Agustín Vicanio asserted that the rebels said they would execute "all those who excuse themselves from the rebellion [which was] in the service of their King Tupamaru," while another asserted that she had carried a sling only because it was "by . . .

order . . . that everyone carry them."[146] Other natives in Chichas, such as Lope Fernández and Ubaldo Dávila, likewise claimed that they had only joined the rebellion out of fear of being killed by the very forces they were joining.[147] During their invasion of Tinquipaya, the rebels of Challapata told the Indians there that they must join the rebellion, as "if not they will be lost."[148] Other rebels also claimed that they had been conscripted in the assaults on Arque and San Pedro de Buenavista.[149]

Like many other leaders, Túpac Catari also used press ganging to augment his forces. In Sicasica, he "ordered with capital punishment [that the residents] leave to the . . . city of La Paz to destroy it and devour all of its residents."[150] In another decree directed to the residents of Sicasica, he commanded "plebian Indians and Creoles" between the ages of 14 and 70 to come to El Alto or be killed.[151] One confessant claimed that Túpac Catari routinely used "rigor and threats" to build his forces.[152] Overall, many of the rebels under Túpac Catari were, in the words of a cleric held captive by the rebel, "truly . . . exasperated with full knowledge of the cactus patch in which he had stuck them."[153]

In Chayanta, a putative order of Túpac Amaru ensured that to "those who were rebels [against the Inca] he would show his rigor and those who were humble he would reward."[154] Whether or not it was issued by the Inca is unclear, although his decrees in his own theater of operations had a similar tone and often utilized the same phrases.[155] Both Andrés and Diego Túpac Amaru were blunt concerning conscription. In edicts in Pacajes, Sicasica, and other provinces, Andrés decreed that all "Indians from seven years old and up [be] put . . . in a body of militia."[156] Diego commanded that his subordinates "punish and behead" anyone who showed "the least resistance or repugnance" to his orders.[157] Although it is not revealed in the documents studied here, it may be that apostasy was less prevalent among the conscripts. Even once conscripted, insufficient enthusiasm for the conflict could bring punishment. In the village of Aymaia, near San Pedro de Buenavista, a native who only observed while other insurgents clubbed the priest Dionicio Córtes to death was himself beaten by one rebel who demanded to know "why don't you help?"[158] In the village of Guanachaca, the rebel Manuel Espinoza was also struck because he had failed to kill any Hispanics.[159]

It would not be surprising if most Indians captured during and after the rebellion asserted that they were conscripted. What is surprising is that in many of the confessions studied here, they did not.[160] The viceroy of Peru, Augustín de Jáuregui, recognized that many of those led by Túpac Amaru had been forced to join the rebellion.[161] In the region of La Paz, Commander Reseguín also acknowledged that many natives obeyed Túpac Catari because they were quite "fearful of the fury of his inhumanity."[162]

The threat of force was also utilized to ensure that Indians in rebel-controlled zones adhered to the demands of the new order. In Chayanta, the Cataristas Tiburcio Rios, José Roque, and Domingo Lope threatened to execute any person who paid either tribute or ecclesiastical dues.[163] A decree in Chichas, written in Túpac Amaru's name, threatened that anyone who opposed him would "experience their ruin, converting my gentleness into fury [and] reducing this province into ashes."[164] When he commissioned his lieutenants, Túpac Catari authorized them to "behead and hang," or condemn "to gallows and knife," anyone who did not comply with rebel orders.[165] Overall, threats of this nature appear to have been common throughout the rebellion.

As in New Mexico, the rebel forces also appear to have been divided along lines of status and age. After Corregidor Alós was released from captivity by the Indians upon Tomás Catari's liberation and confirmation as curaca, the corregidor remarked that the eldest and highest-ranking Indians present during his captivity sought to protect him. The elders advocated for Alós's release, insisting that he was not to blame for Catari's imprisonment.[166] Overall, those Indians who held the higher positions in the indigenous hierarchy tended to be more conservative than younger natives with less status.[167]

Conflicts among Indians were endemic to the insurrection. Some of this revolved around what to do with curacas, such as when in September 1780 the rebels in Macha argued over whether to kill Florencio Lupa, the curaca of Moscari, or to let Father Merlos take custody of him. Lupa became involved in an almost literal tug-of-war, and after Merlos gained custody of him twice, the rebels seized him again and killed him on a hilltop.[168] Merlos's efforts, often with Tomás Cataris's support, to have captives spared appear to have caused considerable friction with and among the rebels.[169]

Internal divisions among the insurgents only increased as the rebellion spread. Of the nineteen rebels who died during their occupation of Oruro, most were killed by other insurgents due to "robberies and resentments." After the rebels had been ousted from Oruro, one observer in Paria wrote that such were the divisions that they were about to "finish off one another due to the differences that have been caused by the distribution of lands and ranches ceded by those of Oruro."[170] One contemporary observed that the insurgency was also a means for many natives to settle old scores, while another said that those of Chayanta often fought "like dogs and cats" among themselves.[171]

Royalist offers of pardon, and the increasing success of the Hispanic campaign, exacerbated schisms among the rebels and helped to doom their cause. The pardon in Upper Peru had been announced very early in the uprising by the audiencia of La Plata, on September 28, 1780, and continued in force throughout the rebellion. It called for the natives to hand over ringleaders, who were not included in the pardon, to swear obedience to the Spanish king, and to go back to their homes and previous occupations.[172] The lure of getting a reward rather than the noose led many insurgents to betray most of their leaders, such as Túpac Amaru, Dámaso and Nicolás Catari, Túpac Catari, Santos Mamani, and Simón Castillo.[173] The fact that many rebels had been reluctantly swept up in the conflict due to conscription or deceit also increased the effect of the pardon in precipitating desertions, further helping the Spanish cause.[174]

Even before the pardon in Upper Peru was officially issued on September 27, 1780, more than 300 Indians approached the priest of San Pedro de Buenavista asking for forgiveness for their role in looting the town and for having demanded that the cleric hand over the mestizos and curacas gathered in the church.[175] During the siege of Oruro, after the Hispanics had inflicted heavy losses on the rebels, many asked Jacinto Rodríguez for pardon.[176] Others from Sorasora asked Rodríguez for amnesty, as they "were afraid of dying at the hands of the Challapata" Indians.[177] As the royalists reasserted their control in the region of Cochabamba, numerous Indians were "on bended knees asking pardon for their excesses."[178] Interestingly, it was loyalists from Cochabamba who noted that other rebels ate at the foot of the gallows and showed no fear of death. Clearly, many preferred the assurance of pardon to the hope of resurrection.[179] As Hispanic-led forces twice made their way to La Paz from Oruro to break the siege of the city, they found many rebels seeking pardon, especially during the second push toward the besieged city. The effort to secure a pardon had clear risks, however, as hard-core rebels were likely to try to kill those who sought it.[180]

In addition to divisions as a result of age, status, deception, or conscription, there were also strong ideological schisms among the rebels. Throughout the area of the rebellion, many rebels who voluntarily joined the rebellion sought to eliminate the Hispanic presence in the region and be ruled by their Inca king, finally free of the onerous burdens of repartimientos, tribute, taxes, ecclesiastical dues, and the mita. Many insurgents also anticipated gaining the lands and many of the possessions of their enemies, as well as the resurgence of native worship, perhaps with some Catholic influences. The actions of the insurgents were consistently focused on these aims, as they executed Hispanics, took Hispanic lands, refused to pay taxes and dues, violated the sanctuary of and desecrated churches, and ignored the appeals of clerics. But these actions and goals were quite different from the objectives of Tomás Catari and Túpac Amaru.

As the rebellion spread, it quickly escaped the grasp of these leaders, who increasingly became nominal in the entire process.[181] Before his assassination, it appears that Tomás Catari was trying to avoid escalating the conflict. Of the curacas brought to Macha for judgment, to the consternation of his followers, he generally sided with Father Merlos in having them spared. Certainly, he did order some curacas deposed and often had them brought to him, though he seems not to have wanted blood on his hands.[182] Furthermore, while Tomás did order a reduction of tribute levels by about a third, which was the amount he believed was being pocketed by corrupt officials, he is not recorded as ever telling his supporters to stop paying all tribute. In addition, he made known to royal authorities that he was willing to see that alcabalas were paid and that the mita was served, although he did call for the abolition of reparto. There is no indication that he promised his supporters lands or an end to Catholicism. Tomás was a reformist at heart, and he sought neither independence nor the extermination of non-Indians. It was his followers who projected upon him the revolutionary and exterminatory goals of the insurgency.[183]

Like Tomás Catari, Túpac Amaru was also separated from his followers by an ideological gulf. He endeavored to create a multiethnic coalition of Creoles, mestizos, Negroes, and Indians against the Spaniards. To generate Creole support, he promised that those who supported him would retain their lands in the new order, and he also sought to minimize looting of Creole interests. His efforts in this regard not only were inefficacious but alienated many of his Indian supporters. While he did call for the abolition of the hated repartos and corregidors, he planned to retain tribute, ecclesiastical dues, and the quinto real, or royal fifth of mineral extraction, upon his anticipated victory. This highlights the enduring nature of his Catholic faith, which, to at least some degree, came about from his Jesuit education in Cuzco. During the rebellion, he frequently attended mass and met with priests while on campaign. When his followers requested that he expel clerics from the areas under rebel control, he reportedly asked, "Who would absolve us in the matter of death?" And when he was imprisoned in Cuzco before his execution, he called out for help from the Virgin Mary as he was tortured. His conservativism is also shown by the fact that his inner circle was devoid of Indians and was formed by relatives, mestizos, and Creoles.[184]

Flores Galindo recognizes the gap between leaders and followers among the Amaristas when he notes, "The masses [wanted] the rebirth of the traditional Andean culture . . . without more Western influences, in difference to the leaders . . . [who] tried to project themselves into the future, trying to visualize a society without Spanish."[185] His observation can also be applied to Upper Peru. As the first group of leaders was captured and leadership fell to individuals such as Dámaso and Nicolás Catari, Miguel Bastidas, and Andrés and Diego Túpac Amaru, the gap between leaders and followers was reduced.

Unlike Túpac Amaru and Tomás Catari, Túpac Catari's ideology was much more closely aligned with his supporters. His exterminatory brand of millennial nativism appealed to many Indians and perhaps helps to explain his rise to power despite his humble background. One area where there does seem to be some gap concerned his relation with Catholicism. Seeking a monopoly on all divine power, he generally preferred to imprison priests, although he did have one executed. His followers, on the other hand, executed several clerics and often refused the last rites upon their own execution. Generally, such was the radicalism of his followers that they often "exceeded in fulfilling his orders."[186]

Discipline, Desertion, and the Hispanic Coalition in the Great Rebellion

Like the insurgents, the Hispanic forces were riddled by internal divisions. We have already noted the role of the Bourbon reforms in sowing discord among the ruling elite and in igniting brief Creole-mestizo uprisings in La Paz, Cochabamba, La Plata, Cuzco, and Arequipa in the years preceding the Great Rebellion.[187] During the insurgency, the officers of Hispanic military forces were plagued by insubordination and lack of discipline. In their eagerness to loot, in one case they "abandoned their weapons to run more lightly."[188] When enduring the siege of La Paz, Sebastián de Segurola, the Spanish commander, lamented on more than one occasion the defenders' fixation on looting and their "common lack of obedience," which led them to flee the scene of battle "with their accustomed disorder [and] abandoning everything." On another occasion he plaintively remarked that his troops fled "with an imponderable precipitation and disorder." The absence of discipline was patently apparent when, on one occasion as the rebels approached an entrance to the city, the troops panicked and ran "without knowing where they were going."[189]

Although Ignacio Flores succeeded in briefly breaking the siege of La Paz in June 1781, he was left with few alternatives other than retreating to Oruro a month later to gather "more respectable" soldiers than the hundreds who had deserted, eager to return to Cochabamba to sell their looted coca leaves.[190] After Colonel Reseguín had led his troops, many from Tucuman, to definitively break the siege of La Paz, great numbers deserted to Oruro where they looted property, murdered seven mestizos, and used "force with the women." They were in fact so unruly that one observer there was concerned that they might defect to the Indian side.[191] Such was the desertion that Reseguín had to contend with that when he arrived in La Paz on October 17, 1781, he led 4,400 soldiers, but by December 4 this number had dwindled to under 400.[192]

To the south, the widows of curacas in Tapacari protested that the soldiers in the relief expeditions sent from Cochabamba had taken their silver, clothing, sheep, and cattle, and similar complaints were lodged by people from Carasi.[193] Looting could also be a matter of pride, as one Cochabambino military leader proudly proclaimed that his expedition had cost the treasury nothing, given that its costs were "entirely satisfied from the spoils" of war.[194] Lack of discipline and desertion were not the only indicators of Hispanic divisions. As the tide of insurgency engulfed the region, in Cochabamba on February 24, 1781, Ambrosio Pando de Figueróa, the administrator of tobaccos, found it necessary to abolish a recent tobacco price increase in an effort to put a stop to increasing sedition in the town.[195] Despite the obvious and imminent threat posed by the insurgency, in Cochabamba and Oruro, treasury agents were often hesitant to provide funds to aid in their defense.[196] In Oruro and Tupiza, competition for political power, distrust, and mutual resentments led to barracks uprisings directed against ruling groups.[197]

The suppression of the revolt relied heavily on loyal curacas who managed to retain the allegiance of the communities they led. Most of the defenders of Cuzco were Indians commanded by loyalist curacas, and as the rebels besieged La Plata, curacas from Yamparáez and Porco provinces brought Indian loyalists to help defend the town.[198] In April 1781, in the vicinity of Tapacari, a group of eighty loyalist Indians were defeated by the rebels. Indians from the villages of Apillapampa, Yotala, and Tocosalla supported the Hispanic cause by providing information about the rebels.[199] In Yura, the curaca Roque Argote led loyal Indians against the rebels, while the Indian curaca Pascual Calli died fighting the insurgents in Palca.[200] Recognizing his loyalty and bravery, royal officials commended Calli for being "worthy of eternal memory" and declared all of his descendants exempt from tribute.[201] Curacas and their communities were also crucial in defeating the insurgency in the area of Tupiza. The curaca Esteban de Luna of Puna, as well as the curacas of Escoma and Santiago de Cotagaita, fought with and captured many rebels.[202] Overall, in appreciation of their loyalty, many curacas who opposed the rebels were awarded medals with much "pomp and ceremony."[203]

To Siege or to Storm: Indian Warfare in the Andes

The rebels in Peru and Upper Peru were often nominally under the leadership of major rebel leaders such as Túpac Amaru, Tomás, Dámaso, and Nicolás Catari, Túpac Catari, Simón Castillo, Santos Mamani, and others. Rebels, however, operated with a considerable degree of autonomy and were at least initially oriented to achieving local goals, such as eliminating the Hispanic presence in their communities and appropriating many of their goods. Throughout the rebellion, although they employed firearms whenever they could, they also used knives and stones thrown with slings.[204] As in Yucatán, the rebels spared some Hispanics who could serve their cause as scribes and as operators of weapons. In taking a town, the rebels would generally first dominate the surrounding countryside and then mass on the target, an event which usually caused the resident Hispanics and their allies to seek refuge in the village church. Once this had taken place, they usually would lead an assault on the building after demanding the surrender of those inside. As is shown in Colcha, Palca, Ayopaia, San Pedro de Buenavista, and numerous other towns, people did surrender and, with the occasional exception of women, who were enslaved, they were then killed. If they did not surrender, the rebels would force their way into the building and kill those inside. This was the basic modus operandi, played out time and again in Peru and Upper Peru.

Unlike in Yucatán, the rebels conducted sieges with very little success. While that of Sorata was brought to a crescendo with the flooding of the town, generally the sieges were lackluster and relatively easily broken by the Hispanics. This was the case in Cuzco and La Plata, and although the sieges were longer in Oruro and La Paz, they were nevertheless unsuccessful.[205] Overall, the rebels in the Great Rebellion sought to limit their exposure to casualties, and perhaps for this reason they never led an all-out assault on the major cities they had under siege. Unlike in Yucatán, where the rebels were organized into companies with rank, the organization in Peru and Upper Peru seems to have been less formal. As in New Mexico, conscription was used extensively to swell the rebel ranks.

A Discordant Confederation: Rebel Leadership in Yucatán

Despite the advances made by the rebels in 1847–48, and their recovery from numerous and severe defeats to establish their own state, they too were plagued by division from quite early in the rebellion. Overall, as in the Pueblo Revolt and Great Rebellion, the support of Indian village leaders and kin groups was critical in the organization of and mobilization for the rebellion.[206] The objectives of the war, however, were the cause of considerable division among the rebel leadership. Reed sums it up well when he notes that while "Pat wished to replace the Ladino government . . . Ay was for driving the white men from the land, and . . . Chi was simply for killing them, down to the last woman and child." Despite their differences, the genocidal objective initially prevailed, and Reed adds that as the crackdown on the Indians in anticipation of the uprising progressed in August 1847, Chi, Pat, and other rebel leaders conferred at Pat's ranch in Culumpich "to declare a war of total extermination . . . against the white race."[207] Like Túpac Catari, Cecilio Chi was of humble origins and among the most radical of the leaders. Baqueiro asserts that Chi's goal was "the extermination of the white race," an objective shared by Venancio Pec.[208] The Mexican general Severo del Castillo recognized the differing objectives of the rebel leaders and wrote that Chi's "only end was always . . . [the] extermination . . . of the whites."[209] Rugeley notes that among the rebel leadership, some were oriented to "political advantage, improved conditions, and local autonomy, and not at the extermination of the Spanish race. In talking to the masses, however, the leadership used incendiary rhetoric that liberated long-simmering racial animosities."[210] While such calls to action may have included promises of divine protection, charismatic leadership became institutionalized in the cult of the speaking cross, which assured the faithful that they were immune to bullets and that their triumph was inevitable.[211]

Just as there were differences in objectives among the rebel leaders, there were also differences of racial origin. Unlike the Indian Chi, Pat was a "mulatto or mestizo, but not an Indian of pure race."[212] In this sense, he was like many of the other rebel leaders. For example, José María Barrera, the originator of the speaking cross, was described by a contemporary as being "a very ladino mestizo," and Dionicio Zapata and Leandro Santos were also mestizos.[213] Likewise, Bonifacio Novelo, formerly a trader in the Valladolid region, was said to be a mulatto, although he was also described as a "lighter shade of color than the generality of the Indians."[214] Crescencio Poot, however, was "extremely dark, whether or not of African admixture, and unusually tall."[215] Despite the genotypic differences, ethnically all were considered Indians by those whom they led. Again, language, occupation, cultural orientation, dress, actions in the insurgency, and some degree of native blood were crucial factors in determining ethnicity.

Jacinto Pat was one rebel leader who was more interested in personal political gain and Indian betterment than in Hispanic extermination. The fact that he was a wealthy batab also distinguished him from Chi. Baqueiro describes Pat as an "Indian very distinct from the others, because his relations with the best of the commercialists of Tekax, Mérida, and Campeche, [and] . . . the considerable fortune he enjoyed, had softened his instincts."[216] Even General Severo del Castillo, who was no friend of the rebels, asserted that Pat was initially reluctant to join the rebellion. Once implicated, however, he and his supporters were hunted and he became swept up in the course of events.[217] Ancona notes that Pat sought political goals involving domination over the whites but did not seek their extermination. He asserts that when Pat and Chi met after the Hispanics had burned Tepich, Pat "tried to dissuade the rebels from their ideas of extermination and made all the efforts possible that the insurrection would have a political color, which would satisfy more his personal ambitions." But, like Túpac Amaru, he had little control over his supporters, who operated "under their own inspirations and committed worse atrocities than" other leaders. In fact, many Indian groups operated autonomously, and one contemporary noted that in 1848 in the region to the north of Tekax "now there is no stone left upon a stone: ranches, haciendas, sugar plantations and everything that could be gripped by flames, has been condemned to fire by these [Indians who] did not belong to Pat or the other leaders."[218]

Pat's control of troops directly under his command was quite tenuous. When Father José Canuto Vela went to negotiate what became the short-lived Treaty of Tzucacab, he and his commission were received by the rebels in Pat's camp "with murmurs of disapproval." Pat nevertheless received them well, and they drank chocolate, dined, and discussed peace terms throughout the night. They were interrupted several times "with shouts and insults, [and the Indians] tried to revolt toward dawn, and it was necessary that Pat go out and contain them. These demonstrations clearly show how unpopular among the mass of rebels was the idea of celebrating peace."[219] Baqueiro notes that the treaty failed "for the very simple reason of the lack of influence of Jacinto Pat over the disorganized masses who surrounded him."[220] Pat himself saw this, and in a letter in which he discussed the negotiations, he stated that "if we arrive at a definite agreement, it is absolutely necessary that I obey what my troops advise."[221]

Soon after the negotiations at Tzucacab, Pat departed to Tekax, leaving Juan Moo in charge in the town. Very soon after Pat's departure, however, the rebels jailed Moo and then killed him and dragged his body through the village. The Indian who had served as an intermediary during the Tzucacab negotiations, Manuel Ignacio Tuz, was also subsequently killed by José María Barrera and Marcelo Pat, a son of Jacinto.[222] The issue of peace continued to be the source of friction among the rebels. In early 1850, as the Hispanics encouraged peace negotiations led by Father Vela, the rebel answer to one letter was the execution of Isidro Blanco, who had delivered it.[223]

Pat was among the first to pay the price for supporting peace. The negotiation of the Treaty of Tzucacab was the beginning of his downfall, which would end with his execution in September 1849 by the hard-liners Florentino Chan, Venancio Pec, and Crescencio Poot.[224] In January 1850, Atanasio Espadas, who had led the assault on Chi's assassin, took advantage of the amnesty, underscoring the value of pardons in promoting divisions among the rebels.[225] In 1851, the negotiations with Angelino Itza that led to the establishment of the Pacífico communities in the south provoked such outrage among the Cruzob that José María Barrera attacked and burned Chichenja before bringing many prisoners to Chan Santa Cruz. The accord with the Pacíficos was an important step forward for the Hispanics, however, as they reduced the number of rebels by up to a half and the Hispanics could now focus their forces on the Cruzob. Pacífico-Cruzob relations continued to be characterized by ongoing conflict that resulted in the relocation of many Pacíficos to Icaiche and the sustained occupation of Chichenja by the indios bravos after their third attack on it in 1863.[226]

The issue of whether or not to negotiate peace with the Mexican authorities would continue to divide the Cruzob leadership in the 1860s. In December 1863, Venancio Puc, who was reputed to have ordered the execution of over 6,000 prisoners over the years, ordered the execution of all of the captives held in Chan Santa Cruz. This was to be done on December 30, 1863, and would coincide with the departure of a 5,000-man rebel force that was to attack Tekax, Oxkutzcab, and Tinum before storming Mérida. He further ordered that any prisoners taken in the engagements were to be killed. Advocates of a negotiated solution with the Hispanics, the generals Dionisio Zapata and Leandro Santos, balked at the plan. On December 23, 1863, they led a coup, first silencing the cross by capturing its voice, José Nah, and then killing Puc. The success of the coup initially seemed in doubt, as no one would obey the new leaders until they had seen Puc executed. This done, they enhanced their popularity by distributing his wealth and giving the other generals control over the town's alcohol still. Shared control over the still had also been a source of conflict between the military leaders, who derived revenue from it by selling its product to their soldiers at six reales a bottle.

As the new leaders sought to advance the cause of peace, they found that the forces for the extermination of the Hispanics were not only resilient but organized, and several months later both Zapata and Santos were themselves killed in a coup that brought Bonifacio Novelo and Bernabé Cen to power. Seeking to capitalize on the late Puc's popularity, Cen soon journeyed to Tulum in an effort to gather support there by convincing people he was the reincarnation of the deceased leader.[227] Dumond notes, "The achievement of power by the cult of the cross was apparently . . . at the expense of the original politico-military leadership, which had earlier included Venancio Puc, Florentino Chan, and Calixto Yam, and in which commanders of long standing such as Bonifacio Novelo and Crescencio Poot should clearly have been in line to succeed. . . . Thus the traditional leadership must have been sidetracked through the activities of Venancio Puc and the prestige he gained for the cross." Now with Novelo and Poot ascendant, the "old military guard" was back in control.[228]

The sermons of the speaking cross offer a window on the religious-military divisions. In 1850 Juan de la Cruz complained to the generals that before one engagement "it would have been good to give you my blessing so that they rise up to fight . . . but none of you came to receive my advice." He then went on to lash out at the military leadership, complaining that "the generals [only] make injustices, because you know . . . that all of my creatures on the earth are asking me for justices." In another sermon, he complained that "the generals [almost always] cause injustice," and after summoning them, "these generals did not come because they do not respond to my call, they say that my words are not true . . . none of my creatures take into account my words."[229]

In 1850 and 1887, Juan de la Cruz promised that "those who do not believe in my commandments, will be eternally punished, without end and everyone who will obey my orders, will receive my affection." This seems to have been directed, at least in part, toward the military leaders, as he went on to complain that "there are very few generals that come because none of [them] believe in any of my ordinances and the generals say that there is no truth whatever in my orders." He also suggested that class played a role in the divisions when he wrote that "my lord did not put me with the rich, because my lord did not put me with the generals, nor with the Commanders, because my lord did not put me with any who says he has lots of money . . . but he placed me with the poor, with the very poor." He went on to write that "all my families know that they have to serve the chiefs, but should serve them for pay, for they ought not to serve them for nothing."[230]

Such divisions caused by Indians working for free for the military leaders appear to have generated friction quite early on. In the summer of 1848 while among the rebels, Father Sierra noted that in the north of the peninsula the Indians would welcome "the entrance of the whites, because they told me, that they pay them when they serve them, and in the present state, they work for the comandantes."[231] By the 1860s, such abuses had led to the flight of over 10,000 former Cruzob to British Honduras.[232] As time went on, things did not get better for the speaking cross. In 1903, after the cult was defeated, the secretary of the cross desperately wrote, "I am getting ready to go on a trip because it was so ordered by my true Lord and my Holy Lady." The frustration was evident when he wrote, "I know you are deceiving me . . . [and] the hour is nearing for me to ask you one by one, why do not you obey any longer my true Lord and my true sacred Lady? I am therefore calling you one by one to punish you with fifty [lashes] because you are talking about mixing with the enemy."[233]

Not only did the rise of the cult of the cross marginalize the military leaders, it also provoked divisions within the overall leadership structure and could lead to the humiliation of men of high military standing. When the Indians recaptured Bacalar in 1858, most of the military men were in favor of ransoming the Hispanic captives. However, the Tatich, through the speaking cross, ordered their deaths instead. About a month later the Tatich ordered an attack on Valladolid. On the way the soldiers found a still on a ranch they attacked, and they got drunk before being routed by the Hispanics. As a result, upon their return to Chan Santa Cruz, the cross "ordered that all the delinquents, including Generals and Officers, be then and there whipped." This no doubt strained military-religious relations, especially when the military leaders knew the cult was a ruse. Once, during a gathering with the cross, a drunken General Leandro Santos interrupted it, shouting, "Stop talking, Brulio, we have enough of sorcery." Brulio was the voice of the cross and son of Tata Nazario. Such an insult immediately resulted in Santos being arrested, flogged, and warned that he would be executed if he ever again showed disrespect for the cross or cult.[234] In the end it was not blasphemy that led to Santos's death but his support of the peace faction, and he was killed in 1863 along with Dionisio Zapata and Augustín Barrera by forces loyal to the hard-liners Poot, Novelo, and Cen.[235] Santos had had his share of factional disputes over the years, and in 1858 he said that some of the other commanders had "always [been] my strong enemies."[236]

If the Tatich had frictions with his generals, and the generals had problems with each other, they also had problems having their orders obeyed. As the Hispanic Colonel Rosado noted in 1848, "each captain works independently. Everything is confusion among them and a chaos of disorder."[237] Reed notes that the rebels "fought as an aggregation of independent companies, with captains and commandants deciding if they would obey the orders of generals."[238] Overall, divisions were "a chronic and salient characteristic of [insurgent] society from the beginning of the rebellion."[239] While it made problems for military discipline, the degree of autonomy of military units also made it more difficult to crush the insurgency.[240] For their part, the leaders of the Pacíficos had little control over their subjects, and their communities were also highly fragmented.[241]

Just as the issue of peace led to Poot becoming the military leader of the Cruzob, so it was the same issue, twenty years later, that would lead to his downfall. Having led a countercoup against the peace faction, he well knew the risks of membership in it. Nevertheless, his views changed over the years, and by 1884 he had agreed to a peace treaty with Mexico that enshrined the status quo. Poot ended up rejecting the treaty before it had been ratified, putatively over an insult from Mexican General Theodosius Canto, and perhaps out of concern for the repercussions of his own actions. It was, however, too late, and in August 1885 he was killed in a coup by Aniceto Dzul, who would serve as the military leader of the Cruzob until 1890.[242] As factions contested power within Chan Santa Cruz, it was increasingly rivaled in the mid- to late 1880s by the rise of a new cult of a speaking cross in Tulum led by María Uicab. Adding to the fragmentation in Chan Santa Cruz was the increasing dispersion of the rebel population in the region, which further reduced the power of the leadership.[243]

The rebel forces were divided, but so were the Indians generally. As we have seen in the reconquest of New Mexico and in the Great Rebellion, the Hispanics in Yucatán relied heavily upon loyal Indians to help suppress the uprising. Those Indians in the region of Mérida, as well as many in Motul, Izamal, Tecoh, Tunkás, Maxcanú, and Calkiní, remained loyal to the Hispanics and were granted the honorific title of hidalgo.[244] As Cline notes, natives who remained loyal were generally those who had longest been assimilated into Hispanic society.[245]

Despair, Division, and Mutiny among the Hispanics in Yucatán

The frictions and divisions among the rebel leadership paled in comparison to those of the Hispanic forces. We have already seen how their political divisions, whether directed against Spain during the independence wars or against Mexico City during the Mexican-American War, or within the peninsula itself, led to their repeated involvement of Indians in these conflicts. Once the Caste War had erupted, the Hispanics were plagued by "unpreparedness, pestilence, faulty leadership, cowardice, political bickering [and] emigration."[246]

The soldiers were ill-fed, ill-clothed, often without a doctor, and rarely paid. As one Hispanic military leader noted, "not few were the cases . . . of scandalous riots in the moment of marching against the enemy, of insubordination . . . and . . . desertion." [247] Sometimes the troops simply refused to fight, such as in late 1847 when Dzonotchel fell to the rebels.[248] After the chaotic abandonment of Valladolid in 1848, the Campeche troops rebelled and insisted upon returning to their homes.[249] By the spring of 1848, Hispanic troops were deserting "in flocks," and among the "infinite [number] of officers and soldiers" who had deserted, some had joined the rebel ranks, exchanging their military skills for their survival among the Cruzob.[250] By April 1853, when Hispanic forces invaded Chan Santa Cruz, the rebels were assisted by "a good number" of Hispanic deserters who both had trained the rebels and helped direct their attacks.[251] Desertion continued to be a significant problem in 1860.[252]

Mutiny, often preceding desertion, also plagued the Hispanic military leaders. For example, in October 1848, troops under Colonel Augustín Leon in Tinum demanded leave to visit their families in Campeche. Despite orders to the contrary, 350 of the 500 troops there soon deserted.[253] In March 1851 in Bacalar, a soldier who planned to desert was executed "with the end of ending these so common crimes."[254] In July 1851, the Hispanic troops in Tihosuco rebelled as they were not receiving the one real per day they were due, in addition to their food and clothes. Shouting "Death to the Commanders and Officers," they captured Colonel Rosado, who nevertheless managed to get reinforcements and then capture and execute the ringleaders. The next month, surveying his forces, General Díaz de la Vega noted the widespread problem of desertion and found the garrisons of Espita, Tizimin, Calotmul, and Valladolid highly disorganized, of low morale, rife with resentment against their commanders, and lacking records concerning troop numbers and supplies.[255]

Deplorable conditions and, initially, frequent rebel victories also produced abysmal morale among the Hispanic troops, who often "trembled in the presence of the Indians."[256] In 1848 Colonel Rosado wrote that "every day . . . I fear more an uprising of the troops that I command than the bullets of the savage enemy." He added, "I am persuaded that [the rebels] lack munitions, but they do not need [them] to impose [fear] on the whites . . . with twenty-five Indians hidden with twenty machetes and five rifles, it is sufficient to contain two hundred whites and make an entire town run. This is not a story; I have already seen it with my own eyes."[257] In February 1858, when the Indians recaptured Bacalar, one reason that it happened so quickly was that after the death of a Hispanic officer, the troops "went into dispersion."[258] One military leader, referring to Hispanic troop morale in 1860, asserted that most of the rank and file saw the rebels as "invincible" and "it is not possible that they sustain a fire-fight for ten minutes against the [Indians], as before they finish they are seen fleeing terrified, [and] . . . no human force can contain them . . . they prefer to be sacrificed . . . fleeing than die fighting" as they are "completely blinded by fear."[259]

Political divisions within the Hispanic military forces also undermined their efforts to defeat the insurgency. In February and March 1848, the rebels attacked and eventually took Yaxcaba and Sotuta. The defense of these neighboring towns was gravely impaired as the troops in one refused to assist or field troops with the other. This was because many Méndez supporters, who were leading the defense of Yaxcaba, resented the fact that the military headquarters was located among the Barbachanistas in Sotuta. In the end, both towns were lost to the rebels, in addition to Tixcacaltuyú, which straddled them.[260] Such divisions were not at all uncommon, as commanders often refused assistance to other military leaders who were of a different political persuasion.[261] Such factionalism, and the resulting lack of cooperation or coordination, led to the fall of Izamal to the rebels in May 1848.[262] Overall, such divisions among the Hispanics strengthened the rebel forces both relatively and absolutely.

At One with the Jungle: Rebel Tactics in Yucatán

The Yucatecan rebels were masters of reversing the initiative of their adversaries. Having allowed their enemy into a location, they would then isolate and exhaust them militarily and in terms of morale. Having eroded their ability and willingness to resist, the balance would shift from resistance and hope to exhaustion and desperation. The tipping point reached, the rebels would decimate the Hispanics as they tried to flee in disorder and panic. Only rarely did the rebels engage in frontal assaults, instead opting for sieges, flanking actions, and ambushes, especially as the Hispanics were in retreat.[263] One captive among the rebels noted in 1873, "It never enters into their calculations to defend a settlement. Rather, their tactic is to allow the enemy to enter in order to immediately close off all roads so that at the moment of defeat, the troops, finding no way out, fall into their power."[264] As another captive among the rebels noted, the rebel soldiers are "active, agile, astute and generally magnificent marksmen . . . they almost never keep up an open battle, and they have a great ability for taking advantage of whatever opportunity to do as much harm as possible without serious risk to themselves. When they attack a town or try to assault a fortification in a defended area, it is always through surprise and darkness. Very rarely do they try a direct frontal assault and in the light of day."[265]

The forest was where they felt most comfortable fighting, and, unlike the

Hispanics, they avoided strong buildings such as churches in which they could be trapped.[266] To assist them in killing retreating troops, often after a siege, they would often lay logs and thorny brush on the escape route to slow their enemy and make them easier prey.[267] They would also make use of the abundant limestone in the region for barricades and shields. Lying on their backs, they would roll boulders forward with their feet, creating a mobile fortification.[268] To communicate among themselves, they frequently used a tunkul, or wooden drum, which could be heard for miles.[269] Often they would scream and clap to intimidate and demoralize their Hispanics, and used women and children for this purpose so that their forces would appear larger than they were.[270] One Mexican military commander noted the "admirable instinct of these Indians of Yucatán for war."[271] The rebels also used biological warfare, specifically cholera, to their advantage. When forces under Lieutenant Colonel Lázaro Ruz invaded Chan Santa Cruz in April 1854, the rebels left cholera-contaminated water in the town. Not long after the thirsty soldiers drank it, so many took ill and died that it decimated the Hispanic ranks.[272]

At the advent of the war, the rebels were poorly organized and had machetes and "shovels and pikes," in addition to some guns. By 1866, however, in the words of one of their enemies, they were "perfectly armed, and better than those [troops] of Yucatán, they are organized in battalions, and they carry out their marches and expeditions with admirable order [and] . . . like any military expedition directed by men of the profession."[273] In the decentralized and somewhat autonomous military organization of the rebels, the company served, and even supplanted the village, as a focal point of loyalty.[274] In 1866 the Cruzob had about 4,000 men under arms, in addition to a great number who served in a support capacity and could make "barricades with an extraordinary ease and rapidity." These support troops were also adept at cutting trees and bush to block roads, preparing the land for ambushes, and constructing cane walls to impede bayonet charges. Many would also take up weapons as others fell, to maintain a constant number of men under arms. Women and even children would help in these tasks.[275]

Conclusion

In all of the rebellions studied here, leadership was critical for the organization and implementation of the insurgency. Charismatic leadership, whether by people or the institution of the speaking cross, claimed to benefit from divine guidance, assistance, and protection and to be leading their people to a promised land free of the Hispanic oppressors. In the cases of the Great Rebellion and the Caste War in Yucatán, a cyclical concept of time and a prophetic tradition ensuring the divinely ordained inevitability of rebel victory helped leaders mobilize the insurgents and maintain their morale.

But just as leadership can be a uniting force, so too can it promote divisions. We have seen how Popé alienated many of the pueblos through his visits and tribute demands and how Tupatu's authority was rejected in many pueblos. In the Great Rebellion, Túpac Amaru and Tomás Catari were far more conservative than their followers, and long-simmering resentments between Indian communities rose to the fore during the insurgency. In Yucatán, leaders were also divided over the goals of the rebellion and, related to this, whether or not to seek some negotiated solution with the Hispanics. Although the speaking cross struggled to maintain the unity of the Cruzob, it was often ignored by the generals, who were over time increasingly characterized by internecine quarrels.

It is also interesting to note that in the two cases where the rebellions succeeded in achieving independence, the leaders soon began to practice what they condemned. Popé not only extracted tribute from his subjects, but further alienated them by his insistence that they receive him as they had the Hispanics. In Yucatán, the military leaders insisted that many Indians work for them for free and were quick to exercise their authority in controlling commerce. In the end it appears that the rebels changed their oppressors more effectively than they ended their oppression.

7 Atrocity as Metaphor
The Symbolic Language of Rebellion

While most rebels left no written word of their sources of inspiration or of their goals, in many ways their actions were their written word. Many were anything but inarticulate and expressed themselves clearly through the symbolic nature of their actions. Symbolic language preceded that of oral and written expression, and that it would be used by traditional peoples should come as no surprise, especially when we consider that the vast majority were illiterate. Claude Lévi-Strauss argued that people "communicate by means of symbols and signs. For anthropology . . . all things are symbol and sign which act as intermediaries between two subjects," and such symbols are chosen from differing alternatives of expression.[1] This deliberate choosing of one form of expression out of the universe of options is key to understanding the relation between rebel action and symbolic expression. The symbolic content of rebel actions and their corroborative value in demonstrating exterminatory objectives were most evident in the ways in which rebels chose, treated, and killed their victims as well as what they did with their victims' property.

Deed as Word among the Pueblo

The Pueblo Indians often expressed their hostility to the Hispanics, and especially friars, through the use of symbolic expression. In 1632, when the Indians of Zuni rebelled, they not only killed Friar Francisco Letrado but underscored their dominance by scalping him.[2] In the early 1670s, when Apaches attacked Abó, they not only burned the monastery but killed Friar Pedro de Ayala, after "stripping him of his clothing, putting a rope around his neck, flogging him most cruelly, and finally killing him with blows of the macana; after he was dead they surrounded the body with dead white lambs, and covered the privy parts, leaving him in this way."[3] Clearly, burning the mission is a symbolic act requiring little explanation, and by surrounding his body with dead lambs the Apaches may have wanted to send a warning that a similar fate awaited his flock. The rebels also used physical abuse and humiliation to symbolically express their hatred of and dominance over Hispanics. During the 1680 rebellion, in Jemez, Friar Jesús Morador was captured in his bed, tied up naked on a pig's back, and paraded throughout the pueblo as the Indians beat him. Then at least one Indian rode him as one would a horse, spurring him before he was finally killed.[4]

Stripping victims, which was quite frequent in the rebellion, was a form of humiliation that demonstrated native power. It may also have been a means of symbolically stripping them of their wealth and appropriating it themselves. Symbolically converting the clergyman to a beast of burden only underscored native dominance. Six miles to the south of San Felipe, on the ranch of Cristó-bal de Anaya, as well as that nearby of Pedro de Cuellar, both men and their families were killed and stripped of their clothing.[5] The religious clothing of priests was also taken by the rebels and used "in their dances, and [placed] with their trophies of . . . other church paraphernalia." Otermín noted that many of the victims of the uprising were mutilated.[6] While the manner is unknown, mutilation requires deliberate effort and usually has some symbolic content.

The rebels would superimpose symbols to convey a message. For example, in Santo Domingo, the friars Juan de Talaban, Antonio de Lorenzana, and Joseph Montes de Oca were attacked in the mission and brought to the church where they were killed and piled on one another at the altar.[7] While their being placed at the altar communicated the death of Hispanic spiritual and temporal dominion, there was also a superimposition of the offering of Hispanic religious blood where that of Christ was symbolically offered. Overall, the church's inherent symbolism of an alien religion and power offered the rebels a rich theater for what was often blunt symbolic expression. In Sandía, the

> sculptured images were desecrated with human excrement, two chalices hidden in a trunk were covered with manure, the crucifix of the incarnation was desecrated; the place of the sacred communion table on the main altar [was] desecrated with human excrement, and a sculptured image of Saint Francis [was] broken by blows from an ax.[8]

Otermín noted that the church had been filled with straw for burning, and "everything was broken to pieces and destroyed."[9]

During the entrada of 1681, as the Hispanics made their way through Senecú in early November, the soldiers found "the holy temple and convent burned," and in the cemetery they found a bell with its clapper removed. Also in the cemetery were a bronze cannon and a pine cross that had been in the plaza, while in the sacristy they found the "hair and crown from a crucifix, thrown on the ground and an altar and two pieces of another."[10] Otermín believed that the town had been the victim of Apache attacks. Whatever the case, by scalping a statue of Christ and breaking an altar, they were conveying the destruction of Hispanic and Catholic power. By removing the clapper from a bell that had for years commanded their presence and service, the Indians in effect castrated a symbol of Hispanic authority. Its placement in the cemetery, along with the cross and cannon, drives home the point that in their view Catholicism and the military might that supported it were dead.

During the same entrada, in late November, the Hispanics found Socorro deserted and the mission and church burned, and again the clappers had been removed from the two bells, which were still in the towers. In the sacristy they "found a crown of twigs and two pieces of the arm of a holy image of Christ," while on the plaza they found an "entire thigh, leg and foot of a holy image of Christ, in one piece, all the rest of the divine image being burned to charcoal and ashes, also some bases of other images and many pieces of burned crosses. One large cross of pine which had been in the cemetery they had cut down at the base with axes and had burned the arms and most of the rest of it in the plaza of the said pueblo."[11] Otermín believed that the rebels, as opposed to Apaches, had burned the temple, images, and crosses. Clearly, burning religious symbols conveyed the figurative and physical destruction of Catholicism as well as the impotence of the Catholic god. Similar symbolic expressions were found when they arrived in Alamillo on December 1. The town was "entirely deserted, and the church, convent, and crosses burned, not one being in evidence," although they did find a bell with its clapper removed.[12]

Arriving three days later in Cebolleta, which had been deserted due to "fear of the Apaches," the soldiers found "the hermitage where the holy sacraments were administered . . . entirely demolished, and the wood from it made into an underground estufa," or kiva.[13] Not only had the power of the Catholic god been destroyed but its vestiges were now at the service of the native gods.

On December 17, 1681, Otermín entered Sandía, where he encountered "the church and convent entirely . . . demolished" along with "two broken bells, in five pieces" as well as a "small broken crown." The symbols of Catholic and in many ways Hispanic authority were literally in pieces. In one house there they found

> a trophy . . . painted on a panel, the image of the Immaculate Conception of
> Our Lady with a dragon at her feet, which work had served as an altar piece
> for the main altar of the said church, and it is said that the divine eyes and
> mouth of the figure were ruined, and that there were signs on the other parts
> of the body of it having been stoned, while the accursed figure at her feet
> was whole and unspoiled.

Clearly, these were deliberate actions, conveying the resurgence of the native gods and the demise of Catholic power, which the Indians had symbolically blinded and muted. The same basic message was conveyed through the destruction of other liturgical items, as they found "some fragments of ornaments and things" of the church there.[14]

As Vargas led his entrada in the region in October 1692 and approached the refuge of the Indians from Jemez, the Indians offered resistance, "making all the gestures they use in their fighting." After seeing the Hispanics stand their ground, they insisted that their display of hostility was in fact a sign of welcome.[15] Kessell asserts that this "may represent a form of military salute or welcome" and notes a similar event around 1846 or 1847. General Stephen Watts Kearny led a group of American officials to Santo Domingo and was "told that young men, dressed for war, were coming to receive them and cautioned not to fire. In a cloud of dust and with war whoops, warriors swept by the soldiers on each side at full speed, firing volleys under the 621 horses' bellies." A similar event occurred in 1850 with Lieutenant J. H. Simpson at Zuni.[16] Hostility became ritual, symbolizing at once native bravery and their acceptance of superior power that did not flee in the face of it.

As his entrada progressed, Vargas found much the same symbolic expressions as had Otermín eleven years previously. Among the Zuni in November 1692, Vargas found bells with the clappers removed, and when he finally expelled the Indians from Santa Fe in December 1693, he found a cross that had been in the plaza now broken to pieces as well as "an image of Our Lady, the head of which was hit and broken with a macana."[17] His reconquest gave voice to other rebel goals. When he was preparing to assault Santa Fe, also in December 1693, the rebels defiantly promised they would kill all of the Hispanics, but they would spare some priests. They asserted that "the friars will for a short time be our servants, we will make them carry firewood and bring it from the woods, and after they have served us we will kill all of them."[18] They further sought to invert the colonial order when they said they were "going to kill . . . [the Hispanics] and make slaves of their women and children."[19] This was no idle threat, as this is what they had done with many Hispanic women in 1680.[20]

Similar events played out during the 1696 rebellion. Generally, it was clear what little the Indians wanted of the Hispanics. In July 1696, one friar noted that the Indians "are interested only in obtaining the equipment of the ministers, the livestock, and everything with regard to the divine religious . . . they broke to pieces and profaned."[21] In March 1696, the guardian of Picurís reported that "he has seen them stone the patron saint," while another in Cochiti was told by an Indian that "he will drink from the chalice."[22] Again we find native resentment and power expressed through the deliberate physical destruction of religious artifacts, as well as the Indian desire to invert relationships and place at the service of the natives that which had served the Hispanics. Also, by drinking from the chalice, one may have sought to appropriate whatever power was left of the Catholic god.

The 1696 rebellion also saw the destruction of missions and the stripping of victims. In San Ildefonso the rebels razed the mission and church and killed eight Hispanics inside the complex, while in Nambé the convent had been cast asunder and the rebels had taken the "sacred vessels and vestments" and left the beaten and naked bodies of four people at the door of the church. A contemporary also noted that "Our Lady of the Conception was found placed in the high altar with the bell, which was hanging."[23] Although it is not clear what was intended by this, it is evident that it was calculated and had some purpose. More obvious were the actions of the inhabitants of San Diego de Jemez during the 1696 rebellion. There the rebels "pulled off even the crosses and rosaries that they had hanging from their necks and threw them to the ground."[24] In the mission of San Juan de los Jemez, the Hispanics "found . . . the images of the saints destroyed and in pieces and the crosses broken. And in the church it was the same, the rosaries thrown on the ground and covered with feathers, ashes, and some rabbit skins."[25] By covering the rosaries with items of native worship, the rebels demonstrated the superior power of the native gods.

In San Cristóbal during the 1696 rebellion, Friars Arbizu and Carbonel were killed and then placed by the Indians "on the ground, placed in the form of a cross, face up" and found in their "underclothing."[26] Again, this appears to be deliberate and perhaps suggests that just as the friars were dead and stripped of power and clothing, so was the Catholic Church dead and stripped of its trappings and power. In San Diego de Jemez, the rebels killed Friar Francisco de Jesús, after tricking him to come out to confess a putatively dying person. Once outside of the mission, they "caught him and killed him next to a cross that the said religious had set up in the cemetery; and on many occasions the said religious was heard to say, and I heard him say, that he had it so that they could crucify him on it, and although these wishes were not attained, he succeeded in expiring at the foot of the cross."[27] Again, we find the tendency to superimpose like upon like, in this case, the priest, the cross, and the field of death.

In July 1696, near Pecos, the alcalde mayor found that Indians, perhaps Navajo or Yuta, had left a "cross they had . . . drawn on the ground by hand. There was also a club and a long line drawn across the trail. The Pecos Indians interpreted the cross to mean that they should understand that those who had made the tracks were not Christians, as they were, and not Apaches, which they were not. They said the club and the line meant that they had to kill however many of them who, because they were Christians, might follow the Spaniards, and that the Pecos were too cowardly to go beyond the line."[28] The drawing and its rapid and complex interpretation by the Indians suggest that they were accustomed to communicating symbolically.

The rebels also employed symbolic language to make peace with the Hispanics, speaking their enemy's own symbolic language. When Vargas and Luís Tupatú met on September 15, 1692, Tupatú was "dressed in the Spanish style," adorned with a rosary and "showed . . . a small, silver image of Christ he had in his hands with a small piece of taffeta, which I saw had the printed image of Our Lady of Guadalupe."[29] In October 1692, as Vargas arrived among the

Zuni, they welcomed him with gifts of sheep, watermelon, and tortillas, the first two of which were brought to the region by the Hispanics.[30]

Transcendent Expression in the Andes

The rebels in the Great Rebellion also used symbolic means to express their goals and desires, and sometimes they were eloquent in their simplicity. For example, Andrés Túpac Amaru, in the area of La Paz and Sicasica, mandated that whenever rebels encountered medals with the bust of Carlos III that had been awarded to loyal curacas, these medals should be hanged from a gallows.[31] Clearly, the symbolic message was that the age of Spanish dominion was over, as would be the lives of those who defended it. When the rebels attacked Pocoata and the escort of Corregidor Alós on August 26, 1780, they chopped off the hand of his scribe, Mateo Tellez, and also cut out the tongue of the corregidor's advisor, Josef Benavides. Both men were then killed, but only after they had been symbolically stripped of their ability to perform their roles in society, to write and speak.[32] Such actions were deliberate, these people had to be identified and captured, and their mutilation was clearly associated with the roles they had played in oppressing the Indians. In at least one case a cleric suffered a similar fate. In Colcha, prior to his execution, a priest had his tongue cut out by the rebels, practically and symbolically preventing him from ministering.[33] Similarly, by doing battle with the whirlwinds on the altiplano, Túpac Catari was not only demonstrating his putative mastery over the forces of nature but, more subtly, also preventing the Christian god from assisting the Hispanics, who were believed to have come from the underworld to which the dust devils served as a link.[34]

Symbolic expression often communicated the implosion of the Hispanic world. For example, when Corregidor Bodega met his demise in Challapata in January 1781 in the midst of a melee, he was not killed on sight but captured and brought to the rollo. Once there, the Indians had his own slave behead him.[35] A similar event happened on the shores of Lake Titicaca, in Juli, where the rebels tied the curaca Fermín Llagua to the rollo, and placed his head at his feet after they had killed him. The curaca Rafael Paca was also beheaded, and his head was placed atop the rollo, thereby symbolically communicating the decapitation of Spanish authority.[36] In Chucuito, the rebels beheaded all of the Hispanic women and, after stringing their heads like beads, hung them like a necklace from the rollo.[37]

The rollo, curaca, and corregidor were all symbols of Hispanic power and exploitation and were easily superimposed on one another symbolically. To decapitate a Hispanic official at the rollo suggests the collapse and decapitation of Spanish power. The message was made more cogent by superimposing one on the other. In the case of Bodega, the Indians staged the event in such a manner that Bodega was actually killed by his own property, his slave. As a result, on a symbolic level, it was Hispanic property that was destroying Spanish authority. These were not arbitrary acts. The rebels deliberately chose to execute these people in this way. In Oruro, the rebels not only prohibited the burial of their victims but also gathered the cadavers and left them at the foot of the rollo.[38] This took time and was a deliberate act, and by doing so the insurgents had gathered up and superimposed all of the dead in one place: Hispanics, Hispanic power, and the power of the Church, which the rollo also represented. Such actions also underscored the inversion of long-standing power relationships.

Beheading Hispanic officials at the rollo was not the only way in which the rebels expressed their belief that the system which had so long oppressed them was imploding. During the slaughter in Tapacari on February 25, 1781, several rebels captured a Spaniard who had been hiding with his family behind an altar. They offered to spare him, but only if he executed his six sons in the presence of his wife. Refusing, he was quickly killed, along with his sons, in front of his spouse.[39] The demand that a father kill his children has within it the idea of internally generated collapse. Like Spanish property destroying Spanish authority in Challapata, Spanish life destroying itself was another means of expressing implosion. Of course, it was the rebels who were orchestrating the scene, but there seems to be an interest on at least the part of some that they would preside over the implosion of the Hispanic order as part of the pachacuti.

Throughout the rebellion, the manner in which people were usually killed, through beheading, also underscored the exterminatory nature of the rebellion. By such acts, the rebels expressed their belief that those killed would never reincarnate or return to the region.[40] Not to do so, or to bury them too soon, would leave open the possibility that the Hispanics would one day return to dominate the region. Sending the heads of victims to leaders such as Túpac Amaru also served as a symbolic means of expressing their support for the Inca.[41] The Spaniards learned the hard way about the perceived relationship between beheading and resurrection. When Viceroy Toledo ordered the execution of Túpac Amaru I in 1572, the Inca was not beheaded. As a result, this opened the way for the belief that he would one day return, a popular perception which the later Túpac Amaru would use to cultivate his image as a demigod in 1780.[42]

We have previously noted the Indian view that in many ways the rebellion was also an expression of a contest between Hispanic and indigenous spiritual forces. Although the rebel forces appear to have had their share of apostates, many insurgents in the Great Rebellion sought a reformulation of Catholicism which would be responsive to and advance native interests. Whatever their differing views of the alien god, as the rebellion radicalized in the early months of 1781, the insurgents consistently violated the long-standing tradition of church sanctuary. We have seen time and again, in the sad tales of Oruro, San Pedro de Buenavista, Tapacari, Yura, Colcha, Palca, Tarata, and other towns, how the rebels would storm the churches if the besieged did not leave them and hand themselves over to almost certain death.[43]

Partly, the church as battleground reflected the fact that it was usually the strongest building in a village and most able to resist a rebel attack. As a result, the flow of events led to the use of churches by Hispanics for defense and by rebels for symbolic language. The assault of, and killing in, churches made it clear to all involved that neither the Christian god nor his priests commanded respect; much less could they impede the pachacuti. As in New Mexico, by executing people on altars, as happened in Tapacari in Upper Peru, both the individual and Catholicism itself were sacrificed in the same place where the blood of Christ and the host were offered.[44] Here again we find two levels of death superimposed, of individual and institution, as we did with the executions or gathering of the dead at the rollo.

As the rebellion progressed, priests increasingly were targeted for death by the rebels. Initially, insurgent hostility toward clerics was expressed through threats, intimidation, and humiliation. For example, on February 12, 1781, when Dámaso Catari and Ramón Paca led the assault on Yura, after they had killed the curaca and others, they permitted the priest to flee only after he had been stripped naked. Paca perpetrated the same deed in Anasayas.[45] Other clerics had a worse fate, as we have seen with the death of numerous priests during the rebellion in Tapacari, San Pedro de Buenavista, Oruro, Poopó, Aymaia, Songo, Chucuito, El Alto, and other towns.[46] The fact that in Palca the insurgents executed more than 400 men, women, and children, leaving "some on top of the others . . . [and] many in a shameless position," suggests that there was some symbolic content to the manner of execution or its aftermath.[47] In Tapacari, Oruro, and other places the rebels also mutilated their victims, although it is not always clear what the role of the victims had been in colonial society.[48]

While the violation of church sanctuary and the killing of priests may be evidence of nothing more than zealous prosecution of the rebellion, the use of symbolic expression suggests that in at least some cases the rebels were, as one contemporary put it, "trying to put an end to the Christian name and return to their ancient infidelity."[49] As in New Mexico, although the insurgents would often seize religious objects that had some utility, such as chalices, in many cases they destroyed items that had value only for Catholics. In Oruro, the rebels not only sacked many churches but destroyed many religious images. The rebels who subsequently besieged the town were candid in their desire to cut "off the head of the image of Our Lady of Rosario" upon their anticipated victory.[50] In San Pedro de Buenavista, after the rebels had taken the silver and jewels from the church, they stripped the images of Mary and Jesus of their clothing before destroying them and the monstrance.[51] After overrunning Tapacari, the rebels removed the crowns from the statues of Mary and Jesus, symbolically stripping them of their authority, before making a pyre of them and other religious statues in the plaza.[52] In Condocondo, a monstrance was destroyed through stoning, and in Palca another was placed in the service of the rebels when they adorned it with offerings of coca leaves.[53] These actions communicated that the pachacuti was destroying not only the Hispanics but also their god.

The forced adoption of indigenous dress by those whom the rebels spared, often briefly, was a symbol not only of the new dominance of native ways and traditions but also of the inversion of previous power relationships. Even at the beginning, when Corregidor Alós was marched in captivity, he was forced to don Indian garb.[54] As the rebellion engulfed the region, in Colcha, Arque, Tapacari, Sacaca, Sicasica, Chocaya, and Oruro, the insurgents consistently commanded that all those subject to them wear exclusively Indian clothing, speak the native language, and generally adhere to native customs such as the chewing of coca leaves.[55] This shift was especially dramatic in Oruro with the rapid breakdown of the alliance between the Creoles and Indians, as the rebels demanded that all individuals dress in the native manner, greet each other in Aymara, and chew coca.[56] In Tapacari and Sorata, the Hispanic women spared by the rebels were also forced to adopt Indian clothing.[57] The importance of adopting native ways was also shown by those who did not, and in many cases people were killed for wearing shirts.[58]

The insurgents also employed ridicule to express their hostility toward Catholicism and priests. In Pintatora, the rebels "made fun" of the assistant priest as he tried to calm the rebels while holding a crucifix, and in Sacaca the Indians maltreated another cleric and forced him to wear a crown of thorns.[59] In Oruro at least one Indian shouted that the Christ of Burgos was only a piece of wood, while in Palca an Indian ridiculed the host as nothing more than simple bread.[60] Dancing over corpses, which was reported in Oruro and Tapacari, was also a means of ridiculing their enemies and expressing their newfound power.[61]

In addition to employing symbolic language to demonstrate the implosion of the colonial order or to humiliate their enemies, the insurgents utilized it to underscore the inversion of power and social relationships. Stripping people of their clothing was one means of inverting the established order. In Challapata, once the rebels had killed the corregidor, they allowed his armed escort to flee only after they had been stripped of their clothing and property. In February 1781, priests were stripped of their vestments in Yura and Anasayas.[62] During the assault on Oruro, the Spanish treasury official Salvador Parilla was stripped by the Indians in the Convent of Santo Domingo.[63] Inversion and humiliation were not the only reasons to strip people, as the natives equated nakedness with poverty. By stripping them of their clothing, the natives were bringing their enemies to the level of poverty that they knew so well. Indeed, in Aymaia, when insurgents were beating the cleric Dionicio Cortés to death, one Indian exclaimed, "Priest! Thief! It is because of you that we are naked."[64] Just as stripping people of their clothing inverted previous relationships, so too did the rebel use of the clothes of their enemies. By appropriating their clothing, as happened in La Paz, Sicasica, and San Pedro de Buenavista, they showed their power over their enemies and further underscored the changes being wrought by the pachacuti.[65]

Just as the rebels sought to turn power relationships on their head by the rebellion, they also sought to invert social relationships. When Simón Castillo invaded San Pedro de Buenavista on Christmas Day, 1780, he demanded that all Spaniards leave the town within eight days or "be sent to the mines of Potosí."[66] When the rebels took Carangas, they placed the treasury official Juan Manuel de Guemes y Huesles in a place many Indians knew well—the stocks—before finally executing him. Similarly, in Chocaya the Spaniard Gerónimo Alquisalete was jailed for a day prior to his execution.[67] Sparing Hispanic women to have them as captive-servants for the rebels also dramatically inverted previous relationships. As women were considered chattel, the rebels were further stripping men of what was considered their property. The experiences of many of these captives are hard to determine as the sources rarely offer detail in this regard. We do know that Hispanic women were used as servants and many were subsequently executed, as we have seen in Tapacari, San Pedro de Buenavista, Palca, Lipes, Sicasica, and La Paz.[68] Under threat of death, the widowed Hispanics of Chocaya came out of their hiding places to kneel and kiss the feet and hands of the rebel leaders before they were rescued by a relief column.[69] Many contemporaries, perhaps reluctant to write of sexual assault, often only wrote that many "outrages which the pen is horrified to repeat" occurred during rebel attacks.[70] Others stated that it "scandalizes the ears" or "horrifies the tongue" to repeat the atrocities committed.[71] Given the brutality of the rebellion, there is little left to infer in this regard.

Inversion and assimilation of colonial elements are evident by the rebel eagerness to appropriate silver during the looting sprees that always accompanied Indian attacks. Silver was a symbol and expression of wealth in colonial society, and by possessing it and other useful items of the Hispanics, the insurgents underscored the inversion of the colonial order. In addition, in San Pedro de Buenavista, El Alto, and elsewhere, by using silver chalices to drink chicha, or by adorning monstrances with coca leaves, the insurgents demonstrated the inversion of cosmological relationships. Such acts also symbolically appropriated whatever remaining power the Catholic god had by employing in native worship that which had served Christianity.[72]

War and Metaphor in Yucatán

During the Caste War of Yucatán, the rebels not only communicated their exterminatory objectives through action, such as killing Hispanics, making slaves of some, razing the towns of their enemies, and establishing their own domain, but they also communicated through symbolic means. Again, we find the use of mutilation to communicate attitudes and objectives. According to Reed, "castration was a favorite form of mutilation," which was quite widespread in the rebellion and symbolically expressed the rebel desire to extinguish the Hispanic race.[73] Apparently, mutilation was also used in at least one case to communicate the inversion of previous relationships or gender, or to express their view of their enemies. In Tiholop in 1853, upon coming out of his hiding place after the rebel assault, one Hispanic survivor found the corpses "horribly mutilated; the madness that the Indians had made between one sex and the other."[74] The Hispanics who returned to Dzilbalchén in late spring 1848, and were subsequently captured by the rebels, were "sacrificed with the most refined cruelty," suggesting that there was some degree of calculation and symbolic expression in the manner in which they were killed.[75] When the rebels overran Maní in April 1848, many of the over 200 victims were left "in pieces," and in the following month victims in Ticul were quartered and those in Sacalum were "horribly mutilated."[76]

As in the Pueblo Revolt and the Great Rebellion, rape was used to express dominance over Hispanics and the inversion of the previous order. During the 1847 attack on Valladolid, the "Indians committed the most brutal acts of lasciviousness, profaning the wives and daughters in front of the husband and their parents."[77] The rebels also inverted the social order by keeping Hispanic women as concubines, while Hispanic men who were held captive served the Indians as laborers and as skilled workers.[78] Political and social inversion was evident in March 1848, when Miguel Huichim captured his godfather, Colonel Victoriano Rivero, just outside of Valladolid. After seizing him, Huichim swapped hats and jackets with his Hispanic captive, underscoring the inversion of relations between them.[79] Also as we have seen in the Pueblo Revolt and the Great Rebellion, in at least one case, that of Tekax in September 1857, the rebels demonstrated their power, and perhaps tried to appropriate that of their enemies, by stripping their victims of all of their clothing.[80]

During the rebel attack on Chancenote in February 1848, after killing and mutilating the defenders and raping many women, the rebels stormed the church and took the saints, religious clothing, and even some of the altars outside and burned them before burning the town itself. While this may have been an act of revenge against Hispanic abuses of sacred native articles, it also was a means of demonstrating that the Christian god could no longer protect the Hispanics.[81] Likewise, during the 1853 attack on Yaxcaba, in addition to the usual activities, the rebels set fire to the church ornamentation.[82]

As in the Great Rebellion, ridicule complemented inversion and humiliation as means of symbolically demonstrating rebel power. When the rebels were preparing to execute the military leaders who had been captured in Valladolid by Miguel Huichim, they humiliated and showed their power over their adversaries by "amus[ing] themselves as if it was a bullfight."[83] In Ticul, when Colonel Cetina was besieged by the rebels in May 1848, they showed their confidence and derision of their enemies by coming in front of the Hispanic lines and doing traditional dances, some in blackface, some in uniforms of dead soldiers, and some dressed as women.[84] There is also an indication that the rebels sought to preside over the implosion of the old order. Just as in the Great Rebellion when a Hispanic father was commanded by the rebels to execute his sons, so too in Sacaba, in mid-1848, the rebels made the local judge burn his own property.[85]

The rebels anticipated using symbolism to celebrate their hoped-for victory over the Hispanics. In 1851, when the speaking cross ordered an attack after the Hispanics had captured the original speaking cross, the interpreter of the cross promised that a string of victories would follow, culminating in the placing of a rooster wind vane on the cathedral of Mérida.[86] The Cruzob also retained Hispanic artillery to express their own power, though they did not use it against their enemies. In 1873, the rebels' captured artillery was "useless for anything more than ceremonial discharges during their celebrations, [but] they are the first things they protect when they have notice of an impending invasion."[87]

For their part, the Hispanic forces to some extent used symbolic language to communicate to the rebels. As the Hispanic counterattack got under way in the summer of 1848, in Santa Elena they not only closed the well of the village after casting a child in it, but after hanging an Indian they "left him . . . seated on an elevated platform with a pen in his hand, because . . . he had served the Indians" as a scribe.[88]

Overall, while it surfaces to differing degrees in the documents, the rebels employed symbolic language to communicate not only their hatred of the old order but also their power and goals. Decapitating victims, castrating men, keeping Hispanic women as concubines, stripping people, having Hispanics destroy what they held dear, dancing over victims, and destroying religious articles were just some of the ways the rebels in each of these rebellions used inversion, implosion, superimposition, and humiliation to express their exterminatory objectives and aspirations for the new order that they were seeking to create.

8 Cultural Assimilation in the Native World

Although each of the movements studied here was exterminatory in terms of their millennially inspired objective of eliminating the Hispanic presence in their lands, the rebels had assimilated, to differing degrees, elements of the culture that they were seeking to eliminate. While this appears contradictory, such assimilation is not at all unusual in such movements generally, and that which was assimilated was generally oriented to that which would support the survival and reproduction of the natives or increase their comfort over the long term.[1]

Rebels and Hispanic Assimilation in New Mexico

Despite the efforts of the Pueblo rebel leaders, through their actions and edicts, to eliminate the Hispanic influence in the Pueblo world, they were only partially successful. We have seen how the Indians had long assimilated horses into their culture and how many Indians had continued to cultivate crops introduced by the Hispanics. The rebels were also eager to appropriate the weapons of their enemies. Exemplary of this tendency was when the Indians began to mass on Santa Fe in 1680: the Indian Juan went to tell Otermín that he and the Hispanics could flee or die, and the rebel appeared "on horseback, wearing a sash of red taffeta which was recognized as being from the missal of the convent of Galisteo, and with harquebus, sword, dagger, leather jacket, and [other] . . . arms of the Spaniards."[2] We have also seen how Hispanic women were forced into the native society as captive concubines. It appears that paternity was important in determining ethnicity, as the offspring of these unions were not killed but assimilated into the society of the independent Indians before many Hispanic women and their children were rescued by Vargas in 1692.[3]

Often what the leaders demanded of their subjects they themselves did not adhere to. For example, Popé moved into the governor's house in Santa Fe and used his coach to travel around town. When he visited other villages, he insisted on being received in the manner of his Spanish predecessors. He also at least once presided over a feast where he and Alonso Catiti played the roles of the Spanish governor and the custodian.[4] During the 1681 entrada, Hispanic forces under Juan Domínguez de Mendoza found extensive collections of Hispanic articles in Santo Domingo, Alameda, Puaray, and San Felipe.[5]

In addition, some Indians may have secretly retained their Catholic faith, or perhaps their belief in the efficacy of Catholic ceremonies, during the period of Indian independence. During the entrada in 1681, in the sacristan's house in Alameda, the Hispanics found the holy oils and some bells that had been buried by Christian Indians to prevent them from falling into rebel hands. They also found some chickens there, originally brought by the Spanish.[6] During the same entrada, in Senecú the Hispanics found crosses in some of the houses, "all of which were standing and without a sign of being burned."[7] While this may suggest that they were not apostates, it is also very possible that they left these articles as a symbolic means to discourage the Hispanics from looting or razing the pueblo.

Assimilation in the Andes

Unlike in New Mexico where there was a concerted effort to eliminate almost all vestiges of Catholic influence, 100 years later in Upper Peru the focus was more on redefining Catholicism to suit native ends than on its outright rejection. This redefinition reflected the success of the missionary endeavor in Peru and Upper Peru, but it also reflected the native belief that while the Christian god was still powerful, it was then being eclipsed by the resurgent power of native deities. This resurgence was tied to the pachacuti, which was, in rebel eyes, then reordering the native universe.[8] This process of reformulation illustrates and partially explains the differing ways in which Catholicism and its ministers were treated during the rebellion. The influence that clerics had at the beginning of the rebellion, which they successfully used to prevent or forestall rebel attacks on civilians in Ocuri, Pintatora, and San Pedro de Buenavista, soon declined to the point where many priests became victims of the rebellion.[9] That not all Indians wholly rejected Christianity is shown by the extensive assimilation of Catholicism by Túpac Amaru and Túpac Catari and by the fact that when Father Menéndez absolved the rebels outside of Oruro, many knelt. In addition, some communities, such as Arque, wanted priests, though different ones than had been there previously.[10] As mentioned earlier, apostasy may have been higher among voluntary rebels than among those who had been conscripted.

Despite the eagerness to rid the region of Hispanics and their rule, many rebels in the Great Rebellion retained a desire for Hispanic goods and had long assimilated many other Hispanic characteristics. As early as the mid-seventeenth century, huacas were discovered that had beards and were clothed in the Hispanic fashion. Silverblatt observes, "Although the language of indianism was ferociously anti-Spanish, it was, at the same time, pervasively . . . hispanified."[11] The native desire for the silver, weapons, alcohol, and even clothing of their enemies underscores the importance of antinomy and assimilation in the rebellion. Among the most sought-after items were firearms, not surprising given their role in helping to bring about the pachacuti. Many Hispanics were held prisoner specifically due to their ability to operate cannons and other weapons. The colonial experience had also given many natives a hearty appreciation for alcoholic drinks stronger than the traditional chicha.[12]

The use of Hispanic clothing could either mark one for death or show one's dominance over one's enemies. We have seen how throughout the rebellion people were killed if they wore shirts, and captives and others found donning native garb their best chance for survival. While Túpac Catari often dressed in the fashion of native nobility, he also was seen to wear a black Hispanic velvet shirt and similar clothing.[13] Many of his supporters also wore Hispanic garb.[14] While some rebels may have worn the uniforms of their Hispanic enemies as part of a ruse to lure them into combat or to show their dominance over the Hispanics, they may also have believed that by wearing such uniforms they harnessed the power of their enemies while simultaneously demonstrating the inversion of previous relationships.[15] In the village of Caloya, in Sicasica province, the cleric Fernando Arancivia observed that "various Indians were dressed like Spaniards, with red and blue cloaks and sabers . . . in hand."[16] In all likelihood, only those who were beyond any doubt committed to the rebel cause would have been safe in Hispanic clothing. Despite his fervent anti-Hispanicism, Túpac Catari referred to himself as "viceroy," his lieutenants as oidores, or judges, his headquarters as a cabildo, or city hall, and the rebels celebrated their dominance of La Paz by holding many bullfights.[17]

Similarly, appropriating the property of the Hispanics was another way for the rebels to obtain what they had been denied in colonial society, whether it was property, power, or, in the case of Túpac Catari, direct contact with the Christian god.[18] The desire for social mobility would also apply to the Amarista leadership and other leaders such as Simón Castillo, whom Father Merlos described as "very ladino," or Hispanicized, as well as the secretary of the unusually light-skinned Túpac Catari who changed his given, Indian, name from Bonifacio Chuquimamani to the Hispanic Manuel Clavijo.[19] Again, we find antinomy where rebels often sought personally what they rejected on a social level.

Too Late to Turn Back: Rebels and Hispanic Culture in Yucatán

Although the rebels sought, at least initially, the extermination of the Hispanic population of Yucatán, much of Hispanic culture had been assimilated into their own. Cruzob society was a reflection of their worldview and had both pre-Hispanic and Hispanic influences. Unlike the oral history tradition and legends of the Andes, as Howard Cline notes, the Indians "preserved little or no memory of the classic Maya civilization or events of the conquest, though a substantial substratum of agricultural and every-day custom has been preserved."[20] The former included a speaking deity, the theocratic nature of Cruzob rule, and its focus in a town that was dedicated to native worship, occupied by the leadership, and populated by rotating contingents of servants.[21] Previous speaking crosses included a pre-Hispanic one in Cozumel, another in Sotuta in 1597, and one in Tayasal in 1697, which was destroyed by its erstwhile adepts as it had failed to impede a Spanish invasion. Another speaking oracle was found in the region of Valladolid in the 1700s.[22] Such speaking deities reflected "practices and ideas already deeply rooted in religious tradition."[23] After the appearance of the speaking cross in Chan Santa Cruz, others appeared in Tulum, Chancah, Chunpom, and San Antonio Muyil.[24] Reed describes the emergence of a new cult in 1985 built around a stone that speaks, led by Cipriano Tamax in Dzulá, and notes that "the tradition of divine voices in Yucatán is ancient, widespread, and continuing."[25] The existence of speaking deities in Maya history helps to explain why the cult of the cross met with so much success, and why Bonifacio Novelo failed as he tried to rally adherents and inspire devotion by showing an image of a virgin, which he said had come from heaven.[26]

Despite these pre-Hispanic foundations and influences in Cruzob society, 350 years of Hispanic and Catholic influence had left its mark. Chan Santa Cruz was itself laid out in the Hispanic fashion with a church and official buildings centered on a plaza.[27] The fact that in the cult it was a cross that spoke underscores the intersection between the pre-Hispanic tradition of speaking deities and the Catholic cross. Also reflecting the impact of Catholicism were the celebration by the Cruzob of the Day of the Holy Cross on May 3, that of the Virgin of Conception on December 8, and Easter. Such celebrations also had other Hispanic influences, including bullfights, and the Cruzob also used guitars, violins, and other nonnative instruments.[28] Catholic influences are further shown by the holding of mass in a church, although they used a tortilla as a host, and the speaking of an interpreted form of Latin during that and other ceremonies.[29] These influences also reflect the fact that many natives who served as priests among the rebels had previously been maestro cantores, or assistants to Catholic priests.[30]

The rebel treatment of priests also is indicative of the degree to which the rebels had assimilated Catholicism and believed that the god of the Catholics still retained some power. It was priests whom the Hispanics sent out to try to persuade the rebels to negotiate, because their lives were generally spared by the insurgents.[31] After the ruse in Valladolid in March 1848 that resulted in

Colonel Victoriano Rivero and other military officers being taken prisoner along with Father Sierra, the officers were marched while bound and on foot, whereas Sierra rode freely on a horse.[32] During the seven months Father Sierra spent among the rebels, he traveled extensively throughout the rebel-controlled areas, usually carried in a litter, and his services of mass, confession, and catechism were in such demand by the Indians that he noted "all the towns were clamoring for me."[33] In September 1857, when the Cruzob assaulted Tekax, almost every Hispanic was killed. The priest Marín, however, was not only untouched but walked freely among the rebels.[34] In September 1861, when Crescencio Poot captured Tunkás, he showed his respect for the priest Manuel Castellanos by offering him a seat as the rebels gathered up the captives.[35]

Not all priests, however, were respected or spared by the rebels. In late September 1847, during the attack on Tixcacalcupul, the rebels killed the priest Eusebio Rejón, who had seized community lands, along with the Hispanic population there.[36] Just before the fall of Valladolid, the priest Alejandro Vilamil of Uayma was found hanged with his eyes gouged out.[37] Likewise, the priest of Tunkás, Manuel Castellanos, was hacked to death outside Chan Santa Cruz, an event which led Dionicio Zapata to become more critical of the cult and to favor peace.[38] In February 1848, during the siege of Sotuta, the Hispanics sent out two priests, Juan de la Cruz and José Antonio Monforte, in an effort to start negotiations with the rebels. They approached the rebels wearing "their most luxurious vestments . . . but as the clergy was beginning already to lose prestige among the Indians, they received outrages instead of the veneration they expected. The first fled terrified back to the plaza, and the second went as far as the trenches" to negotiate.[39] As they approached the rebels, one Indian reproached the others, saying, "Don't take your hats off for these dogs," which was what caused the one priest to flee.[40]

Some rebels also adopted a Hispanic style of dress. When Crescencio Poot took the population of Tunkás captive in September 1861, he was dressed in a frock coat and pants, and when Miguel Huichim took Colonel Victoriano Rivero prisoner, he took his captive's hat and jacket.[41] The Cruzob imitated their enemies in their use of similar military grades and in their use of captured military band members, who performed for them and instructed Indians in the art.[42] There was also a company of white deserters who not only instructed the Cruzob in military arts but also fought for them.[43] Overall, Villa Rojas argues that the blending of preconquest, colonial, and nineteenth-century attributes produced a new and distinctive culture."[44]

The assimilation of elements of the society that the rebels were seeking to exterminate is a paradox of these movements and many nativist and millennial endeavors.[45] It reflects the acculturation and internalization resulting from generations of interaction with the colonizers. In each of these movements, we find increasing degrees of assimilation, especially in the area of religion. While the Pueblo Revolt all but eliminated Catholicism in New Mexico for twelve years, in the Great Rebellion the rebels sought a syncretic reformulation of Catholicism, and in the Caste War of Yucatán, the cult of the speaking cross reflected a high degree of assimilation of Catholic elements. Also contributing to this was the belief by many rebels that, at least until the respective rebellions, the Catholic god did have significant power. As a result, in the Great Rebellion and the Caste War of Yucatán, to the degree to which it could be "tamed" and brought to serve the rebels, it complemented rather than replaced native rites and rituals. Divine assistance, even from alien gods, was acceptable, even welcome, if it seemed to serve survival and reproduction. Clearly, the assimilation of firearms and horses also helped to ensure the survival of the natives. Some other elements, however, were assimilated that did not serve these purposes. Examples include alcohol, silver articles, and Hispanic clothing. Such Hispanic objects may have been seen as increasing the quality of life of the natives, and in the case of the last two, they also served as trophies that highlighted the Indian dominance and victory over their enemies.

Ambivalent Attitudes: The British Role in the Caste War

It is highly unlikely that the Indian rebels of Yucatán would have been able to carry out and maintain their de facto secession with only machetes. Guns (including Enfield rifles), shot, and powder were a critical element of their success. The majority of munitions came from British Honduras, which treated the rebels and later the Cruzob as any other nation friendly to Her Majesty.[46] Such sales occurred despite British assurances in February 1848 to Yucatecan emissary Alonso Peon that the British authorities would not permit them.[47] Despite this pledge, in the same month, the British superintendent noted that he was unable "to prohibit the export of gunpowder from the Settlement."[48] Indeed, the British wasted no time as early as May 1848 in responding favorably to the requests of the new Indian masters of Bacalar to continue trade relations.[49] British powder went not only to the Cruzob but also to the Pacíficos. In 1880, after the death of Marcus Canul and somewhat improved relations with the Pacíficos, the lieutenant governor wrote the Icaiche leader Santiago Pech that "there is no objection to his purchasing guns, powder or caps in the Colony."[50]

For those involved in these affairs, despite the dangers, it was a lucrative trade, and in many cases it facilitated other commerce. For some, if they were to cease the arms trade with the Indians of Yucatán, they would also in all likelihood have lost their logging concessions in Cruzob territory and even be exposed to attack in British territory.[51] Even before the uprising, residents in British Honduras had logging contracts with landowners in the region of Bacalar, and they also imported considerable amounts of food from there.[52] As early as 1849, the British company Vaughn and Christie signed an agreement with rebel authorities to extract mahogany from the vicinity of Bacalar and began to provide munitions. In 1857 the British company Young and Toledo also signed a similar agreement.[53]

The population of British Honduras was small, and its white population was a fraction of it. The British government, first through the superintendent, and later, when it became a colony in 1867, through the lieutenant governor, was half-hearted at best in their efforts to halt the flow of arms, to the continuing outrage of Mexican and Yucatecan officials.[54] To some extent this reflected the cohesive nature of the white community there, and the reluctance of the government to interfere with the livelihood of the fellow elite. In their view it was better to turn a blind eye than alienate individuals who had not only economic but also political power.[55] As the superintendent noted in 1850, "In any other state of society than that of British Honduras these parties must have been prosecuted before the legal tribunals."[56] Unfortunately, they were turning a blind eye to their own participation in a genocide.

The war in Yucatán also led to the agricultural development of British Honduras. Many Hispanic refugees began to arrive as early as 1848, settling in Punta Consejo and elsewhere, and the British authorities assured them that they would "receive every protection" there.[57] By 1850, 4,000 of the 5,000 population between the Northern River and the Hondo in British Honduras were immigrants, and in 1855 the superintendent noted that many Hispanics were "following the occupation of agriculture . . . [and] the district will become the most valuable portion of the Settlement."[58] In 1857, the town of Corozal had a population of 4,500, most of whom were immigrants from Yucatán and 1,500 of whom had arrived that year alone.[59] The population of the district, which included Hispanics and Indians, was about 8,000 then, not including loggers, and were seen by the British authorities as quite industrious.[60] By 1861, 40 percent of the population of British Honduras, or 10,000 people, were born in Yucatán.[61] In Orange Walk, Corozal, and many other towns and hamlets, thousands of refugees of different races had settled, and through their efforts agriculture flourished in British Honduras. In addition, Cruzob occasionally came to British Honduras to earn wages during the sugar harvest.[62]

Apart from the economic benefits of good relations with the Cruzob, which in addition to logwood extraction from Mexican territory included the sale of food and manufactured goods to both Cruzob and Pacífico communities, there were other considerations. Chief among these was the risk of poor relations with the Cruzob and, for that matter, the Pacíficos.[63] As one British troop commander wrote in 1877, "It is most essential to our interests to preserve and improve our friendly relations with the Santa Cruz Indians."[64] This fear is salient in the documents, and frequent incursions by the Cruzob and Pacíficos to capture individuals, usually over debts and desertion, aroused fear throughout the colony.[65] In 1857 the superintendent wrote to the governor in Jamaica, expressing his fear that if Pacífico attacks, led by José María Tzuc, continued, they would result in a "demoralized effect if mahogany operations are abandoned in consequence of these raids and exactions. Alarm would spread throughout the Settlement, and in addition to valuable mahogany works 22 villages would be lost."[66] In 1858, after the Cruzob had retaken Bacalar and decided to slaughter their prisoners instead of ransoming them, panic spread through the community, and Corozal residents fled, fearing that the Cruzob would invade to capture the now deposed Hispanic commandant. A resident of Corozal, Edmund Burke, wrote, "I can convey . . . no idea of the terror and alarm which pervades the entire population. . . . I firmly believe that reckless of the consequences they would at the bidding of their oracle . . . make an incursion into Corozal for the purpose of rapine and murder."[67] The superintendent noted a couple of months later that relations with the Cruzob had declined considerably since 1848 and feared the consequences of a complete breakdown of these relations.[68] This may have reflected the rising strength and confidence of the Cruzob and their declining interest in peace initiatives. Although the British would increase the military presence in the northern region, there were two unattributed attempts to burn Corozal in August and September 1858. In addition, efforts to raise a militia had been a "perfect failure," as no one, including the many immigrant Hispanics, had been willing to join.[69]

Pacífico attacks on Quam Hill and San Pedro in 1866, Orange Walk in 1867, and Corozal in 1870 and 1872 led by Marcus Canul showed just how vulnerable British interests were, and a concerted offensive by the more numerous, more experienced, and better armed Cruzob could cause immeasurable damage.[70] Pacífico attacks had instilled "abject terror" among the inhabitants of Orange Walk.[71] On the other hand, a strong Cruzob were quite useful in limiting Pacífico attacks on British Honduras, as was demonstrated in 1870 when they assisted in repelling the Pacífico invasion of Orange Walk.[72] There was no shortage of reminders just how tenuous this situation was. When the Hispanics retook Bacalar in 1848, many Indian rebels used British Honduras as a base for continued attacks against the Mexicans.[73] Later, the reason that Lieutenants Twigge and Plumridge made their unfortunate journey to Chan Santa Cruz was because the Tatich, Venancio Puc, had ignored previous complaints that had threatened "most effective measures" concerning Cruzob cattle rustling incursions into, and sniping incidents along the border with, British Honduras.[74] British Honduras was also subject to numerous incursions and property seizures by Hispanic forces, usually in an effort to stem the flow of munitions to the rebels.[75]

Despite Britain's insistence on their "strict neutrality" in the matter, arms and munitions sales by entrepreneurs in British Honduras were crucial for their good relations with the Cruzob, and to let go could have terrible consequences.[76]

While the British clearly contributed to the bloodshed in Yucatán, they also had a leading role as mediators between the Cruzob and the Mexicans. As we have seen, toward the end of 1849, Jacinto Pat and Venancio Pec requested British mediation to end the conflict, something to which the British and Mexican governments agreed.[77] Meeting in late November with Superintendent Charles Fancourt in Ascención Bay, Chan and Venancio Pec insisted that they would never believe that the Mérida government would honor an agreement, and they demanded their own nation from Bacalar in the south to the Gulf of Mexico in the north. Barring that, they expressed their support for being placed under British rule, with Fancourt as their governor. Seeing that the Mexicans would never agree to either proposal, Fancourt encouraged the rebels to seek autonomy, instead of either proposal, or their third, which was mass emigration of the rebels to British Honduras. In the end the Yucatecan legislature rejected an arrangement that would have given the rebels autonomy, fearing that the region under rebel control would then be annexed by the British.[78]

In 1853, the British superintendent F. G. Woodhouse led the mediation that resulted in a peace treaty with José María Tzuc, signed in Belize in September of that year. Although Tzuc would not honor the agreement for long, most of the southern Indians would, thereby isolating the Cruzob and allowing the Hispanics to concentrate their resources upon them.[79] Such efforts continued, and in November 1867, Captain John Carmichael met with Indian leaders in Chan Santa Cruz. He was "very favorably impressed with the character and disposition of the three Principal Chiefs," who inquired as to whether they could bring their realm into the British Empire.[80] The Mexican government was ever-suspicious of British efforts in this regard, especially when they involved Cruzob proposals to be annexed by the British, such as that sought in 1849 by Chan and Puc and in 1867 by Bonifacio Novelo.[81] Even as late as 1884, the British had served as intermediaries between the Mexican government and the Cruzob under Crescencio Poot. An agreement that would have largely granted autonomy to the Cruzob was prepared for ratification. Poot rejected it, putatively as a result of a drunken insult by the lead Mexican negotiator, though perhaps also due to opposition by the Cruzob generals.[82]

Just as economic and security considerations led to trade and support for the Cruzob by the British, the same considerations led to a decline in relations between the two. Throughout the 1880s and 1890s, as British investments in Mexico continued to increase, in order to protect and expand them, the British increasingly lent a sympathetic ear to Mexican complaints concerning their support for the Cruzob. Although they still were worried about Cruzob attacks, in July 1893 the British signed the Spencer-Mariscal treaty, which at long last delineated the border between British Honduras and Mexico. Inherent in this agreement was a recognition of the legitimate existence of British Honduras, something long rejected by Mexico. As a result of the treaty, trade with the Cruzob finally ended when, in January 1898, the fortress-barge *Chetumal* dropped anchor on the Mexican side of the Hondo.[83] This was a decision that had clear costs in British Honduras. Of the 24,000 tons of wood exported from British Honduras in 1895, 16,000 of it came from Cruzob and hence Mexican territory.[84] In the end, just as British policy had led to the protraction of the Caste War, so did it lead to its end.

9 Conclusion

Although the rebellions examined in this work were expressions of different cultures and separated by time and distance, they share a great deal in common. All of them were millennially inspired, subaltern exterminatory movements that responded to a history of antagonistic interethnic relations, severe socioeconomic disparity, and pressures that threatened the well-being or very existence of the cultures and peoples who led or participated in them. All were led or sustained by leaders who either claimed or had imputed to them divine guidance and support in their effort to destroy the established order and create an idealized society on earth. The rebellions themselves were part of this process of creation and underscored the imminence of the new order, which did indeed come about in the cases of the Pueblo Revolt and the Caste War in Yucatán. All also followed an internal, if brutal, logic: the utopia that the rebels were seeking to create was largely irreconcilable with the continued presence of Hispanics and much of their culture. As such, millennial elements and goals became fused with exterminatory objectives and became the central tendency of the movements. Those who were targeted for death became so due to race and, in many cases, ethnic attributes such as language, dress, religion, and place of residence, which suggested racial orientation or affinity. Race also was closely tied to class in Latin America, and genocide and class conflict in many cases became superimposed.

Ethnicity also helps to explain why many rebel leaders were of mixed blood. Francisco "El Ollita," Nicolás Jonva, and Alonso Catiti were Coyotes, or of Indian and mestizo origins, while Túpac Amaru, Dionisio Zapata, and Leandro Santos were mestizos, and Crescencio Poot, Bonifacio Novelo, and Jacinto Pat were black. All, however, had Indian blood and fought for Indian independence. It is interesting to note that in Hispanic America, the only Indian rebellions that were successful in restoring native rule for a significant period were of an exterminatory nature.

In the years leading to the outbreak of the Pueblo Revolt, the natives had continually suffered from welfare value–based decremental deprivation, or a declining ability to satisfy relatively unchanging precolonial expectations, among the pueblos.[1] Not only had population levels plummeted by up to 80 percent, but surpluses eroded as a result of the mutually reinforcing effects of droughts, Hispanic exploitation, and attacks by nomadic Indians.[2] Facing terrestrial and cosmological collapse, and clearly in a zero sum game situation, the rebels took inordinate risks in an attempt to save what was left of their population and culture.[3] While welfare values collapsed for the Indians overall, the caciques found their power and interpersonal values constricted by the appointment of native governors by the Hispanics. More important, they had been unable to reverse what was a catastrophic situation.[4]

Even more affected than the caciques in terms of power and interpersonal value–based decremental deprivation were the medicine men, who were also unable to reverse the decline and were persecuted by the friars and often by Hispanic civil authorities. Their decline was even steeper than the caciques', and given their role as the nexus between the terrestrial and spiritual worlds, it had greater effect, both for them and for their communities.[5] It appears that the 1675 roundup and general assault on the medicine men under Governor Treviño threatened, in their eyes, their own survival as a class as well as that of those whom they represented.[6] Indian strength came not only from the skillful planning and organization that went into the rebellion but also from the history of polarizing divisions among the Hispanics as well as their few numbers.[7]

With the eradication of the Hispanics, their culture, and Catholicism, Popé promised a new era where the natives would once again be in harmony with their gods through the resurgence of native religious ceremonies and rituals, as well as other traditions. With this, he assured them, would come bountiful harvests in a society that would be protected by native deities from further intrusion by the Hispanics.[8] Indeed, Popé promised that as a result of the rebellion, they would be "regaled like the religious and Spaniards, and would gather a great many provisions and everything they needed."[9] Others were told that "by living under the laws of their ancients they would raise a great quantity of corn and beans, large bolls of cotton, pumpkins and watermelons . . . and that their houses would be filled, and they would have good health and plenty of rest; and . . . the people . . . [would be] overjoyed, living in pleasure."[10]

Although the creation of a new society was imminent with the outbreak of the rebellion, it had mixed results. Some of the new order was as many had hoped. Kivas were reconstructed, native rituals practiced openly, and the Indians were finally free of the friars and encomenderos who had oppressed them. But the new society came with Popé's heavy hand as he made numerous demands for tribute upon the pueblos while systematically seeking to eradicate almost all vestiges of Hispanic rule and culture.[11] The hardships of independence and Popé's leadership style served as a catalyst for the autonomous inclinations of the pueblos to come to the fore, and Popé's, and later Tupatú's, efforts to subject them to a centralized authority only exacerbated the process of division and disintegration. Instead of an earthly paradise, the Indians found oppression, division, attacks from nomadic Indians, famine, and death.[12]

Despite the outcome, the hope for an earthly native utopia was what inspired many rebels to participate in what was an exterminatory endeavor. In the case of the Pueblo Revolt, we have seen how the rebels killed almost every Hispanic they encountered, sparing only some Hispanic women who became rebel concubines. While the numbers of those killed, 401, are small compared with the other rebellions, so was the total Hispanic population there, which probably did not exceed 2,000.[13] Not only would this represent 20 percent of the nonnative population in the region, but it is important to recognize that the killing was indiscriminate, as noncombatant men, women, and children were slaughtered in the uprising. Furthermore, the events in the field demonstrate that the intent of many rebels was to kill all of the Hispanics, except some women. In Río Arriba almost all of those who did not make it to Santa Fe in time were killed, and in Río Abajo the same played out for almost all of those who were unable to link up with Lieutenant General Alonso García's party. As the survivors under Governor Otermín made their way south from Santa Fe toward the Río Grande, they were shadowed by rebels who sought to ambush and finish them off.[14]

The exterminatory nature of the rebellion is demonstrated in rebel actions and words, which were candid concerning the intent of the insurgents. Emblematic is the exhortation of a rebel emissary who, arriving in San Diego de Jemez on the night of August 10, 1680, called upon the inhabitants to "kill the Spaniards and friars who are here," so that "none of the Spaniards will remain alive" in the realm.[15] Similarly, another rebel would later report that Popé had commanded "all the pueblos to rebel and to swear that they would do so; that no religious or no Spanish person must remain."[16]

As in New Mexico, the Great Rebellion of Peru and Upper Peru was a millennially inspired exterminatory movement. For the elite, however, this uprising was a product of divergent deprivation. This consisted of welfare value–based progressive deprivation, or the partial reversal of socioeconomic betterment in a context of increasing expectations engendered by the previous improvement, combined with power-based decremental deprivation and interpersonal value–based aspirational deprivation.[17] For most Indians, welfare value–based progressive deprivation appears to have had a strong influence. Prior to the rebellion, the native population had been slowly increasing, as had been expressions of native identity and cultural affirmation.[18] But with the Bourbon reforms and the ensuing increase and effective collection of many taxes; the expansion of the reparto; Hispanic encroachment on Indian lands; increased religious fees; and greater exploitation in mines, haciendas, and obrajes, the gains of previous years were increasingly threatened and reversed as welfare values eroded. All of this translated into more rigorous exploitation of the Indians generally and underscored the zero sum game under way. Only slightly more insulated, much of the native elite found themselves displaced from hereditary curacazgos (the office of curaca) and their relative prosperity through commerce and muleteering increasingly eroded through taxation.[19] All of this was occurring against the backdrop of an indigenous cyclical concept of time and a vibrant prophetic tradition that foresaw the inevitable and divinely assisted return of native rule to the region.[20] While they submitted to the yoke of colonialism, to some degree they still measured their lives against the long-lost norm of Indian independence, kept alive by oral tradition and ceremonies.

For their part, the Creoles suffered from divergent deprivation caused by welfare value–based decremental deprivation and power and interpersonal value aspirational deprivation. Increased taxes as well as competition for Indian labor and surplus among the Hispanics only heightened a preexisting frustration of power value aspirations due to the secondary role in relation to the Hispanics to which they were relegated. The spread of Enlightenment ideas, the war of independence in the United States, and perceptions that Spain was vulnerable to British attack all served to convert many Creoles to new values and to exacerbate their discontent and delegitimize Spanish rule. While Creole welfare values were subject to decremental deprivation, power and interpersonal values reflected aspirational deprivation.[21]

Although the causes differed from the Pueblo Revolt, the Great Rebellion was also a millennial movement that sought the long-awaited and divinely assisted reestablishment of native rule in the region. The cyclical concept of time, in which the world was periodically destroyed and re-created in a pachacuti, inspired many Indians to believe that not only was the return of Indian dominion inevitable but it was also at hand. The violence of the uprising, nominally led by Túpac Amaru as Inkarrí, the Incaic "sleeping emperor," was, in Indian eyes, clear evidence of this.[22] As the rebellion spread, they increasingly believed that the Christian god could no longer protect the Hispanics, as they were killed in churches, cemeteries, and wherever else they were found, and that native deities were finally resurgent. Many of those rebels who died in the fight perished with the belief that they would in short order be resurrected to enjoy the new world they were creating.[23] As in New Mexico, the death of the Hispanics was essential for the creation of this new world, and while some were spared to serve their erstwhile subjects, the rebels killed most Hispanic men, women, and children they encountered.

In Yucatán, we have seen how the batabs were subject to the forces of divergent deprivation, in this case involving the decline of previously stable welfare and interpersonal values in the context of increasing power value aspirations. On the one hand, their welfare and interpersonal values were subject to decremental deprivation as abilities declined in the face of reduced commission revenues from obventions and the ensuing erosion of the distinction between elite and mass.[24] On the other hand, their power and interpersonal values also reflected aspirational deprivation, because expectations had continually increased as they had been involved in numerous conflicts dating from the independence wars, to Imán's 1839 revolt, to their 1843 support of Barbachano against Santa Anna, and to their involvement in the 1847 conflict between Mérida and Campeche.[25] Broken Hispanic promises left their desires unsatisfied, and their power, no longer latent, was applied for their own interests in the Caste War.

Like their leaders, the mass of Indians also suffered from divergent deprivation. Their involvement in these previous conflicts had also demonstrated their own potential to themselves, stimulating aspirational deprivation in terms of power and interpersonal value expectations. This was juxtaposed, however, against decremental deprivation in terms of abilities as a result of declining welfare values, as church fees and land encroachment increased while they continued to be oppressed by other civil taxes and forced labor demands.[26] These divergent forces, increasing power and interpersonal value aspirations in the face of actually declining welfare value abilities, not only spawned frustration but repeated cycles of it as the civil authorities routinely failed to keep their promises to the Indians regarding land distribution and reduced taxes and church dues.[27] Not only did involvement in the conflicts that preceded the Caste War increase their hopes of reward, but it also legitimated violence. In the case of the Huits, the forces of decremental deprivation appear to be decisive in inspiring their participation in the revolt. The expansion of the sugar industry and with it the sale of community lands and water sources, and the increasing population in frontier areas consistently eroded the Huits' ability to meet what had been long-standing and stable expectations.[28]

As in the Great Rebellion, the insurgents utilized prophecies and an apocalyptic, cyclical concept of time to inspire rebels with a belief that their undertaking was protected by divine forces and destined to triumph. The Chilam Balam of Maní and that of Chumayel prophesied the return of an Indian savior-king who would destroy the interlopers and initiate a new time cycle of native dominion.[29] We find the same elements at play as in the other rebellions: supernatural forces combined with rebel action would lead to the imminent creation of a new native order free from the oppressors and oppression of the past. The creation of Cruzob society resulted from a concerted and deliberate attempt to eliminate those who were seen as Hispanic. During the rebellion, the rebels did not just attack military targets and personnel, but consistently targeted Hispanic women and children. Later, perhaps seeking to increase agricultural production and population, as well as to highlight the inversion of the old order, Hispanics were often enslaved by the Cruzob.[30] As in New Mexico, the rebellion was successful, and Indian rule returned to the areas they controlled. Native customs were now practiced openly, although Chan Santa Cruz and the cult of the speaking cross reflected both native and Hispanic characteristics resulting from centuries of Hispanic dominance.

Central for the success of these rebellions was charismatic leadership. While Popé in New Mexico and Túpac Amaru and Túpac Catari in Peru and Upper Peru all claimed divine protection, charisma was institutionalized in Yucatán with the cult of the speaking cross. Popé claimed to communicate with and receive divine instructions from the spirits Caudi, Tilini, and Theume.[31] While Tupatú and others may have made similar claims, they have not been found in the documents studied here. As we have seen, Popé's abuses of authority in conjunction with continuing famine and raids by nomadic Indians prevented him from delivering on his promises and led to his overthrow. In Peru and Upper Peru, Túpac Amaru and Túpac Catari both capitalized on the belief in the rising of huacas to establish a new realm. Túpac Catari also claimed direct, divine contact with and revelation from both native and Christian gods, and he claimed the ability to control the elements, as he sought to maintain a monopoly of divine power. Tomás Catari does not appear to have made claims of divine power, although his repeated escapes from captivity led his followers to imbue him with special powers which led to the widespread belief that he had been resurrected.[32] In Yucatán, leaders such as Chi and Pat successfully mobilized thousands of supporters, although the degree to which these leaders made promises of divine protection is unclear. Charisma did become institutionalized, however, with the cult of the cross, which communicated the divine will, inspired the natives, and directed the affairs of the rebel society for a half-century.

Charismatic leadership, and the shared hopes that insurgents projected upon them, could dampen, but not eliminate, divisions among the rebels. Insurgent orders, whether in the planning or operational phases, were generally issued under pain of death, and many natives were reluctant rebels who were forced to participate in the rebellion. A degree of coercion within the ranks of the perpetrators is found in almost all genocidal movements and may be an intrinsic element of them.[33] In New Mexico, Popé's promises led to expectations among the rebels that he could not fulfill. Instead of bountiful harvests, there was famine. Instead of peace, there were Apache and Yuta attacks and Hispanic incursions. His demands for tribute and emulation of the ways of the Hispanics only gave added impetus to the resurgence of the autonomous ways historically embraced by the pueblos. In Peru and Upper Peru, the conservativism of Túpac Amaru, who sought a Catholic multiethnic society, and that of Tomás Catari, who was more partial to reform than revolution, reflected the gulf between them and many of their adherents who had more extreme and exterminatory aims. Túpac Catari was much closer to his followers, both in origins and objectives, than the two leaders from which he forged his nom de guerre.[34] The Great Rebellion also brought to the surface divisions between Indians over the spoils of war. Further evidence of division is shown by the extensive use of coercion and disinformation in both New Mexico and Peru as a means to swell the rebel ranks and promote unity.[35]

In Yucatán, there were also gaps between the rebel leaders and between them and their followers. While Chi was focused on extermination, Pat sought political gain, and in the end Pat had difficulty controlling his troops and was among the first to die in the internecine struggles that would come to characterize the Cruzob military leadership.[36] There were divisions not only among the military but between them and the religious authorities. The issue of negotiating with the Hispanics also became a major point of division among the Cruzob. It also appears that there were divisions on the basis of class, with many Indians resentful of being made to work without pay for the Cruzob commanders.[37] In Peru, Upper Peru, and Yucatán, leadership was often clan-based, and in all cases we have seen how the natives were further divided between those who fought, willingly or not, for the Hispanics and those who fought for the rebels.

We have seen how, despite their own divisions, the rebels were strengthened in a relative manner by schisms among their enemies. In New Mexico, discord was endemic among the Hispanic civil and religious leaders since the early years of colonization, and civil authorities also contended with internal divisions. Although this was somewhat reduced after the rebellion, it nevertheless remained, as people refused to obey the orders of governors and bickered over whether or not to conduct an entrada and how to conduct it.[38] In Peru and Upper Peru, the Bourbon reforms created divisions among the Hispanics over how they could extract surplus from the natives, and once the rebellion erupted, the cohesion and discipline among the Hispanic forces was abysmal.[39] The depth and intensity of the divisions among the Hispanics in Yucatán resembled that of the Hispanics in New Mexico, although religious authority played less of a part. Civil strife, and involving the natives in it, opened the door to the insurgency by demonstrating Hispanic weakness and allowing the Indians to realize their long-latent power. Once the rebellion exploded, Hispanic morale was nonexistent, at least until the counterattack in June 1848, and even after that mutiny, desertion, and hopelessness continued to plague the Hispanic troops.[40]

In addition to the sanguinary events of the uprisings and the statements of many rebels, the rebel use of symbolic language corroborates the exterminatory nature of these insurgencies. Often this symbolic expression took the form of humiliation, inversion, and superimposition. Victims were frequently humiliated before or after their death, as the rebels in all of the uprisings mutilated or castrated them or danced over their corpses.[41] In Jemez during the Pueblo Revolt, the rebels captured Friar Jesus Morador and stripped and bound him before parading him around the pueblo on a pig while the rebels beat him.[42] In Yura and Anasayas, Upper Peru, rebels under Ramón Paca humiliated priests by stripping them, and in Pintatora the lieutenant priest was abused and mockingly forced to wear a crown of thorns.[43] During the Caste War, in Ticul in May 1848, the rebels ridiculed their enemies by dressing in the uniforms of dead soldiers or as women and dancing in front of Hispanic lines.[44] Castration, which was a widespread practice among the insurgents during the Caste War, not only expressed power over another but also had clear implications concerning the continuance of a race.[45]

In each of the rebellions, inversion highlighted the rebel goal of reordering their world. Hispanic women were kept as concubines by rebels in all of the cases studied here, and in late 1693, as Vargas prepared to retake Santa Fe, the Indians who occupied the town promised that they would "fight until all of the Spaniards die" and that "not one will escape us. The friars will for a short time be our servants, we will make them carry firewood and bring it from the woods, and after they have served us we will kill all of them just like when we threw out the Spaniards the other time" in 1680.[46] In the Great Rebellion, Hispanic captives were forced to wear Indian clothing, to chew coca, and to serve the rebels.[47] The same practice played out in the Caste War, as Hispanic captives were enslaved as field hands, servants, and concubines for the Cruzob.[48]

Superimposition also was used to layer symbolism. For example, during the Pueblo Revolt in Santo Domingo, three friars were killed in the church and left at the altar, symbolizing the death of Christian power and superimposing the blood of friars where that of Christ had been ritually offered.[49] In the Great Rebellion, by executing people at, or bringing corpses to, the rollo, the death of Hispanics and the loss of their power were superimposed.[50] Overall, symbolic language both demonstrates that the rebels in these uprisings were articulate and sheds light on their objectives. Removing clappers from bells, casting excrement on religious articles, beheading people so they can never be resurrected, and castrating and mutilating victims demonstrate that these were not simply reformist efforts gone awry but components of a concerted effort to eliminate a people and their culture.

As with most nativistic movements, these rebellions possessed a degree of antinomy, as many rebels sought to retain some of the cultural elements and even people who were otherwise being extirpated or exterminated. Whatever was retained, such as weapons and horses, tended to enhance the ability of the natives to survive and continue as a people and culture. This reflects a desire not to preserve the old culture but to ensure the continuity and comfort of that of the rebels. Cultural artifacts, and the formerly dominant people, were also retained or spared as a means of underscoring the inversion of the preexisting order and the new power of the rebels. Sometimes inversion and enhanced possibilities of native survival went hand in hand, as we have seen in the case of the Caste War of Yucatán where hundreds of Hispanics were kept as prisoners to work as slaves for the Cruzob, while others had much greater liberty and fought on behalf of the Indians in their own military company.[51] Generally, however, such practices were the exception to the rule, as in all of the rebellions those Hispanics who were killed greatly outnumbered those who were spared. Assimilation was also used to highlight native power, as we saw when Popé took up residence in the governor's house in Santa Fe and used his coach for transport.[52] Similarly, the clothing of Hispanic enemies was occasionally used by the rebels in essence as trophies.[53] Assimilation could be used to augment the lifestyle of the rebels, as alcohol, silver, and household items were often taken as loot by the insurgents. Catholicism is indicative of the degree to which the natives had become acculturated to Hispanic ways. While in the Pueblo Revolt it was largely extirpated, in the Great Rebellion the insurgents sought its reformulation to suit and complement native needs, and in Yucatán, Cruzob society realized such a syncretic reformulation and built their society around it.

The fact that not every Hispanic was killed in these rebellions, that rebels relied on deceit and coercion to build their forces, and that to varying degrees elements of the cultures they sought to destroy were assimilated into that of the insurgents does not detract from the fundamentally exterminatory nature of these insurgencies. Few genocides are entirely successful, almost all rely on coercion to some degree, and it is not at all unusual for nativistic movements to retain elements of the culture which they are otherwise trying to eradicate.[54] All of these movements sought the practical elimination of a people, culture, language, and, to varying degrees, belief system. As genocidal movements, they urge a reconsideration of conventional views of the term. While two rebellions did achieve self-rule and create a government, this success came only after the genocide. As a result, the genocides were not initially committed by a state, and while they reflected concerted and often methodical effort, they were not done in a bureaucratic manner. In addition, the rebels were generally not as well armed as their adversaries, and they certainly did not have a "preponderant access to power."[55] Finally, despite varying degrees of success in the New Mexican and Yucatecan cases, these uprisings offer rare examples of cases where the victim groups were ultimately the victors. In the end, we must recognize that these are examples of retributive genocide, which erupted in response to the genocide of conquest and the persistent Hispanic policy of ethnocide against the native peoples. While nothing can justify the murder of innocents, genocide can beget genocide.

Appendix 1
Chronology of the Pueblo Revolt

1538	Alvar Nuñez Cabeza de Vaca arrives in Mexico with news of the Pueblos of New Mexico.
1539	Friar Marcos de Niza leads an expedition into the Pueblo region.
1540–42	Francisco Vázquez de Coronado leads an expedition into the Pueblo region.
1598	Juan Oñate leads an entrada into the region of New Mexico.
1610	Santa Fe is founded.
1616	Office of the custodian is introduced in New Mexico.
1618–25	Governor Eulate allows Indians to practice native religious ceremonies.
1626	The Inquisition begins in New Mexico.
1643	Assessment of Indian tribute changes from a household to individual basis, and taxes are increased.
1660	Governor López increases tolerance of native rituals.
1661	Spaniards increasingly attempt to end native rituals.
1666–69	The Pueblo region is ravaged by drought and famine.
1671	Increasing nomadic Indian raids of pueblos.
1675	Governor Treviño orders arrest of forty-seven Indian medicine men, including Popé.
Aug. 10, 1680	Pueblo revolt begins.
Aug. 21, 1680	Hispanics abandon Santa Fe.
Sept. 29, 1680	Hispanics conduct muster at La Salineta.
Nov. 7, 1681–Feb. 11, 1682	Otermín leads entrada into Pueblo region.
1691	Governor Vargas arrives in El Paso region.
Aug.–Dec. 1692	Vargas leads his first entrada into the Pueblo region.
Oct. 1693	Vargas leads Hispanics to resettle the Pueblo region.
Dec. 30, 1693	Vargas retakes Santa Fe.
June 4, 1696	Second pueblo revolt begins, led by Tiwas, Tewas, Tanos, and Keres Indians.
Nov. 1696	Second Pueblo revolt is suppressed.
July 1697	Governor Pedro Rodríguez de Cubero arrives in Santa Fe, and Vargas is soon jailed.
July 1700	Vargas journeys to Mexico City to clear his name.
Aug. 1703	Vargas arrives in New Mexico to serve second term as governor.
Apr. 1704	Vargas dies in Bernalillo.

Appendix 2
Chronology of the Great Rebellion

1777	Túpac Amaru goes to Lima in an unsuccessful attempt to reduce repartimiento and mita burdens for Indians in Tinta and neighboring provinces in Peru.
1778	Tomás Catari journeys to Buenos Aires to petition the viceroy for reduced repartimiento burdens for the Indians of Macha. He also requests that he be confirmed as curaca of Macha by right of heredity.
1779	Tomás Catari returns to Macha and claims to have been confirmed as curaca by royal decree. After he orders a reduction of tribute levels, he is arrested and jailed in Chayanta, Potosí, and La Plata.
Aug. 26, 1780	Supporters of Tomás Catari capture Corregidor Joaquín Alós. In exchange for his freedom, Catari is released from jail and legally confirmed as curaca of Macha.
Aug.–Dec. 1780	Tomás Catari again declares reduction of tribute. His supporters capture and kill curacas in Chayanta and Yamparaez provinces and abolish the repartimiento, mita, and all taxes.
Sept. 10, 1780	Head and heart of curaca Florencio Lupa appear on a cross outside of La Plata, inspiring great fear of the Indian uprising in the city.
Nov. 4, 1780	Túpac Amaru captures Corregidor Arriaga near Tinta.
Nov. 10, 1780	Túpac Amaru executes Arriaga.
Nov. 18, 1780	Túpac Amaru and supporters defeat loyalists at Sangarará, and 576 royalists perish. Túpac Amaru and all supporters are excommunicated. Death of Creoles in the battle instills fear of rebellion in this group, causing them to withhold their support.
Dec. 28, 1780–Jan. 10, 1781	Túpac Amaru leads unsuccessful siege of Cuzco.
Jan. 8, 1781	Tomás Catari is killed at Chataquila while in transit to La Plata as a prisoner. Catarista leadership passes to his cousins Dámaso and Nicolás Catari. In Challapata, Indians kill their corregidor, Manuel de Bodega.
Jan. 25, 1781	Indians in Carangas kill Corregidor Mateo Ibañez Arce.
Feb. 10, 1781	Creoles lead rebellion in Oruro.
Feb. 12, 1781	Dámaso Catari and Ramón Paca attack Yura.
Feb. 13–17, 1781	Catarista siege of La Plata from near La Punilla.
Feb. 19–25, 1781	Rebels overrun towns of Tinquipaya, Colcha, Palca, Ayopaia, Arque, and Tapacari.

Feb. 27, 1781	Rebels execute Corregidor Francisco de Revilla in Lipes.
Feb. 28, 1781	Indians take town of Tarata.
March 6, 1781	Luís Laso de la Vega leads uprising in Tupiza and surrounding area.
March 9, 1781	Rebels take town of San Pedro de Buenavista.
March 14, 1781	Túpac Catari begins the siege of La Paz.
Apr. 1, 1781	Nicolás Catari is brought to La Plata as a prisoner.
Apr. 5, 1781	Túpac Amaru is captured near Tinta.
Apr. 27, 1781	Dámaso Catari is executed in La Plata.
May 7, 1781	Nicolás Catari and Simón Castillo are executed in La Plata.
May 18, 1781	Túpac Amaru is executed, along with his wife, Micaela Bastidas, and many family members in Cuzco.
June 30, 1781	Ignacio Flores leads forces, briefly lifting the siege of La Paz.
July 5, 1781	Andrés Túpac Amaru takes Sorata.
Aug. 5, 1781	Túpac Catari resumes the siege of La Paz.
Aug.–Sept. 1781	Andrés Túpac Amaru and Amarista forces join Cataris in the siege of La Paz.
Sept.–Oct. 1781	Miguel Bastidas Túpac Amaru replaces Andrés Túpac Amaru to lead the Amaristas in the La Paz siege.
Oct. 17, 1781	Siege of La Paz is definitively broken by forces under José de Reseguín.
Nov. 13, 1781	Túpac Catari is executed.
Jan. 27, 1782	Amaristas peace accord is signed at Sicuani, largely ending the uprising.

Appendix 3
Chronology of the Caste War of Yucatán

Jan. 1847	Indians attack Valladolid.
July 1847	Fears of race war spread throughout Yucatán.
July 26, 1847	Manuel Antonio Ay is executed.
July 30, 1847	Rebels led by Cecelio Chi attack Tepich and begin the Caste War.
Dec. 1847	Rebels take Ichmul.
Feb. 1848	Peto and Yaxcaba fall to the rebels.
March 1848	Valladolid and Sotuta fall to the rebels; Barbachano is named governor.
Apr. 1848	Pat agrees to a peace treaty, but it is soon rejected by other rebel leaders.
May 1848	Ticul, Izamal, and Bacalar to the south are taken by the insurgents.
June 1848	Planting season begins, many Indians return to tend their fields, and the Hispanic counteroffensive gets under way.
July–Dec. 1848	Hispanics retake Izamal, Tekax, Valladolid, Ichmul, and Tihosuco.
Dec. 1848	Cecelio Chi is assassinated by his secretary.
May 1849	Hispanics retake Bacalar.
Sept. 1849	Jacinto Pat is assassinated.
1850	Chan Santa Cruz and the cult of the speaking cross emerge.
Jan. 1851	Chan Santa Cruz continues to grow; rebels attack Kampocolche.
March 1851	Hispanics attack Chan Santa Cruz.
Aug. 1851	Hispanics conclude treaty with Chichenja insurgents, leading to their being known as the Pacíficos del Sur.
Feb. 1852	Hispanics attack Chan Santa Cruz.
May 1852	Hispanics attack Chan Santa Cruz.
Dec. 1852	Death of José María Barrera.
Apr. 1854	Hispanics attack Chan Santa Cruz.
May 1854	Hispanics attack Chan Santa Cruz.
Nov. 1854	Hispanics attack Chan Santa Cruz.
Sept. 1857	Cruzob kill almost all of the population of Tekax.
Feb. 1858	Cruzob retake Bacalar.
Jan. 1860	Hispanics attack and are routed from Chan Santa Cruz.

Sept. 1861	Cruzob attack and capture population of Tunkás.
Dec. 1863	Venancio Puc is killed in Cruzob coup.
1865, 1867, 1870, 1871	Marcus Canul leads attacks on British Honduras.
1870	Death of Bonifacio Novelo.
1872	Canul is killed in raid in British Honduras.
1886	Crescencio Poot dies in coup that brings Aniceto Dzul to power.
July 1893	Spencer-Mariscal treaty is signed, delineating border between Mexico and British Honduras and presaging a decline in trade between the Cruzob and British Honduras.
1897	Armed barge *Chetumal* closes Cruzob supply route on the Río Hondo.
1901	General Bravo occupies Chan Santa Cruz, and Cruzob territory is made into the state of Quintana Roo.

Glossary

alabado: Choral praising of the Sacrament.

alcabala: A sales tax on textiles and foodstuffs.

alcalde or alcalde mayor: A mayor, and leader of a city council, who also occasionally served as a judge.

audiencia: A judicial court with executive and administrative powers.

auto: A judicial order.

Barbachanista: A partisan of Yucatecan Governor Miguel Barbachano.

batab: An Indian village leader in Yucatán.

cabildo abierto: A town meeting that would often include the adult Spanish and Creole population.

cacique: A village chief, such as a curaca or batab.

casas reales: Governor's compound in Santa Fe.

chapetón: A denigratory term for a Spaniard.

chicha: A fermented corn drink.

cholo: An Indian or person of Indian descent who has adopted Spanish cultural characteristics; a ladino.

corregidor: A royal governor possessing executive, judicial, and administrative duties.

Coyote: An individual of Indian and mestizo descent.

Cruzob: Followers of the speaking cross in Yucatán.

curaca: A chief of an Indian village or area.

curacazgo: The office of curaca.

curandero: A healer or medicine man.

custodian: A Franciscan who is in charge of a custody, or jurisdiction subject to a province.

diezmero: A tithe collector.

diezmo: A tithe.

encomendero: An individual who receives Indian labor in exchange for Christianizing Indians and being at the ready to defend the crown.

encomienda: A grant by the crown of Indian labor to a Spaniard or Creole.

entrada: A military expedition.

fagina: A levy of forced labor of four to six days per year.

fiscal: Generally a prosecutor, though in New Mexico also a native official who assists the priest in maintaining discipline.

forasteros: Indians who had left their place of origin.

guerrilla: A small, mobile, autonomous military unit.

hacendado: The owner of an agricultural estate.

hacienda: An agricultural estate.

huaca: A shrine to a native deity.

indios bravos: Cruzob Indians who followed the cult of the speaking cross in eastern Yucatán.

Inkarrí: A hero-savior who would defeat the Hispanics and preside over a utopian era of indigenous rule in the Andes.

jilaqata: An originario-elected Indian village council.

junta de guerra: A war council.

justicia mayor: A judge with judicial, administrative, and executive authority, often appointed in the absence of a corregidor.

kachina, cachina: A Native American ritual dance.

kiva: A subterranean chamber for use in native ceremonies and rituals.

ladino: An Indian who has adopted Spanish cultural characteristics.

macana: A club, usually a weapon made of wood.

maestro cantor: A lay assistant to a Catholic priest.

mestizo: An individual of mixed Spanish or Creole and Indian parentage.

mita: An obligatory labor system for Indians assessed on a community-wide basis.

mulatto: An individual of mixed Hispanic and African descent.

obraje: A textile-making center.

obvention: A religious tax.

oidor: A judge on an audiencia.

originarios: Indians who were native to their place of residence.

pachacuti: A cataclysmic, cyclical destruction of the established order.

Pacíficos del Sur: "Peaceful Ones of the South," also known as "Pacíficos," former rebels in southern Yucatán who recognized Mexican authority.

partido: A district or province.

primicía: An in-kind, agricultural religious tax.

quinto real: The royal fifth on metals extracted from the earth. The actual percentage varied, however, as a function of crown efforts to stimulate mining.

repartimiento: A system of forced Indian labor for the settlers.

reparto: The forced purchase of goods by Indians; also called repartimiento de mercancías.

rollo: A stone column topped by a cross that symbolized Spanish authority.

Tatich: The Great Father, spiritual and overall leader of the Cruzob, also known as Nohoch Tata.

virrey: A viceroy.

yanacona: A hacienda-bound laborer exempt from tribute.

Notes

Archivo General de Indias, Seville (AGI)
Archivo Nacional de Bolivia, Sucre (ANB)

1. Introduction

1. Leon Campbell, "Ideology and Factionalism during the Great Rebellion, 1780–1782," in Steve Stern, ed., *Resistance, Rebellion, and Consciousness in the Andean Peasant World, Eighteenth to Twentieth Centuries* (Madison: University of Wisconsin Press, 1987), 133; Steve Stern, "The Age of Andean Insurrection, 1742–1782: A Reappraisal," ibid., 35.

2. Vittorio Lanternari, *The Religions of the Oppressed* (New York: Knopf, 1963), 247; Michael Adas, *Prophets of Rebellion: Millenarian Protest Movements against the European Colonial Order* (Chapel Hill: University of North Carolina Press, 1979), 9; Ralph Linton, "Nativistic Movements," *American Anthropologist* 45, no. 2 (April–June 1943): 231.

3. Frances Levine, *Our Prayers Are in This Place: Pecos Pueblo Identity over the Centuries* (Albuquerque: University of New Mexico Press, 1999); Carroll Riley, *The Kachina and the Cross: Indians and Spaniards in the Early Southwest* (Salt Lake City: University of Utah Press, 1999); John Kessell, "Spaniards and Pueblos: From Crusading Intolerance to Pragmatic Accommodation," in D. H. Thomas, ed., *Columbian Consequences*, vol. 1 (Washington, D.C.: Smithsonian Institution Press, 1989); Daniel Reff, *Disease, Depopulation, and Culture Change in Northwestern New Spain, 1518–1764* (Salt Lake City: University of Utah Press, 1991). For a study of the differences between ethnic identity and its perception by others, see John Kessell, "Esteban Clemente, Precursor of the Pueblo Revolt," *El Palacio* 86, no. 4 (1980): 16–17; and on the difficulties occasionally encountered in determining ethnicity, see Angelico Chávez, "Pohe-yemo's Representative and the Pueblo Revolt of 1680," *New Mexico Historical Review* 42 (January 1967): 85–126.

4. Marcello Carmagnani, *El regreso de los dioses: el proceso de reconstitución de la identidad étnica en Oaxaca. Siglos xvii y xviii* (Mexico City: El Colegio de México and Fondo de Cultura Económica, 1988); Norma Angélica Castillo Palma, *Cholula: sociedea mestiza en ciudad India: Un análisis de las consecuencias demográficas, económicas y sociales del mestizaje en una ciudad novohispana, 1649–1796* (Mexico City: Universidad Autónoma Metropolitana, 2001). For works with a broader geographical view, see Patricio Silva and Kees Koonings, *Construcciones étnicas y dinámica sociocultural en América Latina* (Quito: Abya-Yala, 1999); Mercedes Durán-Cogan and Antonio Gómez-Moriana, eds., *National Identities and Sociopolitical Changes in Latin America* (New York: Routledge, 2001); Jorge Domínguez, ed., *Race and Ethnicity in Latin America* (New York: Garland, 1994); and Peter Wade, *Race and Ethnicity in Latin America* (Chicago: Pluto Press, 1997).

5. Thomas Abercrombie, *Pathways of Memory and Power: Ethnography and History*

among an Andean People (Madison: University of Wisconsin Press, 1998); Brooke Larson, *Colonialism and Agrarian Transformation in Bolivia: Cochabamba, 1550–1900* (Princeton: Princeton University Press, 1990); see also her "Rural Rhythms of Class Conflict in Eighteenth-Century Cochabamba," *Hispanic American Historical Review* 60, no. 3 (August 1980): 407–30. For a synthetic approach to the interplay between assimilation, evangelism, and identity in South Africa, see Jean and John Comaroff, *Of Revelation and Revolution, 1: Christianity, Colonialism and Consciousness in South Africa* (Edinburgh: Edinburgh University Press, 2000), and *Of Revelation and Revolution, 2: The Dialectics of Modernity on a South African Frontier* (Chicago: University of Chicago Press, 1997).

6. Lorenzo Huertas, *La religión en una comunidad andina* (Ayacucho, Peru: Universidad Nacional de San Cristóbal de Huamanga, 1981); Kenneth Mills, *Idolatry and Its Enemies: Colonial Andean Religion and Extirpation, 1640 to 1750* (Princeton: Princeton University Press, 1997).

7. Nicholas Griffiths, *The Cross and the Serpent: Religious Repression and Resurgence in Colonial Peru* (Norman: University of Oklahoma Press, 1996).

8. Serge Gruzinski, *Man-Gods in the Mexican Highlands: Indian Power and Colonial Society, 1520–1800* (Stanford: Stanford University Press, 1989); William B. Taylor, *Magistrates of the Sacred: Priests and Parishioners in Eighteenth-Century Mexico* (Stanford: Stanford University Press, 1996).

9. Charlotte Zimmerman, "The Cult of the Holy Cross: An Analysis on Cosmology and Catholicism in Quintana Roo," *History of Religions* 3, no. 1 (Summer 1963): 50–71; Alfonso Villa Rojas, *The Maya of East Central Quintana Roo*, Publication 559 (Washington, D.C.: Carnegie Institution of Washington, 1945); Victoria Bricker, *The Indian Christ, the Indian King: The Historical Substrate of Maya Myth and Ritual* (Austin: University of Texas Press, 1981).

10. Andrew Knault, *The Pueblo Revolt of 1680: Conquest and Resistance in Seventeenth-Century New Mexico* (Norman: University of Oklahoma Press, 1995); Riley, *Kachina and the Cross*; Franklin Folsom, *Indian Uprising on the Rio Grande: The Pueblo Revolt of 1680* (Albuquerque: University of New Mexico Press, 1973).

11. Marco Curatola, "Mito y milenarianismo en los andes: del Taqui Onqoy a Inkarrí," *Allpanchis* 10 (Cuzco, 1977): 65–92; Alberto Flores Galindo and Manuel Burga, "La utopía andina," *Allpanchis* 20 (Cuzco, 1982): 85–102; Rosalind Gow, "Inkarrí and Revolutionary Leadership in the Southern Andes," *Journal of Latin American Lore* 8, no. 2 (1982): 197–223; Mercedes López Baralt, *El Retorno del Inca Rey: Mito y profecía en el mundo andino* (La Paz: Hisbol, 1989). See also Franklin Pease, "El mito de Inkarrí y la visión de los vencidos," in Juan Ossio, ed., *Ideología mesiánica del mundo andino* (Lima: I. Prado Pastor, 1973).

12. Jan Szeminski, *La utopía Tupamarista* (Lima: Pontífica Universidad Católica del Perú, 1984); idem, "Why Kill the Spaniard? New Perspectives on Andean Insurrectionary Ideology in the Eighteenth Century," in Stern, *Resistance*; Steve Stern, "New Approaches to the Study of Peasant Rebellion and Consciousness: Implications of the Andean Experience," and "Age," both ibid.; Jorge Hidalgo Lehunde, "Amarus y Cataris: aspectos mesiánicos de la rebelión indígena de 1781 in Cusco, Chayanta, La Paz, y Arica," *Chungara* 10 (Arica, March 1983): 117–38; Ossio, *Ideología mesiánica del mundo andino*; Nicholas Robins, *El mesianismo y la*

semiótica indígena en el Alto Perú: La Gran Rebelión de 1780–1781 (La Paz: Hisbol, 1998).

13. María Eugenia Valle del Siles, *Historia de la rebelión de Túpac Katari, 1781–82* (La Paz: Editorial Don Bosco, 1990); María Eugenia Valle del Siles, "Túpac Katari y la rebelión de 1781: Radiografía de un caudillo aymara," *Anuario de Estudios Americanos* 34 (1977): 633–64. On the religious orientation of Túpac Amaru, see Severo Aparicio Quispe, *El clero y la rebelión de Túpac Amaru* (Cuzco: Imprenta Amauta, 2000).

14. David Cahill, "The Inca and Inca Symbolism in Popular Festive Culture: The Religious Processions of Seventeenth-Century Cuzco," in Peter Bradley and David Cahill, eds., *Hapsburg Peru: Images, Imagination, and Memory* (Liverpool: Liverpool University Press, 2000); see also his "The Virgin and the Inca: An Incaic Procession in the City of Cuzco in 1692," *Ethnohistory* 49, no. 3 (2002): 611–49, and "Popular Religion and Appropriation: The Example of Corpus Christi in Eighteenth-Century Cuzco," *Latin American Research Review* 31, no. 2 (Spring 1996): 67–111; also John Rowe, "El movimiento nacional Inca del siglo XVIII," *Revista Universitaria* 43, no. 107 (1954): 17–40.

15. Ward Stavig, *The World of Túpac Amaru* (Lincoln: University of Nebraska Press, 1999). See also Ann Wightman, *Indigenous Migration and Social Change: The Forasteros of Cuzco, 1570–1720* (Durham: Duke University Press, 1990).

16. Nelson Reed, *The Caste War of Yucatán* (Stanford: Stanford University Press, 1988); Don Dumond, *The Machete and the Cross: Campesino Rebellion in Yucatán* (Lincoln: University of Nebraska Press, 1997).

17. Ward Stavig, "Ambiguous Visions: Nature, Law, and Culture in Indigenous-Spanish Land Relations in Colonial Peru," *Hispanic American Historical Review* 80, no. 1 (2000): 77–111; see also Stavig's *World of Túpac Amaru*. Concerning subtle and individual, as opposed to collective and violent, approaches to subversion, see James Scott, *Weapons of the Weak: Everyday Forms of Peasant Resistance* (New Haven: Yale University Press, 1985).

18. Lillian Estelle Fisher, *The Last Inca Revolt: 1780–1783* (Norman: University of Oklahoma Press, 1966); Carlos Daniel Válcarcel, *La rebelión de Túpac Amaru* (Mexico City: Fondo de la Cultura Económica, 1970); Sergio Serulnikov, *Revindicaciones indígenas y legalidad colonial. La rebelión de Chayanta (1777–1781)* (Buenos Aires: Centro de Estudios de Estado y Sociedad, 1989), and *Tomás Catari y la producción de justicia* (Buenos Aires: Centro de Estudios de Estado y Sociedad, 1988); Claudio Andrade Padilla, *La Rebelión de Tomás Catari* (Sucre, Bolivia: IPTK/CIPRES, 1994).

19. Scarlett O'Phelan Godoy, *Rebellions and Revolts in Eighteenth-Century Peru and Upper Peru* (Cologne: Bohlau, 1985); Sinclair Thomson, *We Alone Will Rule: Native Andean Politics in the Age of Insurgency* (Madison: University of Wisconsin Press, 2002); Jürgen Golte, *Repartos y Rebeliones: Túpac Amaru y las contradicciones de la economía colonial* (Lima: Instituto de Estudios Peruanos, 1980); Stavig, *World of Túpac Amaru*. For a different view of the repartimiento as a means of credit used to enhance Indian production and autonomy, see Jeremy Baskes, *Indians, Merchants, and Markets: A Reinterpretation of the Repartimiento and Spanish-Indian Economic Relations in Colonial Oaxaca, 1750–1821* (Stanford:

Stanford University Press, 2000). On the interrelations between ethnicity and class in the Andean context, see Xavier Albó, "Etnicidad y clase en la gran rebelión Aymara/Quechua: Kataris, Amarus, y bases 1780–81," in Fernando Calderón and Jorge Dandler, eds., *Bolivia: la fuerza histórica del campesinado* (La Paz: Centro de Estudios de la Realidad Económica y Social, 1986).

20. Howard F. Cline, "The Sugar Episode in Yucatán, 1825–1850," *Inter-American Economic Affairs* 1, no. 4 (1948): 79–100; Reed, *Caste War*; Terry Rugeley, ed., *Yucatán's Maya Peasantry and the Origins of the Caste War* (Austin: University of Texas Press, 1996). See also Rugeley's "Rural Political Violence and the Origins of the Caste War," *Americas* 53, no. 4 (April 1997): 469–96. On the role of henequen, see Allen Wells and Gilbert Joseph, *Summer of Discontent, Seasons of Upheaval: Elite Politics and Rural Insurgency in Yucatán, 1876–1915* (Stanford: Stanford University Press, 1996).

21. Dumond, *Machete*.

22. William B. Taylor, *Drinking, Homicide, and Rebellion in Colonial Mexican Villages* (Stanford: Stanford University Press, 1979); Eric Van Young, *The Other Rebellion: Popular Violence, Ideology, and the Mexican Struggle for Independence, 1810–1821* (Stanford: Stanford University Press, 2001); Kevin Gosner, *Soldiers of the Virgin: The Moral Economy of a Colonial Maya Rebellion* (Tucson: University of Arizona Press, 1992).

23. Charles Walker, *Smoldering Ashes: Cuzco and the Creation of Republican Peru* (Durham: Duke University Press, 1999).

24. Young, *Other Rebellion*.

25. Gosner, *Soldiers of the Virgin*.

26. Paul Vanderwood, *The Power of God against the Guns of Government: Religious Upheaval in Mexico at the Turn of the Nineteenth Century* (Stanford: Stanford University Press, 1998).

27. Frank Chalk and Kurt Jonassohn, "The Conceptual Framework," in Chalk and Jonassohn, eds., *The History and Sociology of Genocide: Analyses and Case Studies* (New Haven: Yale University Press, 1990), 9.

28. "Representación del Dr. Manuel Reque cura acerca de los robos, saqueos y profanaciones del templos," La Paz, July 5, 1783, Archivo Nacional de Bolivia (hereafter ANB), SGI.1783.206, 5; "Carta del Cabildo de Cochabamba al Rey," Cochabamba, January 31, 1782, Archivo General de Indias (hereafter AGI), Charcas 595, 2.

29. "Carta del Cabildo de Cochabamba al Rey," 2; "Carta de Arequipa con fecha 2 de Maya de 1781 que refiere los estragos executados por los indios alzados en varios pueblos de las provincias de ambos virreyenatos," Arequipa, May 2, 1781, in Cárlos Daniel Válcarcel, *Colección Documental de la Independencia del Perú*, book 2 (Lima: Comisión Nacional del Sesquicentenario de la Independencia del Perú, 1971), 1:692.

30. D. T. Reff, "The 'Predicament of Culture' and the Spanish Missionary Accounts of the Tepehuan and Pueblo Revolts," *Ethnohistory* 42, no. 1 (Winter 1995): 69.

31. "Luis Granillo, Interrogation of Francisco Témprano," Santa Fe, June 13, 1696, in John L. Kessell, Rick Hendricks, and Meredith Dodge, eds., *Blood on the Boulders:*

The Journals of Don Diego de Vargas, New Mexico, 1694–97 (Albuquerque: University of New Mexico Press, 1998), 2:758 (hereafter *Blood*).

32. "Auto of Antonio de Otermín," Fray Cristóbal, September 13, 1680, in Charles Wilson Hackett, ed., *Revolt of the Pueblo Indians of New Mexico and Otermín's Attempted Reconquest, 1680–1682*, translations of original documents by Charmion Clair Shelby (Albuquerque: University of New Mexico Press, 1942), 8:114 (hereafter *Revolt*); "Auto of Antonio de Otermín, Santa Fe, August 21, 1680," ibid., 8:17; Hackett, "Revolt of the Pueblo Indians of New Mexico in 1680," *Texas State Historical Association Quarterly* 15 (October 1911): 142–43; Hackett, *Revolt*, 8:xciv.

33. "Confesión de Gregoria Apasa" and "Confesión de Ascencia Flores," Santuario de Nuestra Señora de las Peñas, October 18, 1781, AGI, Charcas 595, 2 and 12.

2. Millennialism, Nativism, and Genocide

1. Norman Cohn, *The Pursuit of the Millennium* (New York: Oxford University Press, 1957), 15.

2. Mark Hagopian, *The Phenomenon of Revolution* (New York: Dodd, Mead, 1974), 25.

3. Cohn, *Pursuit of the Millennium*, 35.

4. Hagopian, *Phenomenon of Revolution*, 25–28.

5. Linton, "Nativistic Movements," 230.

6. Ibid., 231–33.

7. Hagopian, *Phenomenon of Revolution*, 22–23.

8. Lanternari, *Religions of the Oppressed*, 253.

9. Ibid., 131.

10. Ibid., 240.

11. Ibid., 28, 133, 243–44.

12. Ibid., 245.

13. Adas, *Prophets of Rebellion*, 175–78; Fisher, *Last Inca Revolt*, 384–87; Campbell, "Ideology," 118.

14. Michael Barkun, *Disaster and the Millennium* (New Haven: Yale University Press, 1974), 166–67; Cohn, *Pursuit of the Millennium*, 109; Campbell, "Ideology," 117; Alberto Flores Galindo, "In Search of an Inca," in Stern, *Resistance*, 201; López Baralt, *El Retorno del Inca Rey*, 40; Nathan Wachtel, *The Vision of the Vanquished* (New York: Barnes and Noble, 1977), 183. See also Adas, *Prophets of Rebellion*, 180–82.

15. Lanternari, *Religions of the Oppressed*, 252.

16. Adas, *Prophets of Rebellion*, 93.

17. Barkun, *Disaster and the Millennium*, 56.

18. Lanternari, *Religions of the Oppressed*, 247; Adas, *Prophets of Rebellion*, 9; Linton, "Nativistic Movements," 231; Anthony Wallace, "Mazeway Disintegration: The Individual's Perception of Socio-Cultural Disorganization," *Human Organization* 16, no. 2 (Summer 1957): 23–24; Anthony Wallace, "Revitalization Movements," *American Anthropologist* 58, no. 1 (February 1956): 270, 273.

19. Hagopian, *Phenomenon of Revolution,* 280.

20. Ibid., 32, 90; Cohn, *Pursuit of the Millennium,* 32. See also Lanternari, *Religions of the Oppressed,* 240.

21. Gow, "Inkarrí and Revolutionary Leadership in the Southern Andes," 197; Szeminski, *La utopía Tupamarista,* 98; Campbell, "Ideology," 112.

22. Wallace, "Mazeway Disintegration," 23; F. P. Kilpatrick, "Problems of Perception in Extreme Situations," *Human Organization* 16, no. 2 (Summer 1957): 21; Barkun, *Disaster and the Millennium,* 106.

23. Len Oakes, *Prophetic Charisma: The Psychology of Revolutionary Religious Personalities* (Syracuse: Syracuse University Press, 1997), 128–29; Robert C. Tucker, "The Theory of Charismatic Leadership," *Daedalus* 97 (1968): 731, 735, 742–43, 745, 747; H. H. Gerth and C. Wright Mills, *From Max Weber: Essays in Sociology* (New York: Oxford University Press, 1946), 52, 245, 249–50, 295–96.

24. Oakes, *Prophetic Charisma,* 27, 28.

25. Eric Hoffer, *The True Believer: Thoughts on the Nature of Mass Movements* (New York: Harper and Row, 1951), 97–98, 16–17; Barkun, *Disaster and the Millennium,* 105; Ervin Staub, *The Roots of Evil: The Origins of Genocide and Other Group Violence* (New York: Cambridge University Press, 1989), 266.

26. Hoffer, *True Believer,* 16–17, 60.

27. Barkun, *Disaster and the Millennium,* 116.

28. Ibid., 116–17; see also Eric J. Hobsbawm, *Primitive Rebels: Studies in Archaic Forms of Social Movement in the Nineteenth and Twentieth Centuries* (Manchester: University of Manchester Press, 1965), 150–51.

29. Tucker, "The Theory of Charismatic Leadership," 742–43; Gerth and Mills, *From Max Weber,* 246, 296; Lanternari, *Religions of the Oppressed,* 242.

30. Cohn, *Pursuit of the Millennium,* 85–86, 88; Adas, *Prophets of Rebellion,* 112; Barkun, *Disaster and the Millennium,* 86.

31. Lanternari, *Religions of the Oppressed,* 240, 242; Oakes, *Prophetic Charisma,* 129.

32. Adas, *Prophets of Rebellion,* 117–19, 121; Oakes, *Prophetic Charisma,* 13.

33. Hobsbawm, *Primitive Rebels,* 58–59.

34. Oakes, *Prophetic Charisma,* 2.

35. Cohn, *Pursuit of the Millennium,* 15; Barkun, *Disaster and the Millennium,* 18–19.

36. Adas, *Prophets of Rebellion,* 173–78; Stern, "Age," 62–63; Campbell, "Ideology," 118.

37. Hoffer, *True Believer,* 86.

38. Adas, *Prophets of Rebellion,* 79. See also Hagopian, *Phenomenon of Revolution,* 24.

39. Lanternari, *Religions of the Oppressed,* 240.

40. Frank Chalk and Kurt Jonassohn, preface to *History and Sociology of Genocide,* xvii.

41. See, e.g., Irving Louis Horowitz, *Taking Lives: Genocide, State Power, and Mass Murder* (New Brunswick: Transaction Books, 1980); Leo Kuper, *Genocide: Its Political Use in the Twentieth Century* (New Haven: Yale University Press, 1981); Michael Freeman, "Genocide in World-Historical Perspective," Essex Papers in

Politics and Government (Essex: University of Essex, April 1984). For a thorough bibliography on genocide, see Israel Charny, ed., *Genocide: A Critical Bibliographical Review* (New York: Facts on File, 1988); and Chalk and Jonassohn, *History and Sociology of Genocide*, 430–61; concerning the prediction and avoidance of genocide, see part 5 of Israel Charny, *Toward the Understanding and Prevention of Genocide: Proceedings of the International Conference on the Holocaust and Genocide* (Boulder: Westview Press, 1988); Jeffery Gayner, "The Genocide Treaty," *Journal of Social and Political Studies* 2 (Winter 1977): 235–45; Barbara Harff, *Genocide and Human Rights: International Legal and Political Issues*, Monograph Series in World Affairs, Graduate School of International Studies (Denver: University of Denver, 1984); Leo Kuper, *The Prevention of Genocide* (New Haven: Yale University Press, 1985); F. H. Littell, "Essay: Early Warning," *Holocaust and Genocide Studies* 3 (1988): 483–90; and Nevitt Sanford, Craig Comstock, et al., *Sanctions for Evil* (San Francisco: Jossey Bass, 1973).

42. Rafael Lemkin, *Axis Rule in Occupied Europe* (Washington, D.C.: Carnegie Endowment for International Peace, 1944), xi, 79.

43. Chalk and Jonassohn, "The Conceptual Framework," 10.

44. Ibid., 11.

45. Barbara Harff and Ted Gurr, "Toward Empirical Theory of Genocides and Politicides: Identification and Measurement of Cases since 1945," *International Studies Quarterly* 32 (1988): 360.

46. Horowitz, *Taking Lives*, 17.

47. Vahakn Dadrian, "A Typology of Genocide," *International Review of Modern Sociology* 5 (Fall 1975): 201, 204.

48. Yehuda Bauer, "The Place of the Holocaust in Contemporary History," in Jonathan Frankel, ed., *Studies in Contemporary Jewry* (Bloomington: University of Indiana Press, 1984), 1:213.

49. Dadrian, "A Typology of Genocide," 203. See also Chalk and Jonassohn, "Carthage," in Chalk and Jonassohn, *History and Sociology of Genocide*, 75–76; idem, "The Christians in Japan," ibid., 130–41; J. Saunders, "The Mogul Conquests," ibid., 96–114.

50. Chalk and Jonassohn, "The Conceptual Framework," 23.

51. Ibid., 24.

52. Pieter Drost, *The Crime of State* (Leyden: A. W. Sythoff, 1959), 2:125.

53. Peter du Preez, *Genocide: The Psychology of Mass Murder* (London: Boyars/Bowerdean, 1994), 4.

54. Helen Fein, "Scenarios of Genocide: Models of Genocide and Critical Responses," in Charny, *Toward the Understanding and Prevention of Genocide*, 4.

55. Dadrian, "A Typology of Genocide," 201; Horowitz, *Taking Lives*, 17.

56. Chalk and Jonassohn, "The Conceptual Framework," 9; Israel Charny, "Toward a Generic Definition of Genocide," in George Andreopoulos, ed., *Genocide: Conceptual and Historical Dimensions* (Philadelphia: University of Pennsylvania Press, 1994), 85. On linguicide in the Ukraine and Canada, see J. B. Rudnyckyj, "Lin-

guicide: Concept and Definition," in Charny, *Toward the Understanding and Prevention of Genocide,* 218-20.

57. Dadrian, "A Typology of Genocide," 205-206.

58. Du Preez, *Genocide,* 48; Harff and Gurr, "Toward Empirical Theory of Genocides and Politicides," 363.

59. Leo Kuper, "Theoretical Issues Relating to Genocide," in Andreopoulos, *Genocide,* 65-66.

60. Chalk and Jonassohn, "The Conceptual Framework," 42.

61. Dadrian, "A Typology of Genocide," 201, 205-10; Roger Smith, "Human Destructiveness and Politics: The Twentieth Century as an Age of Genocide," in Isidor Walliman and Michael Dobkowski, eds., *Genocide and the Modern Age: Etiology and Case Studies of Mass Death* (Westport: Greenwood Press, 1987), 24-27.

62. Smith, "Human Destructiveness," 24-27; Harff and Gurr, "Toward Empirical Theory of Genocides and Politicides," 363.

63. Chalk and Jonassohn, "The Conceptual Framework," 29.

64. Smith, "Human Destructiveness," 24-27, 35, 39-40; Harff and Gurr, "Toward Empirical Theory of Genocides and Politicides," 363; Chalk and Jonassohn, "The Armenians in Turkey," in Chalk and Jonassohn, *History and Sociology of Genocide,* 249-50; Chalk and Jonassohn, "Indonesia," ibid., 379-81; Chalk and Jonassohn, "Cambodia," ibid., 402-404; Stanley Meisler, "Holocaust in Burundi," ibid., 384-85. See also du Preez, *Genocide,* 5-6; and Kuper, *Genocide: Its Political Use,* 11-18.

65. Harff and Gurr, "Toward Empirical Theory of Genocides and Politicides," 363-64; see also Kuper, *Genocide: Its Political Use,* 11-18.

66. Du Preez, *Genocide,* 1, 2, 14, 68-70, 77-78.

67. Kuper, *Prevention of Genocide,* 150.

68. Israel Charny, *How Can We Commit the Unthinkable?* (Boulder: Westview Press, 1982), 190.

69. Neil Kressel, *Mass Hate: The Global Rise of Genocide and Terror* (New York: Plenum Press, 1996), 10, 199; Charny, *How Can We Commit the Unthinkable?* 190; Staub, *Roots of Evil,* 5, 234.

70. Du Preez, *Genocide,* 81-83; Kressel, *Mass Hate,* 251-52; H. C. Kelman, "Violence without Moral Restraint: Reflections on the Dehumanization of Victims and Victimizers," *Journal of Social Issues* 29, no. 4 (1973): 44, 48, 50; see also F. H. Littell, "Essay: Early Warning," *Holocaust and Genocide Studies* 3 (1988): 483-90; Chalk and Jonassohn, "The Conceptual Framework," 28; Fein, "Scenarios of Genocide," 6.

71. Chalk and Jonassohn, "The Conceptual Framework," 28; Staub, *Roots of Evil,* 43; Israel Charny, *How Can We Commit the Unthinkable?* 195.

72. Charny, *How Can We Commit the Unthinkable?* 10, 115.

73. Ibid., 24-26.

74. Ibid., 168-69; Kressel, *Mass Hate,* 3, 171; Kelman, "Violence without Moral Restraint," 25; Israel Charny, "Genocide and Mass Destruction: A Missing Dimen-

sion in Psychopathology," in Charny, *Toward the Understanding and Prevention of Genocide*, 162–63; du Preez, *Genocide*, 90.

75. Staub, *Roots of Evil*, 28.

76. Kressel, *Mass Hate*, 59–60; Staub, *Roots of Evil*, 13, 15, 17, 23.

77. Chalk and Jonassohn, "The Conceptual Framework," 7, 27, 41.

78. Roberto Mario Salmón, *Indian Revolts in Northern New Spain: A Synthesis of Resistance (1680–1786)* (New York: University Press of America, 1991), 37.

79. Meisler, "Holocaust in Burundi," 384, 390; see also Roger Smith, "Fantasy, Purity, Destruction: Norman Cohn's Complex Witness to the Holocaust," in Alan Berger, ed., *Bearing Witness to the Holocaust, 1939–1989* (Lampeter, Wales: Edwin Mellen Press, 1991), 120–21.

80. Chalk and Jonassohn, "Cambodia," 402–406; Chalk and Jonassohn, "East Timor," in Chalk and Jonassohn, *History and Sociology of Genocide*, 409.

81. Charny, *How Can We Commit the Unthinkable?* 19–20.

82. Chalk and Jonassohn, "Indians of the Americas, 1492–1789," in Chalk and Jonassohn, *History and Sociology of Genocide*, 173–74.

3. Creation through Extermination

1. Marc Simmons, "History of Pueblo-Indian Relations to 1821," in Alfonso Ortíz, ed., *The Southwest*, vol. 9 of *Handbook of North American Indians* (Washington, D.C.: Smithsonian Institution, 1979), 178, 184; Knault, *Pueblo Revolt*, 65–66, 68–70, 155, 157, 160–61; D. E. Worcester, "The Beginnings of the Apache Menace of the Southwest," *New Mexico Historical Review* 16, no. 1 (1939): 5–6; Levine, *Our Prayers Are in This Place*, 21. For other narratives of the Pueblo Revolt, see Knault, *Pueblo Revolt*; Robert Silverberg, *The Pueblo Revolt* (New York: Weybright and Talley, 1970); and the introductory chapter in Ralph Emerson Twitchell's *Spanish Archives of New Mexico*, 2 vols. (Cedar Rapids: Torch Press, 1914).

2. France Scholes, "The Supply Service of the New Mexican Missions in the Seventeenth Century, Part 2," *New Mexico Historical Review* 5, no. 2 (April 1930): 193; Knault, *Pueblo Revolt*, 54–55. The Pueblo region that fell under Spanish dominion encompassed three linguistic groups, those of the Zuni, Keres, and Tanos, the last of which included the Tano, Piro, Tiwa, Tewa, and Jemez Indians. The Zuni were concentrated in Hawikuh, while the Keres were grouped in Acoma and also to the north of the confluence of the Rio Grande and Río Jemez in the towns of Cochití, Santo Domingo, San Felipe, Santa Ana, and Zía. Of the Tanos, the Piros resided in Sevilleta, Senecú, Socorro, and Alamillo, while the Tiwa pueblos included those of Taos, Picurís, Puaray, Sandía, Alameda, and Isleta. The Tewas inhabited San Ildefonso, Santa Clara, San Juan, Tesuque, Pojoaque, and Nambé. Tano pueblos also included Galisteo, San Cristóbal, and San Lázaro. The Jemez Indians lived predominantly in Pecos and San Diego de Jemez, although some pueblos comprised a mix of groups, such as San Marcos and La Ciénega, which had both Tanos and Keres residents. At the time of the 1680 uprising there were about 3,000 Picuris, 2,000 Tanos, 5,000 Jemez, 2,200 Tewa, and 2,000 Pecos. Gen-

erally each pueblo had about 200–300 inhabitants. Some, however, were considerably larger, such as Sandía, which had a population of 3,000, and Isleta, with about 2,000. See Hackett, "Revolt of the Pueblo Indians," 100, 110, 115, 120–21, 127; Hackett, *Revolt*, 8:cx; Charles Wilson Hackett, "The Retreat of the Spaniards from New Mexico in 1680, Beginnings of El Paso II," *Southwestern Historical Quarterly* 16, no. 3 (January 1913): 268.

3. "Report to the Viceroy by the Cabildo of Santa Fe, New Mexico," Santa Fe, February 21, 1639, in Charles Wilson Hackett, ed., *Historical Documents Relating to New Mexico, Nueva Vizcaya, and Approaches Thereto, to 1773*, collected by Adolph and Fanny Bandelier (Washington, D.C.: Carnegie Institution, 1937), 4:67, 72; "Opinion of the Cabildo of the Villa of Santa Fe in New Mexico in Regard to Affairs of the Religious," Santa Fe, February 14, 1639, ibid., 4:62; Knault, *Pueblo Revolt*, 77–78; Hubert H. Bancroft, *History of Arizona and New Mexico, 1530–1888*, vol. 17 of *The Works of Hubert Howe Bancroft* (San Francisco: History Company, 1889), 174; France Scholes, "Church and State in New Mexico, 1610–1650," *New Mexico Historical Review* 11, no. 1 (January 1936): 24. See also articles of the same title in issues 2, 3, and 4 of volume 11 and issue 1 of volume 12 of the *New Mexico Historical Review*; France Scholes, "Civil Government and Society in New Mexico in the Seventeenth Century," *New Mexico Historical Review* 10, no. 2 (April 1935): 97.

4. Scholes, "Church and State," 103–104.

5. "Report to the Viceroy by the Cabildo of Santa Fe, New Mexico," 4:71; Scholes, "Church and State," 24; Knault, *Pueblo Revolt*, 88–89; Salmón, *Indian Revolts in Northern New Spain*, 35.

6. Hackett, *Historical Documents*, 4:15; Knault, *Pueblo Revolt*, 90; Manuel J. Espinosa, *The Pueblo Indian Revolt of 1696 and the Franciscan Missions in New Mexico: Letters of the Missionaries and Related Documents* (Norman: University of Oklahoma Press, 1988), 14–15; France Scholes, "Problems in the Early Ecclesiastical History of New Mexico," *New Mexico Historical Review* 7, no. 1 (January 1932): 42; France Scholes, "The First Decade of the Inquisition in New Mexico," *New Mexico Historical Review* 10, no. 3 (July 1935): 198; John L. Kessell, Rick Hendricks, and Meredith Dodge, eds., *By Force of Arms: The Journals of Don Diego de Vargas, 1691–1693* (Albuquerque: University of New Mexico Press, 1992), 7–8; Scholes, "Church and State," 24.

7. "Hearing of February 21, 1661," Mexico City, in Hackett, *Historical Documents*, 4:134; "Deposition of Nicolás de Aguilar," n.p., May 8, 1663, in Hackett, *Historical Documents*, 4:169–70; France Scholes, "Troublous Times in New Mexico, 1659–1670," *Historical Society of New Mexico Publications in History* 11 (January 1942): 74; Riley, *Kachina and the Cross*, 21; Silverberg, *Pueblo Revolt*, 72; Alvin M. Josephy, *The Patriot Chiefs: A Chronicle of American Indian Leadership* (New York: Viking Press, 1961), 56.

8. "Report to the Viceroy by the Cabildo of Santa Fe, New Mexico," 4:71; Scholes, "Church and State," 24; Knault, *Pueblo Revolt*, 88–89; Salmón, *Indian Revolts*, 35.

9. Knault, *Pueblo Revolt*, 73–75.

10. Salmón, *Indian Revolts*, 37.

11. "Statement of Pedro García," El Alamillo, September 6, 1680, in Charles Wilson Hackett, *Revolt*, 8:62.

12. Espinosa, *Pueblo Indian Revolt*, 10.

13. "Petition of Father Juan de Prada," Convent of San Francisco, Mexico, September 26, 1638, in Hackett, *Historical Documents*, 4:106; Hackett, *Historical Documents*, 4:12; Knault, *Pueblo Revolt*, 58–60, 62–64; Scholes, "Troublous Times in New Mexico," 131.

14. Simmons, "History of Pueblo-Indian Relations to 1821," 182–83.

15. Knault, *Pueblo Revolt*, 69–70. For more on the relations between the Athapaskans and the Spaniards, see Jack D. Forbes, *Apache, Navaho, and Spaniard* (Norman: University of Oklahoma Press, 1994).

16. Knault, *Pueblo Revolt*, 65–66, 68–70, 153–54, 157, 160–61; Worcester, "The Beginnings of the Apache Menace of the Southwest," 5–6.

17. Simmons, "History of Pueblo-Indian Relations to 1821," 184; Levine, *Our Prayers Are in This Place*, 21; Knault, *Pueblo Revolt*, 155, 157.

18. "Carta del Padre Fray Silvestre Velez de Escalante," Santa Fe, April 2, 1778, in *Documentos para servir a la historia del Nuevo Mexico, 1538–1778* (Madrid: Ediciones José Porrua Turanzas, 1962), 307 (hereafter *Documentos*); Bancroft, *Arizona and New Mexico*, 17, 170; Knault, *Pueblo Revolt*, 161, 163.

19. Bancroft, *Arizona and New Mexico*, 165, 174; Knault, *Pueblo Revolt*, 163–64.

20. "Declaration of Sargento Mayor Luís de Quintana," Río del Norte, December 22, 1681, in Hackett, *Revolt*, 9:289–90; Knault, *Pueblo Revolt*, 164; Hackett, "Revolt of the Pueblo Indians," 99.

21. "Declaration of Diego López Sambrano," Hacienda of Luis de Carbajal, December 22, 1681, in Hackett, *Revolt*, 9:301; Bancroft, *Arizona and New Mexico*, 170–71; Knault, *Pueblo Revolt*, 164; Josephy, *Patriot Chiefs*, 88.

22. Bancroft, *Arizona and New Mexico*, 166.

23. Knault, *Pueblo Revolt*, 101.

24. Espinosa, *Pueblo Indian Revolt*, 19, 24.

25. Bancroft, *Arizona and New Mexico*, 168.

26. Ibid., 175.

27. Scholes, "Troublous Times in New Mexico," 2; "Testimony of Pedro Naranjo," Río del Norte, December 18, 1681, in Twitchell, *Spanish Archives*, 2:62.

28. "Testimony of Pedro Naranjo," 62.

29. Ibid.

30. Ibid.; "Declaration of Diego López Sambrano," 9:299.

31. Kessell, "Esteban Clemente," 16; "Declaration of Diego López Sambrano," 9:299–300; Bancroft, *Arizona and New Mexico*, 168; Knault, *Pueblo Revolt*, 166–67.

32. "Carta del Padre Fray Silvestre Velez de Escalante," 1778, *Documentos*, 308; Folsom, *Indian Uprising on the Rio Grande*, 61.

33. "Statement of Pedro García," 8:62; "Auto of Antonio de Otermín," Alamillo, Sep-

tember 6, 1680, in Twitchell, *Spanish Archives*, 2:21; Carlos de Siguenza y Gongora, "Mercurio Volante con la noticias de la recuperación de las Provincias del Nuevo Mexico," 1693, in *Documentos*, 84; Bancroft, *Arizona and New Mexico*, 175.

34. Silverberg, *Pueblo Revolt*, 99; Chávez, "Pohe-yemo's Representative and the Pueblo Revolt of 1680," 99, 105.

35. Josephy, *Patriot Chiefs*, 87.

36. Bancroft, *Arizona and New Mexico*, 175; Knault, *Pueblo Revolt*, 167–68; Hackett, "Revolt of the Pueblo Indians," 99.

37. "Testimony of Pedro Naranjo," 62; Espinosa, *Pueblo Indian Revolt*, 34.

38. Knault, *Pueblo Revolt*, 168; Riley, *Kachina and the Cross*, 71; Hackett, "Revolt of the Pueblo Indians," 99; Josephy, *Patriot Chiefs*, 70; Chávez, "Pohe-yemo's Representative and the Pueblo Revolt of 1680," 120–22.

39. "Testimony of Pedro Naranjo," 62–63; "Autos Drawn Up as a Result of the Rebellion of the Christian Indians," Santa Fe, August 9, 1680, in Hackett, *Revolt*, 8:5; Reff, "The 'Predicament of Culture,'" 76; for a presentation of the case that Popé was of African descent, see Chávez, "Pohe-yemo's Representative and the Pueblo Revolt of 1680," 85–126.

40. Reff, "The 'Predicament of Culture,'" 63.

41. "Carta del Padre Fray Silvestre Velez de Escalante," *Documentos*, 308; "Interrogatories and Depositions of Three Indians of the Tehua Nation, Taken by the Order of Don Antonio Otermín," Río del Norte, December 28, 1681, in Twitchell, *Spanish Archives*, 2:51; "Autos Drawn Up as a Result of the Rebellion of the Christian Indians," Hackett, *Revolt*, 8:5.

42. "Testimony of José," Río del Norte, December 19, 1681, in Twitchell, *Spanish Archives*, 2:57.

43. Reff, "The 'Predicament of Culture,'" 65.

44. Hackett, "Revolt of the Pueblo Indians," 102, in Hackett, *Revolt*, 8:xxv.

45. "Interrogatories and Depositions of Three Indians of the Tehua Nation," 2:51.

46. "Testimony of Pedro Naranjo," 63; "Testimony of José," in Twitchell, *Spanish Archives*, 2:52–53; Knault, *Pueblo Revolt*, 168–69; Charles Hackett, "Revolt of the Pueblo Indians," 104.

47. Knault, *Pueblo Revolt*, 168–70; Bancroft, *Arizona and New Mexico*, 175–76; Hackett, "Revolt of the Pueblo Indians," 100, 102, 117; Riley, *Kachina and the Cross*, 206; Joe Sando, "The Pueblo Revolt," 195; Chávez, "Pohe-yemo's Representative and the Pueblo Revolt of 1680," 85, 89, 95; "Carta del Padre Fray Silvestre Velez de Escalante," *Documentos*, 308; Salmón, *Indian Revolts*, 38.

48. Hackett, "Revolt of the Pueblo Indians," 103; Bancroft, *Arizona and New Mexico*, 177; Knault, *Pueblo Revolt*, 4.

49. Bancroft, *Arizona and New Mexico*, 177; Knault, *Pueblo Revolt*, 4, 6, 170; Hackett, "Revolt of the Pueblo Indians," 103; "Letter from the Governor and Captain-General, Don Antonio de Otermín, from New Mexico," September 8, 1680, in Hackett, *Historical Documents*, 4:328; "Autos Drawn Up as a Result of the Rebellion of the Christian Indians," Hackett, *Revolt*, 8:3.

50. Hackett, "Revolt of the Pueblo Indians," 105, 110, 117; Knault, *Pueblo Revolt*, 6, 169; "Letter from the Governor and Captain-General, Don Antonio de Otermín, from New Mexico," 328–329; "Autos Drawn Up as a Result of the Rebellion of the Christian Indians," 8:3; Bancroft, *Arizona and New Mexico*, 177–78.

51. Hackett, "Revolt of the Pueblo Indians," 109, 114, 119; Scholes, "Troublous Times in New Mexico," 7; "Letter from the Governor and Captain-General, Don Antonio de Otermín, from New Mexico," in Hackett, *Historical Documents*, 329–30; "Auto of Antonio de Otermín," n.p., n.d., in Twitchell, *Spanish Archives*, 2:17.

52. "Letter from the Governor and Captain-General, Don Antonio de Otermín, from New Mexico," 330.

53. Hackett, "Revolt of the Pueblo Indians," 109, 114; Scholes, "Troublous Times in New Mexico," 7.

54. "Letter from the Governor and Captain-General, Don Antonio de Otermín, from New Mexico," 329–30; "Auto of Antonio de Otermín," n.p., n.d., in Twitchell, *Spanish Archives*, 2:17; Hackett, "Revolt of the Pueblo Indians," 119.

55. Bancroft, *Arizona and New Mexico*, 177–78; Hackett, "Revolt of the Pueblo Indians," 106–107, 112–13, 123–24, 135; "Answer Presented by the Lieutenant-General, Alonzo García, in His Own Behalf," Isleta, August 14, 1680, in Twitchell, *Spanish Archives*, 2:24; "Declaration of Pedro Hidalgo, Soldier," Santa Fe, August 10, 1680, in Hackett, *Revolt*, 8:5–7; "Auto of Antonio de Otermín," Santa Fe, August 10, 1680, ibid., 8:7; Knault, *Pueblo Revolt*, 7–8; "Judicial Process and Declaration," Santa Fe, August 10, 1680, in Hackett, *Revolt*, 8:8; "Auto and Declaration of Maestre de Campo Francisco Gómez," Santa Fe, August 12, 1680, in Hackett, *Revolt*, 8:9; "Letter from the Governor and Captain-General, Don Antonio de Otermín, from New Mexico," 329.

56. Bancroft, *Arizona and New Mexico*, 177–78; Hackett, "Revolt of the Pueblo Indians," 106–107, 114, 120, 133, 136, 137; Knault, *Pueblo Revolt*, 7–8; "Letter from the Governor and Captain-General, Don Antonio de Otermín, from New Mexico," 329; "Auto of Antonio de Otermín," Santa Fe, August 10, 1680, in Hackett, *Revolt*, 8:11.

57. "Letter from the Governor and Captain-General, Don Antonio de Otermín, from New Mexico," September 8, 1680, in Hackett, *Historical Documents*, 4:328; "Auto of Antonio de Otermín," Santa Fe, August 10, 1680, in Hackett, *Revolt*, 8:11; Bancroft, *Arizona and New Mexico*, 178.

58. "Letter of the Govenor and Captain-General, Don Antonio de Otermín, from New Mexico to Fray Francisco de Ayeta, in Which He Gives Him a Full Account of What Has Happened to Him since the Day the Indians Surrounded Him," n.p., September 8, 1680, in Hackett, *Revolt*, 8:95.

59. "Letter from the Governor and Captain-General, Don Antonio de Otermín, from New Mexico," 328, 330.

60. Ibid., 330; "Auto and Judicial Process," Santa Fe, August 13–20, 1680, in Hackett, *Revolt*, 8:12–13; Bancroft, *Arizona and New Mexico*, 179; Knault, *Pueblo Revolt*, 9; Hackett, "Revolt of the Pueblo Indians," 138.

61. Knault, *Pueblo Revolt*, 9–10.

62. Ibid., 10.

63. "Letter from the Governor and Captain-General, Don Antonio de Otermín, from New Mexico," 330–31; "Auto and Judicial Process," Santa Fe, August 13–20, 1680, 8:13–14; Siguenza y Gongora, "Mercurio Volante," *Documentos,* 85.

64. "Auto of Antonio de Otermín," n.p., n.d., in Twitchell, *Spanish Archives,* 2:33.

65. "Letter from the Governor and Captain-General, Don Antonio de Otermín, from New Mexico," 331; Knault, *Pueblo Revolt,* 10.

66. "Auto of Antonio de Otermín," n.p., n.d., in Twitchell, *Spanish Archives,* 2:32.

67. "Auto and Judicial Process," Santa Fe, August 13–20, 1680, 8:14; Hackett, "Revolt of the Pueblo Indians," 140; Knault, *Pueblo Revolt,* 10–11; Twitchell, *Spanish Archives,* 1:464.

68. "Letter from the Governor and Captain-General, Don Antonio de Otermín, from New Mexico," 332–33; "Carta del Padre Fray Silvestre Velez de Escalante," *Documentos,* 309; "Auto of Antonio de Otermín," n.p., n.d., in Twitchell, *Spanish Archives,* 2:33; "Auto and Judicial Process," Santa Fe, August 13–20, 1680, 8:15.

69. "Letter from the Governor and Captain-General, Don Antonio de Otermín, from New Mexico," 333.

70. Ibid.

71. Ibid., 333–34; "Carta del Padre Fray Silvestre Velez de Escalante," 309; Hackett, "Revolt of the Pueblo Indians," 142.

72. "Letter from the Governor and Captain-General, Don Antonio de Otermín, from New Mexico," 334; Knault, *Pueblo Revolt,* 11–12.

73. "Letter from the Governor and Captain-General, Don Antonio de Otermín, from New Mexico," 334.

74. Knault, *Pueblo Revolt,* 12.

75. "Letter from the Governor and Captain-General, Don Antonio de Otermín, from New Mexico," 334; "Auto of Antonio de Otermín," n.p., n.d., in Twitchell, *Spanish Archives,* 2:32.

76. "Salida para el Paso del Norte, 23 de Agosto, hasta 5 de Octubre de 1680," Antonio de Otermín, Arroyo de San Marcos, in Twitchell, *Spanish Archives,* 2:14; "Auto of Antonio de Otermín," n.p., n.d., ibid., 2:14–15; "Auto of Antonio de Otermín," n.p., n.d., ibid., 2:16; "Declaration of an Indian Rebel," Arroyo de San Marcos, August 23, 1680, in Hackett, *Revolt,* 8:20–21; "Auto of the March and Halting Places," August 24–26, 1680, ibid., 8:22.

77. "Auto of Antonio de Otermín," n.p., n.d., in Twitchell, *Spanish Archives,* 2:21–22; Hackett, *Revolt,* 8: xciv, xcvi; Knault, *Pueblo Revolt,* 13–14.

78. Bancroft, *Arizona and New Mexico,* 178–79.

79. "Opinion of Luís Granillo," Near Socorro, August 26, 1680, in Hackett, *Revolt,* 8:82; "Answer Presented by the Lieutenant-General, Alonzo García, in His Own Behalf," Isleta, August 14, 1680, in Twitchell, *Spanish Archives,* 2:24, 28–29; Hackett, "Revolt of the Pueblo Indians," 128–29.

80. "Answer Presented by the Lieutenant-General, Alonzo García, in His Own Behalf," Isleta, August 14, 1680, in Twitchell, *Spanish Archives,* 2:26, 30; "Auto of Antonio de Otermín," n.p., n.d., ibid., 2:23; "Carta del Padre Fray Silvestre Velez

de Escalante," *Documentos,* 309; Hackett, "Revolt of the Pueblo Indians," 146; "Auto of Antonio de Otermín," Fray Cristóbal, September 13, 1680, in Hackett, - *Revolt,* 8:121.

81. Hackett, *Revolt,* 8:lxxi–lxxiii.

82. Ibid., 8:lxxiv–lxxviii; Charles W. Hackett, "The Retreat of the Spaniards from New Mexico in 1680, Beginnings of El Paso I," *Southwestern Historical Quarterly* 16, no. 2 (October 1912): 144.

83. "Auto of Antonio de Otermín," n.p., n.d., in Twitchell, *Spanish Archives,* 2:21–22; Knault, *Pueblo Revolt,* 13–14; Hackett, *Revolt,* 8:xciv, xcvi.

84. "Auto of Antonio de Otermín," n.p., n.d., in Twitchell, *Spanish Archives,* 2:40–41; Anne Hughes, *The Beginnings of Spanish Settlement in the El Paso District* (Berkeley: n.p., 1914), 301, 310–11, 370.

85. "Letter from the Governor and Captain-General, Don Antonio de Otermín, from New Mexico," September 8, 1680, in Hackett, *Historical Documents,* 4:328, 334; Hackett, *Revolt,* 8:cix–cx; "Auto for Passing Muster, Reviewing Arms and Horses, and Other Things," opposite La Salineta, September 29, 1680, ibid., 8:134; "The Count Continues, on October 2, 1680, in the Said Place," La Salineta, October 2, 1680, ibid., 8:157–59; "Auto de Junta de Guerra," La Salineta, October 2, 1680, ibid., 8:161; Bancroft, *Arizona and New Mexico,* 179; Knault, *Pueblo Revolt,* 14, 133.

86. "To the Governor and Captain General," La Salineta, October 3, 1680, in Twitchell, *Spanish Archives,* 2:45.

87. "Letter from the Governor and Captain-General, Don Antonio de Otermín, from New Mexico," 328; "Letter of Antonio de Otermín to Fray Diego de Parraga," Near Socorro, September 8, 1680, in Hackett, *Revolt,* 8:90; "Auto of Antonio de Otermín," Place opposite la Salineta, October 1, 1680, ibid., 8:153.

88. "Opinion of the Cabildo," Fray Cristóbal, September 14, 1680, in Hackett, *Revolt,* 8:120; "Opinions Given in the Junta de Guerra," La Salineta, October 2, 1680, ibid., 8:166; "To the Governor and Captain General," 2:45.

89. "The Viceroy of New Spain Makes Report to Your Majesty of the General Uprising of the Indians of the Provinces of New Mexico, and of the Measures and Means Which Have Been Adopted for Their Restoration," Mexico City, February 28, 1681, in Hackett, *Historical Documents,* 4:339; "To the Governor and Captain General," 2:44; "List and Memorial of the Religious Whom the Indians of New Mexico Have Killed," n.p., n.d., in Hackett, *Revolt,* 8:108; Bancroft, *Arizona and New Mexico,* 8:179; Knault, *Pueblo Revolt,* 14–15; Hackett, "Revolt of the Pueblo Indians," 129.

90. Knault, *Pueblo Revolt,* 15.

91. "Auto and Judicial Proceeding," La Salineta, September 18, 1680, in Hackett, *Revolt,* 8:130–31; "Auto of Antonio de Otermín," n.p., n.d., in Twitchell, *Spanish Archives,* 2:40–42; "Letter of Father Fray Francisco de Ayeta, Written to the Father Commissary General," Real Chico, December 20, 1680, in Hackett, *Revolt,* 8:212–13, 215; Hackett, *Revolt,* 8:lxxiv, ci–cvi; Hackett, "The Retreat of the Spaniards from New Mexico in 1680, Beginnings of El Paso I," 259–361; "Another Letter of the Same [Don Bartolomé de Estrada] of la Nueva Vizcaya, in Which He Advises the Viceroy How He Has Ordered, under Severe Penalties, that No Person

from New Mexico Be Admitted into That Kingdom, Because of the Governor Having Informed Him that the Spaniards Were Deserting Him," Parral, September 25, 1680, in Hackett, *Revolt,* 8:133; "Order of the Governor and Captain-General of El Parral," San Joseph del Parral, September 24, 1680, in Hackett, *Revolt,* 8:185; "Autos de Junta de Guerra," El Paso, April 5, 1681, in Hackett, *Revolt,* 9:17; "The Viceroy of New Spain Makes Report," 4:343; "Letter of Ayeta to the Viceroy in Which He Advises Him that the Governor Is Alive, and of How He Had Escaped, What Happened to Him as Regards the Indians, and How He Was Going to Aid Them with Provisions and to Care for the Spaniards in Order to Relieve Them in Part after the Many Hardships They Were Suffering and Had Suffered," El Paso, September 16, 1680, in Hackett, *Revolt,* 8:127; "Petition of Luís Granillo," La Salineta, October 5, 1680, in Hackett, *Revolt,* 8:184; "Reply of the Señor Fiscal," Mexico City, January 3, 1681, in Hackett, *Revolt,* 8:222; "Order of the Governor and Captain-General of El Parral," San Joseph del Parral, September 24, 1680, in Hackett, *Revolt,* 8:185; "Letter of Father Fray Francisco de Ayeta," 8:214; "Autos de Junta de Guerra," 9:17; Knault, *Pueblo Revolt,* 172; Hackett, *Revolt,* cxviii; "Auto and Judicial Proceeding," La Salineta, September 22, 1680, in Hackett, *Revolt,* 8:133.

92.   "Auto of Antonio de Otermín," El Paso, September 2, 1681, in Hackett, *Revolt,* 9:87; "Auto for Passing Muster," El Ancón de Fray García, November 7, 1681, ibid., 9:190; "Copy of the Order that Was Given to the Lieutenant General of Cavalry, Juan Domínguez de Mendoza," La Isleta, December 8, 1681, ibid., 8:215-17; "Letter of Juan Domínguez de Mendoza to Antonio de Otermín," Alameda, December 9, 1681, ibid., 9:219-20; "Letter of Juan Domínguez de Mendoza to Antonio de Otermín," Sandía, December 10, 1681, ibid., 9:225; "Declaration of Lieutenant General of Cavalry," Río del Norte, December 20, 1681, ibid., 9:258-61; "Declaration of Captain Pedro Marquez," Río del Norte, December 21, 1681, ibid., 9:279; "Declaration of Sargento Mayor Sebastián de Herrera," Río del Norte, December 21, 1681, ibid., 9:273; "Declaration of Sargento Mayor Luís de Quintana," ibid., 9:289; "Opinions Given in the Junta de Guerra," Hacienda of Luis de Carbajal, December 23, 1681, ibid., 9:319-28; "Continuation of the Opinions of the Junta de Guerra," Hacienda of Luis de Carbajal, December 24, 1681, ibid., 9:330-37; "Judgment and Opinions," opposite La Isleta, December 31, 1681, ibid., 8:349-51; "Certifications of Francisco Xavier," opposite La Isleta, January 1, 1682, ibid., 9:357-58; Knault, *Pueblo Revolt,* 173; Hackett, *Revolt,* 8:cx-cxvi, clxxxi-cxc, cxcix, ccx; Bancroft, *Arizona and New Mexico,* 186-87, 189-90; Knault, *Pueblo Revolt,* 172; "Testimony of Juan of Tesuque," Río del Norte, December 28, 1681, in "Interrogatories and Depositions of Three Indians of the Tehua Nation," Twitchell, *Spanish Archives,* 2:55; "Testimony of José," Río del Norte, December 19, 1681, ibid., 2:58; "Testimony of Juan Lorenzo and Francisco Lorenzo," Paso del Norte, December 20, 1681, ibid., 2:67-68.

93.   "Royal Cedula. To the Viceroy of New Spain, Approving the Presidio with Fifty Soldiers Which He Has Formed in the Place Called El Río del Norte for the Conservation and Defense of the Provinces of New Mexico, and [Directing that] He Is to Carry Out the Rest that He May Be Ordered," Madrid, September 4, 1683, in Hackett, *Historical Documents,* 4:350; "Memorandum and List of the Things . . . Needed for the New Conquest of New Mexico," El Paso, October 12, 1680, in

Hackett, *Revolt,* 8:200; "Junta general de hacienda," Mexico, January 17, 1681, ibid., 8:250; Manuel J. Espinosa, *First Expedition of Vargas into New Mexico, 1692* (Albuquerque: University of New Mexico Press, 1940), 29; Diego de Vargas, campaign journal, New Mexico, August 9–October 15, 1692, in Kessell et al., *By Force of Arms,* 51, 365, 373–84, 386, 388, 393–99, 403–10, 417, 435–48; Diego de Vargas, campaign journal, New Mexico, October 16–December 27, 1692, ibid., 510–34, 538; "Don Juan, the Governor of Pecos, Arrives with the Four Indians Who Came to See Me; Record of the Letter I Wrote My Lieutenant and His Answer of Today; They Give Me Important Information as Soon as They Arrive, as Is of Record," November 25, 1693, in John L. Kessell, Rick Hendricks, and Meredith Dodge, eds., *To the Royal Crown Restored: The Journals of Don Diego de Vargas, New Mexico, 1692–1694* (Albuquerque: University of New Mexico Press, 1995), 437–39; "Information the Governor of Pecos, Don Juan, Gives about the Bad Will of the Tewa and Tano Indians; They Are Having a Meeting and Have Feigned the Obedience They Rendered to Achieve the Treachery in Their Hearts More Effectively," Santa Fe, December 17, 1693, ibid., 473–74; "The Cabildo of Santa Fe to Diego de Vargas, Petition," Santa Fe, December 17, 1693, ibid., 495–500; "War Breaks Out the Following Day, and the Combat Lasts until Night," Santa Fe, December 29, 1693, ibid., 529–33; "The Indian Bartolo from the Keres Pueblo of Zía Comes and Reports that the Jemez Nation, the Keres, and Cieneguilla Pueblo of Cochiti of Captain Malacate and Others Who Are Their Followers Have Been Called Together, and that This Group Held a Junta with the Navajo Apaches," Santa Fe, December 31, 1693, ibid., 538; "The Cabildo of Santa Fe to the Conde de Galve," Santa Fe, January 1694, ibid., 561–62; "Entry into This Town of Santa Fe by Said Governor and Captain General," in Twitchell, *Spanish Archives,* 2:106; "The Governors of Zía and Santa Ana Arrive and Report that the Rebels Struck Their Pueblos from Ambush; They Asked for Aid for the Safety of Their Pueblos," in Kessell et al., *Blood,* 1:276; "Word from the Captain of San Felipe that the Enemy Attacked the Milpas of His Pueblo and Killed an Adult Indian Male and a Boy; For This Reason, He Asks that He Be Given the Five Men in His Pueblo as an Escort," Santa Fe, June 20, 1694, ibid., 1:278; "Statement of Agustín de Salazar," Santa Fe, December 28, 1693, ibid., 1:525; Siguenza y Gongora, "Mercurio Volante," *Documentos,* 88–98; "Carta del Padre Fray Silvestre Velez de Escalante," ibid., 319–20; "Este cuaderno se cree ser obra de un religioso de la provincia del Santo Evangélico," n.p., n.d., ibid., 324–26; "Extracto de la carta en que con fecha de 16 de octubre de 1692, da cuenta Vargas a S.E.," Santa Fe, ibid., 327–29, 331, 333–34; "Tercer cuaderno [of Fray Salvador de San Antonio]," Santa Fe, December 18, 1693, ibid., 343–46; "El Proveido de D. Diego de Vargas Sobre la petición espresada del Padre Custodio y demas religiosos misioneros dice," ibid., 357–58.

94.   Diego de Vargas, campaign journal, New Mexico, October 16–December 27, 1692, in Kessell et al., *By Force of Arms,* 559–97; "Diego de Vargas to the Conde de Galve, Transmittal Summary," El Paso, January 8, 1692, ibid., 607; Siguenza y Gongora, "Mercurio Volante," *Documentos,* 100–111; "Extracto de la carta en que con fecha de 16 de octubre de 1692, da cuenta Vargas a S.E.," 337; Kessell et al., *To the Royal Crown Restored,* 181.

95.   "Vargas to Viceroy Count de Galves," Paso del Norte, October 13, 1693, in Twitchell, *Spanish Archives,* 2:89; "Tercer cuaderno," 343–44.

96. "Tercer cuaderno," 343–46; "Don Juan, the Governor of Pecos, Arrives with the Four Indians Who Came to See Me," 437–39; "Entry into This Town of Santa Fe by Said Governor and Captain General," in Twitchell, *Spanish Archives*, 2:106; "Tercer cuaderno," 347, 349; "Information the Governor of Pecos, Don Juan, Gives about the Bad Will of the Tewa and Tano Indians," 473–74; "El Proveido de D. Diego de Vargas Sobre la petición espresada del Padre Custodio y demas religiosos misioneros dice," 353–54, 357–58, 360, 371–73, 377–80, 383, 385–88; "The Cabildo of Santa Fe to Diego de Vargas, Petition," Santa Fe, December 17, 1693, in Kessell et al., *To the Royal Crown Restored*, 495–500; "War Breaks Out the Following Day," ibid., 529–33; "The Indian Bartolo," ibid., 538; "The Cabildo of Santa Fe to the Conde de Galve," Santa Fe, January 1694, ibid., 561–62; "Statement of Agustín de Salazar," Santa Fe, December 28, 1693, in Kessell et al., *Blood*, 1:525; "Statement of Lucia," January 11, 1694, Santa Fe, ibid., 1:47; "The Governors of Zía and Santa Ana Arrive," Santa Fe, June 14, 1694, ibid., 1:276; "Word from the Captain of San Felipe," Santa Fe, June 20, 1694, ibid., 1:278.

97. "Fray Francisco de Vargas, Petition," Santa Fe, March 7, 1696, in Kessell et al., *Blood*, 2:674; "The Cabildo of Santa Fe, petition," Santa Fe, November 9, 1695, ibid., 1:649; "Diego de Vargas to Fray Francisco de Vargas, Reply to Petition," Santa Fe, March 8, 1696, ibid., 2:678; "Sesto cuaderno y primero del año de 1695," in *Documentos*, 395, 397.

98. "Letter of Fray José Arbizu," San Cristóbal, March 9, 1696, in Espinosa, *Pueblo Indian Revolt*, 171; "Letter of Fray Blás Navarro," Picurís, March 9, 1696, ibid., 173; "Letter of Fray José García Marín," Santa Clara, March 9, 1696, ibid., 174; "Sesto cuaderno y primero del año de 1695," 395, 397; "Diego de Vargas, Proceeding," Santa Fe, March 14, 1696, in Kessell et al., *Blood*, 2:682–86; "Letter of Fray José Diez," San Diego de Tesuque, March 9, 1696, in Espinosa, *Pueblo Indian Revolt*, 175; "Letter of Fray Antonio Carbonel," Nambé, March 31, 1696, ibid., 220–21; "Auto of Governor Vargas," Santa Fe, November 23, 1696, ibid., 285.

99. "Letter of Fray Antonio Carbonel," 220–21; "Auto of Governor Vargas," Santa Fe, November 23, 1696, in Espinosa, *Pueblo Indian Revolt*, 285.

100. "Letter of Fray Miguel Trizio," Bernalillo, April 17, 1696, in Espinosa, *Pueblo Indian Revolt*, 226.

101. "Sesto cuaderno y primero del año de 1695," 398–99; Diego de Vargas, campaign journal, June 4–5, 1696, in Kessell et al., *Blood*, 2:728–29, 732, 734; Diego de Vargas, campaign journal, June 12, 1696, ibid., 2:747.

102. Diego de Vargas, campaign journal, June 4–5, 1696, in Kessell et al., *Blood*, 2:724; Diego de Vargas, campaign journal, June 30–July 2, 1696, ibid., 2:786.

103. "Sesto cuaderno y primero del año de 1695," 399–403; "Miguel de Lara to Diego de Vargas," Zia, July 1, 1696, in Kessell et al., *Blood*, 2:797; Diego de Vargas, campaign journal, August 30–September 6, 1696, ibid., 2:1,010; Kessell et al., *Blood*, 965.

104. "The Community of Santa Fe to the Viceroy, Petition," Santa Fe, June 20, 1696, in Kessell et al., *Blood*, 2:851; "The Cabildo of Santa Fe, Decree," Santa Fe, June 20, 1696, ibid., 2:853; "Letter of Fray Francisco de Vargas to the Provincial," Santa Fe, July 21, 1696, in Espinosa, *Pueblo Indian Revolt*, 255–56.

105. "Primer cuaderno Sobre el Levantamiento de los Zunis," n.p., n.d., in *Documen-*

tos, 414; "Segundo cuaderno sobre la muerte de tres vecinos en Zuni," n.p., n.d. , ibid., 415–18, 420–22; "Segundo cuaderno sobre la muerte de tres vecinos en Zuni," 422; "Segundo gobierno de Vargas," n.p., n.d., ibid., 423–24; Kessell, "Spaniards and Pueblos," 127, 134; Riley, *Kachina and the Cross,* 232.

106. O'Phelan Godoy, *Rebellions and Revolts,* 1, 11–12, 14, 16–18, 23, 27, 101; Herbert Klein, *Bolivia: The Evolution of a Multi-ethnic Society* (New York: Oxford University Press, 1982), 41–42, 51–52; Stavig, *The World of Túpac Amaru,* 742–43; Fisher, *Last Inca Revolt,* 8, 11–12, 23, 39, 43. For general treatments of the rebellion, see Carlos Daniel Válcarcel, *La rebelión de Túpac Amaru* (Mexico City: Fondo de la Cultura Económica, 1970), and Boleslao Lewin, *La rebelión de Túpac Amaru y los origines de la independencia de Hispanoamérica* (Buenos Aires: Sociedad Editora Latino Americana, 1967).

107. "Expediente formado en virtud de una provisión real en la causa seguida por Blas Canaviri, indio principal y Gobernador del allyu Canasa de los indios del pueblo de Belén de Tinquipaya, provincia Porco contra Juan Antonio Guruchaga, Corregidor de Porco, sobre extorsiones y encarcelamiento," La Plata, January 15, 1776, ANB, ECad.1776, 2, 3; "Indios de Hilave de la Provincia de Chucuito contra el Gobernador sobre repartos," Chucuito, December 23, 1780, ANB, SGI.1780.111, 1–2. See also "Damiana Guezo contra el corregidor de Yamparáez por robo," La Plata, June 13, 1780, ANB, EC.1780.143; "Dn. José Saavedra en nombre del cura de la provincia de Asangaro Dr. José Escobedo da a conocer los motivos por las cuales la provincia se hallaba siempre pertubada," Azángaro, November 16, 1778, ANB, EC.1778.250, 1; "Expediente seguido por Dn. Cipriano Santos Luna contra el Corregidor de Sicasica Dn. Juan Carillo de Alboróz sobre exceso de repartos," La Plata, January 30, 1779, ANB, EC.1779.8, 1–3; "Sobre el exceso de los corregs. en sus repartos," La Plata, March 17, 1780, ANB, ECad.1780.6, 2; "Informe y documentos que remite el Corregidor de la Provincia de Cochabamba Dn. Félix José de Villalobos sobre los efectos que internó en la provincia para vender a los Provincianos," Cochabamba, April 7, 1780, ANB, EC.1780.67, 1; "Testimonio en f16 de las cartas de los rebeldes, comisiones e informe que Diego Cristóbal Túpac-Amaru hizo al Exmo. Sr. Virrey de Lima, en respuesta del indulto Gral que libro," Peñas, November 15, 1781, ANB, SGI.1781.248, 4; "Lista del reparto hecho en la provincia de Chayanta, por el Corregidor de ella, Dn. Joaquín Alós," Chayanta, April 14, 1780, ANB, SGI.1780.43, 1, 43, 50; Stern, "Age," 39; O'Phelan Godoy, *Rebellions and Revolts,* 99, 25, 99–103, 109, 119; Fisher, *Last Inca Revolt,* 12. See also Scarlett O'Phelan Godoy, "Elementos étnicos y de poder en el movimiento Tupacamarista, 1780–81" (Torino: Nova Americana, 1982), 89; Scarlett O'Phelan Godoy, "Hacía una tipología y un enfoque alternativo de las revueltas y rebeliones del Perú colonial (siglo XVIII)," in R. Konetzke and Hermann Kellenbenz, eds., *Jahrbuch für Geschiste,* vol. 21, ed. (Cologne: Bohlau, 1984), 148; Klein, *Bolivia,* 70; Válcarcel, *La rebelión de Túpac Amaru,* 18.

108. "Expediente de Dn. Manuel de Bodega y Llano Corregidor de Poopó," Paria, April 29, 1783, ANB, SGI.1785.123, 16; "Dn. Augustín Cusicanqui contra el escribano de Pacajes," Pacajes, October 1, 1779, ANB, EC.1779.61, 1, 3, 4; "Recurso de Ambrocio Mamani y Tomás Llacsavanca indios principales y originarios del pueblo de Laja, partido de Omasuyos, La Paz, ante el Fiscal Protector General, sobre las molestias, vejaciones y agravios que ellos y demás indios de dicha comu-

nidad padecen de Enrique Gisbert y demás hermanos," La Plata, October 26, 1789, ANB, ECad.1789.16, 1; "Dn. Augustín Cusicanqui contra el escribano de Pacajes," 1, 3.

109. "Testimonio en fi6 de las cartas de los rebeldes, comisiones e informe que Diego Cristóbal Túpac-Amaru hizo al Exmo. Sr. Virrey de Lima, en respuesta del indulto Gral que libro," 8–9; O'Phelan Godoy, *Rebellions and Revolts*, 111, 114–16; "Provisión real dirigida al Corregidor y Justicia Mayor de la Provincia de Yamparáez, en la causa de los indios y cacique del pueblo de San Miguel de Aullagas y Uruquillas, provincia de Paria, como dueños de las tierras de Cainaca que poseen en la doctrina de Pocpo, provincia Yamparáez, contra el diezmero, por excesos," La Plata, June 7, 1773, ANB, ECad.1773.17, 1; "Información recivida en la Prova de Chayanta sobre aberiguar quienes han hido los principales caudillos de la sublevcn de dichos pueblos," Moromoro, April 30, 1781, ANB, SGI.1781.160, 8; "Expediente seguido por el cacique de Aullagas Don Cárlos Tiburcio Chuquimia contra el cura de Pocpo Don Benito Ulloa sobre injustos pensiones y servicios," La Plata, July 24, 1774, ANB, EC.1780.39, 1, 3–4.

110. "Autos seguidos sobre el alborato que acasido en el pueblo de Calcha de la prova. de Chichas," Chichas, August 31, 1781, ANB, SGI.1781.25, 6, 12; "Capítulos seguidos contra el Doctor Gregorio Josef de Merlos, por algunas Yndios del Beneficio de Coroma," San Francisco de Coroma, September 22, 1770, Archivo-Biblioteca Arquidiocesanos Mos. Taborga, Acusaciones, Merlos, Gregorio José, 1–3, 10–14, 44; see also chapter 9 in Juan and Ulloa for additional descriptions of clerical abuses.

111. "Autos sobre la petición de varios Indios de Cochabamba contra el Mestizo Francisco Javier de Nadena sobre agravios," Cochabamba, October 3, 1780, ANB, EC.1779.100, 55; "Testimonio formado por el Corregidor de Cochabamba en virtud de derechos de los indios de Tapacari sobre que se les cobra excesibos derechos Parroquiales el señor cura," Cochabamba, April 4, 1781, ANB SGI.1781.181, 1–3, 11; "Cuarto cuaderno de pruebas producidas a pedimiento del abogado de los caciques de Tapacari, y sus mujeres con citación del abogado fiscal," Tapacari, July 26, 1781, ANB, SGI.1781.218, 3; "Provisión real dirigida al Corregidor y Justicia Mayor de la Provincia de Yamparáez," 1; "Información recivida en la Prova de Chayanta sobre aberiguar quienes han hido los principales caudillos de la sublevcn de dichos pueblos," Moromoro, April 30, 1781, ANB, SGI.1781.160, 8; Expediente seguido por el cacique de Aullagas Don Cárlos Tiburcio Chuquimia contra el cura de Pocpo Don Benito Ulloa sobre injustos pensiones y servicios," 1, 3–4.

112. "Carta de Benito Mata Linares a Josef de Galvez," Cuzco, June 3, 1783, AGI, Cuzco 29, 1–2; see also "Capítulos puestos al cura de Curaguara Dn. Miguel de Vera que contiene una lista abrumadora de acusaciones por abusos que el cometió," Carangas, February 17, 1784, ANB, SGI.1784.2, 18.

113. "Autos seguidos, en el pueblo de Pocoata, ante el Corregidor de la Provincia de Chayanta, por sus principales y comunidades de la parcialidad de Anansaya, contra su Gobernador Andrés Ayra y Coñaca, sobre excesos y malversaciones," Pocoata, April 7, 1772, ANB, ECad.1772.3, 1, 2; "Sobre las diligencias por Dn. Pedro Ulloa sobre la usurpación de Tributos imputada al Cacique Dn. Florencio Lupa," La Plata, June 2, 1779, ANB, EC.1779.5, 14; "Autos sobre la petición de varios Indios de Cochabamba contra el Mestizo Francisco Javier de Nadena sobre agra-

vios," Cochabamba, October 3, 1780, ANB, EC.1779.100, 28–30; "Testimonio de los autos seguidos contra Tomás de la Cruz, cacique del pueblo de Jesús de Machaca, provincia de Pacajes, sobre usurpación de tributos," Pacajes, February 23, 1773, ANB, ECad.1773.8, 1; "Pablo Pumacusi, indio de la doctrina de Huata, ante el fiscal y Protector General, sobre no se le cobre el tributo de su hijo muerto, Fermin Pumacusi," Huata, September 18, 1787, ANB, ECad.1787.14, 3; "Pruebas introducidas por los Indios de pocoata sobre los capítulos puestos al Cacique Florencio Lupa," La Plata, March 31, 1779, ANB, EC.1779.195, 1–3, 5; "Recurso de Dn. Toribio Chaves y PeñAlósa Teniente del partido de Mocomoco de la Provincia de Larecaja, sobre excesos del casique Dn. Juan Miranda," Larecaja, April 21, 1780, ANB, EC.1780.57, 1, 2, 3, 4–16; "Testimonio e información de oficio sobre las tropelias del Corregidor de Challapata Ambrosio Condori," La Plata, October 19, 1780, ANB, EC.1780.104, 2, 12, 16, 22, 24, 26; "Expediente seguido por la comunidad de Macha contra el cacique Blas Daria Bernal por varios excesos," La Plata, December 15, 1780, ANB, SGI.1780.194, 1–2; "El lisenciado D. Diego Frnz Mariano representa a V.M. como teniente de cura de la Doctrina de Condocondo, Provincia de Paria," Condocondo, July 12, 1774, in "Expediente informado de la contaduría y respondiendo del Sor. Fiscal sobre excesos del corregidor de Paria Dn Manuel de la Bodega," AGI, Charcas 528, 1; "Confesión de Alvento Arze," La Plata, October 3, 1780, AGI, Charcas 596, 69; "Memoria de Ylario Caguasiri," San Pedro de Buenavista, November 24, 1780, AGI, Charcas 596, 49; "Declaración de Ignacio Salguero," La Plata, April 4, 1781, AGI, Charcas 603, 14; see also Larson, *Colonialism and Agrarian Transformation in Bolivia,* 154, 166. For a discussion of Indiancuraca relations in Quispicanchis and Canas and Canchis, see Stavig, *The World of Túpac Amaru,* 754–62.

114. Klein, *Bolivia,* 45, 47.

115. "Real Provisión de la Audencia de Charcas, al Corregidor de la provincia de Mizque a solicitud de José Santos Encinas, indio principal de la parcialidad de los Chues, sobre la deposición del empleo de cacique que obtenía y del nombramiento de Marcelo Velázques, Mestizo forastero, para que se le confiera interinamente el gobierno de la citada provincia," La Plata, December 7, 1779, ANB, ECad.1779.14, 1–2; "Información recivida en la Prova de Chayanta sobre aberiguar quienes han hido los principales caudillos de la sublevcn de dichos pueblos," 8, 11–12, 15; O'Phelan Godoy, *Rebellions and Revolts,* 117; Stavig, *The World of Túpac Amaru,* 760. For a discussion of the changing nature of the curacazgo, see Thomson, *We Alone Will Rule.* For documents describing the abuses of curacas and Indian governors, see "Mateo Vilca de Tapacari sobre despojo de tierras," Porco, October 12, 1778, ANB, EC.1778.97, 1, 3, 4; ANB, SGI.1778.174, n.t., n.p., October, 7, 1778; "Dn. Juan Vela y demás indios del Pueblo de Viacha, contra los hijos del cacique Manuel mercado," La Plata, June 12, 1780, ANB, EC.1780.108; "Dn. Blas Layme, indio principal y Dn. Cayetano Lillo, vecinos de la doctrina de Potobamba sobre tierras," Porco, April 1, 1781, ANB, EC.1781.97, 1; "El común de indios del pueblo de Andamarca, provincia Carangas, ante el Fiscal Protector General, contra su cacique, Juan de la Cruz Centeno, por agravios, extorsiones y otros excesos," La Plata, July 17, 1771, ANB, ECad.1771.47, 1, 2; "Autos seguidos, en el pueblo de Pocoata, ante el Corregidor de la Provincia de Chayanta, por sus principales y comunidades de la parcialidad de Anansaya, contra su Gobernador Andrés

Ayra y Coñaca, sobre excesos y malversaciones," Pocoata, April 7, 1772, ANB, ECad.1772.3, 1, 2; "Sobre las diligencias por Dn. Pedro Ulloa sobre la usurpación de Tributos imputada al Cacique Dn. Florencio Lupa," 14; "Autos sobre la petición de varios indios de Cochabamba," 28–30; "Testimonio de los autos seguidos contra Tomás de la Cruz, cacique del pueblo de Jesús de Machaca, provincia de Pacajes, sobre usurpación de tributos," 1; "Pablo Pumacusi, indio de la doctrina de Huata, ante el fiscal y Protector General, sobre no se le cobre el tributo de su hijo muerto, Fermin Pumacusi," Huata, September 18, 1787, ANB, ECad.1787.14, 3; "Pruebas introducidas por los Indios de pocoata sobre los capítulos puestos al Cacique Florencio Lupa," 1–3, 5; "Recurso de Dn. Toribio Chaves y Peñalosa Teniente del partido de Mocomoco de la Provincia de Larecaja, sobre excesos del casique Dn. Juan Miranda," 1, 2, 3, 4–16; "Testimonio e información de oficio sobre las tropelias del Corregidor de Challapata Ambrosio Condori," 2, 12, 16, 22, 24, 26; "Expediente seguido por la comunidad de Macha contra el cacique Blas Daria Bernal por varios excesos," 1–2; "El lisenciado D. Diego Frnz Mariano representa a V.M.," 1; "Confesión de Alvento Arze," 69; "Memoria de Ylario Caguasiri," 49; "Declaración de Ignacio Salguero," 14; Larson, *Colonialism and Agrarian Transformation in Bolivia*, 154, 166.

116. "Carta de Ignacio Florez a Gerónimo Manuel de Ruedas," La Plata, January 2, 1781, AGI, Charcas 594, 2; Leona Ruth Auld, "Discontent with the Spanish Systems of Control in Upper Peru: 1730–1809" (Ph.D. diss., University of California, Los Angeles, 1963), 55; Fisher, *Last Inca Revolt*, 69.

117. "Levantamiento de la Provincia de Chayanta o Charcas . . . y lo acaecido en el pueblo de Pocoata de dha provincia a su corregidor Dn. Joaquín Alós," La Plata, September 29, 1780, in Cárlos Daniel Válcarcel, ed., *Colección Documental de la independencia del Perú,* book 2, 1:235; "El lisenciado D. Diego Frnz Mariano representa a V.M.," 1; "Relación de los hechos más notables acaecidos en la sublevación general fraguada en los reynos del Perú, por el indio José Gabriel Túpac Amaru, gobr. del pueblo de Tungasuca en la Provincia de Tinta, que asociado de otros sequaces, causó horrosos estragos desde el año 1780, hasta el de 1782 en que se reprimo el orgullo de la conjuración," *Revista de archivos y bibliotecas nacionales* 3, no. 5 (Lima, September 30, 1900): 143; "Información recibida en la Prova de Chayanta sobre aberiguar quienes han hido los principales caudillos de la subleven de dichos pueblos," 16; "Levantamiento de la Provincia de Chayanta o Charcas," 237; "Representación del indio Tomás Catari," Macha, November 12, 1780, AGI, Charcas 595, 1; Sergio Serulnikov, *Tomás Catari y la producción de justicia,* 20–23; Fisher, *Last Inca Revolt,* 53; Andrade Padilla, *La Rebelión de Tomás Catari,* 69.

118. "Levantamiento de la Provincia de Chayanta o Charcas," 237; "Expediente obrado a solicitud de los indios de la Prova. de Chayanta impetrando perdón sus excesos," La Plata, March 5, 1781, ANB, SGI.1781.50, 1; "Carta a Ignacio Flores," Rosario, January 19, 1781, ANB, SGI.1781.53, 2; "Información recibida en la Prova de Chayanta sobre aberiguar quienes han hido los principales caudillos de la subleven de dichos pueblos," 14, 17; "Representación del indio Tomás Catari," 1; Serulnikov, *Tomás Catari y la producción de justicia,* 22–24; Fisher, *Last Inca Revolt,* 53, 57.

119. "Diario y relación prolija jurada que yo el General Don Juan Gelly hago de todos

los pasajes y sucesos acaecidos en varias distritos y lugares," La Plata, AGI, Charcas 594, 1; "Levantamiento de la Provincia de Chayanta o Charcas," 238.

120. "Diario y relación prolija," 3; "Anexo al diario y relación prolija jurada que yo el general Don Juan Gelly hago de todos los pasajes y sucesos acaecidos en varios distritos y lugares," La Plata, September 9, 1780, AGI, Charcas 594, 1; "Copia de carta acordada dirijida al Corregidor de Chayanta," La Plata, August 22, 1780, ANB, AchLA.11.1780, 952; "Relación de los hechos más notables," 145, 147; "Levantamiento de la Provincia de Chayanta o Charcas," 239–41; Fisher, *Last Inca Revolt*, 58; O'Phelan Godoy, *Rebellions and Revolts*, 243; Andrade Padilla, *La Rebelión de Tomás Catari*, 57, 67.

121. "Diario trunco de los sucesos desde el 4 febo. hasta Octr. 16 de 1780 en Chuquisaca," La Plata, October 16, 1780, ANB, Ruck.1780.96, 2; "Anexo al diario," 1; "Oficio de Merlos a Vertíz," Macha, November 14, 1780, in Lewin, *La rebelión de Túpac Amaru*, 734.

122. "Carta de Ignacio Florez a Juan José Vertíz," La Plata, May 13, 1781, AGI, Charcas 596, 5; "Orden de Tomás Catari," Macha, October 21, 1780, AGI, Charcas 596, 80; "Relación de los hechos más notables," 159; "Recurso de Lope Limachi, gobernador de Tacabamba sobre haberse resistido los indios al page de la contribución de los RR tributos," La Plata, January 22, 1781, ANB, SGI.1781.51, 1, 6; "Causa seguida contra Sebastián Aysa y otros por varios delitos en el pueblo de Condocondo," La Plata, October 9, 1781, ANB, SGI.1781.145.

123. "Informe del oidores Pedro Antonio Zernudas y Lorenzo Blanco Ciceron," La Plata, March 14, 1781, AGI, Charcas 596, 1; "Representación de Juan de Dios Pinapi," La Plata, October 20, 1780, AGI, Charcas 596, 18; "Fragment of Informe," n.p., n.d., AGI, Charcas 594, 1; "Confesión de Asensio Pacheco," La Plata, April 18, 1781, AGI, Charcas 603, 20.

124. "Auto de Tomás Catari," Macha, October 21, 1780, AGI, Charcas 596, 1; "Confesión de Dámaso Catari," La Plata, April 1, 1781, in Manuel de Odriozola, ed., *Documentos históricos del Perú en las épocas del coloniaje despúes de la conquista y de la independencia hasta la presente* (Lima: Tipografia de Aurelio Alfaro, 1863), 1:305–306, 313 (hereafter *Documentos históricos*); "Informe del Fiscal Juan Pino del Manrique," La Plata, March 12, 1781, AGI, Charcas 596, 18; "Exp. seguido contra los indios José Gregorio Arroyo y demás complices de la sublevación del pueblo de Challapata," La Plata, September 30, 1781, ANB, SGI.1781.64, 3; "Dn. Gerónimo Manuel de Ruedas sobre la sublevación del pueblo de Tarabuco provincia de la frontera de Tomina," La Plata, February 2, 1781, ANB, SGI.1781.95, 1; "Carta de Ignacio Florez a Gerónimo Manuel de Ruedas," La Plata, December 1, 1780, AGI, Charcas 594, 1; "Confesión de Alvento Arze," 67; "Informe de Gregorio Josef de Merlos," Macha, October 7, 1780, AGI, Charcas 596, 11; "Informe de Tomás Catari," Macha, October 7, 1780, AGI, Charcas 596, 19; "Carta de Gregorio Josef de Merlos a Francisco Ramón de Herbovo y Figueróa," La Plata, January 23, 1781, AGI, Charcas 597, 3; "Carta de Gregorio Josef de Merlos al Licenciado Mariano de la Vega," La Plata, January 27, 1781, AGI, Charcas 597, 4; "Diario trunco," 3; "Petición de Theodora Lupa y Inojosa," La Plata, October 21, 1780, AGI, Charcas 596, 79–80; "Carta de Ignacio Florez a Juan José Vertíz," May 13, 1781, 5; "Información

recibida por el corregidor deesta ciudad por la que consta la voz publicamente esparcida en el vecendario de que era invadida por numerosa multitud de indios que venían a desolarla y a extraer unos presos de la provincia de Paria," La Plata, October 15, 1780, AGI, Charcas 594, 1; "Informe que hace a S.M. el Presidente Regte de la Rl Auda de Charcas [Gerónimo Manuel de Ruedas] con documentos instructiosos," La Plata, September 18, 1780, AGI, Charcas 594, 1; "El Presidente Regente de la R.A. de Charcas Informando de la sublevación de Indios de la provincia de Chayanta," La Plata, October 15, 1780, AGI, Charcas 594, 1; "Representación de la RI Audiencia de Charcas a Josef de Galvez," La Plata, September 15, 1780, AGI, Charcas 594, 2; "Oficio de Merlos a Vertíz," November 14, 735; "Copiense en el libro de acuerdos los votos en este . . . se refiere la parte que legalmte coresponde con la nota qe en el se expresa," La Plata, September 28, 1780, ANB, SGI.1780.135, 4; "El Presidente Regente de la R.A. de Charcas Informando de la sublevación de Indios de la provincia de Chayanta," La Plata, October 15, 1780, AGI, Charcas 594, 1; "Representación de la Audiencia de Charcas a Josef de Galvez," La Plata, September 15, 1781, AGI, Charcas 594, 2; "Carta de Gerónimo de Ruedas a Josef de Galvez," La Plata, November 15, 1780, AGI, Charcas 596, 1; "Confesión de Nicolás Catari," La Plata, April 10, 1781, in Odriozola, *Documentos históricos*, 1:325; Serulnikov, *Tomás Catari y la producción de justícia*, 17; Serulnikov, *Revindicaciones indígenas*, 7–8; O'Phelan Godoy, *Rebellions and Revolts*, 118–19, 153.

125. Fisher, *Last Inca Revolt*, 4, 23, 25, 30; Szeminski, "Why Kill the Spaniard?" 173–74; O'Phelan Godoy, *Rebellions and Revolts*, 253.

126. Fisher, *Last Inca Revolt*, 33, 35.

127. O'Phelan Godoy, *Rebellions and Revolts*, 168, 207, 218, 260; Fisher, *Last Inca Revolt*, 37, 193, 196, 205; Zuaire Huarte, "Análisis de la rebelión de Túpac Amaru en su bicentenario (1780–1980)," 17, 36.

128. "Confesión de Dámaso Catari," 305–306; "Carta de Dámaso Catari a Dn. Pasqual Llavi," Macha, March 5, 1781, AGI, Charcas 437-b, 56; O'Phelan Godoy, *Rebellions and Revolts*, 210, 244; Campbell, "Ideology," 119; Fisher, *Last Inca Revolt*, 59.

129. "Certificación de actos cometidos por Antonio Oblitas," Cuzco, 1781, in Luís Durand Florez, ed., *Colección documental del bicentenario de la revolución emancipadora de Túpac Amaru* (Lima: Comisión Nacional del Bicentenario de la Rebelión Emancipadora de Túpac Amaru, 1980), 3:555; "Testimonio de los autos formados por el alsamiento del indio José Gabriel Tupa Amaro Cacique del pueblo de Tungasuca provincia de Tinta," n.p., January 30, 1781, ANB, SGI.1781.242, 3; O'Phelan Godoy, *Rebellions and Revolts*, 209; Fisher, *Last Inca Revolt*, 45–46, 95.

130. "Testimonio de la sentencia dada contra el vil traidor Joseph Gabriel Túpac Amaru cazique del pueblo de Tungasuca en la Provincia de Tinta," Cuzco, May 20, 1781, AGI, Charcas 595, 2; "Testimonio de los autos formados por el alsamiento del indio José Gabriel Tupa Amaro Cacique del pueblo de Tungasuca provincia de Tinta," 16, 24; Szeminski, *La utopía Tupamarista*, 246; Fisher, *Last Inca Revolt*, 95–96, 98, 101.

131. Fisher, *Last Inca Revolt*, 102.

132. "Testimonio de los autos formados por el alsamiento del indio José Gabriel Tupa

Amaro Cacique del pueblo de Tungasuca provincia de Tinta," 48; Válcarcel, *La rebelión de Túpac Amaru,* 60; Fisher, *Last Inca Revolt,* 102–103.

133. "Carta de Juan Manuel de Moscoso a Gregorio Francisco de Campos," Huaylla-bamba, July 20, 1782, in Odriozola, *Documentos históricos,* 2:255; Campbell, "Ideology," 124; Fisher, *Last Inca Revolt,* 104; O'Phelan Godoy, *Rebellions and Revolts,* 227.

134. Campbell, "Ideology," 125–26; Boleslao Lewin, *Túpac Amaru, el rebelde, su época, sus luchas y su influencia en el continente* (Buenos Aires: Editorial Claridad, 1943), 201.

135. Fisher, *Last Inca Revolt,* 103, 106, 109, 112, 117; Zuaire Huarte, "Análisis de la rebelión de Túpac Amaru en su bicentenario (1780–1980)," 59.

136. Fisher, *Last Inca Revolt,* 120–21, 122.

137. Ibid., 119, 120–24, 125, 127, 131–32.

138. Fisher, *Last Inca Revolt,* 120–21, 123, 127, 129, 131–32, 212–13.

139. "Representación del indio Tomás Catari," 1–2.

140. "Fragment of Informe," 1; "Carta de Ignacio Florez a Juan José Vertíz," May 13, 1781, 2; "El Rl Auda dela Plata informa a V.M. de lo reciente ocurrido con el Justa Maor nombrado para la Prova de Chayanta y con los reos Thomas Catari y su escrivente Ysidro de Serrano," La Plata, January 15, 1781, AGI, Charcas 594, 1; "Carta de Gerónimo Manuel de Ruedas a Josef de Galvez," La Plata, February 15, 1781, AGI, Charcas 594, 1; "Carta de Juan José Vertíz a Josef de Galvez," Buenos Aires, February 19, 1781, AGI, Charcas 595, 2; Andrade Padilla, *La Rebelión de Tomás Catari,* 128–29, 130.

141. "Oficio de Merlos a Vertíz," February 15, 1781, in Lewin, *La rebelión de Túpac Amaru,* 739.

142. Zuaire Huarte, "Análisis de la rebelión de Túpac Amaru en su bicentenario (1780–1980)," 63; Fisher, *Last Inca Revolt,* 216–19, 222–23; 237–39.

143. Fisher, *Last Inca Revolt,* 252; O'Phelan Godoy, *Rebellions and Revolts,* 212, 255.

144. "Testimonio de Pedro Gonzalez Santalla," in "Expediente seguido sobre el lamen-table estado del pueblo de Sorata por haberse citiada por los indios," Oruro, August 19, 1781, ANB, SGI.1781.244, 1; "Testimonio de Da. Liberata de Mariaca," in "Segundo cuaderno de la sumaria confesión y otras actuaciones de la causa criminal seguida contra Antonio Molina," La Paz, November 4, 1782, ANB, SGI.1782.62, 2.

145. "Testimonio de Pedro Gonzalez Santalla," 1–2; "Testimonio de Gerónimo Gutier-ras," in "Segundo cuaderno de la sumaria confesión y otras actuaciones de la causa criminal seguida contra Antonio Molina," La Paz, November 4, 1782, ANB, SGI.1782.62, 16.

146. "Testimonio de Pedro Gonzalez Santalla," 1–3; "Testimonio de Da. Narcisa San-talla," in "Segundo cuaderno de la sumaria confesión y otras actuaciones de la causa criminal seguida contra Antonio Molina," La Paz, November 4, 1782, ANB, SGI.1782.62, 8–9; see also "Testimonio de Antonio Molina," in "Segundo cua-

derno de la sumaria confesión y otras actuaciones de la causa criminal seguida contra Antonio Molina," La Paz, November 4, 1782, ANB, SGI.1782.62, 56.

147. "Representación de Diego Frnz Mariano," Condocondo, February 12, 1778, in "El lisenciado D. Diego Frnz Mariano representa a V.M.," 1

148. "Dn Pedro Antonio Zernudas y Dn Lorenzo Blanco Ciceron informan," 3; "Carta de Juan José Vertíz a Josef de Galvez," February 19, 1781, 3; "Oficio de Capellán de Challapata, Juan Antonio Beltrán," Challapata, January 18, 1781, AGI, Charcas 595, 1–2; see also "Oficio del regente de la Audiencia de Charcas a Virey de Buenos Aires, con inclusión del Informe del cura de Chayanta en que da noticia de la muerte que dieron los indios de Paria a su corregidor," in Pedro de Angelis, ed., *Relación de obras y documentos relativos ala historia antigua y moderna de las provincias de Río de la Plata* (Buenos Aires: Imprenta del Estado, 1836), 4:259; "Testimonio de Santos Mamani," Oruro, May 25, 1781, AGI, Charcas 601, 72; "Solicitud del Padre Fray Eugenio Gutierres sobre que le atienda en alguna colocación por sus méritos y servicios," Paria, March 4, 1783, ANB, SGI.1783.198, 1; "Dn. Pedro Anto Zernudas y Dn. Lorenzo Blanco Ciceron Oydores de la Rl Auda dela Plata informan a V.M. del estado en que se halla el [sic] rebelión y Alzamto en la prova de Chayanta," La Plata, March 13, 1781, AGI, Charcas 594, 3; "Carta de Juan José Vertíz a Josef Galvez," Buenos Aires, February 19, 1781, AGI, Charcas 595, 3; "Fragment of Informe," 3; "Carta de Juan José Vertíz a Josef Galvez," February 19, 1781, 3; "Testimonio formado sobre la sublevación de los Indios del Pueblo de Challapata y muerte que dieron a su corregidor Dn. Manuel de la Bodega y Llano," La Plata, January 26, 1781, AGI, Charcas 596, 2; "Carta de Capellán Theodoro Gutiérrez de Seballos a Ramón Urrutía y las Casas," Poopó, January 18, 1781, AGI, Charcas 437-b, 5.

149. "Oficio del oficial real de Carangas a la Audiencia de Charcas, en el que avisa haber muerto los indios a su corregidor D. Mateo Ibañez Arco," Carangas, February 17, 1781, in Odriozola, *Documentos históricos,* 1:340; "Diligencias hechas para averiguar los bienes dejados por Manuel Guemes Esles y Mateo Ibañez, oficiales de las cajas reales de Carangas (Oruro), que fueron muertos por los indios durante la rebelión general y quedaron debiendo a la real hacienda," 1789, ANB, EC.1789.104, 1; "Relación verdadera de los lástimos sucesos ocuridos en la villa de Oruro con motivo de haber los mestizos y cholos de ella, procidido inicuamente a quitar la vida a los españoles europeos, que la habitaban," 1781, in Mier, *Noticia y proceso de la muy noble y muy leal Villa de San Felipe de Austria de Oruro* (n.p., 1906), 2:96; "Expediente que contiene el informe del Tesorero Dn. Pable Castilla, hecho a la Rl. A. sobre las muertes ejecutadas por los rebeldes de dicha provincia," La Plata, May 7, 1781, ANB, SGI.1781.249, 1–2.

150. "Información recivida en la Prova de Chayanta sobre aberiguar quienes han hido los principales caudillos de la sublevcn de dichos pueblos," 17; "Confesión de Nicolás Catari," 320; "Carta de Gerónimo Manuel de Ruedas a Josef de Galvez," La Plata, February 15, 1781, AGI, Charcas 594, 1; "Carta de Ignacio Florez a Juan José Vertíz," La Plata, January 29, 1781, AGI, Charcas 595, 1; "Carta de Ignacio Florez a Juan José Vertíz," May 13, 1781, 1; "Representación de Gregorio José de Merlos al Rey," La Plata, March 12, 1782, AGI, Charcas 597, 2; "Fragment of Informe," 2; "Carta de Juan José Vertíz a Josef de Galvez," February 19, 1781, 3;

"Diario trunco," 9; "Confesión de Bonifacio Caisino," La Plata, April 18, 1781, AGI, Charcas 603, 20; "Confesión de Nicolás Achu," La Plata, April 18, 1781, AGI, Charcas 603, 20; "Confesión de Pasqual Canchari," La Plata, April 18, 1781, AGI, Charcas 603, 21; "Carta de Ignacio Florez a Juan José Vertíz," May 13, 1781, 5.

151. "Oficio del oficial real de Carangas," 1:340; "Diligencias hechas para averiguar los bienes dejados por Manuel Guemes Esles y Mateo Ibañez, oficiales de las cajas reales de Carangas (Oruro), que fueron muertos por los indios durante la rebelión general y quedaron debiendo a la real hacienda," 1789, ANB, EC.1789.104, 1; "Relación verdadera," 96; "Expediente que contiene el informe del Tesorero Dn. Pable Castilla," 1–2.

152. "El Presidente Regente de la R.A. de Charcas Informando de la sublevación de Indios de la provincia de Chayanta," 1; "Dn. Pedro Anto Zernudas y Dn. Lorenzo Blanco," 1, 3–4; "Carta de Ignacio Florez a Josef de Galvez," La Plata, December 10, 1782, AGI, Charcas 595, 1; "Carta de Ignacio Florez a Josef de Galvez," La Plata, February 15, 1781, AGI, Charcas 594, 1; "Carta de Gerónimo Manuel de Ruedas a Josef de Galvez," La Plata, September 15, 1780, AGI, Charcas 596, 1–2; "Nueve copias certificadas que acompaña la carta reservada del Yntendante de Buenos Ayres," Buenos Aires, January 14, 1781, AGI, Charcas 594, 1; "Carta de Ignacio Florez a Juan José Vertíz," La Plata, January 27, 1781, AGI, Charcas 595, 1; "Carta de Gerónimo Manuel de Ruedas a Josef de Galvez," La Plata, December 14, 1780, AGI, Charcas 596, 1; "Testimonio del título dado por el excelentísimo sr. Virrey de estas Provincias al sr. Dn. José Flores de Comandante General de las sublevadas de este Perú," La Plata, November 14, 1780, ANB, SGI.1780.87, 1; Andrade Padilla, *La Rebelión de Tomás Catari*, 145.

153. "Actuaciones anteriores a la formación de esta causa de Oruro," La Plata, February 22, 1781, AGI, Charcas 599, 7; "Carta de Capellán Augustín Flores Urito Ledo a Jorge Escobedo," Porco, February 21, 1781, AGI, Charcas 437-b, 25; "Causa criminal contra dos Yndios Reos del Pueblo de Yura sobre la muerte que tumalmte executaron en la persona del Govr. Choquebilca y otros del mismo Yura que son Veliciano Verguera y Jph. Porotaca," Yura, March 22, 1782, ANB, Ruck.1782.105, 1.

154. "Actuaciones anteriores," 7; "Causa criminal contra Ramón Paca, Bentura Pinto, Pedro Copa Cava, y de más reos principales, comprehendidos en la sublevación, muertes y robos perpetrados en este pueblo de Yura y sus ynmediasiones," Porco, October 7, 1781, ANB, SGI.1781.61, 1; "Declaración de Blas Condori," in "Causa criminal contra Ramón Paca," 3; "Declaración de Roque Argote," Potosí, March 7, 1781, AGI, Charcas 596, 9–10.

155. "Relación de los hechos más notables," 165–67; "Confesión de Nicolás Catari," 327; "Carta de Juan Antonio Ruíz Tagle a Jorge Escobedo," La Plata, February 12, 1781, AGI, Charcas 437-b, 9; "Fragment of Informe," 3; "El Regente Presidente de Charcas informa sobre la prissión practicada de la persona de Dor Dn Gregorio Jph de Merlos, cura de la Doctrina de Macha," La Plata, April 15, 1781, AGI, Charcas 444, 1; "Confesión de Dámaso Catari," 307.

156. "Dn. Pedro Anto Zernudas y Dn. Lorenzo Blanco Ciceron Oydores de la Rl Auda dela Plata informan a V.M. del estado en que se halla el [sic] rebelión y Alzamto en la prova de Chayanta," La Plata, March 13, 1781, AGI, Charcas 594, 167–70; "Carta de Ignacio Florez a Juan José Vertíz," May 13, 1781, 1; "Rl. Provisión circu-

lar a los corregidores de Yamparáez, Tomina, Misque y Cochabamba, en que se halla un auto acerca del perdón concedida a los indios sublevados," n.p., June 28, 1781, ANB, SGI.1781.38, 1; "Expediente seguido por Diego Palca, cacique de la Doctrina de Andamarca provincia de Carangas sobre que le confirme en el cucicazgo que obtiene," La Plata, August 16, 1781, ANB, SGI.1781.219, 1; Juan José Vega, *José Gabriel Túpac Amaru* (Lima: Editorial Urquizo, 1969), 152.

157. "Informe con testimonio de autos los graves motivos que ha tenido para quitar a los vezinos de la prova de Sinti el gravemen del doze y medio por ciento que cargaban como nuevo impuesto sobre los aguardientes de sus cosechas," La Plata, April 1781, AGI, Charcas 594, 2.

158. "Relación verdadera," 57, 59, 63–64, 66, 72, 75–76, 77, 78; "Informe del Consejo," 101–14; "Relación de los horribles estragos que en el día 10 de febrero de 1781 hicieron los Cholos e Yndios patricios en Oruro," 1781, in Paz y Guiní, *Guerra Separatista*, 1:342; "Diario fabuloso," 282, 283–84, 288; "De los sucesos más principales acaecidos en la villa de Oruro entre europeos y crillos" (1781), in Marcos Beltrán Avila, *Capítulos de la historia colonial de Oruro* (La Paz: La República, 1925), 294, 310; "Representación de Félix Josef de Villalobos a Gerónimo Manuel de Ruedas," La Plata, March 7, 1781, AGI, Charcas 594, 19; "El corregidor de Oruro, el alcalde de sugundo voto y el administrador de Correos, se dirigen al corregidor de Cochabamba, villa donde se refugiaron, solicitando auxilio contra los rebeldes," Cochabamba, February 1781, in Lewin, *La rebelión de Túpac Amaru*, 879; Lewin, *Túpac Amaru, el rebelde*, 290; "Relación histórica de los sucesos de la rebelión de José Gabriel Túpac-Amaru en las provincias del Perú el año de 1780," in Pedro de Angelis, ed., *Colección de obras y documentos relativos a la historia del Río de la Plata* (Buenos Aires: Librería Nacional de J. Lajouane, 1910), 4:276–79; Ramiro Condarco Morales, "Síntesis Geografía," in *Monografía de Bolivia*, n.a. (La Paz: Biblioteca del sesquicentenario de la república, 1970), 3:121; "Dictamen del Consejo de Indias" (1800), in Mier, *Noticia y proceso de la muy noble y muy leal Villa de San Felipe de Austria de Oruro*, 2:125. See also Fernando Cajias de la Vega, "La rebelión de Oruro," 34.

159. "Relación verdadera," 78; "Diario fabuloso," 288; "De los sucesos más principales," 299.

160. "Relación verdadera," 61, 78–84; "Diario fabuloso," 288–90; "Relación histórica," 17, 24, 26–28; "Relación de los funestros acaecimientos ocuridos en el día 15 del presente mes enero 1781 en el pueblo de Challapata jurisdición de la Provincia de Paria con su corregidor Dn. Manuel de la Bodega, y el 26 de dicho mes en la de Carangas con su corregidor Dn. Matías Ybañez" (1781), in Paz y Guiní, *Guerra Separatista*, 1:340; "Actuaciones anteriores," 178; "Relación traxica de los funestros y ruinosos acaecemientos de la villa de Oruro," Potosí, April 13, 1781, AGI, Charcas 437-b, 3; "Don José Manuel de Santander sobre que le declare de pobre de solemnidad," 1782, ANB, EC.1782.103, 1–2; "Declaración de Pedro Rubén Celis," in "Don José Manuel de Santander sobre que le declare de pobre de solemnidad," 1782, Oruro, ANB, EC. 1782.103, 8; "De los sucesos más principales," 301–302.

161. "Relación de los horribles," 344; Relación verdadera," 84–85; "Relación histórica," 28–29, 31; "Informe del Consejo," 107; "Declaración de Josef Manuel Montesinos," in "Sobre el retiro de los empleados de la villa de Oruro a la ciudad de Cocha-

bamba, con motivo de la sublevación de 10 febrero 1781," 1781, Arque, ANB, EC.1781.138, 58; "Informe del Consejo," 106; "Diario fabuloso," 291; Cajías de la Vega, "Los objectivos," 407, 408, 416.

162. "Relación traxica," 4; "Diario fabuloso," 291-92; "Relación histórica," 29; "Carta del Cabildo de Cochabamba al Rey," Cochabamba, January 31, 1782, AGI, Charcas 595, 1; "Declaración de Don Manuel Parrilla" (Lt. Col. of Militia and Attorney of Oruro to Capt. Salvador Conde), in "Sobre el retiro de los empleados de la villa de Oruro a la ciudad de Cochabamba, con motivo de la sublevación del 10 Febrero 1781," Arque, ANB, EC.1781.138, 54-55; "Causas de Oruro. Testimonio de la acusación del Señor Fiscal de S.M. contra los reos de la sublevación de la villa de Oruro y otras acusaciones," Buenos Aires, 1784, in Mier, *Noticia y proceso de la muy noble y muy leal Villa de San Felipe de Austria de Oruro,* 2:132.

163. "Relación verdadera," 86-87; "Diario fabuloso," 292-93; "Informe del Consejo," 106.

164. "Carta de Ignacio Florez a Dn. Gerónimo Manuel de Ruedas," January 2, 1781, 2; "Oficio de Gregorio Francisco de Campos, Obispo de La Paz, al Rey," La Paz, November 15, 1781, AGI, Charcas 595, 6; "Actuaciones anteriores," 96; "Bando de Andrés Tupacamaro," Lugar de Quincosera, July 13, 1781, AGI, Charcas 595, 1.

165. "Relación histórica," 30; "Informe del Consejo," 107; "Testimonio de Josef Manuel de Santander," in "Causa contra los cabezas de la rebelión de Oruro," La Plata, n.d., AGI, Charcas 599, 180; "Carta de Capellán Theodoro Gutierrez de Seballos," 5.

166. "Informe del Consejo," 106-107.

167. "Testimonio de Santos Maleo," Oruro, April 7, 1781, AGI, Charcas 601, 27; "Carta de Santos Mamani a Jacinto Rodríguez," Sorasora, March 10, 1781, AGI, Charcas 601, 20; Testimonio de Santos Mamani," 72, 73; "Testimonio de Martín Lopes," Oruro, April 7, 1781, AGI, Charcas 601, 26; "Declaración de Manuel Mamani," Oruro, April 7, 1781, AGI, Charcas 601, 29; "Declaración de Nicolás Colque," Oruro, April 7, 1781, AGI, Charcas 601, 30; "Declaración de Philipe Calano," Oruro, April 7, 1781, AGI, Charcas 601, 33; "Relación histórica," 31-32; "Relación verdadera," 93, 98-99; "Expediente seguido por Tomás Carpio por cantidad de pesos que demanda a la Real Hacienda por los cañones que trabajó en el año de la sublevación en la villa de Oruro," 1790, ANB, EC 1790.16, 2; Relación verdadera," 96-98; "Informe del Consejo," 108; "Don José Manuel de Santander sobre que le declare de pobre de solemnidad," 3; "Declaración de Pedro Rubén Celis," 4; "Testimonio de Ventura Balencia," Oruro, April 10, 1781, AGI, Charcas 601, 24; "Sobre los alboratos y sublevación de indios en Cochabamba," Quillacollo, May 26, 1781, ANB, SGI.1781.210, 29; "Actuaciones anteriores," 21, 83, 84-85, 89, 90-91, 95, 123; "Testimonio de Santos Mamani," 73; "Declaración de Francisco Xavier Condori," Oruro, April 10, 1781, AGI, Charcas 601, 24; "Declaración de Juan de Dios Andrade," Oruro, March 10, 1781, AGI, Charcas 601, 20; "Declaración de Antonio Moreno" (Artillery Commander), in "Sobre el retiro de los empleados de la villa de Oruro a la ciudad de Cochabamba, con motivo de la sublevación del 10 Febrero 1781," Arque, ANB, EC.1781.138, 55; "Declaración de Don Manuel Parrilla," 53; "Relación de los sucesos de la Provincia de Cochabamba año de 1781," written by the cabildo of Cochabamba, Cochabamba, December 17, 1781, AGI, Charcas 595, 13; "Declara-

ción de Comandante Pedro Gari," in "Sobre el retiro de los empleados de la villa de Oruro a la ciudad de Cochabamba, con motivo de la sublevación del 10 Febrero 1781," 1781, ANB, EC.1781.138, 55 (also in Mier, *Noticia y proceso de la muy noble y leal villa de San Felipe de Austria de Oruro*, vol. 1, n.p., 1906); Beltrán Avila, *Capítulos*, 188–89; Cajías de la Vega, "Los objectivos," 416, 422; Albó, "Etnicidad y clase en la gran rebelión Aymara/Quechua," 72; Valle del Siles, *Historia de la rebelión de Túpac Katari*, 40.

168.   "Relación verdadera," 96–98; "Actuaciones anteriores," 84; "Relación histórica," 32; "Informe del Consejo," 108; "Don José Manuel de Santander sobre que le declare de pobre de solemnidad," 3; "Declaración de Pedro Rubén Celis," 4; "Testimonio de Ventura Balencia," 24; "Sobre los alboratos y sublevación de indios en Cochabamba," 29; Beltrán Avila, *Capítulos*, 189; Albó, "Etnicidad y clase en la gran rebelión Aymara/Quechua," 72; Cajías de la Vega, "Los objectivos," 416.

169.   "Declaración de Antonio Moreno," 55; "Declaración de Don Manuel Parrilla," 53; "Relación de los sucesos de la Provincia de Cochabamba," 13; "Informe del Consejo," 108; "Declaración de Comandante Pedro Gari," 55; "Don José Manuel de Santander," 3; "Relación verdadera," 99.

170.   Beltrán Avila, *Capítulos*, 193; Válcarcel, *La rebelión de Túpac Amaru*, 195; Lewin, *Túpac Amaru, el rebelde*, 29.

171.   "Relación verdadera," 98; "Testimonio de Santos Mamani," 72; Valle del Siles, *Historia de la rebelión de Túpac Katari*, 40.

172.   "Testimonio del expediente de embargo de los bienes de Dn. Diego Antonio Flores," 1784, ANB, EC.1784.110, 1; "Cuatro oficios del Virey Juan José Vertíz escritos en Montevideo," Montevideo, April 1782, ANB, EC.1782.89, #12, 2; "Informe del Consejo de Indias al Rey, sublevación de Oruro," September 28, 1800, in Mier, *Noticia y proceso de la muy noble y muy leal Villa de San Felipe de Austria de Oruro*, 2:110, 111, 112, 113; "Testimonio del expediente de embargo de bienes de Dn. Diego Antonio Flores," ANB, EC.1784.110, 1; "Causas de Oruro," 2:170–72; Abdon Calderón, *Monografía histórica del departamento de Oruro* (Oruro: n.p., 1947), 34; Válcarcel, *La rebelión de Túpac Amaru*, 192; Beltrán Avila, *Capítulos*, 197–98; Mier, *Noticia y proceso de la muy noble y muy leal Villa de San Felipe de Austria de Oruro*, 2:ix.

173.   "Carta de Capellán Josef Barela y Bohorgues a Jorge Escobedo," Tinquipaia, February 10, 1781, AGI, Charcas 437-b, 7; "Carta de Jorge Escobedo al Regente Gerónimo Manuel de Ruedas," Potosí, February 13, 1781, AGI, Charcas 437-b, 8; "Carta de Jorge Escobedo a Juan José Vertíz," Potosí, February 24, 1781, AGI, Charcas 437-b, 35–36; "Carta de Jorge Escobedo a José Antonio de Areche," Potosí, February 18, 1781, AGI, Charcas 437-b, 15–16; "Decreto de Jorge Escobedo," Potosí, March 4, 1781, AGI, Charcas 437-b, 41; "Representación de Domingo Angeles," 12; "Relación de los hechos más notables," 206; "Carta de Arequipa con fecha 2 de Mayo de 1781 que refiere los estragos executados por los indios alzados en varios pueblos de las provincias de ambos virreyenatos," Arequipa, May 2, 1781, in Cárlos Daniel Válcarcel, ed., *Colección Documental de la independencia del Perú*, book 2, 1:694; "Carta que refiere a los estragos hechos por los Yndios alzados en Suches mineral de la Provincia de Larecaja del Obispado de La Paz; y en los pueblos de Arque, Tapacari, y Colcha en la Provincia de Cochabamba, perteneciente al Arzo-

bispado de la Plata," Cochabamba, February 26, 1781, in Válcarcel, *Colección Documental de la independencia del Perú,* book 2, 1:508–509; "Carta de Arequipa," 694.

174. "Carta de Félix Villalobos a Gerónimo Manuel de Ruedas," Cochabamba, February 24, 1781, AGI, Charcas 596, 7; "Actuaciones anteriores," 5; "Relación de los hechos más notables," 206; "Representación de Francisco Lino y Córdoba a Félix Josef de Villalobos," Cochabamba, March 7, 1781, AGI, Charcas 594, 7.

175. "Relación de los sucesos de la Provincia de Cochabamba," 7.

176. Ibid., 5; "Actuaciones anteriores," 21; "Relación de los hechos más notables," 162; "Carta del Cabildo de Cochabamba al Rey," 1; "Carta de Juan Fernando Pacheco a Félix Joseph de Villalobos," Caraza, September 21, 1780, AGI, Charcas 596, 1; "Carta de Juan Fernando Pacheco al Theniente Coronel Manuel Parilla y Coronel Fsco Mendibal," Caraza, September 21, 1780, AGI, Charcas 596, 1; "Noticias de Cochabamba," Cochabamba, February 24, 1781, AGI, Charcas 437-b, 59; "Relación de los sucesos de la Provincia de Cochabamba," 4; "Actuaciones anteriores," 5, 87, 99, 144; "Declaración de Fray Josef Serbantes," Oruro, April 9, 1781, in "Testimonio del expedientes y diligencias practicadas para averiguar los tumultos meditadas contra Oruro," AGI, Charcas 601, 18; "Oficio de Francisco Javier Beltrán," Potosí, March 14, 1781, AGI, Charcas 437-b, 1; "Confesión de Pedro Choque," in "Autos y causa criminal seguida contra los indios Matías Arreola, Diego Tonacio, Nicolás Capa, Manuel Lerque y Pedro Choque por la muerte que ejecutaron con tumulto en la persona de Dn. Phelipe Tardio y otros azogueros de Guanachaca," Guanachaca, Potosí, June 19, 1781, ANB, SGI.1781.4a, 7, 11; "Legajo contra Mateo Xavier indio de Tolapampa por sublevación y muerte que ejecutó en Dn. Marcos Torres," Porco, August 16, 1781, ANB, SGI.1781.58, 2, 4; "Informe de Josef Atanacio Baspineyro," Potosí, March 14, 1781, AGI, Charcas 437-b, 1–2; "Parte de D. José de Reseguín al Virey de Buenos Aires, sobre la sublevación de la Provincia de Tupiza," Tupiza, March 18, 1781, in Odriozola, *Documentos históricos,* 1:348; "Carta de Jorge Escobedo a Gerónimo Manuel de Ruedas," Potosí, March 11, 1781, AGI, Charcas 596, 22; "Actuaciones anteriores," 17; "Declaración de Francisco Ribera," Potosí, March 10, 1781, AGI, Charcas 437-b, 60; Sebastián Lorete, *Historia del Perú bajo los Borbones* (Lima: Gil y Aubert, 1871), 185–86.

177. "Relación de los sucesos de la provincia de Cochabamba," 4; "Oficio del Regente de la Real Audiencia de la Plata Gerónimo Manuel de Ruedas," La Plata, September 18, 1781, AGI, Charcas 596, 1–2; "Actuaciones anteriores," 6; "Declaración de Martina Rueda," in "El Corregor. Dela Villa de Cochabamba sobre los destrozos que executaron los indios en Tapacari," Oropesa, March 7, 1781, ANB, SGI.1781.62, 3; "Declaración de Da. María Losa," in "El Corregor. Dela Villa de Cochabamba sobre los destrozos que executaron los indios en Tapacari," Oropesa, March 7, 1781, ANB, SGI.1781.62.6, 7; "Declaración de Don Martín Condori," in "El Corregor. Dela Villa de Cochabamba sobre los destrozos que executaron los indios en Tapacari," Oropesa, March 7, 1781, ANB, SGI.1781.62, 2.

178. "Carta que refiere a los estragos," 509; "Declaración de Da. María Crespo," and "Declaración de Da. Magdalena Tribino," both in "El Corregor. de la Villa de Cochabamba sobre los destrozos que executaron los indios en Tapacari," Oropesa, March 7, 1781, ANB, SGI.1781.62, 5, 8–9; "Carta que refiere a los estragos," 508.

179. "Carta que refiere a los estragos," 509; Valentín Abecia Baldivieso, "La insurec-

ción india de Tapacari en 1781," in Cárlos Daniel Válcarcel, ed., *Actas de coloquio Internacional: "Túpac Amaru y su tiempo"* (Lima: Comisión Nacional del Bicentenario de la Revolución Emancipadora de Túpac Amaru, 1982), 41.

180. "Relación de los sucesos de la Provincia de Cochabamba," 5; "Carta de Arequipa," 693, 695.

181. "Dn. Pedro Antonio Cernudas y Dn. Lorenzo Blanco Ciceron oydores en la Rl. Audiencia de Charcas continuan el informe de los sucesos de las provincias cuios naturales incurrieron en el delito de rebelión," La Plata, May 15, 1781, AGI, Charcas 594, 1; "Carta de Pedro Zeberino de San Martín a Jorge Escobedo," Suypacha, March 8, 1781, AGI, Charcas 437-b, 63; "Representación de los vecinos de Tupiza al Comandante General Reseguín pidiendo no deje la provincia por el riesgo que corre con los sublevados," Tupiza, March 17, 1781, in Odriozola, *Documentos históricos,* 1:47; "Oficio de Francisco Javier Beltrán," 1.

182. "Expte. que tiene la sumaria resibida pr el Justa. Mor. de la Prova. de Chichas contra Don Lortenzo Antesana por la complicidad que sele imputa en la sublevación y alboratos de aquella prova," Tupiza, December 19, 1781, ANB, Ruck.1781.104, 1, 3–6, 21, 23, 43.

183. "Carta de Luís de Palacio y Santelices a Gerónimo de Ruedas," Santiago de Cotagaita, March 9, 1781, AGI, Charcas 596, 22, 24; "Declaración de Luís de Palacio y Santelises," La Plata, March 12, 1781, AGI, Charcas 594, 22; "Causa de Augustín Solís," La Plata, March 11, 1781, AGI, Charcas 594, 21; "Fragment of Informe," 5; "Dn. Pedro Antonio Cernudas y Dn. Lorenzo Blanco Ciceron," 1; "Dn Pedro Antonio Zernudas oidor dela Rl Audiencia dela Plata informa," 5; "Carta de Capitán General y Gobernador Andrés Mestre a Josef de Galvez," Salta, June 24, 1781, AGI, Charcas 595, 1; "Noticias de lo acaecido en la provincia de Chichas desde el 6 de Marzo hasta el 3 de Abril de 1781," Remedios, n.d., AGI, Charcas 437-b, 1; "Relación de los hechos más notables," 173; "Oficio de la Audiencia de Charcas a Juan José Vertíz," La Plata, March 15, 1781, AGI, Charcas 594, 1.

184. "Carta de Luís Laso de la Vega a Gobernador Augustín Solís," Tupiza, March 7, 1781, AGI, Charcas 596, 21; "Carta de Pedro Zeberino de San Martín a Jorge Escobedo," 64; "El Regente Presidente de Charcas da cuenta del féliz suceso de la expedn hecha el día 20 de Febrero inmto contra los indios rebeldes," La Plata, May 15, 1781, AGI, Charcas 444, 2; see also "Carta del rebelde D. Pedro de la Cruz Condori a los principales, asi Españoles como naturales y Mestizos criollos de la doctrina de Santiago de Cotagaita," Chocalla, March 19, 1781, in Odriozola, *Documentos históricos,* 1:41; "Carta del Dr. Dn. Francisco López, cura del pueblo de Tupiza, sobre asuntos de la sublevación," Tupiza, March 27, 1781, ANB, SGI.1781.223, 2, 4.

185. "Parte de D. José de Reseguín al Virey de Buenos Aires, sobre la sublevación de la Provincia de Tupiza," March 18, 1781, in Odriozola, *Documentos históricos,* 1:347–48; "Don Josef Reseguín haze presente sus servicios y méritos en las presentes reboluciones de aquel Reyno e incluye el diario de todas sus operaciones," Cochabamba, February 4, 1782, AGI, Charcas 595, 1; "Carta de José de Roseguín a Jorge Escobedo," Tupiza, April 4, 1781, AGI, Charcas 437-b, 26; Odriozola, *Documentos históricos,* 1:36–37, 39–41, 45, 48; "Orden de Jorge Escobedo," Potosí, April 5, 1781, AGI, Charcas 437-b, 17; "Carta de Thomas Villanueva y Lucas Choque a Jorge

Escobedo," Tomabe, April 11, 1781, AGI, Charcas 437-b, 33; "Noticias de lo acaecido en la provincia de Chichas desde el 6 de Marzo hasta el 3 de Abril de 1781," 1–2.

186. "Declaración de Ysidro Josef de Herrera," San Pedro de Buenavista, October 5, 1780, AGI, Charcas 596, 10; "Informe de Pedro Yavira Ylario Caguasiri," San Pedro de Buenavista, December 28, 1780, AGI, Charcas 596, 48, 50–51; "Representación de Marcos Ancienega," San Pedro de Buenavista, September 24, 1780, in "Testimonio de los autos de la sublevación de Chayanta," AGI, Charcas 596, 50–51; "Oficio de Capellán Sebastián de Ballestros al Regente Gerónimo Manuel de Ruedas," San Pedro de Buenavista, September 25, 1780, AGI, Charcas 596, 52–53; "Representación de Polonia Inojosa a Gerónimo Manuel de Ruedas," San Pedro de Buenavista, September 29, 1780, AGI, Charcas 596, 60, 96; "Declaración de Eugenio Moya," La Plata, October 9, 1780, AGI, Charcas 596, 76; "Oficio de Capellán Sebastián de Ballestros," 53; "Informe de Gregorio Josef de Merlos," 11; "Informe de Tomás Catari," 19; "Declaración de Pablo Caquasiri," 75; "Carta de Domingo Angeles a Gerónimo Manuel de Ruedas," La Plata, October 8, 1780, AGI, Charcas 596, 7; "Declaración de Ysidro Josef de Herrera," 10; "Confesión de Nicolás Gueso," La Plata, April 20, 1781, AGI, Charcas 603, 23; "Carta de Ignacio Florez a Dn. Gerónimo Manuel de Ruedas," La Plata, January 2, 1781, AGI, Charcas 594, 3; "Carta a Juan José Vertíz a Josef de Galvez," Buenos Aires, February 19, 1781, AGI, Charcas 595, 2; "Informe de Andrés del Barco y Urcullo," Poopó, October 16, 1780, AGI, Charcas 596, 91; "Representación de Augustín Fernández," Oruro, November 20, 1780, AGI, Charcas 596, 50; "Confesión de Simón Castillo," La Plata, April 25, 1781, AGI, Charcas 603, 32.

187. "Confesión de Simón Castillo," 32; "Juicio criminal seguido de oficio contra Lasaro Apacheta, por haber capitaneado a los indios sublevados," Misque, May 2, 1781, ANB, SGI.1781.1a, 2; "Confesión de Pasqual Tola," La Plata, April 20, 1781, AGI, Charcas 603, 27–28; "Actuaciones anteriores," 23, 24; "Confesión de Sebastiana Mamani," La Plata, April 18, 1781, AGI, Charcas 603, 24; "Confesión de Lázaro Mamani," La Plata, April 18, 1781, AGI, Charcas 603, 24–25; "Confesión de Francisco Gonzalo," La Plata, April 20, 1781, AGI, Charcas 603, 25–26.

188. "Confesión de Francisco Gonzalo," 26; Confesión de Nicolás Gueso," 28; "Confesión de Diego Sosa," La Plata, April 20, 1781, AGI, Charcas 603, 29; "Confesión de Simón Castillo," 32; "Relación de los hechos más notables," 170–71; "Actuaciones anteriores," 23; "Confesión de Josef Daga," La Plata, April 25, 1781, in "Criminales contra Nicolás Catari y otros indios," AGI, Charcas 603, 12; "Carta de Estiban Lidosa a Gerónimo Manuel de Ruedas," La Plata, April 9, 1781, AGI, Charcas 603, 24; "Confesión de Lázaro Mamani," 25; "Confesión de Sebastiana Mamani," 25.

189. "Confesión de Pasqual Tola," 27.

190. "Diario trunco," 11; "Carta de Arequipa," 693; "Relación de los hechos más notables," 170–71; "El Regente Presidente de la Rl. Audiencia de Charcas informa del cuidadoso estado de la rebelión de Indios," La Plata, April 15, 1781, AGI, Charcas 594, 1; "Oficio de Gregorio Francisco de Campos, Obisbo de La Paz al Rey," 6; "Actuaciones anteriores," 23; "Confesión de Josef Daga," 1; "Confesión de Augustín Ventura," La Plata, April 25, 1781, in "Criminales contra Nicolás Catari y otros indios," AGI, Charcas 603, 24; "Confesión de Sebastiana Mamani," 25; "Confesión de Francisco Gonzalo," 25; "Confesión de Nicolás Gueso," 28.

191. "Confesión de Lázaro Mamani," 24; "Carta de Estiban Lidosa," 24; "Confesión de Sebastiana Mamani," 25; "Confesión de Francisco Gonzalo," 25; "Confesión de Pasqual Tola," 27; "Confesión de Thomas Molina," La Plata, April 21, 1781, AGI, Charcas 603, 30; "Diario trunco," 11; "Confesión de Nicolás Catari," 325; "Confesión de Lázaro Mamani," 24; "Confesión de Nicolás Catari," 325; "Confesión de Andrés Mamani," La Plata, April 21, 1781, AGI, Charcas 603, 30; "Confesión de Cárlos Caunachu," La Plata, April 21, 1781, AGI, Charcas 603, 30.

192. "Carta de Fray Matías de la Borda a Sebastián de Segurola," La Paz, May 30, 1781, AGI, Charcas 595, 1; "Copias de documentos citados en el diario," #18, in "Diario del cerco de La Paz en 1781, por Sebastián de Segurola," La Paz, May 30, 1781, ANB, SGI.1781.s.n., 21.

193. "Copias de documentos citados en el diario," #18, 21–22; "Carta de Borda a Segurola," 2.

194. "Confesión de Bacilio Angulo Miranda," La Paz, November 20, 1781, AGI, Charcas 444, 4; "Declaración de Ventura Carbajal," Cuzco, July 7, 1781, in Durand Florez, *Colección documental del bicentenario de la revolución emancipadora de Túpac Amaru*, 3:668; "Declaración del testigo Manuel Linares," Cuzco, July 7, 1781, ibid., 3:666; "Confesión de Isidro Mamani," Cuzco, July 7, 1781, ibid., 3:668.

195. "Diario de Sebastián de Segurola," La Paz, July 1, 1781, AGI, Charcas 595, 5; "Carta de Borda a Segurola," 3; "Confesión de Julián Apasa o Túpac Catari," Santuario de Nuestra Señora de Peñas, November 11 and 13, 1781, AGI, Buenos Aires 320, 24; "Diario que formo yo Esteban Losa escribano de S. Magd. y de guerra de la presente expedición a cargo del Señor Dn. Josef Reseguín Theniente Coronel de Dragones, y Comandante gral della con destino al socorro de la ciudad de La Paz," Oruro, December 22, 1781, AGI, Charcas 595, 10; "Copias de documentos citados en el diario," #18, 25; Valle del Siles, "Túpac Katari y la rebelión de 1781," 645, 648; O'Phelan Godoy, "Elementos étnicos," 86; Válcarcel, *La rebelión de Túpac Amaru,* 192; Campbell, "Ideology," 131.

196. "Diario del cerco de La Paz en 1781, por Sebastián de Segurola," 3; Campbell, "Ideology," 129; Hidalgo Lehunde, "Amarus y Cataris," 128.

197. "Diario de Sebastián de Segurola," 6, 17; "Relación verdadera," 98; "Diario del cerco de La Paz en 1781, por Sebastián de Segurola," 16; Valle del Siles, "Túpac Katari y la rebelión de 1781," 653; Valle del Siles, *Historia de la rebelión de Túpac Katari,* 39; O'Phelan Godoy, *Rebellions and Revolts,* 243; O'Phelan Godoy, "Elementos étnicos," 81, 87.

198. "Diario del cerco de La Paz en 1781, por Sebastián de Segurola," 3.

199. "Carta de Joaquín Salgado a José de Galvez," La Paz, November 10, 1781, AGI, Buenos Aires 320, 1; "Diario del cerco de La Paz en 1781, por Sebastián de Segurola," 2, 16; "Noticias de la expedición del Cargo del Tente Coronl dn Ignacio Flores desde del día 24 de Junio hasta el 24 de Julio subministrados por tres desertores del valle de Sacaba Provincia de Cochabamba que marcharon con la misma expedición y salieron de La Paz el citado 24 de Julio," Sacaba, August 1, 1781, AGI, Charcas, Estado 76, no. 46, 2.

200. "Copias de documentos citados en el diario," #18, 28.

201. "Carta de Joaquín Salgado a Josef de Galvez," 1; "Carta Florez a Galvez," 2–3;

"Sobre la fuga y ostilidades que hicieron los de la Prova de Tucuman que hiban al socorro de la ciudad de La Paz y retrocederían de Oruro," Oruro, August 3, 1781, AGI, Charcas 601, 1–3; "Carta de Oruro sobre el auxilio despachado para el socorro de la ciudad de La Paz comandando el ejército Don Josef Reseguín," Oruro, November 5, 1781, in Válcarcel, *Colección Documental de la Independencia del Perú*, book 2, 3:159; "Noticias de la expedición del cargo del Tente. Coronl. Dn. Ignacio Flores," 2.

202. "Carta de Borda a Segurola," 4; "Carta de Túpac Catari a Sebastián de Segurola," El Alto, April 23, 1781, in "Relación de los hechos más notables acaecidos en la sublevación general fraguada en los reynos del Perú, por el indio José Gabriel Túpac Amaru, gobr. del pueblo de Tungasuca en la Provincia de Tinta, que asociado de otros sequaces, causó horrosos estragos desde el año 1780, hasta el de 1782 en que se reprimo el orgullo de la conjuración," in *Revista de archivos y bibliotecas nacionales* 3, no. 5 (Lima, September 30, 1900): 273.

203. Fisher, *Last Inca Revolt*, 100, 243–44; Valle del Siles, *Historia de la rebelión de Túpac Katari*, 6; O'Phelan Godoy, *Rebellions and Revolts*, 212; Campbell, "Ideology," 131–32.

204. "Carta de Túpac Catari a Sebastián de Segurola," El Alto, April 7, 1781, AGI, Charcas 595, 1; "Oficios del Exmo. Sr. Virrey de Lima acompañado de algunas documtos sobre las ocurrencias de la pasada sublevón de indios," La Paz, April 16, 1784, ANB, SGI.1784.58, 8; O'Phelan Godoy, *Rebellions and Revolts*, 211–12; Fisher, *Last Inca Revolt*, 100, 243–44, 248–49, 291, 317–18, 375; Valle del Siles, *Historia de la rebelión de Túpac Katari*, 6; Campbell, "Ideology," 130–31.

205. Campbell, "Ideology," 122; "Decreto de la Real Audiencia de La Plata," March 13, 1781, AGI, Charcas 596, 23.

206. "Perdón concedida a los indios del partido de Calamarca y Sicasica," Calamarca, August 5, 1781, ANB, SGI.1781.60, 1, 4; "Carta de Josef de Reseguín a Sebastián de Velasco," La Plata, February 25, 1782, AGI, Charcas 595, 1; "Testimonio de Domingo Angeles," La Plata, October 9, 1780, AGI, Charcas 596, 1; "Bando del Virrey Augustín Jáuregui," Lima, September 13, 1781, AGI, Charcas 595, 1; Campbell, "Ideology," 133; Fisher, *Last Inca Revolt*, 348, 351, 375, 378–80.

207. Campbell, "Ideology," 133; José Macedonio Urquidi, *Compendio de la historia de Bolivia* (Buenos Aires: Talleres Gráficos EGLH, 1944), 82; Steve Stern, "Age," 35.

208. "Expediente sobre que se erijan escuelas públicas para los indios y se prohiban los diferentes idiomas que se usan," Carangas, September 27, 1777, ANB, ECad.1777.27, 1–2; Campbell, "Ideology," 118; Klein, *Bolivia*, 77; Fisher, *Last Inca Revolt*, 223–24; Chalk and Jonassohn, "The Conceptual Framework," 9.

209. "Recurso por parte de don Pedro Ramírez de la Parra, gobernador y cacique principal del pueblo de Jesús de Machaca, partido de Pacajes, ante el Fiscal protector, de los excesos, vicios y defectos cometidos por el Teniente Asesor de la provincia de La Paz, en el dislinde y amojonamiento de las tierras pertenecientes a su comunidad, con las de doña María Josefa y doña Evarista Ayoroa," La Paz, February 26, 1790, ANB, ECad.1790.3, 1–3; Klein, *Bolivia*, 77–78, 80; Fisher, *Last Inca Revolt*, 384, 387–89.

210. Nelson Reed, "Juan de la Cruz, Venencio Puc, and the Speaking Cross," *The Americas* 53, no. 4 (April 1997): 497.

211. For detailed accounts of the course of the war, see Nelson Reed's seminal *The Caste War of Yucatán* (Stanford: Stanford University Press, 1988), and Don Dumond, *The Machete and the Cross: Campesino Rebellion in Yucatán* (Lincoln: University of Nebraska Press, 1997). For primary source accounts, see Serapio Baqueiro Preve's *Ensayo histórico sobre las revoluciones de Yucatán desde el año 1840 hasta 1864*, ed. Salvador Rodríguez Losa (Mérida, Mex.: Ediciones de la Universidad Autónoma de Yucatán, 1990), and Eligio Ancona's *Historia de Yucatán, desde la época más remota hasta nuestros días*, 5 vols. (Mérida, México: Imprenta de M. Heredia Argüelles, 1878–1905).

212. Cline, "The Sugar Episode in Yucatán," 80; Reed, *Caste War*, 7–8.

213. Cline, "The Sugar Episode in Yucatán," 80, 82, 86, 94; Reed, *Caste War*, 8.

214. Howard F. Cline, "Regionalism and Society in Yucatán, 1825–1847" (University of Chicago Library, Microfilm Collection of Manuscripts on Middle American Cultural Anthopology, no. 32, 1947), 3; Reed, *Caste War*, 9–10, 45.

215. Cline, "Regionalism and Society in Yucatán," 5. For a study on liberal policies in Mexico during the period of the Caste War, see Marcello Carmagnani, *Estado y Mercado: La economía pública del liberalismo mexicano, 1850–1911* (Mexico City: El Colegio de México and Fondo de Cultura Económica, 1994).

216. Reed, *Caste War*, 23.

217. Rugeley, *Yucatán's Maya Peasantry*, xvii; Reed, *Caste War*, 12.

218. Howard F. Cline, "War of the Castes and Its Consequences," University of Chicago Library, Microfilm Collection of Manuscripts on Middle American Cultural Anthopology, no. 32, 1945, 20; Reed, *Caste War*, 23; Rugeley, *Yucatán's Maya Peasantry*, xvi.

219. Reed, *Caste War*, 23–24.

220. Terry Rugeley, "Los mayas yucatecos del siglo XIX," in Leticia Reina, ed., *La reindianización de América, siglo XIX* (Mexico City: Siglo Veintiuno Editores, 1997), 210; Rugeley, *Yucatán's Maya Peasantry*, 92–93.

221. Ancona, *Yucatán*, 3:359–60, 364–66, 368–71, 4:136; Rugeley, *Yucatán's Maya Peasantry*, 92; *Guerra de Castas en Yucatán: su origen, sus consecuencias y su estado actual, 1866*, transcribed by Melchor Campos García (Mérida, Yucatán, Mex.: Universidad Autónoma de Yucatán, 1997), 9; Reed, *Caste War*, 27–28; Cline, "The Sugar Episode in Yucatán," 96.

222. *Guerra de Castas en Yucatán*, 7, 8.

223. Reed, *Caste War*, 28; Cline, "Regionalism and Society in Yucatán," 3.

224. Ancona, *Yucatán*, 4:12; Reed, *Caste War*, 29, 32.

225. Rugeley, *Yucatán's Maya Peasantry*, 165; Reed, *Caste War*, 33.

226. Baqueiro Preve, *Ensayo histórico*, 1:164–68; *Guerra de Castas en Yucatán*, 26; Ancona, *Yucatán*, 3:468–71; Rugeley, *Yucatán's Maya Peasantry*, 168; Reed, *Caste War*, 34, 46; Dumond, *Machete*, 82.

227. "Comunicaciones oficiales, relativos a los asesinatos cometidos el 15 de Enero en Valladolid," Hacienda Tixcacal, January 19, 1847, in Baqueiro Preve, *Ensayo his-*

tórico, 1:357; Ancona, *Yucatán,* 2:471, 473; ibid., 3:470; Reed, *Caste War,* 34, 46; Rugeley, *Yucatán's Maya Peasantry,* 171–72, 174.

228. Baqueiro Preve, *Ensayo histórico,* 1:224; *Guerra de Castas en Yucatán,* 20, 27, 41; "Superintendent to Governor, Mérida," Belize City, February 1, 1848, R. 22b, in Burdon, *Archives,* 3:100; Rugeley, *Yucatán's Maya Peasantry,* 167, 175.

229. "Sentencia de Muerte de Manuel Antonio Ay," Valladolid, July 25, 1847, in Baqueiro Preve, *Ensayo histórico,* 1:371–72; Baqueiro Preve, *Ensayo histórico,* 1:225–28; *Guerra de Castas en Yucatán,* 28; Reed, *Caste War,* 56–57.

230. *Guerra de Castas en Yucatán,* 22, 29–30; Baqueiro Preve, *Ensayo histórico,* 1:233–36; Reed, *Caste War,* 59.

231. Baqueiro Preve, *Ensayo histórico,* 1:237; *Guerra de Castas en Yucatán,* 30–31; Marie Lapointe, *Los mayas rebeldes de Yucatán* (Zamora, Mex: Colegio de Michoacan, 1983), 69.

232. Baqueiro Preve, *Ensayo histórico,* 2:12; Reed, *Caste War,* 59–60.

233. Baqueiro Preve, *Ensayo histórico,* 2:12–15; Ancona, *Yucatán,* 4:42–43.

234. Baqueiro Preve, *Ensayo histórico,* 1:240; ibid., 2:2–8, 81; ibid., 3:7, 62, 114; Ancona, *Yucatán,* 4:38, 67; Reed, *Caste War,* 61–62; Terry Rugeley, ed., *Maya Wars: Ethnographic Accounts from Nineteenth-Century Yucatán* (Norman: University of Oklahoma Press, 2001), 12; Dumond, *Machete,* 133.

235. Baqueiro Preve, *Ensayo histórico,* 2:21–25, 29–31; Ancona, *Yucatán,* 4:39–40, 42, 44; *Guerra de Castas en Yucatán,* 34–35; Reed, *Caste War,* 63; Rugeley, "Los mayas yucatecos del siglo XIX," 217.

236. Ancona, *Yucatán,* 4:36–37; Reed, *Caste War,* 65–66.

237. Baqueiro Preve, *Ensayo histórico,* 2:43; Ancona, *Yucatán,* 4:58.

238. Ancona, *Yucatán,* 4:58, 85.

239. Baqueiro Preve, *Ensayo histórico,* 2:49, 63, 87; Ancona, *Yucatán,* 4:53–54; *Guerra de Castas en Yucatán,* 35; Reed, *Caste War,* 66.

240. Baqueiro Preve, *Ensayo histórico,* 2:49, 4:59.

241. Ibid., 2:65–67, 3:146; Ancona, *Yucatán,* 4:58–59, 63–66; *Guerra de Castas en Yucatán,* 36; Reed, *Caste War,* 68.

242. "Carta particular Del Coronel Rosado, dirigida a Don Santiago Méndez, durante los primeros días del sitio de Peto, comunicándole varios asuntos interesantes," Peto, January 29, 1848, in Baqueiro Preve, *Ensayo histórico,* 2:70–80; Ancona, *Yucatán,* 4:71–72; Reed, *Caste War,* 69–70.

243. Baqueiro Preve, *Ensayo histórico,* 2:110–14, 116–18; Ancona, *Yucatán,* 4:87–93; Reed, *Caste War,* 72–73, 80.

244. "Apuntes escritos," 369; Ancona, *Yucatán,* 4:95–99; *Guerra de Castas en Yucatán,* 48; Reed, *Caste War,* 81–82.

245. Baqueiro Preve, *Ensayo histórico,* 2:131–34; Ancona, *Yucatán,* 4:100–101.

246. Baqueiro Preve, *Ensayo histórico,* 2:134–36; Ancona, *Yucatán,* 4:95, 101–103; *Guerra de Castas en Yucatán,* 48; Reed, *Caste War,* 83–84.

247. Baqueiro Preve, *Ensayo histórico*, 2:97, 100, 136–37; Ancona, *Yucatán*, 4:118, 125; *Guerra de Castas en Yucatán*, 49, 55.

248. Baqueiro Preve, *Ensayo histórico*, 2:145–50, 168–69; Ancona, *Yucatán*, 4:73–74, 109–11, 157–67; Reed, *Caste War*, 79, 85–87.

249. Baqueiro Preve, *Ensayo histórico*, 2:176–79; Ancona, *Yucatán*, 4:115; *Guerra de Castas en Yucatán*, 51–54; Reed, *Caste War*, 88.

250. Baqueiro Preve, *Ensayo histórico*, 2:181–83; Ancona, *Yucatán*, 4:117–19, 230; Reed, *Caste War*, 89.

251. "Mattias Estevas at 'Bar of San Antonio' to the Superintendent," April 20, 1848, R. 28, in Burdon, *Archives*, 3:106; "Superintendent to Officer Commanding Troops," April 23, 1848, R. 22b, ibid., 3:106; "Apuntes escritos," 370; Baqueiro Preve, *Ensayo histórico*, 2:185–87, 190–91, 195, 201; Baqueiro Preve, *Ensayo histórico*, 3:147; Ancona, *Yucatán*, 4:124, 126–27, 230–32; *Guerra de Castas en Yucatán*, 55–56; Karl Sapper, "Independent Indian States of Yucatán," in Charles P. Bowditch and Eduard Seler, *Mexican and Central American Antiquities, Calendar Systems, and History* (Washington, D.C.: Government Printing Office, 1904), 625; Reed, *Caste War*, 92–95.

252. Baqueiro Preve, *Ensayo histórico*, 2:201; ibid., 3:9; Ancona, *Yucatán*, 4:130; *Guerra de Castas en Yucatán*, 15; Reed, *Caste War*, 97.

253. Ancona, *Yucatán*, 4:133; *Guerra de Castas en Yucatán*, 49–50, 57; Reed, *Caste War*, 97.

254. Baqueiro Preve, *Ensayo histórico*, 2:163.

255. Ancona, *Yucatán*, 4:198–201; *Guerra de Castas en Yucatán*, 15; Reed, *Caste War*, 97.

256. "Apuntes escritos," 370–71; Baqueiro Preve, *Ensayo histórico*, 3:26–27; *Guerra de Castas en Yucatán*, 58, 60; Reed, *Caste War*, 99–100, 102–105; Dumond, *Machete*, 132–33; Terry Rugeley, personal correspondence, July 30, 2004.

257. Baqueiro Preve, *Ensayo histórico*, 3:8; *Guerra de Castas en Yucatán*, 61–64, 66.

258. *Guerra de Castas en Yucatán*, 69.

259. Ibid., 72.

260. "Decreto de Unión a Méjico," Mérida, August 17, 1848, in *Guerra de Castas en Yucatán*, 163–66; *Guerra de Castas en Yucatán*, 65; Baqueiro Preve, *Ensayo histórico*, 3:33–36; Ancona, *Yucatán*, 4:169.

261. Baqueiro Preve, *Ensayo histórico*, 3:99; Ancona, *Yucatán*, 4:193–196, 211–15, 276; *Guerra de Castas en Yucatán*, 67–68.

262. Baqueiro Preve, *Ensayo histórico*, 3:112; Ancona, *Yucatán*, 4:173; *Guerra de Castas en Yucatán*, 73–74; "Decreto de fecha de noviembre de 1848, origen de la venta de indios que tantos abusos causó después," Mérida, November 6, 1848, in Baqueiro Preve, *Ensayo histórico*, 3:306–307; "Comunicación Oficial del Gobierno del Estado, desvaneciendo los fundamentos que tuvo el Supremo Gobierno para reprobarle su conducta por las primeras partidas de indios que salieron para La Habana," Mérida, September 12, 1849, in Baqueiro Preve, *Ensayo histórico*, 3:325–26.

263. Baqueiro Preve, *Ensayo histórico*, 2:93.

264. Ibid., 3:114; Ancona, *Yucatán*, 4:237–38; *Guerra de Castas en Yucatán*, 77; Reed, *Caste War*, 117–18.

265. Baqueiro Preve, *Ensayo histórico,* 3:152–58, 174; Ancona, *Yucatán,* 4:238–39; *Guerra de Castas en Yucatán,* 77; Reed, *Caste War,* 117–18.

266. Reed, *Caste War,* 118, 124.

267. "Carta de Tiburcio R. Esteves al gobernador de Yucatán," San Miguel, February 22, 1858, in *Guerra de Castas en Yucatán,* 166; Ancona, *Yucatán,* 4:297.

268. Baqueiro Preve, *Ensayo histórico,* 3:96–99; ibid., 4:77; Ancona, *Yucatán,* 4:139–41, 143, 149; *Guerra de Castas en Yucatán,* 79; Reed, *Caste War,* 109.

269. Baqueiro Preve, *Ensayo histórico,* 3:112; Ancona, *Yucatán,* 4:250–54.

270. Baqueiro Preve, *Ensayo histórico,* 3:100; Ancona, *Yucatán,* 4:260–61; *Guerra de Castas en Yucatán,* 79; Reed, *Caste War,* 109; Dumond, *Machete,* 149–50.

271. Baqueiro Preve, *Ensayo histórico,* 3:92; Ancona, *Yucatán,* 4:190; Reed, *Caste War,* 107.

272. Ancona, *Yucatán,* 4:90, 193; *Guerra de Castas en Yucatán,* 34.

273. "Informe de la muerte de Jacinto Pat," Mérida, August 1, 1850, in Leticia Reina, *Las rebeliones campesinas en México* (Mexico City: Siglo Ventiuno, 1980), 400; Baqueiro Preve, *Ensayo histórico,* 3:196–98; Ancona, *Yucatán,* 4:63–64; *Guerra de Castas en Yucatán,* 79; "Magistrate, Northern District, to Superintendent," October 13, 1849, R. 33, in Burdon, *Archives,* 3:124; Reed, *Caste War,* 122; Dumond, *Machete,* 156–57.

274. Baqueiro Preve, *Ensayo histórico,* 4:4; Ancona, *Yucatán,* 4:102; *Guerra de Castas en Yucatán,* 80; Dumond, *Machete,* 157.

275. "De José Fermín Aké a Paulino Pech," Rancho Candelaria, December 8, 1849, in Fidelio Quintal Martín, *Correspondencia de la Guerra de Castas* (Mérida: Universidad Autónoma de Yucatán, 1992), 54; "De Timoteo Ek y Juan Crisótomo Chablé a . . . ," Cacabdziú, December 27, 1849, ibid., 62; "Magistrate, Santa Helena, to Superintendent," April 12, 1850, R. 33, in Burdon, *Archives,* 3:131; Reed, *Caste War,* 125.

276. *Guerra de Castas en Yucatán,* 82.

277. Baqueiro Preve, *Ensayo histórico,* 4:6.

278. Ibid., 112–14; Ancona, *Yucatán,* 4:311–12; Reed, *Caste War,* 131.

279. Baqueiro Preve, *Ensayo histórico,* 4:119; Ancona, *Yucatán,* 4:314; Reed, *Caste War,* 135.

280. Baqueiro Preve, *Ensayo histórico,* 4:118–19; Ancona, *Yucatán,* 4:316; Miguel Bartolomé and Alicia Barabas, *La resistencia maya* (México, D.F.: Instituto Nacional de Antropología e Historia, Colección Científica, etnología 53, 1977), 30; Reed, *Caste War,* 136.

281. Baqueiro Preve, *Ensayo histórico,* 4:122; Ancona, *Yucatán,* 4:315–17; Reed, *Caste War,* 136.

282. Baqueiro Preve, *Ensayo histórico,* 4:123; Ancona, *Yucatán,* 4:317; Reed, *Caste War,* 137.

283. *Guerra de Castas en Yucatán,* 125–26; Reed, *Caste War,* 138.

284. Wayne M. Clegern, "British Honduras and the Pacification of Yucatán," *The Americas* 18, no. 3 (1962): 246.

285. Ibid., 139.

286. Baqueiro Preve, *Ensayo histórico*, 4:162–63; Ancona, *Yucatán*, 4:322–23; Reed, *Caste War*, 140–41.

287. Baqueiro Preve, *Ensayo histórico*, 4:135–37, 140, 150–51, 170–71; Ancona, *Yucatán*, 4:319–20, 325–26; *Guerra de Castas en Yucatán*, 88; Reed, *Caste War*, 143–44.

288. Baqueiro Preve, *Ensayo histórico*, 4:165–75; Ancona, *Yucatán*, 4:326; *Guerra de Castas en Yucatán*, 89–90.

289. Baqueiro Preve, *Ensayo histórico*, 4:175; Ancona, *Yucatán*, 4:327–28; *Guerra de Castas en Yucatán*, 91.

290. Baqueiro Preve, *Ensayo histórico*, 4:176–78; Ancona, *Yucatán*, 4:300; Reed, *Caste War*, 146–47.

291. Baqueiro Preve, *Ensayo histórico*, 4:179–84; Ancona, *Yucatán*, 4:334–38; *Guerra de Castas en Yucatán*, 93; Reed, *Caste War*, 148–49; Lapointe, *Los mayas rebeldes de Yucatán*, 81.

292. Baqueiro Preve, *Ensayo histórico*, 4:189–99, 203–205; Ancona, *Yucatán*, 4:339–46, 349–50; *Guerra de Castas en Yucatán*, 93–94; Reed, *Caste War*, 150–52.

293. Ancona, *Yucatán*, 4:351–60; *Guerra de Castas en Yucatán*, xxxiv, 94–95, 102–103; Reed, *Caste War*, 152–54.

294. Ancona, *Yucatán*, 4:362–63; *Guerra de Castas en Yucatán*, 104–105; Reed, *Caste War*, 155.

295. "The Captivity Narrative of José María Rosado," in Richard Buhler, ed., *A Refugee of the War of the Castes Makes Belize His Home: The Memoirs of J. M. Rosado* (Belize: Belize Institute for Social Research and Action, 1970), reprinted in Rugeley, *Maya Wars*, 75; Reed, *Caste War*, 160.

296. Reed, *Caste War*, 160, 163.

297. Baqueiro Preve, *Ensayo histórico*, 4:260–61.

298. Ibid., 277.

299. Ibid., 311, 315; *Guerra de Castas en Yucatán*, 110–12; Reed, *Caste War*, 165–66.

300. *Guerra de Castas en Yucatán*, 112.

301. Baqueiro Preve, *Ensayo histórico*, 4:311–14; *Guerra de Castas en Yucatán*, 111–12; "Superintendent to Governor, Jamaica," November 17, 1857, R. 55, in Burdon, *Archives*, 3:199; "Superintendent to Governor, Jamaica," December 17, 1857, R. 55, ibid., 3:199; Reed, *Caste War*, 167–69.

302. "Carta de Tiburcio R. Esteves al gobernador de Yucatán," San Miguel, February 22, 1858, 166; "Carta de Tiburcio R. Esteves al gobernador de Yucatán," Punta Consejo, March 3, 1858, in *Guerra de Castas en Yucatán*, 167; Baqueiro Preve, *Ensayo histórico*, 5:58–59; "The Captivity Narrative of José María Rosado," 69–71; "Captain Anderson to the Superintendent," March 4, 1858, R. 61, in Burdon, *Archives*, 3:202; "Superintendent to Governor, Jamaica," March 13, 1858, R. 55, ibid., 3:202–203; Reed, *Caste War*, 170–71; Dumond, *Machete*, 225.

303. *Guerra de Castas en Yucatán*, 115.

304. Ibid., 122.

305. Baqueiro Preve, *Ensayo histórico*, 5:117–27; *Guerra de Castas en Yucatán*, 121;

"Crown Surveyor to Superintendent," July 6, 1860, R. 71, in Burdon, *Archives*, 3:230; Reed, *Caste War*, 178–80.

306. *Guerra de Castas en Yucatán*, 116.

307. "El Constitucional. Periodico official del estado de Yucatan, no. 457," in *Guerra de Castas en Yucatán*, 170; Reed, "Juan de la Cruz," 512.

308. Baqueiro Preve, *Ensayo histórico*, 5:163–64; *Guerra de Castas en Yucatán*, 116, 118, 170; Reed, *Caste War*, 180; Dumond, *Machete*, 248.

309. *Guerra de Castas en Yucatán*, 118.

310. Reed, *Caste War*, 180–81.

311. *Guerra de Castas en Yucatán*, 127–28; "Lieutenant Governor to Governor, Jamaica," February 10, 1864, R. 81, in Burdon, *Archives*, 3:255; Dumond, *Machete*, 254–56; Reed, *Caste War*, 190.

312. "John Carmichael's Visit to Santa Cruz," from Archives of Belize, record 96, November 15, 1867, Corozal, in Rugeley, *Maya Wars*, 82; Reed, *Caste War*, 200; Lapointe, *Los mayas rebeldes de Yucatán*, 88.

313. Ibid., 221, 223.

314. Ibid., 224, 226–27; Lapointe, *Los mayas rebeldes de Yucatán*, 91–92.

315. Reed, *Caste War*, 227. For a study on Mexican-U.S. relations during this period through the end of the Caste War, see Gilbert Joseph, *Revolution from Without: Yucatán, Mexico, and the United States, 1880–1924* (Cambridge: Cambridge University Press, 1982).

316. Ibid., 227, 236.

317. Ibid., 230–32.

318. Ibid., 235.

319. Ibid., 228, 229, 251.

320. Ibid., 239–42.

321. Sapper, "Independent Indian States of Yucatán," 628; Reed, *Caste War*, 270; Reina, *Las rebeliones campesinas en México*, 392.

4. Nativism, Caste Wars, and the Exterminatory Impulse

1. Linton, "Nativistic Movements," 230.

2. Ibid., 231.

3. Chalk and Jonassohn, "The Conceptual Framework," 9; Charny, "Toward a Generic Definition of Genocide," 85.

4. David Stannard, "Uniqueness as Denial: The Politics of Genocide Scholarship," in Alan S. Rosenbaum, ed., *Is the Holocaust Unique? Perspectives on Comparative Genocide* (Boulder: Westview Press, 1996), 172, 173, 181.

5. Knault, *Pueblo Revolt*, 153–55.

6. "Letter of Juan Domínguez de Mendoza to Antonio de Otermín," Alameda, December 9, 1681, in Hackett, *Revolt*, 9:219–20.

7. "Testimony of Pedro Naranjo," Río del Norte, December 18, 1681, in Twitchell,

Spanish Archives, 2:62; "Declaration of Diego López Sambrano," Hacienda of Luis de Carbajal, December 22, 1681, in Hackett, *Revolt,* 9:299–300; Bancroft, *Arizona and New Mexico,* 166, 168; Knault, *Pueblo Revolt,* 101, 166–67; Espinosa, *Pueblo Indian Revolt,* 19, 24; John Kessell, "Esteban Clemente," 16.

8. Hughes, *The Beginnings of Spanish Settlement in the El Paso District,* 336, 342–45, 347, 349, 352–53, 356.

9. "Testimony of Pedro Naranjo," 64.

10. "Testimony of Juan Lorenzo and Francisco Lorenzo," Paso del Norte, December 20, 1681, in Twitchell, *Spanish Archives,* 2:66; "Testimony of José," Río del Norte, December 19, 1681, ibid., 2:53, 57; "Carta del Padre Fray Silvestre Velez de Escalante," Santa Fe, April 2, 1778, in *Documentos,* 311; "Auto of Antonio de Otermín," La Isleta, December 9, 1681, in Hackett, *Revolt,* 9:219; "Opinion of fray Francisco de Ayeta," Hacienda of Luis de Carbajal, December 23, 1681, ibid., 9:310; "Declaration of Jerónimo, a Tigua Indian," opposite La Isleta, January 1, 1682, ibid., 9:361; "Reply of the Fiscal, Don Martín de Solís Miranda," Mexico, June 25, 1682, ibid., 9:382; Bancroft, *Arizona and New Mexico,* 184; Knault, *Pueblo Revolt,* 174–75.

11. "Testimony of Juan Lorenzo and Francisco Lorenzo," in Twitchell, *Spanish Archives,* 2:65; "Testimony of Juan of Tesuque," Río del Norte, December 28, 1681, ibid., 2:53; "Testimony of José," Río del Norte, December 19, 1681, ibid., 2:57; "Testimony of Lucas, a Piro Indian," Río del Norte, December 18, 1681, ibid., 2:60; "Carta del Padre Fray Silvestre Velez de Escalante," *Documentos,* 311; "Testimony of Pedro Naranjo," 63–64; "Declaration of Sargento Mayor Sebastián de Herrera," Río del Norte, December 21, 1681, in Hackett, *Revolt,* 9:269; Bancroft, *Arizona and New Mexico,* 184; Knault, *Pueblo Revolt,* 174–75.

12. "Testimony of Juan of Tesuque," 53.

13. Bancroft, *Arizona and New Mexico,* 185.

14. "Letter from the Governor and Captain-General, Don Antonio de Otermín, from New Mexico," n.p., September 8, 1680, in Hackett, *Historical Documents,* 4:333.

15. "Answer Presented by the Lieutenant-General, Alonzo García, in His Own Behalf," Isleta, August 14, 1680, in Twitchell, *Spanish Archives,* 25.

16. Simmons, "History of Pueblo-Indian Relations to 1821," 184.

17. Scholes, "Troublous Times in New Mexico, 1659–1670," 16.

18. Simmons, "History of Pueblo-Indian Relations to 1821," 184; "Testimony of José," Río del Norte, December 19, 1681, in Twitchell, *Spanish Archives,* 2:57.

19. "Testimony of José," 57; see also "Auto of Antonio de Otermín," La Isleta, December 9, 1681, in Hackett, *Revolt,* 9:219.

20. "Declaration of Lieutenant General of Cavalry," Río del Norte, December 20, 1681, in Hackett, *Revolt,* 9:260; "Declaration of Diego López Sambrano," 9:292.

21. "Testimony of Juan Lorenzo and Francisco Lorenzo," 2:67.

22. "Letter of Juan Domínguez de Mendoza to Antonio de Otermín," Sandía, December 10, 1681, in Hackett, *Revolt,* 9:225; "Declaration of Lieutenant General of Cavalry," ibid., 9:259; Hackett, *Revolt,* 8:clxv–clxvi.

23. "Letter of Juan Domínguez de Mendoza to Antonio de Otermín," Sandía, December 10, 1681, in Hackett, *Revolt*, 9:225.

24. "Declaration of Lieutenant General of Cavalry," 9:260; "Declaration of Sargento Mayor Sebastián de Herrera," 9:269.

25. "Roque Madrid to Diego de Vargas," Villa Nueva de Santa Cruz, July 15, 1696, in Kessell et al., *By Force of Arms*, 827.

26. Diego de Vargas, campaign journal, August 30–September 6, 1696, in Kessell et al., *Blood*, 2:1034, 1036; see also note on 1037.

27. Bancroft, *Arizona and New Mexico*, 184; Knault, *Pueblo Revolt*, 174–75; Silverberg, *Pueblo Revolt*, 131.

28. Riley, *Kachina and the Cross*, 210–12; Silverberg, *Pueblo Revolt*, 132.

29. "Reply of the Fiscal, Don Martín de Solís Miranda," 9:382.

30. Diego de Vargas, campaign journal, New Mexico, August 9–October 15, 1692, in Kessell et al., *By Force of Arms*, 382.

31. "Declaration of Sargento Mayor Luís de Quintana," Río del Norte, December 22, 1681, in Hackett, *Revolt*, 9:291; "Opinion of Fray Francisco de Ayeta," Hacienda of Luis de Carbajal, December 23, 1681, ibid., 9:309.

32. "Declaration of an Indian," House of Captain Francisco de Ortega, December 27, 1681, in Hackett, *Revolt*, 9:344.

33. Hackett, "Revolt of the Pueblo Indians," 125.

34. "Tercer cuaderno," 350.

35. "Auto of Antonio de Otermín," Santa Fe, August 13, 1680, in Hackett, *Revolt*, 8:13.

36. Ibid., 8:16.

37. "Declaration of Diego López de Sambrano," 9:295.

38. "To the Governor and Captain General," La Salineta, October 3, 1680, in Twitchell, *Spanish Archives*, 2:46.

39. "Testimony of Pedro Naranjo," 63.

40. "Testimony of Juan Lorenzo and Francisco Lorenzo," 66.

41. "Declaration of One of the Rebellious Christian Indians Who Was Captured on the Road," Alamillo, September 6, 1680, 61, in Hackett, *Revolt*, 8:61.

42. "Declaration of Jerónimo, a Tigua Indian," 9:361.

43. "Salida para el Paso del Norte, 23 de Agosto, hasta 5 de Octubre de 1680," Antonio de Otermín, Arroyo de San Marcos, in Twitchell, *Spanish Archives*, 2:13; "Declaration of an Indian Rebel," Arroyo de San Marcos, August 23, 1680, in Hackett, *Revolt*, 8:20.

44. "Salida para el Paso del Norte, 23 de Agosto, hasta 5 de Octubre de 1680," 2:13.

45. Ibid., 2:17.

46. "Answer Presented by the Lieutenant-General, Alonzo García, in His Own Behalf," Isleta, August 14, 1680, in Twitchell, *Spanish Archives*, 28.

47. Hackett, *Revolt*, 8:clxxv.

48. Diego de Vargas, campaign journal, New Mexico, August 9–October 15, 1692, in Kessell et al., *By Force of Arms*, 389.

49. Diego de Vargas to the King, Zacatecas, May 16, 1693, in Kessell et al., *To the Royal Crown Restored*, 186.

50. "El Proveido de D. Diego de Vargas Sobre la peticion espresada del Padre Custodio y demas religiosos misioneros dice," in *Documentos*, 355.

51. "The Cabildo of Santa Fe to the Conde de Galve," Santa Fe, January 1694, in Kessell et al., *To the Royal Crown Restored*, 561.

52. "Statement of Lucía," January 11, 1694, Santa Fe, in Kessell et al., *Blood*, 1:46.

53. "Fray Francisco de Vargas, Petition," Santa Fe, March 7, 1696, in Kessell et al., *Blood*, 2:674–75.

54. "Letter of Fray José Diez," San Diego de Tesuque, March 9, 1696, in Espinosa, *Pueblo Indian Revolt*, 216.

55. "Letter of Fray Alfonso Jiménez de Cisneros," Cochiti, April 21, 1696, in Espinosa, *The Pueblo Indian Revolt of 1696*, 233.

56. Diego de Vargas, campaign journal, June 12, 1696, in Kessell et al., *Blood*, 2:749.

57. "Luis Granillo, Interrogation of Francisco Témprano," Santa Fe, June 13, 1696, in Kessell et al., *Blood*, 756–57.

58. "Alfonso Rael de Aguilar, Interrogation of a Keres Prisoner," Santa Fe, July 3, 1696, in Kessell et al., *Blood*, 2:802.

59. Diego de Vargas, campaign journal, August 20–29, 1696, in Kessell et al., *Blood*, 2:1001–1002.

60. Campbell, "Ideology," 113, 115, 116–18, 129; Szeminski, "Why Kill the Spaniard?" 173; Pease, "El mito de Inkarrí y la visión de los vencidos," in Ossio, *Ideología mesiánica del mundo andino*, 448; Flores Galindo, "In Search of an Inca," 201; Wachtel, *The Vision of the Vanquished*, 183; Gow, "Inkarrí and Revolutionary Leadership in the Southern Andes," 197; López Baralt, *El Retorno del Inca Rey*, 37. See also Curatola, "Mito y milenarianismo en los andes," Ossio, *Ideología mesiánica del mundo andino*, and Sabine MacCormack, "Pachacuti: Miracles, Punishment, and the Last Judgement: Visionary Past and Prophetic Future in Early Colonial Perú," *American Historical Review* 93, nos. 4–5 (October 1988): 960–1006.

61. Flores Galindo, "In Search of an Inca," 201; Gow, "Inkarrí and Revolutionary Leadership in the Southern Andes," 197; López Baralt, *El Retorno del Inca Rey*, 37; Campbell, "Ideology," 117, 127; Leon Campbell, "Banditry and the Túpac Amaru Rebellion in Cuzco, Perú, 1780–84," *Biblioteca Americana* 1, no. 2 (November 1982): 139; Cohn, *The Pursuit of the Millennium*, 32, 72–73.

62. Hidalgo Lehunde, "Amarus y Cataris," 121; Szeminski, "Why Kill the Spaniard?" 179–80; see also Cohn, *The Pursuit of the Millennium*, 35.

63. "Informe de Fr. Alonso Gutiérrez," Oruro, September 9, 1783, AGI, Charcas 597, 1, 4.

64. "Actuaciones anteriores," 91, 95; "Declaración de Fray Josef Serbantes," Oruro, April 9, 1781, in "Testimonio del expedientes y diligencias practicadas para averiguar los tumultos meditadas contra Oruro," AGI, Charcas 601, 18.

65.   Szeminski, "Why Kill the Spaniard?" 182.

66.   "Copias de documentos citados en el diario," #18, 25.

67.   Ibid., 28.

68.   "Carta de Túpac Catari a José de Ayarza," n.p., n.d., in "Relación de los hechos más notables acaecidos en la sublevación general fraguada en los reynos del Perú, por el indio José Gabriel Túpac Amaru, gobr. del pueblo de Tungasuca en la Provincia de Tinta, que asociado de otros sequaces, causó horrosos estragos desde el año 1780, hasta el de 1782 en que se reprimo el orgullo de la conjuración," *Revista de archivos y bibliotecas nacionales* 3, vol. 5 (Lima, September 30, 1900): 230.

69.   "Informe de Fr. Alonso Gutiérrez," Oruro, September 9, 1783, AGI, Charcas 597, 1, 4.

70.   "Carta de Ignacio Florez a Juan José Vertíz," Oruro, October 9, 1781, AGI, Charcas 595, 1.

71.   "Consejo Real de Indias al Sr. Virrey de Buenos Aires," Aranjuez, April 21, 1782, AGI, Charcas 595, 1.

72.   Cohn, *The Pursuit of the Millennium*, 15.

73.   Szeminski, personal correspondence, April 21, 2001.

74.   Alberto Flores Galindo, "Túpac Amaru y la sublevación de 1780," in Alberto Flores Galindo, ed., *Túpac Amaru II: 1780* (Lima: Retablo de Papel Ediciones, 1976), 281; Walker, *Smoldering Ashes*, 47.

75.   Cohn, *The Pursuit of the Millennium*, 15.

76.   "Relación de los sucesos de la Provincia de Cochabamba año de 1781," written by the cabildo of Cochabamba, Cochabamba, December 17, 1781, AGI, Charcas 595, 12.

77.   Campbell, "Ideology," 126; Campbell, "Banditry," 154–55; Szeminski, "Why Kill the Spaniard?" 185–86.

78.   Serulnikov, *Revindicaciones indígenas y legalidad colonial*, 7–8, 16; O'Phelan Godoy, *Rebellions and Revolts*, 118–19, 153.

79.   "Carta de Gregorio Josef de Merlos a Fray Manuel Parraga," Ocuri, January 26, 1781, AGI, Charcas 597, 4; "Confesión de Nicolás Catari," La Plata, April 10, 1781, in Odriozola, *Documentos históricos*, 1:320; "Carta de Pedro Zeberino de San Martín a Jorge Escobedo," Suypacha, March 8, 1781, AGI, Charcas 437-b, 64; "El Regente Presidente de Charcas da cuenta del féliz suceso de la expedn hecha el día 20 de Febrero inmto contra los indios rebeldes," La Plata, May 15, 1781, AGI, Charcas 444, 2; see also Lewin, *Túpac Amaru, el rebelde*, 294–95.

80.   "Carta de Félix Villalobos a Gerónimo Manuel de Ruedas," Cochabamba, February 24, 1781, AGI, Charcas 596, 6–7; "Actuaciones anteriores," 5, 87, 99, 144; "Relación de los hechos más notables," 206; "Representación de Félix Josef de Villalobos a Gerónimo Manuel de Ruedas," La Plata, March 7, 1781, AGI, Charcas 594, 7; "Relación de los sucesos de la Provincia de Cochabamba," 4; "Declaración de Fray Josef Serbantes," Oruro, April 9, 1781, in "Testimonio del expedientes y diligencias practicadas para averiguar los tumultos meditadas contra Oruro," AGI, Charcas 601, 18.

81.   "Fragment of Informe," n.p., n.d., AGI, Charcas 594, 1.

82.   "Carta de Gerónimo Manuel de Ruedas a Juan José Vertíz," La Plata, May 15, 1781,

AGI, Charcas 595, 1; "Carta de Gerónimo Manuel de Ruedas a Josef de Galvez," La Plata, April 19, 1781, AGI, Charcas 594, 1.

83. "Declaración de Ysidro Josef de Herrera," San Pedro de Buenavista, October 5, 1780, AGI, Charcas 596, 10; "Declaración de Pablo Caquasiri," La Plata, October 8, 1780, AGI, Charcas 596, 75; "Carta de Domingo Angeles a Gerónimo Manuel de Ruedas," La Plata, October 8, 1780, AGI, Charcas 596, 7; "Diario trunco de los sucesos desde el 4 febo. hasta Octr. 16 de 1780 en Chuquisaca," La Plata, October 16, 1780, ANB, Ruck.1780.96, 11; "Carta de Arequipa con fecha 2 de Mayo de 1781 que refiere los estragos executados por los indios alzados en varios pueblos de las provincias de ambos virreyenatos," Arequipa, May 2, 1781, in Válcarcel, *Colección Documental de la independencia del Perú,* book 2, 1:693; "Relación de los hechos más notables," 170–71; "El Regente Presidente de la Rl. Audiencia de Charcas informa del cuidadoso estado de la rebelión de Indios," La Plata, April 15, 1781, AGI, Charcas 594, 1; "Oficio de Gregorio Francisco de Campos, Obisbo de La Paz al Rey," La Paz, November 15, 1781, AGI, Charcas 595, 6; "Actuaciones anteriores," 23; "Confesión de Josef Daga," La Plata, April 25, 1781, in "Criminales contra Nicolás Catari y otros indios," AGI, Charcas 603, 1; "Confesión de Augustín Ventura," La Plata, April 25, 1781, in "Criminales contra Nicolás Catari y otros indios," AGI, Charcas 603, 24; "Confesión de Sebastiana Mamani," La Plata, April 18, 1781, AGI, Charcas 603, 25; "Confesión de Francisco Gonzalo," La Plata, April 20, 1781, AGI, Charcas 603, 25; "Confesión de Nicolás Gueso," La Plata, April 20, 1781, AGI, Charcas 603, 28.

84. "Informe del Corregidor de Paria Manuel de Bodega," La Plata, October 21, 1780, AGI, Charcas 596, 92. A cholo is a Hispanicized Indian.

85. "Oficio de Francisco Javier Beltrán," Potosí, March 14, 1781, AGI, Charcas 437-b, 1.

86. "Relación traxica," 2; "Relación verdadera," 85; "Relación histórica," 29; "Confesión de Mariano Quispe," in "Sumaria información recibida de varios indios de Chocaya como sindicados en la sublevación," Chichas, November 23, 1781, ANB, SGI.1781.10, 45; "Carta de Félix Villalobos a Gerónimo Manuel de Ruedas," February 24, 1781, 7; "Actuaciones anteriores," 5, 87, 99, 144; "Relación de los hechos más notables," 206; "Representación de Félix Josef de Villalobos," 7; "Relación de los sucesos de la provincia de Cochabamba," 4; "Declaración de Fray Josef Serbantes," 18; "Confesión de Alvento Arze," La Plata, October 3, 1780, AGI, Charcas 596, 68.

87. "Carta de Arequipa," 694. The same occurred in Calca; see Walker, *Smoldering Ashes,* 48.

88. "Carta de Fray Matías de la Borda a Sebastián de Segurola," La Paz, May 30, 1781, AGI, Charcas 595, 1–2; "Copias de documentos citados en el diario," #18, 21; "Diario de Sebastián de Segurola," La Paz, July 1, 1781, AGI, Charcas 595, 6; Francisco Tadeo Diez de Medina, *Diario del alzamiento del indios conjurados contra la ciudad de Nuestra Señora de La Paz,* transcribed with an introduction by María Eugenia del Valle de Siles (La Paz: Banco Boliviano Americano, 1981), 30.

89. "Relación traxica," 2; "Diario fabuloso del cura de Oruro Doctor Don Patricio Gabriel Menéndez: Relación trajica de los funestos y ruinosos aconticimientos de Oruro," in Beltrán Avila, *Capítulos,* 292–93.

90. "Carta que refiere a los estragos hechos por los Yndios alzados en Suches mineral de la Provincia de Larecaja del Obispado de La Paz; y en los pueblos de Arque, Tapacari, y Colcha en la Provincia de Cochabamba, perteneciente al Arzobispado de la Plata. Cochabamba, February 26, 1781, in Válcarcel, *Colección Documental de la independencia del Perú*, book 2, 1:508; "Relación de los sucesos de la provincia de Cochabamba," 4.

91. "Actuaciones anteriores," 21, 83, 84–85, 89, 90, 123; "Testimonio de Santos Mamani," Oruro, May 25, 1781, AGI, Charcas 601, 73; "Declaración de Francisco Xavier Condori," Oruro, April 10, 1781, AGI, Charcas 601, 24; "Testimonio de Martín Lopes," Oruro, April 7, 1781, AGI, Charcas 601, 26.

92. "Carta que refiere a los estragos," 508–509; "Carta de Arequipa," 693–94; "Relación de los sucesos de la Provincia de Cochabamba," 4–5, 6–7; "Actuaciones anteriores," 5, 6, 21, 23, 87, 99, 144; "Relación de los hechos más notables," 162, 170–73; "Carta del Cabildo de Cochabamba al Rey," Cochabamba, January 31, 1782, AGI, Charcas 595, 1; "El Regente Presidente de la Rl. Audiencia de Charcas informa del cuidadoso estado de la rebelión de Indios," 1; "Confesión de Josef Daga," 1, "Confesión de Augustín Ventura," 12; "Confesión de Sebastiana Mamani," 25; "Carta de Luís de Palacio y Santelices a Gerónimo de Ruedas," Santiago de Cotagaita, March 9, 1781, AGI, Charcas 596, 22; "Causa de Augustín Solís," La Plata, March 11, 1781, AGI, Charcas 594, 21; "Dn. Pedro Antonio Zernudas oidor dela Rl Audiencia de la Plata informa a V.M. haber echo la prisión de Dr. Gregorio de Merlo cura dela Doctrina de Macha," La Plata, March 12, 1781, AGI, Charcas 594, 5; "Informe de Josef Atanacio Baspineyro," Potosí, March 14, 1781, AGI, Charcas 437-b, 1; "Parte de José de Reseguín al Virey de Buenos Aires," Tupiza, March 18, 1781, 348.

93. "Carta de Gerónimo Manuel de Ruedas a Josef de Galvez," April 19, 1781, 1; "El Regente Presidente de la Rl. Audiencia de Charcas informa del cuidadoso estado de la rebelión de indios," 1.

94. "Carta del cabildo de Cochabamba al Rey," 2.

95. "Carta que refiere a los estragos," 508; "Relación de los sucesos de la Provincia de Cochabamba," 4; "Declaración de Fray Josef Serbantes," 18; "Informe de Andrés del Barco y Urcullo," Poopó, October 16, 1780, AGI, Charcas 596, 91.

96. "Testimonio de Florentín Alfaro," in "Testimonio del expediente seguido contra el Presbitero José Vasquez de Velasquez por complice en la sublevación en la provincia de Chichas," La Plata, November 12, 1781, ANB, SGI.1781.12, 13.

97. "Diario del cerco de La Paz en 1781, por Sebastián de Segurola," La Paz, May 30, 1781, ANB, SGI.1781.s.n., 2.

98. "Copias de documentos citados en el diario," #18, 21.

99. "Declaración de Padre Fr. Josef de Uriarte," in "Diversas declaraciones hechas por varios sujetos sobre las disposiciones y sacriligios de los rebeldes de varias provincias ante dr. Esteban de Loza," El Alto, April 17, 1782, ANB, SGI.1782.97, 1.

100. "Diario del cerco de La Paz en 1781, por Sebastián de Segurola," 8.

101. "Carta de Túpac Catari a José de Ayarza," 230; "Copias de documentos citados en el diario," #10, in "Diario del cerco de La Paz en 1781, por Sebastián de Segurola," 19.

102. "Confesión de Gregoria Apasa," Santuario de Nuestra Señora de Peñas, October 18, 1781, AGI, Charcas 595, 1.

103. "Confesión de Augustina Zerna," Santuario de Nuestra Señora de las Peñas, October 18, 1781, AGI, Charcas 595, 5.

104. "Confesión de Josefa Anaya," Santuario de Nuestra Señora de las Peñas, October 18, 1781, AGI, Charcas 595, 5–6.

105. "Confesión de Diego Quispe," Santuario de Nuestra Señora de las Peñas, October 18, 1781, AGI, Charcas 595, 8.

106. "Copias de documentos citados en el diario," #18, 21; "Carta de Borda a Segurola," 1; "Confesión de Diego Estaca," Santuario de Nuestra Señora de las Peñas, October 18, 1781, AGI, Charcas 595, 20–21; O'Phelan Godoy, *Rebellions and Revolts,* 252–54.

107. "Copias de documentos citados en el diario," #18, 21.

108. "Relación verdadera," 98; "Diario de Sebastián de Segurola," 17; "Confesión de Julián Apasa o Túpac Catari," Santuario de Nuestra Señora de Peñas, November 11 and 13, 1781, AGI, Buenos Aires 320, 24; "Carta de Ignacio Florez a Josef de Galvez," La Plata, December 10, 1782, AGI, Charcas 595, 2.

109. Andrade Padilla, *La Rebelión de Tomás Catari,* 231; "Confesión de Alvento Arze," 63.

110. Andrade Padilla, *La Rebelión de Tomás Catari,* 200.

111. "Testimonio de Sebastián Morochi," in "Causa criminal contra Juan Luís y Pascual Condori, como complices principales en la rebelión de los Cataris," Poroma, November 8, 1781, ANB, SGI.1781.13, 3; "Expediente seguido contra various indios del pueblo de Poroma y por complice en la sublevación," La Plata, April 7, 1781, ANB, Ruck.1781.101, 2.

112. "Declaración de Don Martín Condori," in "El Corregor. Dela Villa de Cochabamba sobre los destrozos que executaron los indios en Tapacari," Oropesa, March 7, 1781, ANB, SGI.1781.62, 1.

113. "Confesión de Diego Calsina," Santuario de Nuestra Señora de las Peñas, October 18, 1781, AGI, Charcas 595, 16; "Confesión de Diego Estaca," 20; "Confesión de Nicolás Ramírez," Oruro, 1781, in "Expedientes de las confesiones tomadas por Dn Jacinto Rodríguez de Herrera a distintas indios reos cómplices en los tumultos," AGI, Charcas 601, 1; "Confesión de Juan Solís," Oruro, 1781, in "Expedientes de las confesiones tomadas por Dn Jacinto Rodríguez de Herrera a distintas indios reos cómplices en los tumultos," AGI, Charcas 601, 2; "Confesión de Manuel Mamani," Oruro, 1781, in "Expedientes de las confesiones tomadas por Dn Jacinto Rodríguez de Herrera a distintas indios reos cómplices en los tumultos," AGI, Charcas 601, 3.

114. Cajías de la Vega, "Los objectivos," 418. See also "Expedientes de las confesiones tomadas por Dn Jacinto Rodríguez de Herrera a distintas indios reos cómplices en los tumultos," AGI, Charcas 601.

115. Ibid. See also "Expedientes de las confesiones tomadas por Dn Jacinto Rodríguez de Herrera a distintas indios reos cómplices en los tumultos."

116. "Diario y relación prolija jurada que yo el General Don Juan Gelly hago de todos

los pasajes y sucesos acaecidos en varios distritos y lugares," La Plata, AGI, Charcas 594, 3; "Relación de los hechos más notables," 74; "Levantimiento de la Provincia de Chayanta o Charcas . . . y lo acaecido en el pueblo de Pocoata de dha provincia a su corregidor Dn. Joaquín Alós," La Plata, September 29, 1780, in Válcarcel, *Colección Documental de la independencia del Perú*, book 2, 1:27; "Anexo al diario y relación prolija jurada que yo el general Don Juan Gelly hago de todos los pasajes y sucesos acaecidos en varios distritos y lugares," La Plata, September 9, 1780, AGI, Charcas 594, 1.

117.   "Declaración de Ysidro Josef de Herrera," 10; "Representación de Ylario Caguasiri, Gobernador y Cacique Principal propietario del pueblo de San Pedro de Buenavista," La Plata, n.d., AGI, Charcas 596, 48; "Representación de Marcos Ancienega," San Pedro de Buenavista, September 24, 1780, in "Testimonio de los autos de la sublevación de Chayanta," AGI, Charcas 596, 1; "Declaración de Pablo Caquasini," La Plata, October 8, 1780, AGI, Charcas 596, 75; "Informe de Pedro Yavira Ylario Caguasiri," San Pedro de Buenavista, December 28, 1780, AGI, Charcas 596, 51.

118.   "Informe de Gregorio Josef de Merlos," Macha, October 7, 1780, AGI, Charcas 596, 11; "Informe de Tomás Catari," Macha, October 7, 1780, AGI, Charcas 596, 19; "Carta de Gregorio Josef de Merlos a Francisco Ramón de Herbovo y Figueróa," La Plata, January 23, 1781, AGI, Charcas 597, 3; "Carta de Gregorio Josef de Merlos al Licenciado Mariano de la Vega," La Plata, January 27, 1781, AGI, Charcas 597, 4.

119.   "Relación de los hechos más notables," 163.

120.   Ibid., 162; "Carta de Gregorio Josef de Merlos a Fray Manuel Parraga," Ocuri, January 26, 1781, AGI, Charcas 597, 4; "Carta de Gregorio Josef de Merlos al Rey," La Plata, March 12, 1782, AGI, Charcas 597, 2; "Declaración de Ignacio Salguero," La Plata, April 4, 1781, AGI, Charcas 603, 14; "Confesión de Nicolás Catari," 326; Serulnikov, *Subverting Colonial Authority*, 188.

121.   "Oficio de Capellán de Challapata, Juan Antonio Beltrán," Challapata, January 18, 1781, AGI, Charcas 595, 1–2; "Dn. Pedro Anto Zernudas y Dn. Lorenzo Blanco Ciceron Oydores de la Rl Auda dela Plata informan a V.M. del estado en que se halla el [*sic*] rebelión y Alzamto en la prova de Chayanta," La Plata, March 13, 1781, AGI, Charcas 594, 3.

122.   "Actuaciones anteriores," 13, 45; "Carta de Capellán Augustín Flores Urito a Jorge Escobedo," Porco, February 21, 1781, AGI, Charcas 437-b, 25; "Declaración de Roque Argote," Potosí, March 7, 1781, AGI, Charcas 596, 9–10; "Relación histórica," 24–27; "Diario fabuloso," 289–90; "Relación de los hechos más notables," 170–71; "Confesión de Josef Daga," 12; "Carta que refiere a los estragos," 508, 694; "Relación de los sucesos de la Provincia de Cochabamba," 5, 7, 9.

123.   Szeminski, personal correspondence, March 4, 2001.

124.   "Representación de Gregorio Josef de Merlos al Rey," 2; "Oficio de Gregorio Josef de Merlos a Juan José Vertíz," La Plata, February 15, 1781, in Lewin, *La rebelión de Túpac Amaru*, 738–39; "Relación de los hechos más notables," 167.

125.   "Actuaciones anteriores," 7; "Declaración de Roque Argote," 9–10.

126.   "Diario Fabuloso," 289; "Actuaciones anteriores," 175–77; "Relación traxica," 3; "Relación verdadera," 96; "Relación histórica," 25; Fisher, *Last Inca Revolt*, 72.

127. "Carta que refiere a los estragos," 509, 694; "Relación de los hechos más notables," 206; "Representación de Domingo Angeles a Gerónimo Manuel de Ruedas," La Plata, October 17, 1780, AGI, Charcas 596, 12; "Carta de Arequipa," 694; "Relación de los sucesos de la provincia de Cochabamba," 7.

128. "Carta de Arequipa," 693; "Relación de los hechos más notables," 170–71.

129. "Carta de Borda a Segurola," 2.

130. "Copias de documentos citados en el diario," #18, 24; "Relación de la papeleta remitida a la ciudad de Arequipa por dn. Joaquin de Orellana corregidor de la villa de Puno, en que se refiere los estragos acaecidos por los yndios en Juli y Chucuito," Puno, April 8, 1781, in Válcarcel, *Colección Documental de la independencia del Perú,* book 2, 2:625.

131. Szeminski, personal correspondence, March 4, 2001.

132. "Diario fabuloso," 288.

133. "Relación verdadera," 78.

134. "Actuaciones anteriores," 177.

135. Ibid., 84; "Relación traxica," 2; Cajías de la Vega, "Los objetivos," 418.

136. "Relación de los hechos más notables," 162.

137. "Carta de Arequipa," 693.

138. "Testimonio de Santos Mamani," 73; "Actuaciones anteriores," 175–77; "Relación traxica," 3; "Representación de los vecinos de Tupiza al Comandante General Reseguín pidiendo no deje la provincia por el riesgo que corre con los sublevados," Tupiza, March 17, 1781, in Odriozola, *Documentos históricos,* 1:47.

139. "Actuaciones anteriores," 181.

140. "El regente de la Rl. Audiencia de Charcas informa del cuidadoso estado de rebelión," 1; "Relación de los hechos más notables," 171–72.

141. "Carta que refiere a los estragos," 509; Abecia Baldivieso, "La insurección india de Tapacari en 1781," 41; "Representaciones hechas a la real Audiencia en la Plata por el Corregidor de la Provincia de Chayanta," La Plata, August 25, 1780, AGI, Charcas 594, 6.

142. "Relación del éxito que tuvo la expedición y salida que hizo el corregidor de Puno con las milicias de su provincia acia la de Lampa," Cuzco, January 10, 1781, in Válcarcel, *Colección Documental de la independencia del Perú,* book 2, 1:405–13.

143. "Carta de Dn. Juan Bautista de Zavala que relaciona por mayor las calamidades de La Paz en el segundo sitio," La Paz, November 3, 1781, in Válcarcel, *Colección Documental de la independencia del Perú,* book 2, 3:147–48.

144. Szeminski, "Why Kill the Spaniard?" 186.

145. Szeminski, personal correspondence, March 4, 2001.

146. "Confesión de Pasqual Tola," La Plata, April 20, 1781, AGI, Charcas 603, 27; "Declaración de Ysidro Josef de Herrera," 10; "Declaración de Pedro Caguasiri," 75; Szeminski, *La utopía Tupamarista,* 246, 277.

147. "Confesión de Bartolomé Vello," La Plata, April 21, 1781, AGI, Charcas 603, 34.

148. Abecia Baldivieso, "La insurección india de Tapacari en 1781," 42–43.

149. "Carta de Benito Mata Linares a Josef de Galvez," Cuzco, June 3, 1783, AGI, Cuzco 29, 3.

150. "Relación de los hechos más notables," 172.

151. "Diario fabuloso," 289; "Relación verdadera," 77; "Actuaciones anteriores," 176; "Causas de Oruro. Testimonio de la acusación del Señor Fiscal de S.M. contra los reos de la sublevación de la villa de Oruro y otras acusaciones," Buenos Aires, 1784, in Mier, *Noticia y proceso de la muy noble y muy leal Villa de San Felipe de Austria de Oruro*, 2:141; "Informe del Consejo de Indias al Rey, sublevación de Oruro," September 28, 1800, in Mier, *Noticia y proceso de la muy noble y muy leal Villa de San Felipe de Austria de Oruro*, 2:106; "Causa de Augustín Solís," 21; Szeminski, "Why Kill the Spaniard?" 170.

152. Dumond, *Machete*, 421; Linton, "Nativistic Movements," 230.

153. *Guerra de Castas en Yucatán*, 127, 146; Reed, *Caste War*, 175.

154. E. Rogers, "Appendix: Los Indios de Santa Cruz," in *Honduras Británica: Sus recursos y desarrollo* (Mérida, Mex.: Compañía Tipográfica Yucateca, 1938), 30.

155. "Lieutenant Governor's Message," May 8, 1867, Assembly, in Burdon, *Archives*, 3:288; "Lieutenant Governor to Governor, Jamaica," May 17, 1867, R. 98, ibid., 3:288; Reed, *Caste War*, 204.

156. "The Captivity Narrative of José María Echeverría," Izamal, November 8, 1856, in Rugeley, *Maya Wars*, 63; Reed, *Caste War*, 175; Reed, "Juan de la Cruz, Venencio Puc, and the Speaking Cross," 520.

157. Zimmerman, "The Cult of the Holy Cross," 67.

158. William Miller, "A Journey from British Honduras to Santa Cruz, Yucatán," in *Proceedings of the Royal Geographic Society* (London: n.p., 1889), 1:23.

159. Ibid., 23–25.

160. Ibid., 25–26.

161. Ibid., 27.

162. Ibid., 28.

163. Ibid., 27.

164. Ibid., 27–28.

165. "John Carmichael's Visit to Chan Santa Cruz," in Rugeley, *Maya Wars*, 86.

166. Carl H. Berendt, "Report of Explorations in Central America," in *Smithsonian Institution Annual Report for 1867* (Washington, D.C.: Smithsonian Institution, 1867), 422–23.

167. Ibid., 424.

168. Sapper, "Independent Indian States of Yucatán," 627, 628, 630; Villa Rojas, *The Maya of East Central Quintana Roo*, 23; Reed, *Caste War*, 25.

169. Sapper, "Independent Indian States of Yucatán," 627, 629; Villa Rojas, *The Maya of East Central Quintana Roo*, 25; Cline, "War of the Castes and Its Consequences," 23.

170. Sapper, "Independent Indian States of Yucatán," 632.

171. Villa Rojas, *The Maya of East Central Quintana Roo*, 25.

172. "The Report of José Bartolomé del Granado Baeza," Yaxcabá, 1813, in Rugeley, *Maya Wars*, 20.

173. Baqueiro Preve, *Ensayo histórico*, 104.

174. "An Anonymous Report on Rebel Military Capacity," Mérida, June 1878, University of Texas at Austin, Nettie Lee Benson Library, García Collection, G559, in Rugeley, *Maya Wars*,91.

175. Villa Rojas, *The Maya of East Central Quintana Roo*, 97.

176. Ibid., 101.

177. Ibid., 106, 107.

178. Dumond, *Machete*, 2, 419.

179. Ancona, *Historia de Yucatán, desde la época más remota hasta nuestros días*. 5 vols. (Mérida, México: Imprenta de M. Heredia Argüelles, 1878–1905), 4:36, 92.

180. "Numero 1," in "Comunicación Oficial del Coronel Don Augustín León, participando el éxito de varias relaciones que se tuvieron con el enemigo, y acompañando los documentos que se refiere, bajo los numeros 1, 2 y 3," Valladolid, January 24, 1848, in Baqueiro Preve, *Ensayo histórico*, 2:243.

181. "Nuevamente habla la cruz," ca. October 15, 1850, in Reina, *Las rebeliones campesinas en México*, 410.

182. "De Juan de la Cruz a . . . ," #1, Balamná, October 15, 1850, in Fidelio Quintal Martín, *Correspondencia de la Guerra de Castas*, 87.

183. "Sermon of the Talking Cross," 1887, 1903, in Alfonso Villa Rojas, *The Maya of East Central Quintana Roo*, 163.

184. "Mensaje de Juan de la Cruz, Sermón de Chumpon," 1888, in Bartolomé and Barabas, *La resistencia Maya*, 127.

185. Bartolomé and Barabas, *La resistencia Maya*, 32–33.

186. Bricker, *The Indian Christ, the Indian King*, 6.

187. Ibid., 71.

188. Bartolomé and Barabas, *La resistencia Maya*, 32.

189. Reed, *Caste War*, 34; Villa Rojas, *The Maya of East Central Quintana Roo*, 20.

190. Baqueiro Preve, *Ensayo histórico*, 1:224; see also 229.

191. Villa Rojas, *The Maya of East Central Quintana Roo*, 20.

192. Baqueiro Preve, *Ensayo histórico*, 1:189.

193. Ibid., 2:77.

194. Ancona, *Yucatán*, 4:78.

195. Ibid., 118, 124, 126–27, 230–32; Baqueiro Preve, *Ensayo histórico*, 3:147; ibid., 4:182; *Guerra de Castas en Yucatán*, 55–56.

196. "Apuntes escritos por el antiguo y memorable Vicario de Valladolid D. Manuel Antonio Sierra," n.p., n.d., in Baqueiro Preve, *Ensayo histórico*, 2:368; see also 2:191–93.

197. *Guerra de Castas en Yucatán*, 110.

198. "Proclama del Gobernador Provisional Barret, al Estallar la conspiración tramada por los indios," Mérida, August 5, 1847, in Baqueiro Preve, *Ensayo histórico,* 1:373.

199. *Guerra de Castas en Yucatán,* 10.

200. Ibid., 28.

201. Baqueiro Preve, *Ensayo histórico,* 2:94; ibid., 4:127.

202. "Carta de Don Felipe Rosado, dirigida a Don José Sosa desde el rancho Sacsucil," Sacsucil, February 1, 1848, in Baqueiro Preve, *Ensayo histórico,* 2:295.

203. "Carta de D. José Domingo Sosa, dirigida a D. Santiago Méndez, desde Tekax, acompañádole copia de los artículos del acta que debío servir a Jacinto Pat," Tekax, February 28, 1848, in Baqueiro Preve, *Ensayo histórico,* 2:304.

204. "Military Commandant of Bacalar to the Superintendent," February 19, 1848, R. 28, in Burdon, *Archives,* 3:101.

205. "Exposición de los indígenas de los pueblos de Ucí, muxupip y Kiní del partido de Motul, pidiendo marchar a la campaña," Motul, June 26, 1848, in Baqueiro Preve, *Ensayo histórico,* 3:277.

206. "Governor, Jamaica, to Superintendent," August 19, 1848, R. 30, in Burdon, *Archives,* 3:110.

207. "Governor, Jamaica, to Superintendent," February 21, 1850, R. 35, in Burdon, *Archives,* 3:129.

208. "Lieutenant Governor to Governor, Jamaica," July 21, 1868, R. 98, in Burdon, *Archives,* 3:308.

209. Ancona, *Yucatán,* 4:5, 14.

210. Ibid., 39.

211. Berendt, "Report of Explorations in Central America," 422.

212. Villa Rojas, *The Maya of East Central Quintana Roo,* 20.

213. Cline, "The Sugar Episode in Yucatán," 81.

214. "Diligencias mandadas practicar por el Jefe político del partido de Motul, y remitidas al Gobierno Supremo de la Nación por el Estado, en que consta la decidida protección de los ingleses en favor de los indios sublevados," Motul, July 17, 1848, in Baqueiro Preve, *Ensayo histórico,* 3:287; "Los indios de Santa Cruz," 29; Reed, "Juan de la Cruz," 520.

215. "The Captivity Narrative of José María Echeverría," 63; Rugeley, *Maya Wars,* 62.

216. "The Captivity Narrative of José María Rosado," in Richard Buhler, ed., *A Refugee of the War of the Castes Makes Belize His Home: The Memoirs of J. M. Rosado* (Belize: Belize Institute for Social Research and Action, 1970), reprinted in Rugeley, *Maya Wars,* 71.

217. Baqueiro Preve, *Ensayo histórico,* 3:100; Ancona, *Yucatán,* 4:260–61; *Guerra de Castas en Yucatán,* 79; Reed, *Caste War,* 109; Dumond, *Machete,* 149–50.

218. Baqueiro Preve, *Ensayo histórico,* 4:225; *Guerra de Castas en Yucatán,* 116, 118, 170; "El Constitucional. Periodico official del estado de Yucatán, no. 457," in *Guerra de Castas en Yucatán,* 170; Baqueiro Preve, *Ensayo histórico,* 5:163–64; Reed, *Caste War,* 180; Dumond, *Machete,* 248; *Guerra de Castas en Yucatán,* xxxvi.

219. *Guerra de Castas en Yucatán,* 118.

220. "The Captivity Narrative of José María Echeverría," 63; Reed, *Caste War,* 175; Reed, "Juan de la Cruz, Venencio Puc, and the Speaking Cross," 520; Dumond, *Machete,* 2, 419.

221. "Lieutenant Governor to O. C. Troops," January 5, 1865, R. 91, in Burdon, *Archives,* 3:259.

222. Baqueiro Preve, *Ensayo histórico,* 3:6.

223. "Proclama dirigida á los indios por D. Miguel Barbachano, presidente de la primera comisión nombrada por el gobierno para escuchar sus quejas y procurar la conclusión de la guerra," Tekax, February 17, 1848, in Ancona, *Yucatán,* vol. 4, appendix, v.

224. Baqueiro Preve, *Ensayo histórico,* 3:67.

225. Ibid., 97.

226. "Comunicación Oficial del Gobierno del Estado, desvaneciendo los fundamentos que tuvo el Supremo Gobierno para reprobarle su conducta por las primeras partidas de indios que salieron para La Habana," Mérida, September 12, 1849, in Baqueiro Preve, *Ensayo histórico,* 3:328.

227. *Guerra de Castas en Yucatán,* xix, lxix.

228. Ibid., 37.

229. Ibid., 132.

230. Baqueiro Preve, *Ensayo histórico,* 4:75.

231. Ibid., 76.

232. Reina, *Las rebeliones campesinas en México,* 378.

233. Harff and Gurr, "Toward Empirical Theory of Genocides and Politicides," 364–65.

234. Lemkin, *Axis Rule in Occupied Europe,* 79, xi.

235. Chalk and Jonassohn, "The Conceptual Framework," 10.

236. Fein, "Scenarios of Genocide," 4

237. Drost, *The Crime of State,* 2:125; du Preez, *Genocide,* 4.

238. Bauer, "The Place of the Holocaust in Contemporary History," 213.

239. Chalk and Jonassohn, "The Conceptual Framework," 23–24.

240. Dadrian, "A Typology of Genocide," 201, 204.

241. Ibid.

242. Harff and Gurr, "Toward Empirical Theory of Genocides and Politicides," 360; Horowitz, *Taking Lives,* 17.

243. Dadrian, "A Typology of Genocide," 201, 205–10; Smith, "Human Destructiveness and Politics," 24–27; Harff and Gurr, "Toward Empirical Theory of Genocides and Politicides," 363–64; du Preez, *Genocide,* 14, 68–70.

244. Chalk and Jonassohn, "The Conceptual Framework," 23–24.

245. Lanternari, *The Religions of the Oppressed,* 247; Adas, *Prophets of Rebellion,* 9; Linton, "Nativistic Movements," 231.

5. Rebellion and Relative Deprivation

1. Hagopian, *The Phenomenon of Revolution,* 1–2, 24, 28, 81, 85, 280; see also Hobsbawm, *Primitive Rebels,* 57; Barkun, *Disaster and the Millennium,* 21–23; and Crane Brinton, *The Anatomy of Revolution* (New York: Prentice Hall, 1952), 262.

2. Ted R. Gurr, *Why Men Rebel* (Princeton: Princeton University Press, 1971), 13–14, 24, 123–24, 315–16; Staub, *The Roots of Evil,* 35.

3. Ibid., 24–25, 359.

4. Ibid., 25–26, 358.

5. Ibid., 13, 24, 123–25; Barkun, *Disaster and the Millennium,* 35.

6. Gurr, *Why Men Rebel,* 13, 103–104; Allen Grimshaw, "Interpreting Collective Violence: An Argument for the Importance of Social Structure," in James Short and Martin Wolfgang, eds., *Collective Violence* (Chicago: Aldine-Atherton, 1972), 45; Taylor, *Drinking,* 132, 141.

7. Gurr, *Why Men Rebel,* 304, 319–21, 323–26, 327.

8. Ibid., 46–48; Barkun, *Disaster and the Millennium,* 35–36.

9. Adas, *Prophets of Rebellion,* 44, 46, 62–64, 66, 72, 79.

10. The term was first used by Edward P. Thompson in "The Moral Economy of the English Crowd in the Eighteenth Century," *Past and Present* 50 (1971): 76–136, discussing the English food riots of the 1700s. It has since been more broadly applied to conditions of decremental deprivation which erode long-standing relationships between those of unequal power. See also "The Moral Economy Reviewed," in *Customs in Common* (London: Merlin Press, 1991), for Thompson's views concerning its application. For a critique of Thompson's use of moral economy, calling for greater attention to be paid to the larger political and economic context, see John Bohstedt, "The Moral Economy and the Discipline of Historical Context," *Journal of Social History* 26, no. 2 (Winter 1992): 265–85. For applications of the concept see the edited work of Adrian Randall and Andrew Charlesworth, *Moral Ecomony and Popular Protest: Crowds, Conflict and Authority* (New York: St. Martin's Press, 2000), and James Scott, *The Moral Economy of the Peasant: Rebellion and Subsistence in Southeast Asia* (New Haven: Yale University Press, 1976). For its use in the context of Latin America, see Stavig, "Ethnic Conflict, Moral Economy, and Population in Rural Cuzco on the Eve of the Thupa Amaro II Rebellion," *Hispanic American Historical Review* 64, no. 4 (November 1988): 737–70, as well as his *World of Túpac Amaru,* and also Gosner, *Soldiers of the Virgin.*

11. Taylor, *Drinking,* 132; see also Stavig, "Ethnic Conflict," 738–40, 769.

12. Barrington Moore, *Social Origins of Dictatorship and Democracy: Lord and Peasant in the Making of the Modern World* (Boston: Beacon Press, 1966), 474.

13. Gurr, *Why Men Rebel,* 103–104; Grimshaw, "Interpreting Collective Violence," 42–45; Taylor, *Drinking,* 132; Brinton, *The Anatomy of Revolution,* 55, 60, 63–64; Adas, *Prophets of Rebellion,* 55.

14. Jack Levy, "An Introduction to Prospect Theory," *Political Psychology* 13, no. 2 (1992): 171, 175; Robert Jervis, "Political Implications of Loss Aversion," ibid., 187, 188, 191–92.

15. Barkun, *Disaster and the Millennium*, 1, 19; Wallace, "Revitalization Movements," 265; Wallace, "Mazeway Disintegration," 24.

16. Barkun, *Disaster and the Millennium*, 54–55, 56, 62, 64, 67–69, 91–92; Adas, *Prophets of Rebellion*, 80–83.

17. Barkun, *Disaster and the Millennium*, 65–66.

18. See also Hagopian, *The Phenomenon of Revolution*, 26.

19. Brinton, *The Anatomy of Revolution*, 33; Gurr, *Why Men Rebel*, 104.

20. Hagopian, *The Phenomenon of Revolution*, 171.

21. Brinton, *The Anatomy of Revolution*, 29–30, 78; Gurr, *Why Men Rebel*, 46, 52–56.

22. Hagopian, *The Phenomenon of Revolution*, 174.

23. Gurr, *Why Men Rebel*, 101.

24. Ibid., 102–103, 109–10.

25. Ibid., 56–57, 102. See also Adas, *Prophets of Rebellion*, 77–78, 184.

26. Gurr, *Why Men Rebel*, 47–48, 124; Barkun, *Disaster and the Millennium*, 35–36.

27. Levy, "An Introduction to Prospect Theory," 171, 175; Jervis, "Political Implications of Loss Aversion," 187, 191–192.

28. Gurr, *Why Men Rebel*, 46–48; Barkun, *Disaster and the Millennium*, 35–36.

29. Reff, "The 'Predicament of Culture,'" 70; Daniel Reff, *Disease, Depopulation and Culture Change in Northwestern New Spain, 1518–1764* (Salt Lake City: University of Utah Press, 1991), 229.

30. Levy, "An Introduction to Prospect Theory," 171, 175; Jervis, "Political Implications of Loss Aversion," 187.

31. Gurr, *Why Men Rebel*, 24–26, 358–59.

32. Knault, *Pueblo Revolt*, 68; Simmons, "History of Pueblo-Indian Relations to 1821," 184; Riley, *Kachina and the Cross*, 212.

33. "Auto of Antonio de Otermín," n.p., n.d., in Twitchell, *Spanish Archives*, 2:16.

34. "Declaration of Pedro García, an Indian of the Tagno Nation, a Native of Las Salinas," Near Estancia of Cristóbal de Anaya, August 25, 1680, in Hackett, *Revolt*, 8:24–25.

35. Gurr, *Why Men Rebel*, 24–26, 358–59; Simmons, "History of Pueblo-Indian Relations to 1821," 183, 184; Reff, "The 'Predicament of Culture,'" 70–71; Knault, *Pueblo Revolt*, 7; Hackett, *Revolt*, 8:xxii; Riley, *Kachina and the Cross*, 212.

36. "Testimony of Juan Lorenzo and Francisco Lorenzo," Paso del Norte, December 20, 1681, "Interrogatories and Depositions of Three Indians of the Tehua Nation, Taken by the Order of Don Antonio Otermín," Río del Norte, December 28, 1681, in Twitchell, *Spanish Archives*, 2:66; Hackett, *Revolt*, 8:xxii, clvii; "Declaration of Lieutenant General of Cavalry," Río del Norte, December 20, 1681, ibid., 9:262; "Declaration of Sargento Mayor Luís de Quintana," Río del Norte, December 22, 1681, ibid., 9:289; Diego de Vargas, campaign journal, New Mexico, August 9–

October 15, 1692, in Kessell et al., *By Force of Arms*, 391; Hackett, *Revolt*, 8:xxii, clvii; Knault, *Pueblo Revolt*, 167, 175–76.

37. "Auto of Antonio de Otermín," Alamillo, September 6, 1680, in Twitchell, *Spanish Archives*, 2:20; see also 21.

38. "Declaration of One of the Rebellious Christian Indians Who Was Captured on the Road," Alamillo, September 6, 1680, 61, in Hackett, *Revolt*, 8:60–61.

39. "Declaration of Diego López Sambrano," Hacienda of Luis de Carbajal, December 22, 1681, in Hackett, *Revolt*, 9:301; Bancroft, *Arizona and New Mexico*, 170–71; Knault, *Pueblo Revolt*, 164; Josephy, *Patriot Chiefs*, 88.

40. O'Phelan Godoy, *Rebellions and Revolts*, 109–10, 119, 148, 153, 207, 260, 279–80; O'Phelan Godoy, "Elementos étnicos," 89; O'Phelan Godoy, "Hacía una tipología," 148; Stern, "Age," 39, 75; see also "Representación ante el Fiscal de la Audiencia de Charcas por don José Chirari y Herrera, cacique del Pueblo de Moromoro, provincia Chayanta, por sí y en nombre de su comunidad, sobre las extorciones y agravios que les infieren los receptores de alcabalas en las internaciones de los frutos de sus labranzas," La Plata, October 25, 1771, ANB, ECad.1771.77, 1. For more on the Bourbon reforms, see O'Phelan Godoy, *Rebellions and Revolts;* John Fisher, *Bourbon Peru, 1750–1824* (Liverpool: Liverpool University Press, 2003); John Fisher, Allan Kuethe, and Anthony McFarlane, eds., *Reform and Insurrection in Bourbon New Granada and Peru* (Baton Rouge: Louisiana State University Press, 1990); Jacques Barbier, *Reform and Politics in Bourbon Chile, 1755–1796* (Ottawa: University of Ottawa Press, 1980); Kendall Brown, *Bourbons and Brandy: Imperial Reform in Eighteenth-Century Arequipa* (Albuquerque: University of New Mexico Press, 1985); and Anthony McFarlane, *Colombia before Independence: Economy, Society, and Politics under Bourbon Rule* (New York: Cambridge University Press, 1993).

41. Hagopian, *The Phenomenon of Revolution*, 151.

42. Rowe, "El movimiento nacional Inca del siglo XVIII," 23, 26; see also Bradley and Cahill, *Habsburg Peru*, as well as Cahill's "The Virgin and the Inca: An Incaic Procession in the City of Cuzco in 1692" and "Popular Religion and Appropriation: The Example of Corpus Christi in Eighteenth-Century Cuzco."

43. O'Phelan Godoy, *Rebellions and Revolts*, 118, 258, 261, 266.

44. "Información recibida en la Prov. de Chayanta sobre averiguar quines han sido los principales caudillos de la sublevacn. del dichos pueblos," Moromoro, May 20, 1781, ANB, SGI.1781.160, 2–18; O'Phelan Godoy, *Rebellions and Revolts*, 265.

45. Calderón, *Monografía histórica del departamento de Oruro*, 29.

46. Lewin, *Túpac Amaru, el rebelde*, 9; Lewin, *Túpac Amaru, su época, su lucha, su hado* (Buenos Aires: Ediciones Siglo Veinte, 1973), 122.

47. Lewin, *Túpac Amaru, el rebelde*, 12, 48; see also Lewin, *Los movimientos de emancipación en Hispanoamérica y la independencia de estados unidos* (Buenos Aires: Editorial Raigal, 1952), 121.

48. Zuaire Huarte, "Análisis de la rebelión de Túpac Amaru en su bicentenario (1780–1980)," 36; Fisher, *Last Inca Revolt*, 193, 196, 205.

49. Lewin, *Túpac Amaru, el rebelde*, 21; Lewin, *Los movimientos*, 123; Válcarcel, *La Rebelión de Túpac Amaru*, 18. See also Taylor, *Drinking*, 132.

50. Gurr, *Why Men Rebel*, 101.

51. Ibid., 46; Hagopian, *The Phenomenon of Revolution*, 172; Válcarcel, *La Rebelión de Túpac Amaru*, 68.

52. Calderón, *Monografía histórica del departamento de Oruro*, 29; Fernando Cajías de la Vega, "La rebelión de Oruro y las provincias aledañas en 1781," *Encuentro* 5 (November 1989): 32.

53. Lewin, *Túpac Amaru, el rebelde*, 54–67.

54. Lewin, *Los movimientos*, 131.

55. Rugeley, "Los mayas yucatecos del siglo XIX," 210; Rugeley, *Yucatán's Maya Peasantry*, 92–93.

56. Rugeley, *Yucatán's Maya Peasantry*, 115, 185.

57. Eligio Ancona, *Historia de Yucatán, desde la época más remota hasta nuestros días*, 5 vols. (Mérida, México: Imprenta de M. Heredia Argüelles, 1878–1905), 4:7; *Guerra de Castas de Yucatán*, 3, 12, 31, 93.

58. Rugeley, *Maya Wars*, 10; "Through Fire and Blood: Cecilio Chi's Letter to John Fancourt," ibid., 54; "The Whites Began It: Jacinto Pat's Letter on the Origins of the Caste War," ibid., 51–52; "'They Kill the Poor Indians as They Kill Animals': Jacinto Pat's Letter to Modesto Méndez," July 11, 1848, ibid., 55; Terry Rugeley, "Rural Political Violence and the Origins of the Caste War," *The Americas* 53, no. 4 (April 1997): 494–95; Rugeley, "Los Mayas Yucatecos," 205; Dumond, *Machete and the Cross*, 137.

59. Rugeley, *Yucatán's Maya Peasantry*, 44.

60. *Guerra de Castas en Yucatán*, 9; Ancona, *Historia de Yucatán*, 3:359–60, 364–66, 368–73; Reed, *Caste War*, 27–28; Cline, "The Sugar Episode in Yucatán," 96.

61. Reed, *Caste War*, 28; Cline, "Regionalism and Society in Yucatán," 3.

62. Dumond, *Machete*, 138, 407.

63. Reed, *Caste War*, 9–10, 45; Cline, "The Sugar Episode in Yucatán," 100.

64. Cline, "The Sugar Episode in Yucatán," 100; Grant D. Jones, "La estructura política de los mayas de Chan Santa Cruz: el papel del respaldo ingles," *Amérique Indígena* 31, no. 2 (April 1971): 418; Rugeley, *Yucatán's Maya Peasantry*, xiv.

65. Reed, *Caste War*, 48.

66. Gurr, *Why Men Rebel*, 103–104; Grimshaw, "Interpreting Collective Violence," 45; Taylor, *Drinking*, 132; Brinton, *The Anatomy of Revolution*, 55, 60, 63–64; Dumond, *Machete*, 407.

6. Leadership and Division

1. Adas, *Prophets of Rebellion*, 118–20.

2. "Testimony of Pedro Naranjo," Río del Norte, December 18, 1681, in Twitchell, *Spanish Archives*, 2:64.

3. "Declaration of Diego López Sambrano," Hacienda of Luis de Carbajal, December 22, 1681, in Hackett, *Revolt*, 9:295.

4. Ibid.

5. "Testimony of Pedro Naranjo," 2:64.

6. "Declaration of Jerónimo, a Tigua Indian," opposite La Isleta, January 1, 1682, in Hackett, *Revolt*, 9:361.

7. "Declaration of an Indian," House of Captain Francisco de Ortega, December 27, 1681, in Hackett, *Revolt*, 9:346.

8. "Testimony of Pedro Naranjo," 64.

9. Bancroft, *Arizona and New Mexico*, 184.

10. Kessel, "Esteban Clemente," 16.

11. Knault, *Pueblo Revolt*, 167.

12. "Letter from the Governor and Captain-General, Don Antonio de Otermín, from New Mexico," September 8, 1680, in Hackett, *Historical Documents*, 4:330.

13. Chávez, "Pohe-yemo's Representative and the Pueblo Revolt," 86.

14. "Reply of the Fiscal, Don Martín de Solís Miranda," Mexico, June 25, 1682, in Hackett, *Revolt*, 9:383-84; Kessell et al., *By Force of Arms*, 621; see also Chávez, "Pohe-yemo's Representative and the Pueblo Revolt," 95; "Tercer cuaderno," 346.

15. "El provedio de D. Diego de Vargas sobre la petición espresada del Padre Custorio y demas religiosos misioneros dice," 383.

16. "Testimony of Pedro Naranjo," 63; "Testimony of Juan Lorenzo and Francisco Lorenzo," Paso del Norte, December 20, 1681, in "Interrogatories and Depositions of Three Indians of the Tehua Nation, Taken by the Order of Don Antonio Oter-mín," Río del Norte, December 28, 1681, in Twitchell, *Spanish Archives*, 2:65; "Carta del Padre Fray Silvestre Velez de Escalante," Santa Fe, April 2, 1778, in *Documentos*, 312; Bancroft, *Arizona and New Mexico*, 184-85.

17. "Carta del Padre Fray Silvestre Velez de Escalante," *Documentos*, 312; Bancroft, *Arizona and New Mexico*, 185; Knault, *Pueblo Revolt*, 175.

18. Jane Sánchez, "Spanish-Indian Relations during the Otermín Administration, 1677-1683," *New Mexico Historical Review* 58, no. 2 (April 1983): 145.

19. "Carta del Padre Fray Silvestre Velez de Escalante," *Documentos*, 312.

20. "Declaration of Lieutenant General of Cavalry," Río del Norte, December 20, 1681, in Hackett, *Revolt*, 9:259, 260; "Letter of Juan Domínguez de Mendoza to Antonio de Otermín," Alameda, December 9, 1681, in Hackett, *Revolt*, 9:220.

21. Lanternari, *The Religions of the Oppressed*, 247; Adas, *Prophets of Rebellion*, 9; Linton, "Nativistic Movements," 231.

22. "Carta del Padre Fray Silvestre Velez de Escalante," *Documentos*, 318; Siguenza y Gongora, "Mercurio Volante," in *Documentos*, 96; Bancroft, *Arizona and New Mexico*, 185; Knault, *Pueblo Revolt*, 175; "Declaration of an Indian," House of Captain Francisco de Ortega, December 27, 1681, in Hackett, *Revolt*, 9:344, 346.

23. "Carta del Padre Fray Silvestre Velez de Escalante," *Documentos*, 318; Bancroft, *Arizona and New Mexico*, 185.

24. Siguenza y Gongora, "Mercurio Volante," *Documentos*, 95.

25. Hackett, "Revolt of the Pueblo Indians," 117.

26. "Declaration of Diego López Sambrano," 9:295.

27. "Testimony of Juan Lorenzo and Francisco Lorenzo," 2:66.

28. "Interrogatories and Depositions of Three Indians of the Tehua Nation," 51.

29. "Testimony of Pedro Naranjo," 64.

30. "Interrogatories and Depositions of Three Indians of the Tehua Nation," 53; "Carta del Padre Fray Silvestre Velez de Escalante," *Documentos,* 312, 318; Siguenza y Gongora, "Mercurio Volante," *Documentos,* 96; "Testimony of Pedro Naranjo," 63; "Testimony of Juan Lorenzo and Francisco Lorenzo," 2:65; Bancroft, *Arizona and New Mexico,* 184–85; Knault, *Pueblo Revolt,* 175.

31. "Declaration of Jerónimo, a Tigua Indian," 9:361.

32. "Carta del Padre Fray Silvestre Velez de Escalante," 318; Siguenza y Gongora, "Mercurio Volante," *Documentos,* 96; Bancroft, *Arizona and New Mexico,* 185, 199; Knault, *Pueblo Revolt,* 175, 180; Sánchez, "Spanish-Indian Relations during the Otermín Administration," 133.

33. "Auto of Antonio de Otermín," La Isleta, December 9, 1681, in Hackett, *Revolt,* 9:218.

34. "Declaration of Juan de la Cruz," Hacienda of Luís de Carbajal, December 24, 1681, in Hackett, *Revolt,* 9:330.

35. "Testimony of José," Río del Norte, December 19, 1681, in "Interrogatories and Depositions of Three Indians of the Tehua Nation," in Twitchell, *Spanish Archives,* 2:57, 58; see also "Reply of the Fiscal, Don Martín de Solís Miranda," 9:400.

36. Hackett, *Revolt,* 8:cxlii–cxliii; "Letter of Juan Domínguez de Mendoza to Antonio de Otermín," Alameda, December 9, 1681, ibid., 9:220.

37. "R. No. B. Pueblo de Acoma," September 20, 1869, in Twitchell, *Spanish Archives,* 2:456.

38. Kessell, "Spaniards and Pueblos," 130; see also Knault, *Pueblo Revolt,* xvi.

39. Riley, *Kachina and the Cross,* 219, 238.

40. Diego de Vargas, campaign journal, New Mexico, August 9–October 15, 1692, in Kessell et al., *By Force of Arms,* 385, 426, 428, 432, 449.

41. "Tercer cuaderno," 354, 359, 360–64.

42. "Letter of Fray Gerónimo Prieto," San Juan, March 10, 1696, in Espinosa, *Pueblo Indian Revolt,* 179.

43. "Sesto cuaderno," 413–14.

44. "Letter of Fray Alfonso Jiménez de Cisneros," Cochiti, April 21, 1696, in Espinosa, *Pueblo Indian Revolt,* 245.

45. Diego de Vargas, campaign journal, June 12, 1696, in Kessell et al., *Blood,* 2:751.

46. Ibid., 754.

47. Diego de Vargas, campaign journal, June 17–30, 1696, in Kessell et al., *Blood,* 2:771.

48. "Alfonso Rael de Aguilar, Interrogation of a Keres Prisoner," Santa Fe, July 3, 1696, in Kessell et al., *Blood,* 2:802; "Roque Madrid to Alfonso Rael de Aguilar," Villa Nueva de Santa Cruz, August 9, 1696, in Kessell et al., *By Force of Arms,* 995.

49. Diego de Vargas, campaign journal, August 20–29, 1696, in Kessell et al., *Blood*, 2:1002.

50. Diego de Vargas, campaign journal, September 6–October 18, 1696, in Kessell et al., *Blood*, 2:1030.

51. "Letter of Ayeta to the Viceroy in Which He Advises Him that the Governor Is Alive," in Hackett, *Revolt*, 8:126; "Reply of the Señor Fiscal," Mexico, January 3, 1681, ibid., 8:222.

52. "Letter of Ayeta to the Viceroy in Which He Advises Him that the Governor Is Alive," 125.

53. "Letter from the Governor and Captain-General, Don Antonio de Otermín, from New Mexico," in Hackett, *Historical Documents*, 4:328; "Letter of Antonio de Otermín to Fray Diego de Parraga," Near Socorro, September 8, 1680, in Hackett, *Historical Documents*, 8:90; "Auto of Antonio de Otermín," Place opposite la Salineta, October 1, 1680, in Hackett, *Revolt*, 8:153.

54. "Autos de junta de guerra," El Paso, April 5, 1681, in Hackett, *Revolt*, 9:18–29.

55. "Declaration of Pedro Leiva," San Lorenzo, June 15, 1681, in Hackett, *Revolt*, 9:30–31.

56. "Proclamation of Antonio de Otermín," San Lorenzo, October 1681, in Hackett, *Revolt*, 9:153.

57. "Auto of Antonio de Otermín," El Paso, September 2, 1681, in Hackett, *Revolt*, 9:87.

58. "Autos and Judicial Proceedings Concerning Certain Persons Excusing Themselves from the Royal Service," El Paso, September 29–October 18, 1681, in Hackett, *Revolt*, 9:147–52; "Certified Copy of the Requisition that Was Sent by Señor Don Antonio de Otermín to Francisco Ramírez, Alcalde Mayor of Casas Grandes," El Paso, October 9, 1681, ibid., 9:155.

59. "Opinion of Fray Francisco de Ayeta," Hacienda of Luis de Carbajal, December 23, 1681, in Hackett, *Revolt*, 9:312–14.

60. "Auto of Antonio de Otermín," San Lorenzo, October 20, 1681, in Hackett, *Revolt*, 9:159.

61. "Declaration of maestre de campo Francisco Gómez, lieutenant general, fifty-three years of age," San Lorenzo, October 21, 1681, in Hackett, *Revolt*, 9:169.

62. "Auto of Antonio de Otermín," San Lorenzo, October 26, 1681, in Hackett, *Revolt*, 9:183.

63. "Auto for Passing Muster," El Ancón de fray García, November 7, 1681, in Hackett, *Revolt*, 9:190–91.

64. "Auto of Antonio de Otermín," San Lorenzo, October 20, 1681, in Hackett, *Revolt*, 9:160.

65. Hackett, *Revolt*, 8:cxxx, ccvi–ccvii; "Proclamation," Las Barrancas, December 5, 1681, ibid., 9:213.

66. Sánchez, "Spanish-Indian Relations during the Otermín Administration," 141.

67. "Opinion of Fray Francisco de Ayeta," 9:315–16.

68. "Opinion of the Cabildo," La Salineta, October 3, 1680, in Hackett, *Revolt*, 8:180.

69. "Testimony of José," Río del Norte, December 19, 1681, in "Interrogatories and Depositions of Three Indians of the Tehua Nation," in Twitchell, *Spanish Archives*, 2:58; "Testimony of Juan of Tesuque," Río del Norte, December 28, 1681, ibid., 2:55; "Testimony of Juan Lorenzo and Francisco Lorenzo," Paso del Norte, December 20, 1681, ibid., 2:67–68; "Declaration of Sargento Mayor Sebastián de Herrera," Río del Norte, December 21, 1681, in Hackett, *Revolt*, 9:273; "Declaration of Sargento Mayor Luís de Quintana," Río del Norte, December 22, 1681, in Hackett, *Revolt*, 9:289; "Tercer cuaderno [of Fray Salvador de San Antonio]," Santa Fe, December 18, 1693, in *Documentos*, 346; "Don Juan, the governor of Pecos, arrives with the four Indians who came to see me," November 25, 1693, in Kessell et al., *To the Royal Crown Restored*, 437–39; Kessell, "Esteban Clemente," 16; Knault, *Pueblo Revolt*, 166.

70. "Auto of Antonio de Otermín," Fray Cristóbal, September 13, 1680, in Hackett, *Revolt*, 8:113; "The Viceroy of New Spain Makes Report to Your Majesty of the General Uprising of the Indians of the Provinces of New Mexico, and of the Measures and Means Which Have Been Adopted for Their Restoration," Mexico City, February 28, 1681, in Hackett, *Historical Documents*, 4:340; "Auto of Antonio de Otermín," Alamillo, September 6, 1680, in Twitchell, *Spanish Archives*, 2:32.

71. "Testimony of Sargento Mayor Sebastián de Herrera, Forty-four Years of Age," San Lorenzo, October 21, 1681, in Hackett, *Revolt*, 9:171.

72. "Auto of Antonio de Otermín," n.p., n.d., in Twitchell, *Spanish Archives*, 2:2; "Answer Presented by the Lieutenant-General Alonzo García, in His Own Behalf," Isleta, August 14, 1680, ibid., 25.

73. "Auto of Antonio de Otermín," Fray Cristóbal, September 13, 1680, in Hackett, *Revolt*, 8:114; "Auto of Antonio de Otermín," Santa Fe, August 21, 1680, ibid., 8:17; Hackett, "Revolt of the Pueblo Indians," 142–43.

74. Hackett, *Revolt*, 8:xciv.

75. "Opinion of Luís Granillo," Near Socorro, August 26, 1680, in Hackett, *Revolt*, 8:80; Hackett, "Revolt of the Pueblo Indians," 125.

76. "Answer Presented by the Lieutenant-General Alonzo García, in His Own Behalf," Isleta, August 14, 1680, in Twitchell, *Spanish Archives*, 28; "Opinion of Luís Granillo," 8:80.

77. "Letter of Luís Granillo to Antonio de Otermín," La Isleta, December 24, 1681, in Hackett, *Revolt*, 9:339.

78. "Extracto de la carta en que con fecha de 16 de Octubre de 1692, da cuenta Vargas a S.E.," Santa Fe, in *Documentos*, 333; Diego de Vargas, campaign journal, New Mexico, October 16–December 27, 1692, in Kessell et al., *By Force of Arms*, 538, 557–58.

79. "The Governor, Don Luis, Refers to the Words Spoken by Pedro de Tapia, Which Caused Suspicion, and to the State of Mind of the Tewas and Tanos," Santo Domingo, December 4, 1693, in Kessell et al., *To the Royal Crown Restored*, 458; Diego de Vargas, campaign journal, June 12, 1696, in Kessell et al., *Blood*, 2:755; Diego de Vargas, campaign journal, July 20–25, 1696, in Kessell et al., *Blood*, 2:841; Diego de Vargas, campaign journal, New Mexico, October 16–December 27, 1692,

in Kessell et al., *By Force of Arms*, 538, 557–58; "Extracto de la carta en que con fecha de 16 de Octubre de 1692, da cuenta Vargas a S.E.," 333.

80. Gerth and Mills, *From Max Weber*, 295–96; Tucker, "The Theory of Charismatic Leadership," 731, 742.

81. Szeminksi, "Why Kill the Spaniard?" 174, 175; Campbell, "Ideology," 117–18; Pedro de Angelis, "Discurso preliminar a la revolución de Túpac-Amaru," in Pedro de Angelis, ed., *Colección de obras y documentos relativos a la historia del Río de la Plata* (Buenos Aires, Librería Nacional de J. Lajouane, 1910), 4:269; Campbell, "Banditry," 139; López Baralt, *El Retorno del Inca Rey*, 37, 40; Valle del Siles, "Túpac Katari y la rebelión de 1781," 654.

82. Szeminski, *La utopía Tupamarista*, 198; Szeminski, "Why Kill the Spaniard?" 187.

83. Hobsbawm, *Primitive Rebels*, 58–59; Campbell, "Banditry," 160; Campbell, "Ideology," 127; Válcarcel, *La rebelión de Túpac Amaru*, 145.

84. Adas, *Prophets of Rebellion*, 119.

85. Valle del Siles, "Túpac Katari y la rebelión de 1781," 636, 637, 640, 650, 655.

86. Ibid., 642.

87. Stern, "Age," 80–81.

88. Hidalgo Lehunde, "Amarus y Cataris," 123.

89. Adas, *Prophets of Rebellion*, 119.

90. "Diario trunco," 2; "Representación de Domingo Angeles a Gerónimo Manuel de Ruedas," La Plata, October 17, 1780, AGI, Charcas 593, 12.

91. "Representación de Juan de Dios Pinapi," La Plata, October 20, 1780, AGI, Charcas 596, 18; "Declaración de Bernardo Franco," Potosí, March 24, 1781, AGI, Charcas 437-b, 13.

92. "Carta de Ignacio Florez a Juan José Vertíz," La Plata, May 13, 1781, AGI, Charcas 596, 3.

93. "Declaración de Alvento Arze," Oropesa, Cochabamba, October 2, 1780, AGI, Charcas 596, 70.

94. "Informe del corregidor de Paria Manuel de Bodega," La Plata, October 21, 1780, AGI, Charcas 596, 92–93.

95. Diario y relación prolija jurada que yo el General Don Juan Gelly," 2–3; "Anexo al diario y relación," 1; "Relación de los hechos más notables acaecidos en la sublevación general fraguada en los reynos del Perú, por el indio José Gabriel Túpac Amaru, gobr. del pueblo de Tungasuca en la Provincia de Tinta, que asociado de otros sequaces, causó horrosos estragos desde el año 1780, hasta el de 1782 en que se reprimo el orgullo de la conjuración," in *Revista de archivos y bibliotecas nacionales* 3, no. 5 (Lima, September 30, 1900): 141–47.

96. "Carta de Valeriano Marino a Juan Pino del Manrique," Chayanta, October 11, 1780, AGI, Charcas 596, 72; "Informe de Pedro Yavira Ylario Caguasiri," San Pedro de Buenavista, December 28, 1780, AGI, Charcas 596, 52.

97. "Parte de D. José de Reseguín al Virey de Buenos Aires, sobre la sublevación de Santiago de Cotagaita," Cayza, April 15, 1781, in Odriozola, *Documentos históricos*,

1:345; "Parte de D. José de Reseguín al Virey de Buenos Aires," March 18, 1781, 1:348.

98. "Oficio de Gregorio Josef de Merlos a Juan José Vertíz," La Plata, February 15, 1781, in Lewin, *La rebelión de Túpac Amaru*, 739.

99. "Carta de Joseph Antonio de Areche, Visitador de Tribunales y Superintendente de la Real Hacienda en Perú al Superior Consejo de Indians," Cuzco, May 23, 1781, AGI, Charcas 595, 2.

100. "Diario fabuloso," 289; "Relación verdadera," 77; "Actuaciones anteriores," 176; "Causas de Oruro: Testimonio de la acusación del Señor Fiscal de S.M. contra los reos de la sublevación de la villa de Oruro y otras acusaciones," Buenos Aires, 1784, in Mier, *Noticia y proceso de la muy noble y muy leal Villa de San Felipe de Austria de Oruro*, 2:141; "Informe del Consejo," 106; "Causa de Augustín Solís," La Plata, March 11, 1781, AGI, Charcas 594, 21; "Relación de los sucesos de Cochabamba," 12; Campbell, "Ideology," 126; Campbell, "Banditry," 154–55; Szeminski, "Why Kill the Spaniard?" 170, 185–86.

101. "Oficio de Gregorio Francisco de Campos, Obispo de La Paz, al Rey," La Paz, November 15, 1781, AGI, Charcas 595, 1.

102. "Actuaciones anteriores," 95; "Confesión de Pasqual Tola," La Plata, April 20, 1781, AGI, Charcas 603, 27; "Expediente seguido por los vecinos de la Doctrina de Miculpaya sobre que se les ausilie con armas para la defensa de los indios," Porco, March 16, 1781, ANB, SGI.1781.88, 2.

103. "Carta de Capellán Theodoro Gutiérrez de Seballos a Ramón de Urrutía y las Casas," Poopó, January 18, 1781, AGI, Charcas 437-b, 5.

104. "Declaración de Bernardo Franco," Potosí, March 24, 1781, AGI, Charcas 437-b, 12.

105. "Confesión de Mariano Quispe," in "Sumaria información recibida de varios indios de Chocaya como sindicados en la sublevación," Chichas, November 23, 1781, ANB, SGI.1781.10, 43.

106. "Relación traxica," 1, 15; "Relación verdadera," 84; "Testimonio de Josef Manuel de Santander," in "Causa contra los cabezas de la rebelión de Oruro," La Plata, n.d., AGI, Charcas 599, 231.

107. "Carta que refiere a los estragos hechos por los Yndios alzados en Suches mineral de la Provincia de Larecaja del Obispado de La Paz; y en los pueblos de Arque, Tapacari, y Colcha en la Provincia de Cochabamba, perteneciente al Arzobispado de la Plata," Cochabamba, February 26, 1781, in Carlos Daniel Válcarcel, ed., *Colección Documental de la independencia del Perú*, book 2, 1:509.

108. "Relación verdadera," 84–85; "Relación histórica," 29, 31; Mario Montaño, *Síntesis histórica de Oruro* (n.p., 1972), 83.

109. "Actuaciones anteriores," 123; "Confesión del reo Ventura Pinto," in "Causa criminal contra Ramón Paca, Bentura Pinto, Pedro Copa Cava, y de más reos principales, comprehendidos en la sublevación, muertes y robos perpetrados en este pueblo de Yura y sus ynmediasiones," Porco, October 7, 1781, ANB, SGI.1781.61, 27.

110. "Testimonio de Ventura Balencia," Oruro, April 10, 1781, AGI, Charcas 601, 24; "Carta de Capellán Theodoro Gutiérrez de Seballos a Ramón de Urrutía y las Casas," 5; "Actuaciones anteriores," 11, 42–43, 45, 48, 62; "Testimonio de Santos

Mamani," Oruro, May 25, 1781, AGI, Charcas 601, 37; "Declaración de Francisco Xavier Condori," Oruro, April 10, 1781, AGI, Charcas 601, 12; "Testimonio de Martín Lopes," Oruro, April 7, 1781, AGI, Charcas 601, 13.

111. "Declaración de Luís de Palacio y Santelises," La Plata, March 12, 1781, AGI, Charcas 594, 11; "Causa de Augustín Solís," 11; "Fragment of Informe," n.p., n.d., AGI, Charcas 594, 3; "Dn. Pedro Antonio Cernudas y Dn. Lorenzo Blanco Ciceron oydores en la Rl. Audiencia de Charcas continuan el informe de los sucesos de las provincias cuios naturales incurrieron en el delito de rebelión," La Plata, May 15, 1781, AGI, Charcas 594, 1; "Dn Pedro Antonio Zernudas oidor de la Rl Audiencia dela Plata informa," 3; "Carta de Capitán General y Gobernador Andrés Mestre a Josef de Galvez," Salta, June 24, 1781, AGI, Charcas 595, 1.

112. "Confesión de Dámaso Catari," La Plata, April 1, 1781, in Odriozola, *Documentos históricos*, 1:305–306; see also "Carta de Dámaso Catari a Dn. Pasqual Llavi," Macha, March 5, 1781, AGI, Charcas 437-b, 56.

113. "Carta de Ignacio Florez a Juan José Vertíz," La Plata, May 13, 1781, 5.

114. "Carta de Jorge Escobedo a Juan José Vertíz," Potosí, February 24, 1781, AGI, Charcas 437-b, 2.

115. "Informe de Josef Atanacio Baspineyro," Potosí, March 14, 1781, AGI, Charcas 437-b, 1; "Parte de D. José de Reseguín al Virey de Buenos Aires," March 18, 1781, 1:348.

116. Campbell, "Ideology," 130–31, Valle del Siles, "Túpac Katari y la rebelión de 1781," 657–58; Fisher, *Last Inca Revolt*, 293–94.

117. Irene Silverblatt, "Becoming Indian in the Central Andes of Seventeenth-Century Peru," in Gyan Prakash, ed., *After Colonialism: Imperial Histories and Postcolonial Displacements* (Princeton: Princeton University Press, 1995), 287.

118. "Carta de Borda a Segurola," 6.

119. "Copias de documentos citados en el diario," #18, 26; Valle del Siles, "Túpac Katari y la rebelión de 1781," 653; "Relación de los hechos más notables," 249; "Diario de Sebastián de Segurola," La Paz, July 1, 1781, AGI, Charcas 595, 6; "Confesión de Julián Apasa o Túpac Catari," Santuario de Nuestra Señora de Peñas, November 11 and 13, 1781, AGI, Buenos Aires 320, 14; "Carta de Borda a Segurola," 6; "Oficio de Gregorio Francisco de Campos, Obisbo de La Paz al Consejo Real de Indias," 1; "Carta de Gerónimo de Ruedas a Juan José Vertíz," La Plata, June 15, 1781, AGI, Charcas 596, 1; "Diario que formo yo, Esteban Losa," 10. For a culturally based examination of Túpac Catari, see Thomson, *We Alone Will Rule*, pp. 188–211.

120. Valle del Siles, "Túpac Katari y la rebelión de 1781," 652.

121. "Bando de Túpac Catari," El Alto, April 7, 1781, AGI, Charcas 595, 1; "Carta de Túpac Catari," La Paz, April 7, 1781, in "Relación de los hechos más notables," 263.

122. "Carta de Túpac Catari a Gregorio Francisco de Campos," El Alto, April 3, 1781, in "Relación de los hechos más notables," 263.

123. "Diario que formo yo, Esteban Losa," 10.

124. Szeminski, personal correspondence, March 4, 2001.

125. "Confesión de Julián Apasa o Túpac Catari," 27.

126. "Diario que formo yo, Esteban Losa," 10; "Relación verdadera," 98; Valle del Siles,

"Túpac Katari y la rebelión de 1781," 636, 643; Valle del Siles, *Historia de la rebelión de Túpac Katari*, 39; Campbell, "Ideology," 126; Szeminski, "Why Kill the Spaniard?" 186; Fisher, *Last Inca Revolt*, 167; Ossio, *Ideología mesiánica del mundo andino*, xxvi.

127. "Diario de Sebastián de Segurola," 6; "Diario que formo yo, Esteban Losa," 10.

128. "Copias de documentos citados en el diario," #18, 25; see also "Carta de Borda a Segurola," 4.

129. "Copias de documentos citados en el diario," #18, 24.

130. "Carta de Oruro sobre el auxilio despachado para el socorro de la ciudad de La Paz comandando el ejército Don Josef Reseguín," Oruro, November 5, 1781, in Válcarcel, *Colección Documental de la Independencia del Perú*, book 2, 3:158; Diez de Medina, *Diario*, 66; "Carta de Borda a Segurola," 78; "Copias de documentos citados en el diario," #18, 24; "Carta de Ramón de Moya y Villareal a Juan Jos Vertíz," Arequipa, May 25, 1781, AGI, Charcas 596, 7.

131. "Diario de Sebastián de Segurola," 15; "Carta de Borda a Segurola," 4; "Confesión de Francisco Mamani," Santuario de Nuestra Señora de las Peñas, October 18, 1781, AGI, Charcas 595, 21.

132. "Levantimiento de la provincia de Chayanta o Charcas," 237; "Anexo al diario," 1.

133. "Informe de oidores Pedro Antonio Zernudas y Lorenzo Blanco Ciceron," March 14, 1781, 1; "Representación de Juan de Dios Pinapi," 18; "Carta de Ignacio Florez a Juan José Vertíz," May 13, 1781, 5; "Auto de Tomás Catari," Macha, October 21, 1780, AGI, Charcas 596, 80; "Relación de los hechos más notables," 159.

134. "Representación del indio Tomás Catari," Macha, November 12, 1780, AGI, Charcas 595, 1, 2.

135. "Confesión de Dámaso Catari," 310.

136. "Certificación de actos cometidos por Antonio Oblitas," Cuzco, 1781, in Durand Florez, *Colección documental del bicentenario de la revolución emancipadora de Túpac Amaru*, 3:555; "Testimonio de los autos formados por el alsamiento del indio José Gabriel Tupa Amaro Cacique del pueblo de Tungasuca provincia de Tinta," n.p., January 30, 1781, ANB, SGI.1781.242, 3; "Edicto de Diego Túpac Amaru," Azángaro, August 20, 1781, in Odriozola, *Documentos históricos*, 1:209; O'Phelan Godoy, *Rebellions and Revolts*, 209; Fisher, *Last Inca Revolt*, 45–46, 95–96, 98, 101; Szeminski, "Why Kill the Spaniard?" 167–68.

137. "Confesión de Gregoria Apasa," Santuario de Nuestra Señora de Peñas, October 18, 1781, AGI, Charcas 595, 1.

138. "Declaración de Alvento Arze," 67.

139. "Confesión de Cárlos Pacaja," La Plata, April 18, 1781, AGI, Charcas 603, 18–19.

140. "Confesión de Nicolás Catari," La Plata, April 10, 1781, in Odriozola, *Documentos históricos*, 1:327; "Relación de los hechos más notables," 165–67.

141. "Declaración de Antonio Solís, Tenente de Milicias," in "Expediente seguido criminalmente contra los Yndios de la Provincia de Chayanta, nombrado Antonio, Miguel, Yldefonzo, Bartolomé Cayari y Bartolomé Ramierez," Sacaca, November 14, 1781, ANB, Ruck.1781.107, 2; "Declaración de Juan Josef Teran," in "Expediente

seguido criminalmente contra los Yndios de la Provincia de Chayanta, nombrado Antonio, Miguel, Yldefonzo, Bartolomé Cayari y Bartolomé Ramierez," Sacaca, November 14, 1781, ANB, Ruck.1781.107, 3; "Confesión de Miguel Ildefonzo," in "Expediente seguido criminalmente contra los Yndios de la Provincia de Chayanta, nombrado Antonio, Miguel, Yldefonzo, Bartolomé Cayari y Bartolomé Ramierez," Sacaca, November 14, 1781, ANB, Ruck.1781.107, 9; "Confesión de Bartolomé Ramírez," in "Expediente seguido criminalmente contra los Yndios de la Provincia de Chayanta, nombrado Antonio, Miguel, Yldefonzo, Bartolomé Cayari y Bartolomé Ramierez," Sacaca, November 14, 1781, ANB, Ruck.1781.107, 9.

142. "Actuaciones anteriores," 7; "Relación de los hechos más notables," 163; see also "Expediente seguido contra el indio Tomás Calli por sublevado en el año 1781," Chayanta, August 9, 1781, ANB, SGI.1781.11, 11.

143. "Declaración de Fernando Flores," in "Causa criminal contra Ramón Paca," 7; "Auto de Dámaso Catari," in "Causa criminal contra Ramón Paca," 10.

144. "Representación de Juan de Dios Pinapi," 18; "Informe de Tomás Catari," Macha, October 7, 1780, AGI, Charcas 596, 19; "Carta del rebelde D. Pedro de la Cruz Condori a los principales, asi Españoles como naturales y mestizos criollos de la doctrina de Santiago de Cotagaita," Chocalla, March 19, 1781, in Odriozola, *Documentos históricos,* 1:41.

145. "Testimonio de Pedro Cala," in "Testimonio del expediente seguido contra el Presbitero José Vasquez de Velásquez por complice en la sublevación en la provincia de Chichas," La Plata, November 12, 1781, ANB, SGI.1781.12, 7.

146. "Confesión de Augustín Vicanio," in "Sumaria información recibida de varios indios de Chocaya como sindicados en la sublevación," Chichas, November 23, 1781, ANB, SGI.1781.10, 4; "Confesión de Bernarda Benite," in "Sumaria información recibida de varios indios de Chocaya como sindicados en la sublevación," Chichas, November 23, 1781, ANB, SGI.1781.10, 3.

147. "Confesión de Lope Fernández," in "Sumaria información recibida de varios indios de Chocaya como sindicados en la sublevación," Chichas, November 23, 1781, ANB, SGI.1781.10, 5; "Declaración de Ubaldo Dávila," in "Sumaria información recibida de varios indios de Chocaya como sindicados en la sublevación," Chichas, November 23, 1781, ANB, SGI.1781.10, 8.

148. "Expediente sobre los alboratos de los indios de Yocalla," Porco, April 27, 1781, ANB, SGI.1781.42, 2; see also "Cartas de esta R.A. a Dn. Nicolás Michel sobre las ocurrencias de la sublevación pasada," Oruro, November 2, 1781, ANB, SGI.1781.238, 9–10.

149. "Confesión de Andrés Mamani," La Plata, April 21, 1781, AGI, Charcas 603, 30; "Confesión de Clemente Vasquez," La Plata, April 21, 1781, AGI, Charcas 603, 36.

150. "Carta de Thomas Quispe a Jorge Escobedo," Sicasica, April 24, 1781, AGI, Charcas 437-b, 45.

151. "Auto de Túpac Catari," Sicasica, May 13, 1781, in "Relación de los hechos más notables," 227.

152. "Confesión de Nicolás Ramírez," Oruro, 1781, in "Expedientes de las confesiones tomadas por Dn Jacinto Rodríguez de Herrera a distintas indios reos cómplices en los tumultos," AGI, Charcas 601, 1.

153. "Copias de documentos citados en el diario," #18, 25.

154. "Declaración de Bernardo Franco," 12.

155. "Edicto de Túpac Amaru a los moradores de Cuzco," Tungasuca, November 20, 1781, in Romulo Cuneo-Vidal, *Precursores y mártires de la independencia del Perú* (Lima: Editorial Ignacio Prado Pastor, 1978), 64-65; "Bando de Túpac Amaru. Ayaviri," December 6, 1780, in Válcarcel, *Colección Documental de la Independencia del Perú,* book 2, 1:328; "Edicto [de Túpac Amaru] a los criollos de la ciudad de Arequipa," Tungasuca, November 20, 1781, in Durand Florez, *Colección documental del bicentenario de la revolución emancipadora de Túpac Amaru,* 1:490; "Edicto de Túpac Amaru a los moradores de la Provincia de Chumbivilcas," Tungasuca, November 15, 1780, ibid., 1:418; "Edicto [de Túpac Amaru] a los moradores de la Provincia de Paruro," Tungasuca, November 16, 1780, ibid., 1:489; "Edicto de Túpac Amaru a los moradores de Lampa," Tungasuca, November 25, 1780, ibid., 1:303; "Disposición de Túpac Amaru contra los indios que no le sigan," Velille, January 10, 1781, in Válcarcel, *Colección Documental de la Independencia del Perú,* book 2, 3:95.

156. "Bando de Andrés Tupacamaro," Lugar de Quincosera, July 13, 1781, AGI, Charcas 595, 1.

157. "Edicto de Diego Túpac Amaru," 210.

158. "Confesión de Espíritu Alonso," La Plata, April 25, 1781, AGI, Charcas 603, 36.

159. "Autos y causa criminal seguida contra los indios Matías Arreola, Diego Tonacio, Nicolás Capa, Manuel Lerque y Pedro Choque por la muerte que ejecutaron con tumulto en la persona de Dn. Phelipe Tardio y otros azogueros de Guanachaca," Guanachaca, Potosí, June 19, 1781, ANB, SGI.1781.4a, 5.

160. "Carta de Túpac Catari a José de Ayarza," n.p., n.d., in "Relación de los hechos más notables," 230; "Copias de documentos citados en el diario," #10, 19, 21; "Confesión de Gregoria Apasa," 1; "Confesión de Augustina Zerna," Santuario de Nuestra Señora de las Peñas, October 18, 1781, AGI, Charcas 595, 5; "Confesión de Josefa Anaya," Santuario de Nuestra Señora de las Peñas, October 18, 1781, AGI, Charcas 595, 5-6; "Confesión de Diego Quispe," Santuario de Nuestra Señora de las Peñas, October 18, 1781, AGI, Charcas 595, 8; "Confesión de Diego Estaca," Santuario de Nuestra Señora de las Peñas, October 18, 1781, AGI, Charcas 595, 20-21; "Confesión de Alvento Arze," La Plata, October 3, 1780, AGI, Charcas 596, 63; "Testimonio de Sebastián Morochi," in "Causa criminal contra Juan Luís y Pascual Condori, como cómplices principales en la rebelión de los Cataris," Poroma, November 8, 1781, ANB, SGI.1781.13, 3; "Expediente seguido contra various indios del pueblo de Poroma y por complice en la sublevación," La Plata, April 7, 1781, ANB, Ruck.1781.101, 2; "Declaración de Don Martín Condori," in "El Corregor: Dela Villa de Cochabamba sobre los destrozos que executaron los indios en Tapacari," Oropesa, March 7, 1781, ANB, SGI.1781.62, 1; "Confesión de Diego Calsina," Santuario de Nuestra Señora de las Peñas, October 18, 1781, AGI, Charcas 595, 16; "Confesión de Nicolás Ramírez," 1; "Confesión de Juan Solís," Oruro, 1781, in "Expedientes de las confesiones tomadas por Dn Jacinto Rodríguez de Herrera a distintas indios reos cómplices en los tumultos," AGI, Charcas 601, 2; "Confesión de Manuel Mamani," Oruro, 1781, in "Expedientes de las confesiones tomadas por Dn Jacinto

Rodríguez de Herrera a distintas indios reos cómplices en los tumultos," AGI, Charcas 601, 3.

161. Augustín Jáuregui y Aldecoa, *Relación y documentos de Gobierno del Virrey del Perú, Augustín de Jaregui y Aldecoa (1780–1784)*, ed. Remedio Contreras (Madrid: Instituto "Gonzalo Fernández de Oviedo," 1982), 195.

162. "Perdón concedida a los indios del partido de Calamarca y Sicasica," Calamarca, August 5, 1781, ANB, SGI.1781, 3.

163. "Confesión de Simón Castillo," La Plata, April 25, 1781, AGI, Charcas 603, 32; "Expediente seguido contra el indio cacique José Roque por complice en la sublevación y muerte del cura de Aymaya Dr. Dionisio Córtes," Chayanta, October 9, 1781, ANB, SGI.1781.19, 2.

164. "Edicto [de Túpac Amaru] para la Provincia de Chichas," Lampa, December 23, 1780, in Válcarcel, *Colección Documental de la Independencia del Perú*, book 2, 1:43.

165. "Auto de Túpac Catari," El Alto, April 4, 1781, AGI, Charcas 602, 1; "Orden del 'Virrey' Túpac Catari del 1 de Mayo de 1781, en que manda sea obedecido en todo Francisco Nuno," n.p., May 1, 1781, in Lewin, *La rebelión de Túpac Amaru*, 865; "Cedula del 'Birrey' Túpac Catari, en que nombra por su segundo parta San Francisco de Coroma y su jurisdicción a Miguel Mamani Gualla," El Alto, March 20, 1781, in Boleslao Lewin, *La rebelión de Túpac Amaru*, 876.

166. "Anexo al diario," 1.

167. Klein, *Bolivia*, 45.

168. "Oficio de Merlos a Vertíz," Macha, November 14, 1780, in Lewin, *La rebelión de Túpac Amaru*, 735.

169. "Informe de oidores Pedro Antonio Zernudas y Lorenzo Blanco Ciceron," 1; "Representación de Juan de Dios Pinapi," 18; "Informe del Fiscal Juan Pino del Manrique," La Plata, March 12, 1781, AGI, Charcas 596, 18.

170. "Relación traxica," 2, 3.

171. "Declaración de Bernardo Franco," 13; "Actuaciones anteriores," 99.

172. "Testimonio de Domingo Angeles," La Plata, October 9, 1780, AGI, Charcas 596, 1; "Auto de la Real Audiencia de Charcas," La Plata, February 15, 1781, AGI, Charcas 437-b, 30.

173. "Relación de los hechos más notables," 170; "El Regente Presidente de Charcas informa del buen efecto que han producido las providencias tomadas por la R A y Presidencia para la restablación del sociego," La Plata, May 15, 1781, AGI, Charcas 444, 1; "El Regente Presidente de la RA de Charcas informa del cuidadoso estado de rebelión," 1; "Carta de Ignacio Florez a Juan José Vertíz," May 13, 1781, 1; "Relación verdadera," 98; "Testimonio de Santos Mamani," 72; Valle del Siles, *Historia de la rebelión de Túpac Katari*, 40; Fisher, *Last Inca Revolt*, 218, 318.

174. "El Regente Presidente de Charcas informa del buen efecto que han producido las providencias tomadas por la R A y Presidencia para la restablación del sociego y debida obedencia en las provincias sublevadas," La Plata, May 15, 1781, AGI, Charcas 594, 1.

175. "Declaración de Ysidro Josef de Herrera," San Pedro de Buenavista, October 5, 1780, AGI, Charcas 596, 10.

176. "Actuaciones anteriores," 90.

177. "Expediente de las capitulaciones celebrados para el perdón que solicitaron los indios de diferentes Provincias. Remitido por Dn. Mariano Vargas y Rodríguez," La Plata, April 5, 1781, AGI, Charcas 601, 1.

178. "Relación de los sucesos de la provincia de Cochabamba," 12.

179. "Diario fabuloso," 289; "Relación verdadera," 77; "Actuaciones anteriores," 176; "Causas de Oruro," 141; "Informe del Consejo," 106; "Causa de Augustín Solís," 21; "Relación de los sucesos de Cochabamba," 12; Campbell, "Ideology," 126; Campbell, "Banditry," 154–55; Szeminski, "Why Kill the Spaniard?" 170, 185–86.

180. "Diario que formo yo, Esteban Losa," 2, 5, 11; "Confesión de Diego Calsina," 16; "Confesión de Marcos Poma," Santuario de Nuestra Señora de Peñas, October 18, 1781, AGI, Charcas 595, 16; "Confesión de Francisco Mamani," 21; "Noticias de la expedición del cargo del Tente. Coronl. dn. Ignacio Flores desde del día 24 de Junio hasta el 24 de Julio subministrados por tres desertores del valle de Sacaba Provincia de Cochabamba que marcharon con la misma expedición y salieron de La Paz el citado 24 de Julio," Sacaba, August 1, 1781, AGI, Charcas, Estado 76, number 46, 1–2; see also "Oficio de Sebastián de Segurola a Josef de Galvez," Achacacha, January 3, 1782, AGI, Charcas 595, 1.

181. Scarlett O'Phelan Godoy, "El Mito de la 'Independencia Concedida': Los programas políticos del siglo XVIII y del temprano XIX en el Perú y Alto Perú (1730–1814)," in Inge Buisson et al., eds., *Problemas de la formación del estado y de la nación en Hispano-America* (Cologne: Bohlau, 1984), 56.

182. "Informe de Merlos," 11; "Informe de Tomás Catari," 19; "Carta de Merlos a Francisco Ramón de Herbovo y Figueróa," 3; "Carta de Merlos a Mariano de la Vega," 4.

183. "Representación del indio Tomás Catari," 1; "Carta de Ignacio Florez a Juan José Vertíz," May 13, 1781, 5; "Orden de Tomás Catari," Macha, October 21, 1780, AGI, Charcas 596, 80; "Relación de los hechos más notables," 159.

184. Campbell, "Banditry," 152–53, 156; Szeminksi, *La utopía Tupamarista*, 246, 277; Flores Galindo, "La nación como utopía," 278; "Bando de coronación de Túpac Amaru," n.p., n.d., in Odriozola, *Documentos históricos*, 206; Szeminski, "Why Kill the Spaniard?" 176, 178; Válcarcel, *La rebelión de Túpac Amaru*, 141, 144, 152; Lewin, *Túpac Amaru, su época*, 31; Flores Galindo, "Túpac Amaru y la sublevación de 1780," 282; "Representación del indio Tomás Catari," 1; "Carta de Ignacio Florez a Juan José Vertíz," May 13, 1781, 5; "Orden de Tomás Catari," 80; "Relación de los hechos más notables," 159.

185. Flores Galindo, "La nación como utopía," 59, 62. For more on ideological divisions, see Galindo and Manuel Burga, "La utopía andina," *Allpanchis* 20 (Cuzco, 1982): 85–102.

186. "Carta de Dn. Juan Bautista de Zavala que relaciona por mayor las calamidades de La Paz en el segundo sitio," La Paz, November 3, 1781, in Cárlos Daniel Válcarcel, ed., *Colección Documental de la independencia del Perú*, book 2, 3:147–48; "Carta de Oruro," 158; Diez de Medina, *Diario*, 66; "Diario de Sebastián de Segurola," 11,

29; "Carta de Borda a Segurola," 3, 4; "Confesión de Francisco Mamani," 21; "Relación de los hechos más notables," 249; "Diario que formo yo, Esteban Losa," 10–11.

187. O'Phelan Godoy, *Rebellions and Revolts*, 162–67; Lewin, *Túpac Amaru, el rebelde*, 54–57, 62–67.

188. "Carta de Joaquín Salgado a Josef de Galvez," 1.

189. "Diario del cerco de La Paz en 1781, por Sebastián de Segurola," La Paz, May 30, 1781, ANB, SGI.1781.s.n., 4, 6, 7, 14.

190. Ibid., 2; "Carta de Ignacio Florez a Juan José Vertíz," Oruro, June 6, 1781, AGI, Charcas 596, 1; "Carta de José Reseguín a Sebastián de Segurola," El Alto, November 24, 1781, AGI, Charcas 596, 1; "Los vecinos de La Paz sobre las fuerzas que vinieron en ausilio," La Paz, July 31, 1781, ANB, SGI.1781.237, 1.

191. "Sobre la fuga y ostilidades que hicieron los de la Prova de Tucuman que hiban al socorro de la ciudad de La Paz y retrocederían de Oruro," Oruro, August 3, 1781, AGI, Charcas 601, 1–2.

192. "Diario que formo yo, Esteban Losa," 12.

193. "Expediente seguido por las mugeres de los caciques de Tapacari contra Dn. Pedro Gari y su hermano Dn. Salvador Conde," Tapacari, July 13, 1781, ANB, SGI.1781.34; "Expediente seguido por Juan Taquichiri y Santos Aoca que jandose contra los soldados y demás personas de Misque deque les han quitado sus ganados," La Plata, September 16, 1781, ANB, Ruck.1781.106, 1–2; see also "Expediente sobre el recojo de los bienes de los indios reveldes de la Provincia de Chayanta," Micani, November 11, 1793, ANB, SGI.1793.111, 2, 29.

194. "Sobre los alboratos y sublevación de indios en Cochabamba," Quillacollo, May 26, 1781, ANB, SGI.1781.210, 7.

195. "Actuaciones anteriores," 5; "Relación de los sucesos de la provincia de Cochabamba," 3, 4.

196. "Relación verdadera," 62.

197. Ibid., 63–64, 66; "Relación histórica," 18–19; "Informe del Consejo," 102; "De los sucesos más principales acaecidos en la villa de Oruro entre europeos y criollos" (1781), in Beltrán Avila, *Capítulos,* 294; "Relación de los horribles estragos," 342; "Representación de Félix Josef de Villalobos a Gerónimo Manuel de Ruedas," La Plata, March 7, 1781, AGI, Charcas 594, 19; "Carta de Luís de Palacio y Santelices a Gerónimo de Ruedas," 24; "Declaración de Luís de Palacio y Santelices," 22; "Causa de Augustín Solís," 21.

198. "El Regente Presidente de la Rl. Audiencia de Charcas informa del cuidadoso estado de rebelión de indios," 1; Fisher, *Last Inca Revolt*, 103, 117, 119, 120–24, 125, 127, 131–32; Zuaire Huarte, "Análisis de la rebelión de Túpac Amaru en su bicentenario (1780–1980)," 59.

199. "Relación de los sucesos de la provincia de Cochabamba," 25, 83.

200. "Oficio de Francisco Javier Beltrán," Potosí, March 14, 1781, AGI, Charcas 437-b, 1.

201. "Relación de los sucesos de la Provincia de Cochabamba," 16.

202. "Carta de Jorge Escobedo a Gerónimo Manuel de Ruedas," Potosí, March 11, 1781,

AGI, Charcas 596, 22; "Noticias de lo acaecido en la provincia de Chichas desde el 6 de Marzo hasta el 3 de Abril de 1781," Remedios, n.d., AGI, Charcas 437-b, 2.

203. "El Regente Presidente de Charcas informa del buen efecto que han producido las providencias tomadas," Charcas 444, 1; "Decreto de la Real Audiencia de La Plata," March 13, 1781, AGI, Charcas 596, 23; "Carta de Juan José Vertíz a Josef de Galvez," Montevideo, September 30, 1782, AGI, Buenos Aires, 44, 1; "El Regente Presidente de la Rl. Audiencia de Charcas informa del cuidadoso estado de rebelión de indios," 1.

204. Alberto Crespo, "Las armas de los rebeldes," in *Actas del coloquio internacional "Túpac Amaru y su tiempo"* (Lima: Comisión Nacional del bicentenario de la rebelión emancipadora de Túpac Amaru, 1982), 142–43.

205. "Testimonio de Pedro Gonzalez Santalla," in "Expediente seguido sobre el lamentable estado del pueblo de Sorata por haberse citiada por los indios," Oruro, August 19, 1781, ANB, SGI.1781.244, 2; "Testimonio de Da. Narcisa Santalla," in "Segundo cuaderno de la sumaria confesión y otras actuaciones de la causa criminal seguida contra Antonio Molina," La Paz, November 4, 1782, ANB, SGI.1782.62, 8; "Relación verdadera," 96–98; "Relación histórica," 32; "Informe del Consejo," 108; "Don José Manuel de Santander sobre que le declare de pobre de solemnidad," Oruro, 1782, ANB, EC.1782.103, 3; "Declaración de Pedro Rubén Celis," in "Don José Manuel de Santander sobre que le declare de pobre de solemnidad," 1782, Oruro, ANB, EC. 1782.103, 4; "Testimonio de Ventura Balencia," 29; "Actuaciones anteriores," 21, 83, 84–85, 89, 90–91, 95, 123; "Testimonio de Santos Mamani," 73; "Declaración de Francisco Xavier Condori," 24; "Testimonio de Martín Lopes," 26; "Declaración de Juan de Dios Andrade," Oruro, March 10, 1781, AGI, Charcas 601, 20; Beltrán Avila, *Capítulos*, 189; Cajías de la Vega, "Los objectivos," 416; Albó, "Etnicidad y clase en la gran rebelión Aymara/Quechua," 72; "Dn. Pedro Anto Zernudas oidor de la Rl Audiencia dela Plata informa a V.M. haber echo la prisión de Dr. Gregorio de Merlo cura dela Doctrina de Macha," 1; "Relación de los hechos más notables," 167–70; "Diario que formo yo, Esteban Losa," 12; "Diario de Sebastián de Segurola," 6, 17; Fisher, *Last Inca Revolt*, 119, 120–21, 123–24, 125, 127; Valle del Siles, "Túpac Katari y la rebelión de 1781," 653; Valle del Siles, *Historia de la rebelión de Túpac Katari*, 39; O'Phelan Godoy, *Rebellions and Revolts*, 243; O'Phelan Godoy, "Elementos étnicos," 81, 87; Crespo, 151–52.

206. *Guerra de Castas en Yucatán*, 150.

207. Reed, *Caste War*, 55, 64.

208. Baqueiro Preve, *Ensayo histórico*, 4:181; Ancona, *Historia de Yucatán*, 4:34.

209. *Guerra de Castas en Yucatán*, 44; see also Lapointe, *Los mayas rebeldes de Yucatán*, 71.

210. Rugeley, *Maya Wars*, 11.

211. Baqueiro Preve, *Ensayo histórico*, 4:118–19; Ancona, *Historia de Yucatán*, 4:316; Bartolomé and Barabas, *La resistencia Maya*, 30; Reed, *Caste War*, 136–37.

212. *Guerra de Castas en Yucatán*, 34.

213. Ancona, *Historia de Yucatán*, 4:315; Rugeley, "Los mayas yucatecos del siglo XIX," 215.

214. *Guerra de Castas en Yucatán*, 41; "John Carmichael's Visit to Chan Santa Cruz," in Rugeley, *Maya Wars*, 84; Rugeley, *Yucatán's Maya Peasantry*, 167.

215. Dumond, *Machete*, 306.

216. Baqueiro Preve, *Ensayo histórico*, 2:140.

217. *Guerra de Castas en Yucatán*, 32-34; Rugeley, *Yucatán's Maya Peasantry*, 154.

218. Ancona, *Historia de Yucatán*, 4:34, 74.

219. Ibid., 4, 113, 114.

220. Baqueiro Preve, *Ensayo histórico*, 2:181.

221. "De Jacinto Pat a Felipe Rosado," Peto, April 6, 1848, in Quintal Martín, *Correspondencia de la Guerra de Castas*, 37.

222. Baqueiro Preve, *Ensayo histórico*, 3:81.

223. Ibid., 237; *Guerra de castas de Yucatán*, 83.

224. Ancona, *Historia de Yucatán*, 4:262-64.

225. Baqueiro Preve, *Ensayo histórico*, 3:100; Ancona, *Historia de Yucatán*, 4:260-61, 296; *Guerra de Castas en Yucatán*, 79; Reed, *Caste War*, 109; Dumond, *Machete*, 149-50.

226. Reed, *Caste War*, 140-41, 189.

227. *Guerra de Castas en Yucatán*, 127-28; "Lieutenant Governor to Governor, Jamaica," February 10, 1864, R. 81, in Burdon, *Archives*, 3:255; Dumond, *Machete*, 254-56; Reed, *Caste War*, 190; Reed, "Juan de la Cruz," 520-521; Dumond, *Machete*, 254-57.

228. Dumond, *Machete*, 260.

229. "De Juan de la Cruz a . . . ," #1 and #2, Balamná, October 15, 1850, in Fidelio Quintal Martín, *Correspondencia de la Guerra de Castas*, 86, 88, 90-91.

230. "Sermon of the Talking Cross," 1887, 1903, in Villa Rojas, *The Maya of East Central Quintana Roo*, 161, 163.

231. "Apuntes escritos," 377.

232. Reed, *Caste War*, 205.

233. "Sermon of the Talking Cross," 1903, in Villa Rojas, *The Maya of East Central Quintana Roo*, 164.

234. "The Captivity Narrative of José María Rosado," in Richard Buhler, ed., *A Refugee of the War of the Castes Makes Belize His Home: The Memoirs of J. M. Rosado* (Belize: Belize Institute for Social Research and Action, 1970), reprinted in Rugeley, *Maya Wars*, 71-75.

235. *Guerra de Castas en Yucatán*, 127-28; "Lieutenant Governor to Governor, Jamaica," February 10, 1864, R. 81, in Burdon, *Archives*, 3:255; Dumond, *Machete*, 254-56; Reed, *Caste War*, 190.

236. "The Captivity Narrative of José María Rosado," 77.

237. "Segunda," Peto, January 31, 1848, in "Dos cartas del Coronel Rosado, dirigidas, la primera a don José Domingo Soss y la segunda a D. Santiago Méndez hablandole de varias conferencias que el teniente Coronel Baqueiro había tenido con los indios, así como de otros sucesos de importancia," in Baqueiro Preve, *Ensayo histórico*, 2:282.

238. Reed, "Juan de la Cruz," 507.

239. Dumond, *Machete*, 418.

240. Reed, "Juan de la Cruz," 507.

241. Rugeley, "Los mayas yucatecas," 216.

242. Dumond, *Machete*, 330; Reed, *Caste War*, 221–22.

243. Reed, "Juan de la Cruz," 512, 514; Rugeley, *Maya Wars*, 90; Dumond, *Machete*, 259.

244. Ancona, *Historia de Yucatán*, 4:136–37, 202.

245. Cline, "War of the Castes and Its Consequences," 18.

246. Cline, "War of the Castes and the Independent Indian States of Yucatan," University of Chicago Library, microfilm collection of manuscripts on Middle American Cultural Anthropology, no. 32, 1941, 3; see also "Carta particular del Coronel Rosado, dirigida a Don Santiago Méndez, durante los primeros días del sitio de Peto, comunicándole varios asuntos interesantes," Peto, January 29, 1848, in Baqueiro Preve, *Ensayo histórico*, 2:275.

247. Ancona, *Historia de Yucatán*, 4:63, 131; *Guerra de Castas en Yucatán*, 45.

248. "Segunda," Peto, January 31, 1848, 2:284.

249. Baqueiro Preve, *Ensayo histórico*, 2:134.

250. Ibid., 101; see also 159, also "Carta particular del Coronel Rosado," 2:275; *Guerra de Castas en Yucatán*, 96; "Primera," Peto, January 30, 1848, in "Dos cartas del Coronel Rosado, dirigidas, la primera a don José Domingo Soss y la Segunda a D. Santiago Méndez hablandole de varias conferencias que el teniente Coronel Baqueiro había tenido con los indios, así como de otros sucesos de importancia," in Baqueiro Preve, *Ensayo histórico*, 2:279.

251. *Guerra de Castas en Yucatán*, 102.

252. Baqueiro Preve, *Ensayo histórico*, 5:117–18.

253. Ancona, *Historia de Yucatán*, 4:207.

254. "Parte de la tropa se une a los mayas," Mérida, March 25, 1851, in Leticia Reina, *Las rebeliones campesinas en Mexico*, 405.

255. Baqueiro Preve, *Ensayo histórico*, 4:157–58, 167.

256. *Guerra de Castas en Yucatán*, 108.

257. "Segunda," Peto, January 31, 1848, 2:284.

258. "Carta de Tiburcio R. Esteves al gobernador de Yucatán," Punta Consejo, March 3, 1858, in *Guerra de Castas en Yucatán*, 167.

259. *Guerra de Castas en Yucatán*, 121.

260. Baqueiro Preve, *Ensayo histórico*, 2:95–97; Ancona, *Historia de Yucatán*, 4:79–80.

261. Ancona, *Historia de Yucatán*, 4:131.

262. Baqueiro Preve, *Ensayo histórico*, 2:198.

263. *Guerra de Castas en Yucatán*, 148–49.

264. "A Second Anonymous Report on Rebel Military Capacity," from Tulane University, Yucatecan Collection, 26, box 2, folder 14, in Rugeley, *Maya Wars*, 96. See also Ancona, *Historia de Yucatán*, 4:146.

265. "An Anonymous Report on Rebel Military Capacity," in Rugeley, *Maya Wars,* 91; see also Ancona, *Historia de Yucatán,* 4:82; *Guerra de castas de Yucatán,* 38; Reed, *Caste War,* 73.

266. Ancona, *Historia de Yucatán,* 4:146.

267. Ibid., 88.

268. Baqueiro Preve, *Ensayo histórico,* 2:189, 3:148; Ancona, *Historia de Yucatán,* 4:124, 231.

269. Reed, *Caste War,* 73.

270. Baqueiro Preve, *Ensayo histórico,* 3:12; *Guerra de castas de Yucatán,* 39.

271. *Guerra de castas de Yucatán,* 37.

272. Ancona, *Historia de Yucatán,* 4:352–53.

273. *Guerra de Castas en Yucatán,* 146.

274. Reed, *Caste War,* 162, 219; Reed, "Juan de la Cruz, Venencio Puc, and the Speaking Cross," 507.

275. *Guerra de Castas en Yucatán,* 148.

7. Atrocity as Metaphor

1. Claude Lévi-Strauss, *Structural Anthropology,* trans. Monique Layton (New York: Basic Books, 1976), 2:9, 11.

2. Simmons, "History of Pueblo-Indian Relations to 1821," 184.

3. Knault, *Pueblo Revolt,* 163.

4. Bancroft, *Arizona and New Mexico,* 182.

5. "Auto of Antonio de Otermín," n.p., n.d., in Twitchell, *Spanish Archives,* 2:14; Hackett, "Revolt of the Pueblo Indians," 124.

6. "To the Governor and Captain General," La Salineta, October 3, 1680, in Twitchell, *Spanish Archives,* 2:43; Hackett, "Revolt of the Pueblo Indians," 130–31; "Auto of Antonio de Otermín," Paraje del Río del Norte, October 9, 1680, in Hackett, *Revolt,* 8:194.

7. Hackett, "Revolt of the Pueblo Indians," 123.

8. "To the Governor and Captain General," 2:44; "Auto of Antonio de Otermín," n.p., n.d., in Twitchell, *Spanish Archives,* 2:18; Hackett, "Revolt of the Pueblo Indians," 130–31; "Opinion of the Cabildo," La Salineta, October 3, 1680, in Hackett, *Revolt,* 8:177.

9. "Continuation of Otermín's March, August 26, 1680," in Hackett, *Revolt,* 8:26.

10. "March of the Army from El Paso to La Isleta," November 5–December 8, 1681, in Hackett, *Revolt,* 9:203–204.

11. Ibid., 205.

12. Ibid., 206.

13. Ibid., 207.

14. "Continuation of the March," December 13–18, 1681, in Hackett, *Revolt,* 9:230–31.

15. Diego de Vargas, campaign journal, New Mexico, October 16–December 27, 1692, in Kessell et al., *By Force of Arms,* 521.

16. Kessell et al., *By Force of Arms,* 620.

17. Diego de Vargas, campaign journal, New Mexico, October 16–December 27, 1692, 549; "Tercer cuaderno," 357.

18. "El provedio de D. Diego de Vargas sobre la petición espresada del Padre Custorio y demas religiosos misioneros dice," 355.

19. "The Cabildo of Santa Fe to the Conde de Galve," Santa Fe, January 1694, in Kessell et al., *To the Royal Crown Restored,* 561.

20. "Letter from the Governor and Captain-General, Don Antonio de Otermín, from New Mexico," September 8, 1680, in Hackett, *Historical Documents,* 4:329–30; "Auto of Antonio de Otermín," n.p., n.d., in Twitchell, *Spanish Archives,* 2:17; Siguenza y Gongora, "Mercurio Volante," in *Documentos,* 100–111; Hackett, "Revolt of the Pueblo Indians," 119.

21. "Letter of Fray Francisco de Vargas to the Provincial," Santa Fe, July 21, 1696, in Espinosa, *Pueblo Indian Revolt,* 254; see also "Sesto cuaderno," 398.

22. "Fray Francisco de Vargas, Petition," Santa Fe, March 22, 1696, in Kessell et al., *Blood,* 2:687; "Petition of Fray Francisco de Vargas and the Definitorio to Governor Vargas," Santa Fe, March 22, 1696, in Espinosa, *Pueblo Indian Revolt,* 206.

23. Diego de Vargas, campaign journal, June 4–5, 1696, in Kessell et al., *Blood,* 2:729, 732, 734.

24. "Letter of Fray Francisco de Vargas to the Commissary General," Santa Fe, July 21, 1696, in Espinosa, *Pueblo Indian Revolt,* 244.

25. "Letter of Fray Francisco de Vargas to the Provincial," 252.

26. "Letter of Fray Francisco de Vargas to the Commissary General," 245.

27. "Letter of Fray Francisco de Vargas to the Provincial," 250.

28. Diego de Vargas, campaign journal, July 20–25, 1696, in Kessell et al., *Blood,* 2:836.

29. Siguenza y Gongora, "Mercurio Volante," *Documentos,* 95; Diego de Vargas, campaign journal, New Mexico, August 9–October 15, 1692, in Kessell et al., *By Force of Arms,* 407.

30. "Extracto de la carta con fecha de 16 de Octubre de 1692, da cuenta Vargas a S.E.," Santa Fe, in *Documentos,* 334.

31. "Confesión de Gregoria Apasa," Santuario de Nuestra Señora de Peñas, October 18, 1781, AGI, Charcas 595, 3; "Confesión de Ascencia Flores," Santuario de Nuestra Señora de Peñas, October 18, 1781, AGI, Charcas 595, 23.

32. "Levantimiento de la Provincia de Chayanta o Charcas," 239–41.

33. "Carta que refiere a los estragos hechos por los Yndios alzados en Suches mineral de la Provincia de Larecaja del Obispado de La Paz; y en los pueblos de Arque, Tapacari, y Colcha en la Provincia de Cochabamba, perteneciente al Arzobispado de la Plata," Cochabamba, February 26, 1781, in Carlos Daniel Válcarcel, ed., *Colección Documental de la independencia del Perú,* book 2, 1:508–509; "Carta de

Arequipa con fecha 2 de Mayo de 1781 que refiere los estragos executados por los indios alzados en varios pueblos de las provincias de ambos virreyenatos," Arequipa, May 2, 1781, ibid., 1:694.

34. Szeminski, personal correspondence, March 4, 2001.

35. "Oficio de capellán de Challapata, Juan Antonio Beltrán," Challapata, January 18, 1781, AGI, Charcas 595, 3; "Carta de Capellán Theodoro Gutiérrez de Seballos a Ramón Urrutía y las Casas," Poopó, January 18, 1781, AGI, Charcas 437-b, 10.

36. "Carta de Ramón de Moya y Villareal a Juan José Vertíz," Arequipa, May 25, 1781, AGI, Charcas 596, 4; "Oficio de capellán de Challapata, Juan Antonio Beltrán," 3; "Carta de Capellán Theodoro Gutiérrez de Seballos a Ramón Urrutía y las Casas," 10.

37. "Relación de la papeleta remitida a la ciudad de Arequipa por dn. Joaquin de Orellana corregidor de la villa de Puno," 627.

38. "Testimonio de Josef Manuel de Santander," in "Causa contra los cabezas de la rebelión de Oruro," La Plata, n.d., AGI, Charcas 599, 209–10.

39. "Relación histórica," 292.

40. "Carta de Joseph Antonio de Areche, Visitador de Tribunales y Superintendente de la Real Hacienda en Perú al Superior Consejo de Indios," Cuzco, May 23, 1781, AGI, Charcas 595, 2; "Diario fabuloso," 289; "Relación verdadera," 77; "Actuaciones anteriores," 176; "Causas de Oruro. Testimonio de la acusación del Señor Fiscal de S.M. contra los reos de la sublevación de la villa de Oruro y otras acusaciones," Buenos Aires, 1784, in Mier, *Noticia y proceso de la muy noble y muy leal Villa de San Felipe de Austria de Oruro*, 2:141; "Informe del Consejo," 106; "Causa de Augustín Solís," La Plata, March 11, 1781, AGI, Charcas 594, 21; Szeminski, "Why Kill the Spaniard?" 170; Hidalgo Lehunde, "Amarus y Cataris," 125.

41. "Testimonio de Ventura Balencia," Oruro, April 10, 1781, AGI, Charcas 601, 24; "Carta de Capellán Theodoro Gutiérrez de Seballos a Ramón de Urrutía y las Casas," Poopó, January 18, 1781, AGI, Charcas 437-b, 5; "Actuaciones anteriores," 11, 42–43, 45, 48, 62; "Testimonio de Santos Mamani," Oruro, May 25, 1781, AGI, Charcas 601, 37; "Declaración de Francisco Xavier Condori," Oruro, April 10, 1781, AGI, Charcas 601, 12; "Testimonio de Martín Lopes," Oruro, April 7, 1781, AGI, Charcas 601, 13; "Declaración de Luís de Palacio y Santelices," La Plata, March 12, 1781, AGI, Charcas 594, 11; "Causa de Augustín Solís," 11; "Fragment of Informe," n.p., n.d., AGI, Charcas 594, 3; "Dn. Pedro Antonio Cernudas y Dn. Lorenzo Blanco Ciceron oydores en la Rl. Audiencia de Charcas continuan el informe de los sucesos de las provincias cuios naturales incurrieron en el delito de rebelión," La Plata, May 15, 1781, AGI, Charcas 594, 1; "Dn Pedro Antonio Zernudas oidor de la Rl Audiencia dela Plata informa," 3; "Carta de Capitán General y Gobernador Andrés Mestre a Josef de Galvez," Salta, June 24, 1781, AGI, Charcas 595, 1.

42. Szeminski, *La utopía tupamarista*, 198.

43. "Bando de coronación de Túpac Amaru," n.p., n.d., in Odriozola, *Documentos históricos*, 206; "Actuaciones anteriores," 13, 45; "Carta de Capellán Augustín Flores Urito a Jorge Escobedo," 49; "Declaración de Roque Argote," Potosí, March 7, 1781, AGI, Charcas 596, 18–20; "Relación histórica," 24–27; "Diario fabuloso," 289–90; "Relación de los hechos más notables acaecidos en la sublevación general fra-

guada en los reynos del Perú, por el indio José Gabriel Túpac Amaru, gobr. del pueblo de Tungasuca en la Provincia de Tinta, que asociado de otros sequaces, causó horrosos estragos desde el año 1780, hasta el de 1782 en que se reprimo el orgullo de la conjuración," in *Revista de archivos y bibliotecas nacionales* 3, no. 5 (Lima, September 30, 1900): 170–71; "Confesión de Josef Daga," La Plata, April 25, 1781, in "Criminales contra Nicolás Catari y otros indios," AGI, Charcas 603, 23; "Carta que refiere a los estragos," 508, 694; "Relación de los sucesos de la Provincia de Cochabamba," written by the cabildo of Cochabamba, Cochabamba, December 17, 1781, AGI, Charcas 595, 9, 14, 17–18; Szeminski, *La utopía Tupamarista,* 246, 277; Szeminski, "Why Kill the Spaniard?" 176, 178; Campbell, "Banditry," 152–53.

44. "El corregidor de la villa de Cochabamba sobre los destrozos que executaron los indios en Tapacari," 2.

45. "Actuaciones anteriores," 14; "Declaración de Roque Argote," 18–20.

46. "Diario fabuloso," 289; "Actuaciones anteriores," 351, 354; "Relación traxica," 5; "Carta que refiere a los estragos," 509, 694; "Relación de los hechos más notables," 170–71, 206; "Representación de Domingo Angeles," 23; "Carta de Arequipa," 693–94; "Relación de los sucesos de Cochabamba," 14; "Carta de Oruro sobre el auxilio despachado para el socorro de la ciudad de La Paz comandando el ejército Don Josef Reseguín," Oruro, November 5, 1781, in Válcarcel, *Colección Documental de la Independencia del Perú,* book 2, 3:158; Diez de Medina, *Diario,* 66; "Carta de Fray Matías de Borda a Sebastián de Segurola," 155; "Carta de Ramón de Moya y Villareal a Juan José Vertíz," 13.

47. "Relación de los sucesos de Cochabamba," 24–25.

48. "Relación verdadera," 78; "Diario fabuloso," 288; "De los sucesos más principales acaecidos en la villa de Oruro entre europeos y criollos" (1781), in Beltrán Avila, *Capítulos,* 299; "Relación traxica," 3; "Relación de los sucesos de la Provincia de Cochabamba," 14.

49. "Carta de Félix Villalobos a Gerónimo Manuel de Ruedas," Cochabamba, February 24, 1781, AGI, Charcas 596, 14.

50. "Actuaciones anteriores," 168; "Relación traxica," 4.

51. "El Regente de la Rl. Audiencia de Charcas informa del cuidadoso estado de rebelión de los indios," 1; "Relación de los hechos más notables," 171–72; "El corregidor de la villa de Cochabamba sobre los destrozos," 10.

52. "Carta que refiere a los estragos," 509; Abecia Baldivieso, "La insurección india de Tapacari en 1781," 41.

53. "Representaciones hechas a la real Audiencia en la Plata por el Corregidor de la Provincia de Chayanta," La Plata, August 25, 1780, AGI, Charcas 594, 12; "Carta de Arequipa," 693.

54. "Diario trunco," 1; "Anexo al diario," 1.

55. "Carta de Felíx Villalobos a Gerónimo Manuel de Ruedas," 13–14; "Actuaciones anteriores," 10, 173, 198, 288; "Relación de los hechos más notables," 206; "Representación de Felíx Josef Villalobos a Gerónimo Manuel de Ruedas," 14; "Relación

de los sucesos de la Provincia de Cochabamba," 7; "Declaración de Fray Josef Serbantes," Oruro, April 9, 1781, in "Testimonio del expedientes y diligencias practicadas para averiguar los tumultos meditada contra Oruro," AGI, Charcas 601, 36;
"Anexo al diario," 1; "Declaración de Alvento Arze," Oropesa, Cochabamba, October 2, 1780, AGI, Charcas 596, 135; "Sumaria información recibida de varios indios
de Chocaya como sindicados en la sublevación," Chichas, November 23, 1781,
ANB, SGI.1781.10, 45, 47.

56. "Relación traxica," 4; "Relación histórica," 29; "Carta del Cabildo de Cochabamba al Rey," Cochabamba, January 31, 1782, AGI, Charcas 595, 2.

57. "Relación de los sucesos de la Provincia de Cochabamba," 6; "Declaración de
Da. María Crespo," in El Corregor. dela Villa de Cochabamba sobre los destrozos
que executaron los indios en Tapacari," Oropesa, March 7, 1781, ANB, SGI.1781.62,
5; "Declaración de Dn. Salvador Conde," in "El Corregor. dela Villa de Cochabamba sobre los destrozos que executaron los indios en Tapacari," Oropesa, March
7, 1781, ANB, SGI.1781.62, 10; "Testimonio de Da. Narcisa Santalla," in "Segundo
cuaderno de la sumaria confesión y otras actuaciones de la causa criminal seguida
contra Antonio Molina," La Paz, November 4, 1782, ANB, SGI.1782.62, 9; "Testimonio de Pedro Gonzalez Santalla," in "Expediente seguido sobre el lamentable
estado del pueblo de Sorata por haberse citiada por los indios," Oruro, August 19,
1781, ANB, SGI.1781.244, 2–3.

58. "Carta de Arequipa," 694; "Copias de documentos citados en el diario," #18, 21;
"Carta de Borda a Segurola," 1; "Confesión de Diego Estaca," Santuario de Nuestra Señora de las Peñas, October 18, 1781, AGI, Charcas 595, 20–21; O'Phelan Godoy, *Rebellions and Revolts,* 252–54.

59. "Relación de los hechos más notables," 163; "Declaración de Alvento Arze," 134.

60. "Relación de los horribles," 343; "Diario fabuloso," 289; "Relación histórica," 25;
"Relación traxica," 4; "Relación de los hechos más notables," 162.

61. "El corregidor de la villa de Cochabamba sobre los destrozos que executaron los
indios en Tapacari," 5, 8; "Relación verdadera," 78; "Diario fabuloso," 288; "De los
sucesos más principales," 299; "Relación traxica," 3.

62. "Oficio de Capellán de Challapata," 3; "Carta de Capellán Theodoro Gutiérrez de
Seballos a Ramón Urrutia y las Casas," 10; "Testimonio formado sobre la subleva-
ción de los Indios del Pueblo de Challapata y muerte que dieron a su corregidor
Dn. Manuel de la Bodega y Llano," La Plata, January 26, 1781, AGI, Charcas 596, 3.

63. "Actuaciones anteriores," 24.

64. "Confesión de Espíritu Alonso," La Plata, April 25, 1781, AGI, Charcas 603, 24;
"Confesión de Bartolomé Vello," 67.

65. "Carta de Borda a Segurola," 4–7; "Diario de Sebastián de Segurola," 21; Valle del
Siles, *Historia de la rebelión de Túpac Katari,* 449; "Confesión de Sebastiana
Mamani," La Plata, April 18, 1781, AGI, Charcas 603, 48; "Confesión de Francisco
Gonzalo," La Plata, April 20, 1781, AGI, Charcas 603, 50; "Declaración de Fernando
Arancivia," in "Diversas declaraciones hechas por varios sujetos sobre las dis-
posiciones y sacriligios de los rebeldes de varias provincias ante dr. Esteban de
Loza," El Alto, April 17, 1782, ANB, SGI, 1782.97, 18.

66. "Informe de Pedro Yavira Ylario Caguasiri," San Pedro de Buenavista, December 28, 1780, AGI, Charcas 596, 101; "Confesión de Simón Castillo," La Plata, April 25, 1781, AGI, Charcas 603, 64.

67. "Oficio del oficial real de Carangas a la Audiencia de Charcas, en el que avisa haber muerto los indios a su corregidor D. Mateo Ibañez Arco," Carangas, February 17, 1781, in Odriozola, *Documentos históricos,* 1:340; "Sumaria información recibida de varios indios de Chocaya," 44.

68. "Diario que formo yo Esteban Losa," 2, 4; "Relación de los sucesos de la Provincia de Cochabamba," 11.

69. "Sumaria información recibida de varios indios de Chocaya," 28, 32.

70. "Carta de Cabildo de Cochabamba al Rey," 2.

71. "Carta de Arequipa," 692.

72. "Relación de los sucesos de Cochabamba," 8; "Actuaciones anteriores," 12; "Declaración de Roque Argote," 19–20; "Confesión de Lázaro Mamani," La Plata, April 18, 1781, AGI, Charcas 603, 47; "Carta de Estiban Lidosa a Gerónimo Manuel de Ruedas," La Plata, April 9, 1781, AGI, Charcas 603, 48; "Confesión de Sebastiana Mamani," 50; "Confesión de Francisco Gonzalo," 50; "Confesión de Pasqual Tola," La Plata, April 20, 1781, AGI, Charcas 603, 53; "Confesión de Thomas Molina," La Plata, April 21, 1781, AGI, Charcas 603, 60; "Carta de Arequipa," 693; "Sumaria información recibida de varios indios de Chocaya," 2, 7.

73. Baqueiro Preve, *Ensayo histórico,* 2:109, 188; Ancona, *Historia de Yucatán, desde la época más remota hasta nuestros días,* 5 vols. (Mérida, México: Imprenta de M. Heredia Argüelles, 1878–1905), 4:123; Reed, *Caste War,* 81, 245.

74. Baqueiro Preve, *Ensayo histórico,* 4:260.

75. Ibid., 2:164.

76. Ancona, *Historia de Yucatán,* 4:118; Baqueiro Preve, *Ensayo histórico,* 2:188; ibid., 4:182.

77. Baqueiro Preve, *Ensayo histórico,* 1:168.

78. *Guerra de castas de Yucatán,* 119; Reed, *Caste War,* 175, 200.

79. "Apuntes escritos," 355.

80. Baqueiro Preve, *Ensayo histórico,* 4:314.

81. Reed, *Caste War,* 80.

82. Baqueiro Preve, *Ensayo histórico,* 4:260.

83. Ibid., 2:361.

84. Ibid., 190; Reed, *Caste War,* 92.

85. Baqueiro Preve, *Ensayo histórico,* 3:24.

86. Reed, *Caste War,* 137.

87. "A Second Anonymous Report on Rebel Military Capacity," in Rugeley, *Maya Wars,* 96.

88. Baqueiro Preve, *Ensayo histórico,* 3:18–19.

8. Cultural Assimilation in the Native World

1. Lanternari, *The Religions of the Oppressed,* 247; Adas, *Prophets of Rebellion,* 9; Linton, "Nativistic Movements," 231.

2. "Auto of Antonio de Otermín," Santa Fe, August 13, 1680, in Hackett, *Revolt,* 8:13; Hackett, "Revolt of the Pueblo Indians," 139.

3. "Este cuaderno se cree ser obra de un religioso de la provincia del Santo Evangélico," n.p., n.d., in *Documentos,* 324; Bancroft, *Arizona and New Mexico,* 182, 217.

4. "Carta del Padre Fray Silvestre Velez de Escalante," Santa Fe, April 2, 1778, in *Documentos,* 312.

5. "Declaration of Lieutenant General of Cavalry," Río del Norte, December 20, 1681, in Hackett, *Revolt,* 9:259–60; "Letter of Juan Domínguez de Mendoza to Antonio de Otermín," Alameda, December 9, 1681, ibid., 9:220.

6. "Letter of Juan Domínguez de Mendoza to Antonio de Otermín," Alameda, December 9, 1681, in Hackett, *Revolt,* 9:220; Hackett, ibid., 8:cxlv–cxlvi.

7. "March of the Army from El Paso to La Isleta," November 5–December 8, 1681, in Hackett, *Revolt,* 9:204.

8. Szeminski, personal correspondence, March 4, 2001; Szeminski, "Why Kill the Spaniard?" 179; Rowe, "El movimiento nacional Inca del siglo XVIII," 22; Curatola, "Mito y milenarianismo en los andes," 71. See also Frank Saloman, "Ancestor Cults and Resistance to the State in Arequipa, ca. 1748–1754," in Stern, *Resistance.*

9. "Relación de los hechos más notables acaecidos en la sublevación general fraguada en los reynos del Perú, por el indio José Gabriel Túpac Amaru, gobr. del pueblo de Tungasuca en la Provincia de Tinta, que asociado de otros sequaces, causó horrosos estragos desde el año 1780, hasta el de 1782 en que se reprimo el orgullo de la conjuración," in *Revista de archivos y bibliotecas nacionales* 3, no. 5 (Lima, September 30, 1900): 162; "Carta de Gregorio Josef de Merlos a Fray Manuel Parraga," Ocuri, January 26, 1781, AGI, Charcas 597, 4; "Carta de Gregorio Josef de Merlos al Rey," 2; "Declaración de Ignacio Salguero," La Plata, April 4, 1781, AGI, Charcas 603, 14; "Confesión de Nicolás Catari," La Plata, April 10, 1781, in Odriozola, *Documentos históricos,* 1:326; "Representación de Polonia Inojosa a Gerónimo Manuel de Ruedas," San Pedro de Buenavista, September 29, 1780, AGI, Charcas 596, 60, 96; "Declaración de Eugenio Moya," La Plata, October 9, 1780, AGI, Charcas 596, 76; "Oficio de Capellán Sebastián de Ballestros," 53; "Informe de Gregorio Josef de Merlos," Macha, October 7, 1780, AGI, Charcas 596, 11; "Informe de Tomás Catari," Macha, October 7, 1780, AGI, Charcas 596, 19; "Representación de Marcos Ancienega," San Pedro de Buenavista, September 24, 1780, in "Testimonio de los autos de la sublevación de Chayanta," AGI, Charcas 596, 51; "Declaración de Ysidro Josef de Herrera," San Pedro de Buenavista, October 5, 1780, AGI, Charcas 596, 10; "Confesión de Nicolás Gueso," La Plata, April 20, 1781, AGI, Charcas 603, 23.

10. "Relación de los sucesos de la Provincia de Cochabamba," written by the cabildo

of Cochabamba, Cochabamba, December 17, 1781, AGI, Charcas 595, 4; "Declaración de Fray Josef Serbantes," 18.

11.   Silverblatt, "Becoming Indian," 290.

12.   "Confesión de Sebastiana Mamani," La Plata, April 18, 1781, AGI, Charcas 603, 24; "Confesión de Francisco Gonzalo," 25; "Confesión de Cárlos Caunachu," La Plata, April 21, 1781, AGI, Charcas 603, 30; "Confesión de Thomas Molina," La Plata, April 21, 1781, AGI, Charcas 603, 30; "Confesión de Diego Sosa," La Plata, April 20, 1781, AGI, Charcas 603, 29; "Confesión de Andrés Mamani," La Plata, April 21, 1781, AGI, Charcas 603, 30; "El regente de la Rl. Audiencia de Charcas informa del cuidadoso estado de rebelión," 1; "Relación de los hechos más notables," 171–72; "El corregidor de la villa de Cochabamba sobre los destrozos," 5; "Declaración de Blas Condori," in "Causa criminal contra Ramón Paca, Bentura Pinto, Pedro Copa Cava, y de más reos principales, comprehendidos en la sublevación, muertes y robos perpetrados en este pueblo de Yura y sus ynmediasiones," Porco, October 7, 1781, ANB, SGI.1781.61, 3; "Relación de los hechos más notables," 171–72; "Testimonio de Pedro Gonzalez Santalla," in "Expediente seguido sobre el lamentable estado del pueblo de Sorata por haberse citiada por los indios," Oruro, August 19, 1781, ANB, SGI.1781.244, 3; "Confesión de Lázaro Mamani," La Plata, April 18, 1781, AGI, Charcas 603, 24; "Carta de Estiban Lidosa," 24; "Confesión de Sebastiana Mamani," 25; "Confesión de Francisco Gonzalo," 25; "Confesión de Pasqual Tola," La Plata, April 20, 1781, AGI, Charcas 603, 27–28; "Diario trunco," 11; "Diario del cerco de La Paz en 1781, por Sebastián de Segurola," La Paz, May 30, 1781, ANB, SGI.1781.s.n., 13; "Declaración de Bernardo Franco," Potosí, March 24, 1781, AGI, Charcas 437-b, 12; "Carta de Philipe Ayaviri Cuizana a Félix de Villalobos," Cochabamba, September 28, 1780, AGI, Charcas 596, 66; "Relación traxica," 3; "Actuaciones anteriores," 351; Hidalgo Lehunde, "Amarus y Cataris," 127.

13.   "Carta de Borda a Segurola," 2, 4.

14.   "Diario de Sebastián de Segurola," La Paz, July 1, 1781, AGI, Charcas 595, 4; "Confesión de Julián Apasa o Túpac Catari," Santuario de Nuestra Señora de las Peñas, November 11 and 13, 1781, AGI, Buenos Aires 320, 26; "Diario que formo yo, Esteban Losa," 10; "3er cuaderno de los autos seguidos por Antolín Chavarri contra Bartolomé Jorge indio de Tatasi," Chicas, April 3, 1787, ANB, SGI.1787.17, 5–8; Valle del Siles, *Historia de la rebelión de Túpac Katari,* 448; "Carta de Borda a Segurola," 6.

15.   "Diario de Sebastián de Segurola," 11; Adas, *Prophets of Rebellion,* 140; Valle del Siles, *Historia de la rebelión de Túpac Katari,* 449.

16.   "Declaración de Fernando Arancivia," in "Diversas declaraciones hechas por varios sujectos sobre las disposiciones y sacrilgios de los rebeldes de varias provincias ante dr. Esteban de Loza," El Alto, April 17, 1782, ANB, SGI.1782.97, 18.

17.   "Carta de Borda a Segurola," 3; Diez de Medina, *Diario,* 315; "Copias de documentos citados en el diario," #18, 23.

18.   Sabine MacCormack, personal communication, October 7, 1999.

19.   "Copias de documentos citados en el diario," #18, 23; Fisher, *Last Inca Revolt,* 245, 248.

20.   Cline, "War of the Castes and Its Consequences," 26.

21.   Reed, *Caste War*, 220.

22.   Villa Rojas, *The Maya of East Central Quintana Roo*, 21; Reed, "Juan de la Cruz," 503–504.

23.   Villa Rojas, *The Maya of East Central Quintana Roo*, 21.

24.   Ibid., 23.

25.   Reed, "Juan de la Cruz," 504.

26.   Dumond, *Machete*, 184.

27.   *Guerra de castas de Yucatán*, 127; Reed, *Caste War*, 175.

28.   Baqueiro Preve, *Ensayo histórico*, 2:190; Villa Rojas, *The Maya of East Central Quintana Roo*, 24, 25.

29.   Reed, *Caste War*, 199.

30.   Ibid., 214.

31.   "Apuntes escritos," 334; Baqueiro Preve, *Ensayo histórico*, 2:126–28, 137, 142–44, 177, 3:226–30; *Guerra de Castas en Yucatán*, 48, 83–86; Reed, *Caste War*, 81; Ancona, *Historia de Yucatán*, 4:279–82.

32.   "Apuntes escritos," 355.

33.   Baqueiro Preve, *Ensayo histórico*, 2:191; "Apuntes escritos," 354–55, 357, 364–66, 372, 381.

34.   Reed, *Caste War*, 166.

35.   Baqueiro Preve, *Ensayo histórico*, 5:163–64.

36.   Ibid., 2:43.

37.   Ibid., 112, 122; Ancona, *Historia de Yucatán*, 4:95.

38.   *Guerra de castas de Yucatán*, 127.

39.   Ancona, *Historia de Yucatán*, 4:83.

40.   Baqueiro Preve, *Ensayo histórico*, 2:99.

41.   Ibid., 5:164.

42.   Reed, *Caste War*, 179.

43.   "El Constitutional," 171.

44.   Villa Rojas, *The Maya of East Central Quintana Roo*, 25.

45.   Lanternari, *The Religions of the Oppressed*, 247; Adas, *Prophets of Rebellion*, 9; Linton, "Nativistic Movements," 231.

46.   "Comunicación Official del General en Jefe Llergo, transcribiendo al gobierno del Estado un parte del Corenel Cetina, en que manifiesta la abierta protección de los colonos de Belice en favor de los sublevados," Mérida, September 12, 1849, in Baqueiro Preve, *Ensayo histórico*, 3:331–32; "Correspondencia de los cabecillas Florentino Chan y Venancio Pec, en contestación al decreto del E. Sr. Gobernador," n.p., October 9, 1849, in Baqueiro Preve, *Ensayo histórico*, 3:342; "Superintendent to H.B.M. Minister, Mexico," November 10, 1849, R. 32b, in Burdon, *Archives*, 3:126; "Lieutenant Governor to Governor, Jamaica," June 5, 1866, R. 92, ibid., 3:271; "Lieutenant Governor to Governor, Jamaica," August 14, 1866, R. 92, ibid., 3:272; "Lieutenant Governor to General Santiago Pech," February 9, 1880,

R. 120a, ibid., 3:343; "Diligencias mandadas practicar por el Jefe político del partido de Motul, y remitidas al Gobierno Supremo de la Nación por el Estado, en que consta la decidida protección de los inglese en favor de los indios sublevados," Motul, July 17, 1848, in Baqueiro Preve, *Ensayo histórico*, 3:286; Ancona, *Historia de Yucatán*, 4:220, 233; Lapointe, *Los mayas rebeldes de Yucatán*, 86–87; Grant D. Jones, "La estructura política de los mayas de Chan Santa Cruz: el papel del respaldo inglés," *Amérique Indígena* 31, no. 2 (April 1971): 415–27; Rugeley, *Maya Wars*, 82; Monrad S. Metzgen and Henry E. C. Cain, *Handbook of British Honduras Comprising Historical, Statistical and General Information Concerning the Colony* (London: West India Committee, 1925), 35. For more primary source accounts concerning British relations with both the Cruzob and the Pacificos, see the following, all of which are in Burdon, *Archives*, vol. 3: "Acting Superintendent to Officer Commanding Troops, Corozal," March 14, 1861, R. 72, 3:237; "Acting Superintendent to Officer Commanding Troops, Corozal," March 15, 1861, R. 72, 3:237; "Lieutenants Plumridge and Twigge to Superintendent," April 12, 1861, R. 71, 3:238; "Acting Superintendent to Chief of the Santa Cruz Indians," August 7, 1861, R. 72, 3:242; "Magistrate, Northern District, to Superintendent," April 25, 1861, R. 71, 3:239; "Lieutenant Governor to O. C. Troops," February 5, 1867, R. 91, 3:279; "Chief Justice's Report on the Trial and Conviction of Marcellino Montego and Esteban Toon," April 18, 1867, R. 96, 3:287; "Lieutenant Governor to O. C. Troops," April 18, 1870, R. 108, 3:320; "Lieutenant Governor to Speaker," April 19, 1870, R. 99, 3:320; "O. C. Troops (Major MacKay) to Lieutenant Governor," December 24, 1866, R. 95, 3:275–76; "R. Williamson to Lieutenant Governor," December 26, 1866, R. 89, 3:276; "Garrison Orders. Giving Detail of the Troops Proceeding with the British Honduras Field Force into the Interior," January 25, 1867, R. 95, 3:278; "Lieutenant-Colonel Harley to Lieutenant Governor," February 9, 1867, R. 95, 3:280; "Lieutenant-Colonel Harley to Lieutenant Governor," February 13, 1867, R. 95, 3:280–81; "Lieutenant Governor to Governor, Jamaica," February 25, 1867, R. 92, 3:281; "Captain Delemere to Brigadier-General Harley," March 9, 1867, R. 95, 3:283–84; "Superintendent to H.B.M. Minister, Mexico," November 10, 1849, R. 32b, 3:126; "Lieutenant Governor to Governor, Jamaica," June 5, 1866, R. 92, 3:271; "Lieutenant Governor to Governor, Jamaica," August 14, 1866, R. 92, 3:272; "Lieutenant Governor to General Santiago Pech," February 9, 1880, R. 120a, 3:343; "Superintendent to Principal Magistrate, Bacalar," May 9, 1848, R. 22b, 3:107; "Lieutenant Governor to General Santiago Pech," February 9, 1880, R. 120a, 3:343; "Lieutenant Governor's Speech," July 19, 1880, Leg. Co. 1880, 3:344; "Superintendent to Messrs. Vaughn Christie and Co.," October 25, 1849, R. 32b, 3:125; "Governor, Jamaica, to Superintendent," July 20, 1849, R. 30, 3:121; "Letter from Secretary General, Mérida, forwarded to British Minister, Mexico, to Superintendent," September 12, 1849, R. 33, 3:122; "Governor, Jamaica, to Superintendent," February 21, 1850, R. 35, 3:129; "Mr. J. I. Blockley to Lieutenant Governor," July 10, 1868, R. 102, 3:307; "General-in-Chief of State of Campeche to Lieutenant Governor," May 4, 1870, R. 106, 3:322; as well as "Belize and the Indians of Yucatán," *Colonial Guardian*, Belize, December 8, 1888, n.p.

47.   Ancona, *Historia de Yucatán*, 4:229; "Belize and the Indians of Yucatán."

48.   "Superintendent to Governor, Mérida," Belize City, February 1, 1848, R. 22b, in Burdon, *Archives*, 3:100.

49. "Superintendent to Principal Magistrate, Bacalar," May 9, 1848, R. 22b, in Burdon, *Archives*, 3:107.

50. "Lieutenant Governor to General Santiago Pech," February 9, 1880, R. 120a, in Burdon, *Archives*, 3:343; "Lieutenant Governor's Speech," July 19, 1880, Leg. Co. 1880, ibid., 3:344.

51. Rogers, *Honduras Británica*, 16; Jones, "La estructura política," 422.

52. Jones, "La estructura política," 421.

53. "Superintendent to Messrs. Vaughn Christie and Co.," October 25, 1849, R. 32b, in Burdon, *Archives*, 3:125; Lapointe, *Los mayas rebeldes de Yucatán*, 86.

54. "Governor, Jamaica, to Superintendent," August 19, 1848, R. 30, in Burdon, *Archives*, 3:110; "Governor, Jamaica, to Superintendent," July 20, 1849, R. 30, ibid., 3:121; "Letter from Secretary General, Mérida, forwarded to British Minister, Mexico, to Superintendent," September 12, 1849, R. 33, ibid., 3:122; "Governor, Jamaica, to Superintendent," February 21, 1850, R. 35, ibid., 3:129; "Mr. J. I. Blockley to Lieutenant Governor," July 10, 1868, R. 102, ibid., 3:307; "General-in-Chief of State of Campeche to Lieutenant Governor," May 4, 1870, R. 106, ibid., 3:322; Lapointe, *Los mayas rebeldes de Yucatán*, 86.

55. "Superintendent to Sir Charles Grey," October 12, 1849, R. 31, in Burdon, *Archives*, 3:124.

56. "Superintendent to Governor, Jamaica," July 11, 1850, R. 31, in Burdon, *Archives*, 3:136.

57. "Superintendent to Commandant of Militia, Bacalar," Belize City, February 24, 1848, R. 22b, in Burdon, *Archives*, 3:102; "Superintendent to Governor, Jamaica," January 11, 1850, R. 34, ibid., 3:128.

58. "William Salmon, Magistrate, St. Helena, Río Hondo, to Superintendent," December 30, 1850, R. 20, in Burdon, *Archives*, 3:141; "Superintendent to Governor, Jamaica," June 15, 1855, R. 48, ibid., 3:182.

59. "Superintendent to Governor, Jamaica, Describing the Northern District," November 16, 1857, R. 55, in Burdon, *Archives*, 3:198.

60. "Superintendent's Speech," January 21, 1858, Assembly, in Burdon, *Archives*, 3:200.

61. Dumond, *Machete*, 412.

62. "Belize and the Indians of Yucatán"; "Superintendent to Governor, Jamaica," June 15, 1855, R. 48, in Burdon, *Archives*, 3:182.

63. Ancona, *Historia de Yucatán*, 4:233; Jones, "La estructura política," 422.

64. "O. C. Troops to Lieutenant Governor," November 2, 1877, R. 116, in Burdon, *Archives*, 3:338.

65. "Superintendent to Officer Commanding Troops," March 4, 1848, R. 22b, in Burdon, *Archives*, 3:103; "Superintendent to Principal Magistrate, Bacalar," June 24, 1848, R. 22b, ibid., 3:108; "Petition from the Inhabitants of Punta Consejo," January 1, 1849, R. 28, ibid., 3:114; "Superintendent to Governor, Jamaica," July 16, 1857, R. 55, ibid., 3:196; Superintendent to Governor, Jamaica," September 16, 1857, R. 55, ibid., 3:197; "Superintendent to Governor, Jamaica," February 17, 1858, R. 55, ibid., 3:201; "Edmund Burke to the Superintendent," March 5, 1858, R. 61, ibid.,

3:202; "Superintendent to Governor, Jamaica," March 17, 1858, R. 55, ibid., 3:203; "Superintendent to Governor, Jamaica," May 17, 1858, R. 58, ibid., 3:206; "James Hume Black, J. P. Corozal, to Lieutenant-Governor," April 30, May 5, 1863, R. 83, ibid., 251; "Lieutenant Governor to Speaker," February 17, 1868, R. 99, ibid., 3:300; "Lieutenant Governor to Governor, Jamaica," July 30, 1868, R. 98, ibid., 3:309; "Lieutenant Governor to Governor, Jamaica," November 13, 1869, R. 98, ibid., 3:316; "Undated Petition from the Inhabitants of Corozal to the Lieutenant Governor," received November 24, 1869, R. 105, ibid., 3:317; "Lieutenant Governor to Governor, Jamaica," January 29, 1870, R. 98, ibid., 3:317; "Address to Legislative Assembly by Lieutenant Governor," January 1870, R. 101, ibid., 3:317; "Lieutenant Governor's Speech," July 19, 1880, Leg. Co. 1880, ibid., 3:344; "Lieutenant Governor to Commandant, Volunteer Force," July 3, 1882, R. 117, ibid., 3:349.

66. "Superintendent to Governor, Jamaica," September 16, 1857, R. 55, in Burdon, *Archives*, 3:197; "Lieutenant Governor to Governor, Jamaica," July 13, 1863, R. 81, ibid., 3:253; "Governor Eyre, Jamaica, to Governor, Yucatán," June 22, 1864, R. 86, ibid., 3:256; "J. Hodge, Manager, to British Honduras Co, Ltd. London," September 20, 1864, R. 86, ibid., 3:258; "Chief Justice's Report on the Trial and Conviction of Marcellino Montego and Esteban Toon," April 18, 1867, R. 96, ibid., 3:287; "Lieutenant Governor to Governor, Jamaica," January 11, 1868, R. 98, ibid., 3:298; "Address to Legislative Assembly by Lieutenant Governor," January 30, 1868, R. 101, ibid., 3:299.

67. "Edmund Burke to the Superintendent," March 5, 1858, R. 61, in Burdon, *Archives*, 3:202.

68. "Superintendent to Governor, Jamaica," May 17, 1858, R. 58, in Burdon, *Archives*, 3:206; "Superintendent to Governor, Jamaica," July 17, 1858, R. 55, ibid., 3:207–208.

69. "Superintendent to Governor, Jamaica," April 17, 1858, R. 55, in Burdon, *Archives*, 3:205; "Superintendent to Governor, Jamaica," August 15, 1858, R. 55, ibid., 3:208; "Superintendent to Governor, Jamaica," September 17, 1858, R. 55, ibid., 3:209; "Superintendent's Speech," January 27, 1859, Assembly, ibid., 3:211.

70. "Attorney, British Honduras Company, to Lieutenant Governor," May 2, 1866, R. 93, in Burdon, *Archives*, 3:269; "Lieutenant Governor to Governor, Jamaica," August 14, 1866, R. 92, ibid., 3:272; "Lieutenant Governor to O. C. Troops," December 8, 1866, R. 91, ibid., 3:274; Sapper, "Independent Indian States of Yucatán," 627; Rogers, *Honduras Británica*, 10; Metzgen and Cain, *Handbook of British Honduras*, 36.

71. "Lieutenant Governor to Governor, Jamaica," May 4, 1868, R. 98, in Burdon, *Archives*, 3:303; "Memorial from John Carmichael and 9 Other Property Owners of the Northern District to the Governor and Council of British Honduras," c. 1867, R. 93, ibid., 3:310; "Lieutenant Governor to O. C. Troops," September 3, 1872, R. 108, ibid., 3:327; "Major William Johnston, to Lieutenant Governor," September 11, 1872, R. 111, ibid., 327–29; "Rafael Chan, Chief of the Ychaiches, to Lieutenant Governor," September 26, 1872, R. 111, ibid., 3:329.

72. "Lieutenant Governor to Governor, Jamaica," November 28, 1867, R. 98, in Burdon, *Archives*, 3:297; Metzgen and Cain, *Handbook of British Honduras*, 36; Lapointe, *Los mayas rebeldes de Yucatán*, 88.

73. "Commandant of Bacalar to the Superintendent," December 29, 1848, R. 28, in Burdon, *Archives*, 3:113.

74. E. Rogers, "Appendix: Los Indios de Santa Cruz," 30–33; Miller, "A Journey from British Honduras," 23; "The Captivity Narrative of José de los Angeles Loesa," Archives of Belize, Record 74, August 26, 1861, 174–75, in Rugeley, *Maya Wars*, 79; "The Captivity Narrative of José María Rosado," in Richard Buhler, ed., *A Refugee of the War of the Castes Makes Belize His Home: The Memoirs of J. M. Rosado* (Belize: Belize Institute for Social Research and Action, 1970), reprinted in Rugeley, *Maya Wars*, 68; "Acting Superintendent to the Patron Santa Cruz," March 14, 1861, R. 72, in Burdon, *Archives*, 3:237; Reed, *Caste War in Yucatán*, 181–83.

75. "Superintendent to Commandant, Bacalar," October 3, 1849, R. 32b, in Burdon, *Archives*, 3:124; "Superintendent to Commandant, Bacalar," October 23, 1849, R. 32b, ibid., 3:125; "Superintendent to Governor of Yucatán," November 1, 1849, R. 32b, ibid., 3:126; "Messrs. Hyde Co, to Colonial Secretary," January 17, 1850, R. 33, ibid., 3:135; "Superintendent to Governor, Jamaica," May 11, 1850, R. 31, ibid., 3:135.

76. "Superintendent to Commandant, Bacalar," June 27, 1849, R. 32a, in Burdon, *Archives*, 3:120; Jones, "La estructura política," 422, 424.

77. "Jacinto Pat, Commandant in Chief of the Indians, to Messrs. John Kingdom, Edward L. Rhys, et al.," February 18, 1849, R. 28, in Burdon, *Archives*, 3:116; "British Minister, Mexico, to Superintendent," August 10, 1849, R. 33, ibid., 3:122; "Superintendent to Chief of Indians, Yucatán," September 17, 1849, R. 32h, ibid., 3:122; "Indian Chiefs Puc and Chan to Superintendent," October 1849, n.d., R. 33, ibid., 3:125; "Superintendent to the Chiefs of the Indians in Yucatán," October 30, 1849, R. 32b, ibid., 3:125; "British Minister, Mexico, to Superintendent," January 16, 1850, R. 33, ibid., 3:128; "Superintendent to Commandant of Bacalar," June 10, 1853, R. 40, ibid., 3:167.

78. "British Minister, Mexico, to Superintendent," November 15, 1849, R. 33, in Burdon, *Archives*, 3:126; "Superintendent to Governor, Yucatán," December 10, 1849, R. 32b, ibid., 3:127; Baqueiro Preve, *Ensayo histórico*, 3:226–30; Ancona, *Historia de Yucatán*, 4:277–82.

79. *Guerra de castas en Yucatán*, 98, 101.

80. "Captain John Carmichael B.H. Militia to Lieutenant Governor," November 15, 1867, R. 93, in Burdon, *Archives*, 3:296.

81. Rugeley, *Maya Wars*, 87; Lapointe, *Los mayas rebeldes de Yucatán*, 89.

82. "Treaty of Peace between General Theodosius Canto Representing the Government of the State of Yucatán and John Chuc Representing Don José Cresencio Poot General and Governor of Chan Santa Cruz," January 11, 1884, R. 118, in Burdon, *Archives*, 3:352; "José Cresencio Poot to Administrator," January 30, 1884, R. 118, ibid., 3:352; "Administrator to General Canto," February 11, 1884, R. 118, ibid., 3:353.

83. Reed, *Caste War*, 227, 236.

84. Lapointe, *Los mayas rebeldes de Yucatán*, 94.

9. Conclusion

1. Gurr, *Why Men Rebel,* 46–48; Barkun, *Disaster and the Millennium,* 35–36.

2. Reff, "The 'Predicament of Culture,'" 70; Reff, *Disease, Depopulation, and Culture Change in Northwestern New Spain, 1518–1764,* 229; Knault, *Pueblo Revolt,* 68; Simmons, "History of Pueblo-Indian Relations to 1821," 184; Riley, *Kachina and the Cross,* 212.

3. Levy, "An Introduction to Prospect Theory," 171, 175; Jervis, "Political Implications of Loss Aversion," 187.

4. Gurr, *Why Men Rebel,* 24–26, 358–59; Reff, "The 'Predicament of Culture,'" 70–71; Knault, *Pueblo Revolt,* 7.

5. Reff, "The 'Predicament of Culture,'" 70–71; Knault, *Pueblo Revolt,* 7, 73–75; Simmons, "History of Pueblo-Indian Relations to 1821," 184.

6. "Testimony of Juan Lorenzo and Francisco Lorenzo," 66; Hackett, *Revolt,* 8:xxii, clvii; "Declaration of Lieutenant General of Cavalry," Río del Norte, December 20, 1681, ibid., 9:262; "Declaration of Sargento Mayor Luís de Quintana," Río del Norte, December 22, 1681, ibid., 9:289; Diego de Vargas, campaign journal, New Mexico, August 9–October 15, 1692, in Kessell et al., *By Force of Arms,* 391; "Auto of Antonio de Otermín," Alamillo, September 6, 1680, in Twitchell, *Spanish Archives,* 2:20, see also 21; Gurr, *Why Men Rebel,* 24–26, 358–59; Simmons, "History of Pueblo-Indian Relations to 1821," 184; Riley, *Kachina and the Cross,* 212.

7. "Opinion of the Cabildo of the Villa of Santa Fe in New Mexico in Regard to Affairs of the Religious," Santa Fe, February 14, 1639, in Hackett, *Historical Documents,* 4:62, 64; Bancroft, *Arizona and New Mexico,* 165, 177; Knault, *Pueblo Revolt,* 4–6, 103–104; Hackett, "Revolt of the Pueblo Indians," 103; Scholes, "Church and State in New Mexico, 1610–1650," 25, 102, 283, 286; Scholes, "Troublous Times in New Mexico," 53–54.

8. "Testimony of José," Río del Norte, December 19, 1681, in Twitchell, *Spanish Archives,* 2:57; Bancroft, *Arizona and New Mexico,* 184.

9. "Declaration of Diego López Sambrano," Hacienda of Luis de Carbajal, December 22, 1681, in Hackett, *Revolt,* 9:295.

10. "Testimony of Pedro Naranjo," Río del Norte, December 18, 1681, in Twitchell, *Spanish Archives,* 2:64.

11. "Testimony of José," 53, 57; "Auto of Antonio de Otermín," La Isleta, December 9, 1681, in Hackett, *Revolt,* 9:219; "Testimony of Juan Lorenzo and Francisco Lorenzo," 65–66; "Testimony of Juan of Tesuque," 53; "Testimony of Lucas, a Piro Indian," Río del Norte, December 18, 1681, in Twitchell, *Spanish Archives,* 2:60; "Carta del Padre Fray Silvestre Velez de Escalante," Santa Fe, April 2, 1778, in *Documentos,* 311; "Testimony of Pedro Naranjo," 63–64; "Declaration of Sargento Mayor Sebastian de Herrera," Río del Norte, December 21, 1681, in Hackett, *Revolt,* 9:269; "Opinion of Fray Francisco de Ayeta," Hacienda of Luis de Carbajal, December 23, 1681, ibid., 9:361; "Reply of the Fiscal, Don Martín de Solís Miranda," Mexico, June 25, 1682, ibid., 9:382; Bancroft, *Arizona and New Mexico,* 184;

Knault, *Pueblo Revolt,* 174–75; Simmons, "History of Pueblo-Indian Relations to 1821," 184.

12. "Carta del Padre Fray Silvestre Velez de Escalante," *Documentos,* 312, 318; Siguenza y Gongora, "Mercurio Volante," in *Documentos,* 96; "Testimony of Pedro Naranjo," 63; "Testimony of Juan Lorenzo and Francisco Lorenzo," 65; Bancroft, *Arizona and New Mexico,* 184–85; Knault, *Pueblo Revolt,* 175.

13. "The Viceroy of New Spain Makes Report to Your Majesty of the General Uprising of the Indians of the Provinces of New Mexico, and of the Measures and Means Which Have Been Adopted for Their Restoration," Mexico City, February 28, 1681, in Hackett, *Historical Documents,* 4:339; "To the Governor and Captain General," La Salineta, October 3, 1680, in Twitchell, *Spanish Archives,* 2:44; "List and Memorial of the Religious Whom the Indians of New Mexico Have Killed," n.p., n.d., in Hackett, *Revolt,* 8:108; Bancroft, *Arizona and New Mexico,* 179; Knault, *Pueblo Revolt,* 14; Hackett, "Revolt of the Pueblo Indians," 129.

14. "Salida para el Paso del Norte, 23 de Agosto, hasta 5 de Octubre de 1680," Antonio de Otermín, Arroyo de San Marcos, in Twitchell, *Spanish Archives,* 2:13.

15. Hackett, "Revolt of the Pueblo Indians," 125.

16. "Declaration of Diego López de Sambrano," 9:295.

17. Hagopian, *The Phenomenon of Revolution,* 151.

18. Rowe, "El movimiento nacional Inca del siglo XVIII," 23, 26.

19. "Información recibida en la Prov. de Chayanta sobre averiguar quines han sido los principales caudillos de la sublevacn. del dichos pueblos," Moromoro, May 20, 1781, ANB, SGI.1781.160, 2–18; O'Phelan Godoy, *Rebellions and Revolts,* 118, 258, 261, 265–66.

20. Campbell, "Ideology," 113, 115, 116–18, 129; Pease, "El mito de Inkarrí y la visión de los vencidos," 448; Flores Galindo, "In Search of an Inca," 201; Wachtel, *The Vision of the Vanquished,* 183; Gow, "Inkarrí and Revolutionary Leadership in the Southern Andes," 197; López Baralt, *El Retorno del Inca Rey,* 37; Szeminski, "Why Kill the Spaniard?" 173.

21. Calderón, *Monografía histórica del departamento de Oruro,* 29; Lewin, *Túpac Amaru, el rebelde,* 9, 12, 21 48; Lewin, *Túpac Amaru, su época,* 122; Lewin, *Los movimientos,* 121, 123; Válcarcel, *La Rebelión de Túpac Amaru,* 18, 68; Gurr, *Why Men Rebel,* 46, 101; Hagopian, *The Phenomenon of Revolution,* 172. See also Taylor, *Drinking,* 132.

22. Campbell, "Ideology," 113, 115, 116–18, 129; Campbell, "Banditry," 139; Pease, "El mito de Inkarrí y la visión de los vencidos," 448; Flores Galindo, "In Search of an Inca," 201; Wachtel, *The Vision of the Vanquished,* 183; Gow, "Inkarrí and Revolutionary Leadership in the Southern Andes," 197; López Baralt, *El Retorno del Inca Rey,* 37, 40; Szeminski, "Why Kill the Spaniard?" 173–74, 187; Szeminski, *La utopía Tupamarista,* 198; de Angelis, "Discurso preliminar a la revolución de Túpac-Amaru," 269; López Baralt, *El Retorno del Inca Rey,* 37, 40; Valle del Siles, "Túpac Katari y la rebelión de 1781," 654; Hagopian, *The Phenomenon of Revolution,* 32, 90; Cohn, *The Pursuit of the Millennium,* 32; Lanternari, *The Religions of the Oppressed,* 240.

23. "Relación de los sucesos de Cochabamba," 12; Campbell, "Ideology," 126; Campbell, "Banditry," 154–55; Szeminski, "Why Kill the Spaniard?" 185–86.

24. Rugeley, "Los mayas yucatecos del siglo XIX," 210; Rugeley, *Yucatán's Maya Peasantry,* 92–93, 115, 185.

25. Ancona, *Historia de Yucatán,* 4:7; *Guerra de Castas de Yucatán,* 3, 12, 31, 93.

26. Rugeley, *Maya Wars,* 10; "Through Fire and Blood: Cecilio Chi's Letter to John Fancourt," ibid., 54; "The Whites Began It: Jacinto Pat's Letter on the Origins of the Caste War," ibid., 51–52; " 'They Kill the Poor Indians as They Kill Animals': Jacinto Pat's Letter to Modesto Méndez," July 11, 1848, ibid., 55; Terry Rugeley, "Rural Political Violence and the Origins of the Caste War," *The Americas* 53, no. 4 (April 1997): 494–95; Rugeley, "Los Mayas Yucatecos," 205; Dumond, *Machete,* 137.

27. Rugeley, *Yucatán's Maya Peasantry,* 44; *Guerra de Castas en Yucatán,* 9; Ancona, *Historia de Yucatán,* 3:359–60, 364–66, 368–73; Reed, *Caste War,* 27–28; Cline, "The Sugar Episode in Yucatán," 96; Dumond, *Machete,* 138, 407.

28. Reed, *Caste War,* 9–10, 45, 48; Cline, "The Sugar Episode in Yucatán," 100; Jones, "La estructura política," 418; Rugeley, *Yucatán's Maya Peasantry,* xiv; Gurr, *Why Men Rebel,* 103–104; Grimshaw, "Interpreting Collective Violence," 45; Taylor, *Drinking,* 132; Brinton, *The Anatomy of Revolution,* 55, 60, 63–64; Dumond, *Machete,* 407.

29. Bricker, *The Indian Christ, the Indian King,* 71; Bartolomé and Barabas, *La resistencia Maya,* 32.

30. Ancona, *Historia de Yucatán,* 4:78; Baqueiro Preve, *Ensayo histórico,* 1:189, 224, 229, 2:77; "Lieutenant Governor's Message," May 8, 1867, Assembly, in Burdon, *Archives,* 3:288; "Lieutenant Governor to Governor, Jamaica," May 17, 1867, R. 98, ibid., 3:288; Reed, *Caste War,* 34, 204; Villa Rojas, *The Maya of East Central Quintana Roo,* 20.

31. "Testimony of Pedro Naranjo," 62; Espinosa, *Pueblo Indian Revolt,* 34.

32. "Diario que formo yo, Esteban Losa," 10; "Copias de documentos citados en el diario," #18, 26; "Relación de los hechos más notables acaecidos en la sublevación general fraguada en los reynos del Perú, por el indio José Gabriel Túpac Amaru, gobr. del pueblo de Tungasuca en la Provincia de Tinta, que asociado de otros sequaces, causó horrosos estragos desde el año 1780, hasta el de 1782 en que se reprimo el orgullo de la conjuración," in *Revista de archivos y bibliotecas nacionales* 3, no. 5 (Lima, September 30, 1900): 249; "Diario de Sebastián de Segurola," La Paz, July 1, 1781, AGI, Charcas 595, 6; de Angelis, "Discurso preliminar a la revolución de Túpac-Amaru," 269; Szeminski, "Why Kill the Spaniard?" 174; Campbell, "Ideology," 117–18; Campbell, "Banditry," 139; López Baralt, *El Retorno del Inca Rey,* 37, 40; Valle del Siles, "Túpac Katari y la rebelión de 1781," 653–54; Hidalgo Lehunde, "Amarus y Cataris," 123.

33. Chalk and Jonassohn, "The Conceptual Framework," 28; Charny, *How Can We Commit the Unthinkable?* 195; Staub, *The Roots of Evil,* 43.

34. "Carta de Túpac Catari a Gregorio Francisco de Campos," El Alto, April 3, 1781, in "Relación de los hechos más notables acaecidos en la sublevación general fra-

guada en los reynos del Perú, por el indio José Gabriel Túpac Amaru, gobr. del pueblo de Tungasuca en la Provincia de Tinta, que asociado de otros sequaces, causó horrosos estragos desde el año 1780, hasta el de 1782 en que se reprimo el orgullo de la conjuración," *Revista de archivos y bibliotecas nacionales* 3, no. 5 (Lima, September 30, 1900): 263; "Bando de coronación de Túpac Amaru," n.p., n.d., in Odriozola, *Documentos históricos,* 206; "Representación del indio Tomás Catari," Macha, November 12, 1780, AGI, Charcas 595, 1; "Carta de Ignacio Florez a Juan José Vertíz," La Plata, May 13, 1781, AGI, Charcas 596, 5; Orden de Tomás Catari, Macha, October 21, 1780, AGI, Charcas 596, 80; "Relación de los hechos más notables," 159; Szeminski, *La utopía Tupamarista,* 246, 277; Szeminski, "Why Kill the Spaniard?" 176, 178; Válcarcel, *La rebelión de Túpac Amaru,* 141, 144, 152; Campbell, "Banditry," 152–53; Lewin, *Túpac Amaru, su época,* 31; Flores Galindo, "Túpac Amaru y la sublevación de 1780," 282; Flores Galindo, "La nación como utopía," 278.

35. Diego de Vargas, campaign journal, October 16–December 27, 1692, in Kessell et al., *By Force of Arms,* 2:538; Diego de Vargas, campaign journal, June 12, 1696, ibid., 2:755; Diego de Vargas, campaign journal, July 20–25, 1696, ibid., 2:841; "The Governor, Don Luis, Refers to the Words Spoken by Pedro de Tapia, Which Caused Suspicion, and to the State of Mind of the Tewas and Tanos," Santo Domingo, December 4, 1693, in Kessell et al., *To the Royal Crown Restored,* 458; Diego de Vargas, campaign journal, New Mexico, October 16–December 27, 1692, in Kessell et al., *By Force of Arms,* 557–58; "Extracto de la carta en que con fecha de 16 de Octubre de 1692, da cuenta Vargas a S.E.," Santa Fe, in *Documentos,* 333; "Levantimiento de la provincia de Chayanta o Charcas," 237; "Anexo al diario," 1; "Informe de oidores Pedro Antonio Zernudas y Lorenzo Blanco Ciceron," March 14, 1781, 1; "Representación de Juan de Dios Pinapi," La Plata, October 20, 1780, AGI, Charcas 596, 18; "Carta de Ignacio Florez a Juan José Vertíz," May 13, 1781, 5; "Orden de Tomás Catari," 80; "Relación de los hechos más notables," 159; "Certificación de actos cometidos por Antonio Oblitas," Cuzco, 1781, in Durand Florez, *Colección documental del bicentenario de la revolución emancipadora de Túpac Amaru,* 3:555; "Testimonio de los autos formados por el alsamiento del indio José Gabriel Tupa Amaro Cacique del pueblo de Tungasuca provincia de Tinta," n.p., January 30, 1781, ANB, SGI.1781.242, 3; "Edicto de Diego Túpac Amaru," Azángaro, August 20, 1781, in Odriozola, *Documentos históricos,* 1:209; "Declaración de Alvento Arze," Oropesa, Cochabamba, October 2, 1780, AGI, Charcas 596, 67; "Confesión de Cárlos Pacaja," La Plata, April 18, 1781, AGI, Charcas 603, 18–19; "Confesión de Nicolás Catari," La Plata, April 10, 1781, in Odriozola, *Documentos históricos,* 1:327; "Relación de los hechos más notables," 165–67; "Confesión de Gregoria Apasa," Santuario de Nuestra Señora de las Peñas, October 18, 1781, AGI, Charcas 595, 1; O'Phelan Godoy, *Rebellions and Revolts,* 209; Fisher, *Last Inca Revolt,* 45–46, 95–96, 98, 101; Szeminski, "Why Kill the Spaniard?" 167–68.

36. Ancona, *Historia de Yucatán,* 4:113–14, 263–64; "Informe de la muerte de Jacinto Pat," Mérida, August 1, 1850, in Leticia Reina, *Las rebeliones campesinas en México,* 400; Baquero Preve, *Ensayo histórico,* 3:196–98; *Guerra de Castas en Yucatán,* 79; "Magistrate, Northern District, to Superintendent," October 13, 1849, R. 33, in Burdon, *Archives,* 3:124; Reed, *Caste War,* 55, 122; Dumond, *Machete,* 156–57.

37.   "The Captivity Narrative of José María Rosado," 77; "Apuntes escritos," 377; "Sermon of the Talking Cross," 1887, 163; *Guerra de Castas en Yucatán*, 127–28; "Lieutenant Governor to Governor, Jamaica," February 10, 1864, R. 81, in Burdon, *Archives*, 3:255; Dumond, *Machete*, 254–56; Reed, *Caste War*, 190.

38.   "Opinion of the Cabildo of the Villa of Santa Fe in New Mexico in Regard to Affairs of the Religious," Santa Fe, February 14, 1639, in Hackett, *Historical Documents*, 4:62, 64; "Reply of the Señor Fiscal," Mexico City, January 3, 1681, in Hackett, *Revolt*, 8:222; "Letter of Ayeta to the Viceroy in Which He Advises Him that the Governor Is Alive," ibid., 8:125; "Declaration of Pedro Leiva," San Lorenzo, June 15, 1681, ibid., 9:30–31; "Autos and Judicial Proceedings Concerning Certain Persons Excusing Themselves from the Royal Service," El Paso, September 29–October 18, 1681, ibid., 9:147–52; "Opinion of Fray Francisco de Ayeta," Hacienda of Luis de Carbajal, December 23, 1681, ibid., 9:312–14; Bancroft, *Arizona and New Mexico*, 165, 177; Knault, *Pueblo Revolt*, 4–6, 103–104; Hackett, "Revolt of the Pueblo Indians," 103; Scholes, "Church and State in New Mexico, 1610–1650," 25, 102, 283, 286; Scholes, "Troublous Times in New Mexico," 53–54.

39.   Stern, "Age," 39, 75; O'Phelan Godoy, *Rebellions and Revolts*, 25, 99–103, 109, 119, 207, 260; Fisher, *Last Inca Revolt*, 12; see also "Representación ante el Fiscal de la Audiencia de Charcas por don José Chirari y Herrera, cacique del Pueblo de Moromoro, provincia Chayanta, por sí y en nombre de su comunidad, sobre las extorciones y agravios que les infieren los receptores de alcabalas en las internaciones de los frutos de sus labranzas," La Plata, October 25, 1771, ANB, ECad.1771.77, 1; "El común de indios del pueblo de Andamarca, provincia Carangas, ante el Fiscal Protector General, contra su cacique, Juan de la Cruz Centeno, por agravios, extorsiones y otros excesos," La Plata, July 17, 1771, ANB, ECad.1771.47, 1, 2.

40.   Ancona, *Historia de Yucatán*, 4:7, 63, 131, 207; *Guerra de Castas de Yucatán*, 3, 12, 31, 45, 93, 96, 108; Baqueiro Preve, *Ensayo histórico*, 2:101, 159, 4:157–58; "Primera," Peto, January 30, 1848, ibid., 2:279; "Segunda," Peto, January 31, 1848, ibid., 2:284; "Carta particular del Coronel Rosado, dirigida a Don Santiago Méndez, durante los primeros días del sitio de Peto, comunicándole varios asuntos interesantes," Peto, January 29, 1848, ibid., 2:275; "Carta de Tiburcio R. Esteves al gobernador de Yucatán," San Miguel, February 22, 1858, ibid., 166; "Parte de la tropa se une a los mayas," Mérida, March 25, 1851, in Leticia Reina, *Las rebeliones campesinas en México*, 405.

41.   "Relación de los sucesos de la Provincia de Cochabamba," 6; "Declaración de Da. María Crespo," in "El Corregor. dela Villa de Cochabamba sobre los destrozos que executaron los indios en Tapacari," Oropesa, March 7, 1781, ANB, SGI.1781.62, 5; "Declaración de Dn. Salvador Conde," ibid., 10; "Relación verdadera," 78; "Diario fabuloso," 288; "De los sucesos más principales acaecidos en la villa de Oruro entre europeos y crillos" (1781), in Beltrán Avila, *Capítulos*, 299; Baqueiro Preve, *Ensayo histórico*, 2:109, 188; Ancona, *Historia de Yucatán*, 4:123; Reed, *Caste War*, 81, 245.

42.   Bancroft, *Arizona and New Mexico*, 182.

43.   "Actuaciones anteriores," 14; "Declaración de Roque Argote," 18–20; "Relación de los hechos más notables," 163; "Declaración de Alvento Arze," 134.

44.   Baqueiro Preve, *Ensayo histórico*, 2:190; Reed, *Caste War*, 92.

45. Baqueiro Preve, *Ensayo histórico*, 2:109, 188; Ancona, *Historia de Yucatán*, 4:123; Reed, *Caste War*, 81, 245.

46. "Este cuaderno se cree ser obra de un religioso de la provincia del Santo Evangélico," n.p., n.d., in *Documentos*, 324; "El provedio de D. Diego de Vargas •sobre la petición espresada del Padre Custorio y demás religiosos misioneros dice," 355; Bancroft, *Arizona and New Mexico*, 182, 217.

47. "Diario trunco," 1; "Anexo al diario," 1; "Carta de Félix Villalobos a Gerónimo Manuel de Ruedas," 13–14; "Actuaciones anteriores," 10, 173, 198, 288; "Relación de los hechos más notables," 206; "Relación de los sucesos de la Provincia de Cocha- bamba," 6–7; "Declaración de Fray Josef Serbantes," Oruro, April 9, 1781, in "Tes- timonio del expedientes y diligencias practicadas para averiguar los tumultos meditadas contra Oruro," AGI, Charcas 601, 36; "Declaración de Alvento Arze," 135; "Sumaria información recibida de varios indios de Chocaya como a sindi- cados en la sublevacion," 45, 47; "Relación traxica," 4; "Relación histórica," 29; "Carta del Cabildo de Cochabamba al Rey," Cochabamba, January 31, 1782, AGI, Charcas 595, 2; "Declaración de Da. María Crespo," 5; "Declaración de Dn. Salvador Conde," 10.

48. Ancona, *Historia de Yucatán*, 4:78; Baqueiro Preve, *Ensayo histórico*, 1:189, 224, 229, 2:77; "Lieutenant Governor's Message," May 8, 1867, Assembly, in Burdon, *Ar- chives*, 3:288; "Lieutenant Governor to Governor, Jamaica," May 17, 1867, R. 98, ibid., 3:288; Reed, *Caste War*, 34, 204; Villa Rojas, *The Maya of East Central Quin- tana Roo*, 20.

49. "Answer Presented by the Lieutenant-General, Alonzo García, in His Own Be- half," Isleta, August 14, 1680, in Twitchell, *Spanish Archives*, 24; Hackett, "Revolt of the Pueblo Indians," 123.

50. "Carta de Ramón de Moya y Villareal a Juan José Vertíz," Arequipa, May 25, 1781, AGI, Charcas 596, 4; "Oficio de capellán de Challapata, Juan Antonio Beltrán," Challapata, January 18, 1781, AGI, Charcas 595, 3; "Carta de Capellán Theodoro Gutiérrez de Seballos a Ramón Urrutía y las Casas," 10; "Testimonio de Josef Manuel de Santander," in "Causa contra los cabezas de la rebelión de Oruro," La Plata, n.d., AGI, Charcas 599, 418–19.

51. Baqueiro Preve, *Ensayo histórico*, 4:225, 5:163–64; "Diligencias mandadas practicar por el Jefe político del partido de Motul, y remitidas al Gobierno Supremo de la Nación por el Estado, en que consta la decidida protección de los inglese en favor de los indios sublevados," Motul, July 17, 1848, ibid., 3:287; *Guerra de Castas en Yucatán*, 116, 118, 170; "El Constitucional. Periódico official del estado de Yucatán, no. 457," ibid., 170; "The Captivity Narrative of José María Echeverría," Izamal, November 8, 1856, in Rugeley, *Maya Wars*, 63; "Los indios de Santa Cruz," 29; Dumond, *Machete*, 248; Reed, *Caste War*, 180; Reed, "Juan de la Cruz," 520.

52. "Carta del Padre Fray Silvestre Velez de Escalante," *Documentos*, 312.

53. Valle del Siles, *Historia de la rebelión de Túpac Katari*, 449.

54. Chalk and Jonassohn, "The Conceptual Framework," 23, 28; Charny, *How Can We Commit the Unthinkable?* 195; Staub, *The Roots of Evil*, 43; Linton, "Nativistic Movements," 230–31.

55. Dadrian, "A Typology of Genocide," 201; Horowitz, *Taking Lives*, 17.

Bibliography

Archival Sources

Archivo-Biblioteca Arquidiocesano "Monseñor Taborga," Sucre, Bolivia
  Acusaciones
ANB: Archivo Nacional de Bolivia, Sucre
  Libros de Acuerdos
  Colección Ruck
  Expedientes Coloniales
  Expedientes Coloniales Adiciones
  Sublevación General de Indias
AGI: Archivo General de Indias, Seville, Spain
  Buenos Aires 44, 320
  Charcas 437-b, 444, 528, 594, 595, 596, 597, 599, 601, 602, 603; Estado, 76.
  Cuzco, 29

Published Primary Sources

Ancona, Eligio. *Historia de Yucatán, desde la época más remota hasta nuestros días.* 5 vols. Mérida, México: Imprenta de M. Heredia Argüelles, 1878–1905.

Baqueiro Preve, Serapio. *Ensayo histórico sobre las revoluciones de Yucatán desde el año 1840 hasta 1864.* Vols. 1–5. Ed. Salvador Rodríguez Losa. Mérida: Ediciones de la Universidad Autónoma de Yucatán, 1990.

"Belize and the Indians of Yucatán." *Colonial Guardian*, Belize, December 8, 1888.

Berendt, Carl H. "Report of Explorations in Central America." In *Smithsonian Institution Annual Report for 1867*, 420–26. Washington, D.C.: Smithsonian Institution, 1867.

Burdon, John, ed. *Archives of British Honduras*. Vol. 3. London: Sifton Praed, 1935.

Diez de Medina, Francisco Tadeo. *Diario del alzamiento del indios conjurados contra la ciudad de Nuestra Señora de La Paz.* Transcribed with an introduction by María Eugenia del Valle de Siles. La Paz: Banco Boliviano Americano, 1981.

Documentos para servir a la historia del Nuevo México, 1538–1778. Madrid: Ediciones José Porrua Turanzas, 1962.

"Edicto de Túpac Amaru a los moradores de Cuzco." Tungasuca, November 20, 1780. In Romulo Cuneo-Vidal, *Precursores y mártires de la independencia del Perú*, 64. Lima: Editorial Ignacio Prado Pastor, 1978.

"El Virrey del Río de la Plata da cuenta de que el cura de Macha dn Gregorio Jph de Merlos se halla en Buenos Aires." Buenos Aires, October 7, 1781. AGI, Charcas 594.

"Expedte. que contiene las dilig. actuadas por el Corregor de la Provincia de Porco sobre los insultos que el Cacique de Coroma Don Sebastián José Martínez experimento en su comunidad." La Plata, December 22, 1780. ANB, SGI.1780.206.

Guerra de Castas en Yucatán: su origen, sus consecuencias y su estado actual, 1866. Transcribed by Melchor Campos García. Mérida, Yucatán, Mex: Universidad Autónoma de Yucatán, 1997.

Jáuregui y Aldecoa, Augustín. *Relación y documentos de Gobierno del Virrey del Perú, Augustín de Jauregui y Aldecoa (1780–1784).* Ed. Remedio Contreras. Madrid: Instituto "Gonzalo Fernández de Oviedo," 1982.

"Letter of the Governor and Captain-General, Don Antonio de Otermín, from New Mexico to Fray Francisco de Ayeta, in which he gives him a full account of what has happened to him since the day the Indians surrounded him. September 8, 1680. In *Revolt of the Pueblo Indians of New Mexico and Otermín's Attempted Reconquest, 1680–1682,* ed. Charles Wilson Hackett, translations of original documents by Charmion Clair Shelby, 8:94. Albuquerque: University of New Mexico Press, 1942.

"Lieutenant Governor to Governor, Jamaica." April 13, 1863, R. 81. In *Archives of British Honduras,* ed. John Burdon, 3:251. London: Sifton Praed, 1935.

"Mensaje de Juan de la Cruz, Sermón de Chumpon." 1888. In Miguel Bartolomé and Alicia Barabas, *La resistencia maya,* 125. México, D.F.: Instituto Nacional de Anthopología e Historia, Collección Científica, etnología 53, 1977.

Miller, William. "A Journey from British Honduras to Santa Cruz, Yucatán." *Proceedings of the Royal Geographic Society,* 1:23–28. London: n.p., 1889.

"Numo. 458 Reservado al Sr. Galvez informando que a la sublevación de Chayanta dio ocasión el no administrar prontam.te Just.a la Aud.a de Charcas . . . (Carta del Fiscal)." La Plata, March 15, 1781. In Boleslao Lewin, *Túpac Amaru el Rebelde: Su época, sus luchas y su influencia en el continente,* 436. Buenos Aires: Editorial Claridad, 1943.

Quintal Martín, Fidelio. *Correspondencia de la Guerra de Castas.* Mérida: Universidad Autónoma de Yucatán, 1992.

"Relación histórica de los sucesos de la rebelión de José Gabriel Túpac-Amaru en las provincias del Perú el año de 1780." In *Colección de obras y documentos relativos a la historia del Río de la Plata,* ed. Pedro de Angelis, 4:276. Buenos Aires, Librería Nacional de J. Lajouane, 1910.

Sapper, Karl. "Independent Indian States of Yucatán." In Charles P. Bowditch and Eduard Seler, *Mexican and Central American Antiquities, Calendar Systems, and History.* Washington, D.C.: Government Printing Office, 1904.

"Superintendent to Governor, Jamaica." February 17, 1858. R. 55. In *Archives of British Honduras,* ed. John Burdon, vol. 3, 201. London: Sifton Praed, 1935.

Secondary Sources

Abecia Baldivieso, Valentín. "La insurreción india de Tapacari en 1781." In *Actas de coloquio Internacional: "Túpac Amaru y su tiempo,"* ed. Cárlos Daniel Válcarcel. Lima: Comisión Nacional del Bicentenario de la Revolución Emancipadora de Túpac Amaru, 1982.

Abercrombie, Thomas. *Pathways of Memory and Power: Ethnography and History among an Andean People.* Madison: University of Wisconsin Press, 1998.

Adas, Michael. *Prophets of Rebellion: Millenarian Protest Movements against the European Colonial Order.* Chapel Hill: University of North Carolina Press, 1979.

Albó, Xavier. "Etnicidad y clase en la gran rebelión Aymara/Quechua: Kataris, Amarus, y bases 1780–81." In *Bolivia: la fuerza histórica del campesinado,* ed. Fernando Calderón and Jorge Dandler. La Paz: Centro de Estudios de la Realidad Económica y Social, 1986.

Andrade Padilla, Claudio. *La Rebelión de Tomás Catari*. Sucre, Bolivia: IPTK/CIPRES, 1994.

Aparicio Quispe, Severo. *El clero y la rebelión de Túpac Amaru*. Cuzco: Imprenta Amauta, 2000.

Auld, Leona Ruth. "Discontent with the Spanish Systems of Control in Upper Peru: 1730–1809." Dissertation, University of California, Los Angeles, 1963.

Bancroft, Hubert H. *History of Arizona and New Mexico, 1530–1888*. Vol. 17 of *The Works of Hubert Howe Bancroft*. San Francisco: The History Company, 1889.

Barbier, Jacques. *Reform and Politics in Bourbon Chile, 1755–1796*. Ottawa: University of Ottawa Press, 1980.

Barkun, Michael. *Disaster and the Millennium*. New Haven: Yale University Press, 1974.

Bartolomé, Miguel, and Alicia Barabas. *La resistencia maya*. México, D.F.: Instituto Nacional de Anthopología e Historia, Colección Científica, etnología 53, 1977.

Baskes, Jeremy. *Indians, Merchants, and Markets: A Reinterpretation of the Repartimiento and Spanish-Indian Economic Relations in Colonial Oaxaca, 1750–1821*. Stanford: Stanford University Press, 2000.

Bauer, Yehuda. "The Place of the Holocaust in Contemporary History." In *Studies in Contemporary Jewry*, ed. Jonathan Frankel, vol. 1. Bloomington: Indiana University Press, 1984.

Beltrán Avila, Marcos. *Capítulos de la historia colonial de Oruro*. La Paz: La República, 1925.

Bohstedt, John. "The Moral Economy and the Discipline of Historical Context." *Journal of Social History* 26, no. 2 (Winter 1992): 265–85.

Bradley, Peter, and David Cahill. *Habsburg Peru: Images, Imagination, and Memory*. Liverpool: Liverpool University Press, 2000.

Bricker, Victoria. *The Indian Christ, the Indian King: The Historical Substrate of Maya Myth and Ritual*. Austin: University of Texas Press, 1981.

Brinton, Crane. *The Anatomy of Revolution*. New York: Prentice-Hall, 1952.

Brown, Kendall. *Bourbons and Brandy: Imperial Reform in Eighteenth-Century Arequipa*. Albuquerque: University of New Mexico Press, 1985.

Cahill, David. "Popular Religion and Appropriation: The Example of Corpus Christi in Eighteenth-Century Cuzco." *Latin American Research Review* 31, no. 2 (Spring 1996): 67–111.

———. "The Inca and Inca Symbolism in Popular Festive Culture: The Religious Processions of Seventeenth-Century Cuzco." In *Hapsburg Peru: Images, Imagination, and Memory*. Liverpool: Liverpool University Press, 2000.

———. "The Virgin and the Inca: An Incaic Procession in the City of Cuzco in 1692." *Ethnohistory* 49, no. 3 (2002): 611–49.

Calderón, Abdon. *Monografía histórica del departamento de Oruro*. Oruro: n.p., 1947.

Cajías de la Vega, Fernando. "La rebelión de Oruro y las provincias aledañas en 1781." *Encuentro* 5 (November 1989): 32–40.

———. "Los Objectivos de la revolución indígena de 1781: El Caso de Oruro." *Revista Andina* 1, no. 2 (December 1983): 407–28.

Campbell, Leon. "Banditry and the Túpac Amaru Rebellion in Cuzco, Perú, 1780–1784." *Biblioteca Americana* 1, no. 2 (November 1982): 131–62.

———. "Ideology and Factionalism during the Great Rebellion, 1780–1782." In *Resistance, Rebellion, and Consciousness in the Andean Peasant World, Eighteenth to Twentieth Centuries*, ed. Steve Stern. Madison: University of Wisconsin Press, 1987.

Carmagnani, Marcello. *El regreso de los dioses: el proceso de reconstitución de la identidad étnica en Oaxaca. Siglos xvii y xviii.* Mexico City: El Colegio de México and Fondo de Cultura Económica, 1988.

———. *Estado y Mercado: La economía pública del liberalismo mexicano, 1850–1911.* Mexico City: El Colegio de México and Fondo de Cultura Económica, 1994.

Castillo Palma, Norma Angélica. *Cholula: sociedea mestiza en ciudad India: Un análisis de las consecuencias demográficas, económicas y sociales del mestizaje en una ciudad novohispana, 1649–1796.* Mexico City: Universidad Autónoma Metropolitana, 2001.

Chalk, Frank, and Kurt Jonassohn, eds. *The History and Sociology of Genocide: Analyses and Case Studies.* New Haven: Yale University Press, 1990.

Charny, Israel, ed. *Genocide: A Critical Bibliographical Review.* New York: Facts on File, 1988.

———. "Genocide and Mass Destruction: A Missing Dimension in Psychopathology." In Israel Charny, *Toward the Understanding and Prevention of Genocide: Proceedings of the International Conference on the Holocaust and Genocide.* Boulder: Westview Press, 1988.

———. *How Can We Commit the Unthinkable?* Boulder: Westview Press, 1982.

———. "Toward a Generic Definition of Genocide." In *Genocide: Conceptual and Historical Dimensions,* ed. George Andreopoulos. Philadelphia: University of Pennsylvania Press, 1994.

———. *Toward the Understanding and Prevention of Genocide: Proceedings of the International Conference on the Holocaust and Genocide.* Boulder: Westview Press, 1988.

Chávez, Angelico. "Pohe-yemo's Representative and the Pueblo Revolt of 1680." *New Mexico Historical Review* 42 (January 1967): 85–126.

Clegern, Wayne M. "British Honduras and the Pacification of Yucatán." *The Americas* 18, no. 3 (1962): 243–54.

Cline, Howard F. "Regionalism and Society in Yucatán, 1825–1847." University of Chicago Library, Microfilm Collection of Manuscripts on Middle American Cultural Anthopology, no. 32, 1947.

———. "The Sugar Episode in Yucatán, 1825–1850." *Inter-American Economic Affairs* 1, no. 4 (1948): 79–100.

———. "War of the Castes and Its Consequences." University of Chicago Library, Microfilm Collection of Manuscripts on Middle American Cultural Anthopology, no. 32, 1945.

Cohn, Norman. *The Pursuit of the Millennium.* New York: Oxford University Press, 1957.

Comaroff, Jean, and John Comaroff. *Of Revelation and Revolution.* Chicago: University of Chicago Press, 1991.

Condarco Morales, Ramiro. "Oruro en la Historia." In n.a., *Monografía de Bolivia.* La Paz: Biblioteca del sesquicentenario de la república, 1970. Also in *Perfiles de Oruro,* ed. Elian Delgado Morales. Oruro: Alea Ltda., 1987.

———. "Síntesis Geografía." In n.a., *Monografía de Bolivia,* vol. 3. La Paz: Biblioteca del sesquicentenario de la república, 1970.

Cornblit, Oscar. *Power and Violence in the Colonial City: Oruro and the Mining Renaissance to the Rebellion of Túpac Amaru (1740–1782).* New York: Cambridge University Press, 1995.

Crespo, Alberto. "Las armas de los rebeldes." In *Actas del coloquio internacional "Túpac*

Amaru y su tiempo." Lima: Comisión Nacional del bicentenario de la rebelión emancipadora de Túpac Amaru, 1982.

Curatola, Marco. "Mito y milenarianismo en los andes: del Taqui Onqoy a Inkarrí." *Allpanchis* 10 (Cuzco, 1977): 65–92.

Dadrian, Vahakn. "A Typology of Genocide." *International Review of Modern Sociology* 5 (Fall 1975): 201–12.

De Angelis, Pedro. "Discurso preliminar al la revolución de Túpac-Amaru." In Pedro de Angelis, ed., *Colección de obras y documentos relativos a la historia del Río de la Plata*, vol. 4. Buenos Aires, Librería Nacional de J. Lajouane, 1910.

Domínguez, Jorge, ed. *Race and Ethnicity in Latin America.* New York: Garland, 1994.

Drost, Pieter. *The Crime of State.* Vol. 2. Leyden, Holland: A. W. Sythoff, 1959.

Du Preez, Peter. *Genocide: The Psychology of Mass Murder.* London: Boyars/Bowerdean, 1994.

Dumond, Don E. *The Machete and the Cross: Campesino Rebellion in Yucatán.* Lincoln: University of Nebraska Press, 1997.

Durán-Cogan, Mercedes, and Antonio Gómez-Moriana, eds. *National Identities and Sociopolitical Changes in Latin America.* New York: Routledge, 2001.

Durand Florez, Luís, ed. *Colección documental del bicentenario de la revolución emancipadora de Túpac Amaru.* 5 vols. Lima: Comisión Nacional del Bicentenario de la Rebelión Emancipadora de Túpac Amaru, 1980–92.

Espinosa, J. Manuel. *First Expedition of Vargas into New Mexico, 1692.* Albuquerque: University of New Mexico Press, 1940.

———. *The Pueblo Indian Revolt of 1696 and the Franciscan Missions in New Mexico: Letters of the Missionaries and Related Documents.* Norman: University of Oklahoma Press, 1988.

Fein, Helen. "Scenarios of Genocide: Models of Genocide and Critical Responses." In Israel Charny, *Toward the Understanding and Prevention of Genocide: Proceedings of the International Conference on the Holocaust and Genocide.* Boulder: Westview Press, 1988.

Fisher, John. *Bourbon Peru, 1750–1824.* Liverpool: Liverpool University Press, 2003.

Fisher, John, Allan Kuethe, and Anthony McFarlane, eds. *Reform and Insurrection in Bourbon New Granada and Peru.* Baton Rouge: Louisiana State University Press, 1990.

Fisher, Lillian Estelle. *The Last Inca Revolt, 1780–1783.* Norman: University of Oklahoma Press, 1966.

Flores Galindo, Alberto. "In Search of an Inca." In *Resistance, Rebellion, and Consciousness in the Andean Peasant World, Eighteenth to Twentieth Centuries*, ed. Steve Stern. Madison: University of Wisconsin Press, 1987.

———. "Túpac Amaru y la sublevación de 1780." In *Túpac Amaru II: 1780*, ed. Alberto Flores Galindo. Lima: Retablo de Papel Ediciones, 1976.

Flores Galindo, Alberto, and Manuel Burga. "La utopía andina." *Allpanchis* 20 (Cuzco, 1982): 85–102.

Folsom, Franklin. *Indian Uprising on the Rio Grande: The Pueblo Revolt of 1680.* Albuquerque: University of New Mexico Press, 1973.

Forbes, Jack D. *Apache, Navaho, and Spaniard.* Norman: University of Oklahoma Press, 1994.

Freeman, Michael. "Genocide in World-Historical Perspective." Essex Papers in Politics and Government. Essex: University of Essex, April 1984.

Gayner, Jeffery. "The Genocide Treaty." *Journal of Social and Political Studies* 2 (Winter 1977): 235–45.

Gerth, H. H., and C. Wright Mills. *From Max Weber: Essays in Sociology*. New York: Oxford University Press, 1946.

Golte, Jürgen. *Repartos y Rebeliones: Túpac Amaru y las contradicciones de la economía colonial*. Lima: Instituto de Estudios Peruanos, 1980.

Gosner, Kevin. *Soldiers of the Virgin: The Moral Economy of a Colonial Maya Rebellion*. Tucson: University of Arizona Press, 1992.

Gow, Rosalind. "Inkarrí and Revolutionary Leadership in the Southern Andes." *Journal of Latin American Lore* 8, no. 2 (1982): 197–223.

Griffiths, Nicholas. *The Cross and the Serpent: Religious Repression and Resurgence in Colonial Peru*. Norman: University of Oklahoma Press, 1996.

Grimshaw, Allen. "Interpreting Collective Violence: An Argument for the Importance of Social Structure." In *Collective Violence*, ed. James Short and Martin Wolfgang. Chicago: Aldine-Atherton, 1972.

Gruzinski, Serge. *Man-Gods in the Mexican Highlands: Indian Power and Colonial Society, 1520–1800*. Stanford: Stanford University Press, 1989.

Gurr, Ted Robert. *Why Men Rebel*. Princeton: Princeton University Press, 1971.

Gutiérrez, Ramón A. *When Jesus Came the Corn Mothers Went Away: Marriage, Sexuality, and Power in New Mexico, 1500–1846*. Stanford: Stanford University Press, 1991.

Hackett, Charles Wilson, ed. *Historical Documents Relating to New Mexico, Nueva Vizcaya, and Approaches Thereto, to 1773*. Collected by Adolph and Fanny Bandelier. Vol. 4. Washington, D.C.: Carnegie Institution, 1937.

——. *Revolt of the Pueblo Indians of New Mexico and Otermín's Attempted Reconquest, 1680–1682*. Vols. 8 and 9. Translations of original documents by Charmion Clair Shelby. Albuquerque: University of New Mexico Press, 1942.

——. "The Retreat of the Spaniards from New Mexico in 1680, Beginnings of El Paso I." *Southwestern Historical Quarterly* 16, no. 2 (October 1912): 137–68.

——. "The Retreat of the Spaniards from New Mexico in 1680, Beginnings of El Paso II." *Southwestern Historical Quarterly* 16, no. 3 (January 1913): 259–76.

——. "The Revolt of the Pueblo Indians of New Mexico in 1680." *Texas State Historical Association Quarterly* 15 (October 1911): 93–147.

Hagopian, Mark N. *The Phenomenon of Revolution*. New York: Dodd, Mead, 1974.

Harff, Barbara. *Genocide and Human Rights: International Legal and Political Issues*. Monograph Series in World Affairs, Graduate School of International Studies. Denver: University of Denver, 1984.

Harff, Barbara, and Ted Gurr. "Toward Empirical Theory of Genocides and Politicides: Identification and Measurement of Cases Since 1945." *International Studies Quarterly* 32 (1988): 359–71.

Hidalgo Lehunde, Jorge. "Amarus y Cataris: aspectos mesiánicos de la rebelión indígena de 1781 in Cusco, Chayanta, La Paz, y Arica." *Chungara* 10 (Arica, March 1983): 117–38.

Hobsbawm, Eric J. *Primitive Rebels: Studies in Archaic Forms of Social Movement in the 19th and 20th Centuries*. Manchester: University of Manchester Press, 1965.

Hoffer, Eric. *The True Believer: Thoughts on the Nature of Mass Movements*. New York: Harper and Row, 1951.

Horowitz, Irving Louis. "Genocide and the Reconstruction of Social Theory: Observations on the Exclusivity of Collective Death." *Armenian Review* 37 (1984): 1–21.

——. *Genocide: State Power and Mass Murder*. New Brunswick: Transaction Books, 1980.

———. *Taking Lives: Genocide and State Power*. New Brunswick: Transaction Books, 1997.

Huertas, Lorenzo. *La religión en una comunidad andina*. Ayacucho, Peru: Universidad Nacional de San Cristóbal de Huamanga, 1981.

Hughes, Anne. *The Beginnings of Spanish Settlement in the El Paso District*. Berkeley: n.p., 1914.

Jervis, Robert. "Political Implications of Loss Aversion." *Political Psychology* 13, no. 2 (1992): 187–204.

Jones, Grant D. "La estructura política de los mayas de Chan Santa Cruz: el papel del respaldo inglés." *Amérique Indígena* 31, no. 2 (April 1971): 415–27.

Joseph, Gilbert. *Revolution from Without: Yucatán, Mexico, and the United States, 1880–1924*. Cambridge: Cambridge University Press, 1982.

Josephy, Alvin M. *The Patriot Chiefs: A Chronicle of American Indian Leadership*. New York: Viking Press, 1961.

Kelman, H. C. "Violence without Moral Restraint: Reflections on the Dehumanization of Victims and Victimizers." *Journal of Social Issues* 29, no. 4 (1973): 25–61.

Kessell, John L. "Esteban Clemente, Precursor of the Pueblo Revolt." *El Palacio* 86, no. 4 (1980): 16–17.

———. "Spaniards and Pueblos: From Crusading Intolerance to Pragmatic Accommodation." In *Columbian Consequences*, vol. 1, ed. D. H. Thomas. Washington, D.C.: Smithsonian Institution Press, 1989.

Kessell, John L., Rick Hendricks, and Meredith Dodge, eds. *Blood on the Boulders: The Journals of Don Diego de Vargas, New Mexico, 1694–97*. 2 vols. Albuquerque: University of New Mexico Press, 1998.

———. *By Force of Arms: The Journals of Don Diego de Vargas, 1691–1693*. Albuquerque: University of New Mexico Press, 1992.

———. *To the Royal Crown Restored: The Journals of Don Diego de Vargas, New Mexico, 1692–1694*. Albuquerque: University of New Mexico Press, 1995.

Kilpatrick, F. P. "Problems of Perception in Extreme Situations." *Human Organization* 16, no. 2 (Summer 1957): 20–22.

Klein, Herbert. *Bolivia: The Evolution of a Multi-ethnic Society*. New York: Oxford University Press, 1982.

Knault, Andrew L. *The Pueblo Revolt of 1680: Conquest and Resistance in Seventeenth-Century New Mexico*. Norman: University of Oklahoma Press, 1995.

Kressel, Neil. *Mass Hate: The Global Rise of Genocide and Terror*. New York: Plenum Press, 1996.

Kuper, Leo. *Genocide: Its Political Use in the Twentieth Century*. New Haven: Yale University Press, 1981.

———. *The Prevention of Genocide*. New Haven: Yale University Press, 1985.

———. "Theoretical Issues Relating to Genocide." In *Genocide: Conceptual and Historical Dimensions*, ed. George Andreopoulos. Philadelphia: University of Pennsylvania Press, 1994.

Lanternari, Vittorio. *The Religions of the Oppressed*. New York: Alfred Knopf, 1963.

Lapointe, Marie. *Los mayas rebeldes de Yucatán*. Zamora, Michoacán, Mex: Colegio de Michoacán, 1983.

Larson, Brooke. *Colonialism and Agrarian Transformation in Bolivia: Cochabamba, 1550–1900*. Princeton: Princeton University Press, 1990.

———. "Rural Rhythms of Class Conflict in Eighteenth-Century Cochabamba." *Hispanic American Historical Review* 60, no. 3 (August 1980): 407–30.

Lemkin, Rafael. *Axis Rule in Occupied Europe.* Washington, D.C.: Carnegie Endowment for International Peace, 1944.

Levine, Frances. *Our Prayers Are in This Place: Pecos Pueblo Identity over the Centuries.* Albuquerque: University of New Mexico Press, 1999.

Lévi-Strauss, Claude. *Structural Anthropology.* Vol. 2. Trans. Monique Layton. New York: Basic Books, 1976.

Levy, Jack. "An Introduction to Prospect Theory." *Political Psychology* 13, no. 2 (1992): 171–86.

Lewin, Boleslao. *La rebelión de Túpac Amaru y los orígines de la independencia de Hispanoamérica.* Buenos Aires: Sociedad Editora Latino Americana, 1967.

———. *Los movimientos de emancipación en hispanoamérica y la independencia de estados unidos.* Buenos Aires: Editorial Raigal, 1952.

———. *Túpac Amaru, el rebelde, su época, sus luchas y su influencia en el continente.* Buenos Aires: Editorial Claridad, 1943.

———. *Túpac Amaru, su época, su lucha, su hado.* Buenos Aires: Ediciones Siglo Veinte, 1973.

Linton, Ralph. "Nativistic Movements." *American Anthropologist* 45, no. 2 (April–June 1943): 230–40.

Littell, F. H. "Essay: Early Warning." *Holocaust and Genocide Studies* 3 (1988): 483–90.

López Baralt, Mercedes. *El Retorno del Inca Rey: Mito y profecía en el mundo andino.* La Paz: Hisbol, 1989.

Lorente, Sebastián. *Historia del Perú bajo los Borbones, 1700–1821.* Lima: Gil y Aubert, 1871.

MacCormack, Sabine. "Pachacuti: Miracles, Punishment, and the Last Judgement: Visionary Past and Prophetic Future in Early Colonial Peru." *American Historical Review* 93, no. 4–5 (October 1988): 960–1006.

———. Personal communication. October 7, 1999.

McFarlane, Anthony. *Colombia before Independence: Economy, Society, and Politics under Bourbon Rule.* New York: Cambridge University Press, 1993.

Meisler, Stanley. "Holocaust in Burundi." In Chalk and Jonassohn, *The History and Sociology of Genocide.*

Metzgen, Monrad S., and Henry E. C. Cain. *Handbook of British Honduras Comprising Historical, Statistical and General Information Concerning the Colony.* London: West India Committee, 1925.

Mier, Adolfo. *Noticia y proceso de la muy noble y muy leal Villa de San Felipe de Austria de Oruro.* 2 vols. N.p., 1906.

Mills, Kenneth. *Idolatry and Its Enemies: Colonial Andean Religion and Extirpation, 1640 to 1750.* Princeton, N.J.: Princeton University Press, 1997.

Montaño, A. Mario. *Síntesis Histórica de Oruro.* N.p., 1972.

Moore, Barrington. *Social Origins of Dictatorship and Democracy: Lord and Peasant in the Making of the Modern World.* Boston: Beacon Press, 1966.

Oakes, Len. *Prophetic Charisma: The Psychology of Revolutionary Religious Personalities.* Syracuse: Syracuse University Press, 1997.

Odriozola, Manuel de. *Documentos históricos del Perú en las épocas del coloniaje despúes de la conquista y de la independencia hasta la presente,* ed. Manuel de Odriozola. Lima: Tipografía de Aurelio Alfaro, 1863.

O'Phelan Godoy, Scarlett. "Elementos étnicos y de poder en el movimiento Tupacamarista, 1780–81." Torino: Nova Americana, 1982.

———. "El Mito de la 'Independencia Concedida': Los programas políticos del siglo XVIII y del temprano XIX en el Perú y Alto Perú (1730–1814)." In *Problemas de la formación del estado y de la nación en Hispano-America,* ed. Inge Buisson et al. Cologne: Bohlau, 1984.

———. "Hacía una tipología y un enfoque alternativo de las revueltas y rebeliones del Perú colonial (siglo XVIII)." In *Jahrbuch für Geschiste,* ed. R. Konetzke and Hermann Kellenbenz, vol. 21. Cologne: Bohlau, 1984.

———. *Rebellions and Revolts in Eighteenth-Century Peru and Upper Peru.* Cologne: Bohlau, 1985.

Ossio, Juan, ed. *Ideología mesiánica del mundo andino.* Lima: I. Prado Pastor, 1973.

Paz y Guiní, Melchor de. *Guerra Separatista: Rebeliones de indios en Sur América la sublevación de Túpac Amaru, crónica.* Ed. Luis Antonio Eguiguren. 2 vols. Lima: Imprenta Torres Aguirre, 1952.

Pease, Franklin. "El mito de Inkarrí y la visión de los vencidos." In *Ideología mesiánica del mundo andino,* ed. Juan Ossio. Lima: I. Prado Pastor, 1973.

Randall, Adrian, and Andrew Charlesworth, eds. *Moral Economy and Popular Protest: Crowds, Conflict, and Authority.* New York: St. Martin's Press, 2000.

Reed, Nelson. "Juan de la Cruz, Venencio Puc, and the Speaking Cross." *The Americas* 53, no. 4 (April 1997): 497–523.

———. *The Caste War of Yucatán.* Stanford: Stanford University Press, 1988.

Reff, Daniel. *Disease, Depopulation, and Culture Change in Northwestern New Spain, 1518–1764.* Salt Lake City: University of Utah Press, 1991.

———. "The 'Predicament of Culture' and the Spanish Missionary Accounts of the Tepehuan and Pueblo Revolts." *Ethnohistory* 42, no. 1 (Winter 1995): 63–90.

Reina, Leticia. *Las rebeliones campesinas en México, 1819–1906.* México, D.F.: Siglo Veintiuno, 1980.

Riley, Carroll. *The Kachina and the Cross: Indians and Spaniards in the Early Southwest.* Salt Lake City: University of Utah Press, 1999.

Robins, Nicholas. *El mesianismo y la semiótica indígena en el Alto Perú: La Gran Rebelión de 1780–1781.* La Paz: Hisbol, 1998.

Rogers, E. *Honduras Británica: Sus recursos y desarrollo.* Mérida, México: Compañia Tipográfica Yucateca, 1938.

Rowe, John H. "El movimiento nacional Inca del siglo XVIII." *Revista Universitaria* 43, no. 107 (1954): 17–40.

Rudnyckyj, J. B. "Linguicide: Concept and Definition." In Charny, *Toward the Understanding and Prevention of Genocide.*

Rugeley, Terry. "Los mayas yucatecos del siglo XIX." In *La reindianización de América, siglo XIX,* ed. Leticia Reina. Mexico City: Siglo Veintiuno Editores, 1997.

———, ed. *Maya Wars: Ethnographic Accounts from Nineteenth-Century Yucatán.* Norman: University of Oklahoma Press, 2001.

———. Personal correspondence. July 30, 2004.

———. "Rural Political Violence and the Origins of the Caste War." *The Americas* 53, no. 4 (April 1997): 469–96.

———. *Yucatán's Maya Peasantry and the Origins of the Caste War.* Austin: University of Texas Press, 1996.

Salmón, Roberto Mario. *Indian Revolts in Northern New Spain: A Synthesis of Resistance (1680–1786).* New York: University Press of America, 1991.

Saloman, Frank. "Ancestor Cults and Resistance to the State in Arequipa, ca. 1748–1754."

In *Resistance, Rebellion, and Consciousness in the Andean Peasant World, Eighteenth to Twentieth Centuries,* ed. Steve Stern. Madison: University of Wisconsin Press, 1987.

Sánchez, Jane C. "Spanish-Indian Relations during the Otermín Administration, 1677–1683." *New Mexico Historical Review* 58, no. 2 (April 1983): 133–51.

Sando, Joe S. "The Pueblo Revolt." In *The Southwest,* ed. Alfonso Ortíz, 194–97. Vol. 9 of *Handbook of North American Indians.* Washington, D.C.: Smithsonian Institution, 1979.

Sanford, Nevitt, Craig Comstock, et al. *Sanctions for Evil.* San Francisco: Jossey Bass, 1973.

Saunders, J. "The Mogul Conquests." In Chalk and Jonassohn, *The History and Sociology of Genocide.*

Scholes, France V. "Church and State in New Mexico, 1610–1650." *New Mexico Historical Review* 11, no. 1 (January 1936): 9–76.

———. "Church and State in New Mexico, 1610–1650." *New Mexico Historical Review* 11, no. 2 (April 1936): 145–78.

———. "Church and State in New Mexico, 1610–1650." *New Mexico Historical Review* 11, no. 3 (July 1936): 283–94.

———. "Church and State in New Mexico, 1610–1650." *New Mexico Historical Review* 11, no. 4 (October 1936): 297–349.

———. "Church and State in New Mexico, 1610–1650." *New Mexico Historical Review* 12, no. 1 (January 1937): 78–106.

———. "Civil Government and Society in New Mexico in the Seventeenth Century." *New Mexico Historical Review* 10, no. 2 (April 1935): 71–111.

———. "Problems in the Early Ecclesiastical History of New Mexico." *New Mexico Historical Review* 7, no. 1 (January 1932): 32–74.

———. "The First Decade of the Inquisition in New Mexico." *New Mexico Historical Review* 10, no. 3 (July 1935): 195–241.

———. "The Supply Service of the New Mexican Missions in the Seventeenth Century. Part 1." *New Mexico Historical Review* 5, no. 1 (January 1930): 93–115.

———. "The Supply Service of the New Mexican Missions in the Seventeenth Century. Part 2." *New Mexico Historical Review* 5, no. 2 (April 1930): 186–210.

———. "The Supply Service of the New Mexican Missions in the Seventeenth Century. Part 3." *New Mexico Historical Review* 5, no. 4 (October 1930): 386–404.

———. "Troublous Times in New Mexico, 1659–1670." *Historical Society of New Mexico Publications in History* 11 (January 1942): 1–270.

Scott, James. *The Moral Economy of the Peasant: Rebellion and Subsistence in Southeast Asia.* New Haven: Yale University Press, 1976.

———. *Weapons of the Weak: Everyday Forms of Peasant Resistance.* New Haven: Yale University Press, 1985.

Serulnikov, Sergio. "Customs and Rules: Bourbon Rationalizing Projects and Social Conflicts in Northern Potosí during the 1770s." *Colonial Latin American Review* 8, no. 2 (1999): 245–74.

———. *Revindicaciones indígenas y legalidad colonial. La rebelión de Chayanta (1777–1781).* Buenos Aires: Centro de Estudios de Estado y Sociedad, 1989.

———. *Subverting Colonial Authority: Challenges to Spanish Rule in Eighteenth-Century Southern Andes.* Durham: Duke University Press, 2003.

——. *Tomás Catari y la producción de justicia*. Buenos Aires: Centro de Estudios de Estado y Sociedad, 1988.

Silva, Patricio, and Kees Koonings. *Construcciones étnicas y dinámica sociocultural en América Latina*. Quito: Abya-Yala, 1999.

Silverberg, Robert. *The Pueblo Revolt*. New York: Weybright and Talley, 1970.

Silverblatt, Irene. "Becoming Indian in the Central Andes of Seventeenth-Century Peru." In *After Colonialism: Imperial Histories and Postcolonial Displacements*, ed. Gyan Prakash. Princeton: Princeton University Press, 1995.

Simmons, Marc. "History of Pueblo-Indian Relations to 1821." In *The Southwest*, ed. Alfonso Ortíz, 178–223. *Handbook of North American Indians*, vol. 9. Washington, D.C.: Smithsonian Institution, 1979.

Smith, Roger. "Human Destructiveness and Politics: The Twentieth Century as an Age of Genocide." In *Genocide and the Modern Age: Etiology and Case Studies of Mass Death*, ed. Isidor Walliman and Michael Dobkowski. Westport: Greenwood Press, 1987.

——. "Fantasy, Purity, Destruction: Norman Cohn's Complex Witness to the Holocaust." In *Bearing Witness to the Holocaust, 1939–1989*, ed. Alan Berger. Lampeter, Wales: Edwin Mellen Press, 1991.

Stannard, David. "Uniqueness as Denial: The Politics of Genocide Scholarship." In *Is the Holocaust Unique? Perspectives on Comparative Genocide*, ed. Alan S. Rosenbaum. Boulder: Westview Press, 1996.

Staub, Ervin. *The Roots of Evil: The Origins of Genocide and Other Group Violence*. New York: Cambridge University Press, 1989.

Stavig, Ward. "Ambiguous Visions: Nature, Law and Culture in Indigenous-Spanish Land Relations in Colonial Peru." *Hispanic American Historical Review* 80, no. 1 (2000): 77–111.

——. "Ethnic Conflict, Moral Economy, and Population in Rural Cuzco on the Eve of the Thupa Amaro II Rebellion." *Hispanic American Historical Review* 64, no. 4 (November 1988): 737–70.

——. *The World of Túpac Amaru*. Lincoln: University of Nebraska Press, 1999.

Stern, Steve. "New Approaches to the Study of Peasant Rebellion and Consciousness: Implications of the Andean Experience." In Stern, *Resistance, Rebellion, and Consciousness*.

——. "The Age of Andean Insurrection, 1742–1782: A Reappraisal." In Stern, *Resistance, Rebellion, and Consciousness*.

——. *Resistance, Rebellion, and Consciousness in the Andean Peasant World, Eighteenth to Twentieth Centuries*. Madison: University of Wisconsin Press, 1987.

Szeminski, Jan. *La utopía Tupamarista*. Lima: Pontífica Universidad Católica del Perú, 1984.

——. Personal correspondence, March 4, 2001.

——. Personal correspondence, April 27, 2001.

——. "Why Kill the Spaniard? New Perspectives on Andean Insurrectionary Ideology in the Eighteenth Century." In Stern, *Resistance, Rebellion, and Consciousness*.

Taylor, William B. "Banditry and Insurrection: Rural Unrest in Central Jalisco, 1790–1816." In *Riot, Rebellion and Revolution: Rural Social Conflict in Mexico*, ed. Friedrich Katz. Princeton: Princeton University Press, 1988.

——. *Drinking, Homicide, and Rebellion in Colonial Mexican Villages*. Stanford: Stanford University Press, 1979.

——. *Magistrates of the Sacred: Priests and Parishioners in Eighteenth-Century Mexico.* Stanford: Stanford University Press, 1996.

Thompson, Edward P. *Customs in Common.* London: Merlin Press, 1991.

——. "The Moral Economy of the English Crowd in the Eighteenth Century." *Past and Present* 50 (1971): 76–136.

Thomson, Sinclair. *We Alone Will Rule: Native Andean Politics in the Age of Insurgency.* Madison: University of Wisconsin Press, 2002.

Tucker, Robert C. "The Theory of Charismatic Leadership." *Daedalus* 97 (1968): 731–56.

Twitchell, Ralph Emerson, comp. *The Spanish Archives of New Mexico.* 2 vols. Cedar Rapids: Torch Press, 1914.

Urquidi, José Macedonio. *Compendio de la historia de Bolivia.* Buenos Aires: Talleres Graficos EGLH, 1944.

Válcarcel, Carlos Daniel. *La rebelión de Túpac Amaru.* Mexico City: Fondo de la Cultura Económica, 1970.

——, ed. *Colección Documental de la Independencia del Perú.* Book 2, vols. 1–3. Lima: Comisión Nacional del Sesquicentenario de la Independencia del Perú, 1971.

Valle de Siles, María Eugenia del. *Historia de la rebelión de Túpac Katari, 1781–82.* La Paz: Editorial Don Bosco, 1990.

——. "Túpac Katari y la rebelión de 1781: Radiografía de un caudillo aymara." *Anuario de Estudios Americanos* 34 (1977): 633–64.

Vanderwood, Paul. *The Power of God against the Guns of Government: Religious Upheaval in Mexico at the Turn of the Nineteenth Century.* Stanford: Stanford University Press, 1998.

Van Young, Eric. *The Other Rebellion: Popular Violence, Ideology, and the Mexican Struggle for Independence, 1810–1821.* Stanford: Stanford University Press, 2001.

Vega, Juan José. *José Gabriel Túpac Amaru.* Lima: Editorial Universo, S.A., 1969.

Villa Rojas, Alfonso. *The Maya of East Central Quintana Roo.* Publication 559. Washington, D.C.: Carnegie Institution of Washington, 1945.

Wachtel, Nathan. *The Vision of the Vanquished.* New York: Barnes and Noble, 1977.

Wade, Peter. *Race and Ethnicity in Latin America.* Chicago: Pluto Press, 1997.

Walker, Charles. *Smoldering Ashes: Cuzco and the Creation of Republican Peru.* Durham, N.C.: Duke University Press, 1999.

Wallace, Anthony. "Mazeway Disintegration: The Individual's Perception of Socio-Cultural Disorganization." *Human Organization* 16, no. 2 (Summer 1957): 23–27.

——. "Revitalization Movements." *American Anthropologist* 58, no. 1 (February 1956): 264–81.

Wells, Allen, and Gilbert Joseph. *Summer of Discontent, Seasons of Upheaval: Elite Politics and Rural Insurgency in Yucatán, 1876–1915.* Stanford: Stanford University Press, 1996.

Wightman, Ann. *Indigenous Migration and Social Change: The Foresteros of Cuzco, 1570–1720.* Durham: Duke University Press, 1990.

Worcester, D. E. "The Beginnings of the Apache Menace of the Southwest." *New Mexico Historical Review* 16, no. 1 (1939): 1–14.

Zimmerman, Charlotte. "The Cult of the Holy Cross: An Analysis on Cosmology and Catholicism in Quintana Roo." *History of Religions* 3, no. 1 (Summer 1963): 50–71.

Zuaire Huarte, Eulogio. "Análisis de la rebelión de Túpac Amaru en su bicentenario (1780–1980)." *Revista de Indios,* no. 159 (1980): 13–79.

Index

NICHOLAS A. ROBINS received his Ph.D. in Latin American Studies in 1994 from Tulane University. He is presently a visiting scholar in the Center for Latin American and Caribbean Studies at Duke University.